Ruling Passions

Ruling Passions

POLITICAL OFFICES AND DEMOCRATIC ETHICS

Andrew Sabl

PRINCETON UNIVERSITY PRESS

PRINCETON AND OXFORD

Copyright © 2002 by Princeton University Press
Published by Princeton University Press, 41 William Street, Princeton, New Jersey 08540
In the United Kingdom: Princeton University Press, 3 Market Place,
Woodstock, Oxfordshire OX20 1SY

Library of Congress Cataloging-in-Publication Data

Sabl, Andrew, 1969–
Ruling passions : political offices and democratic ethics / Andrew Sabl.
p. cm.
Includes bibliographical references and index.
ISBN 0-691-08830-6 — ISBN 0-691-08831-4 (pbk. : alk. paper)
1. Politics, Practical—United States. 2. United States—Politics and
government. 3. Politicians—United States. 4. Political ethics. I. Title.

JK1764 .S2 2002
324′.0973—dc21   2001050016

British Library Cataloging-in-Publication Data is available

This book has been composed in Janson

Printed on acid-free paper. ∞

www.pupress.princeton.edu

Printed in the United States of America

10 9 8 7 6 5 4 3 2 1

10 9 8 7 6 5 4 3 2 1
(Pbk.)

For my parents

"I have not said this to diminish in any way the infinite distance there is between vices and virtues: God forbid! I have only wanted to make it understood that not all political vices are moral vices and that not all moral vices are political vices, and those who make laws that run counter to the general spirit should not be ignorant of this."

—Montesquieu

Contents

Preface and Acknowledgments

THIS BOOK BEGAN with two pursuits, and with an insight that came from pursuing them both at once.

The first pursuit was ethical. When arguing the big questions of public debate (abortion, welfare, affirmative action, war and peace, the death penalty) I have always felt a genuine perplexity. While I had strong opinions, and could certainly be loud and partisan in arguing them, I never quite forgot that many disagreed with these opinions for what seemed to them very good reasons. I wanted to know who and what was right, or at least what to do if no one knew the answer to that. When I first started to look at ethical and moral philosophy, I hoped it would help me deal with these issues. I expected ethics, whatever its tone or approach (sage-like or critical, gentle or slashing), to be motivated by a need to address the "big questions" of real-world argument—though (with luck) humble about the certainty of its answers.

While most ethicists are motivated by similar concerns, however, the attention of moral philosophy as an academic field has not always focused on them. At one extreme, moral philosophy has tended to concentrate on "metaethics," the study of what ethical argument is all about. As a result, real-world issues are neglected, at times even actively rejected as too far removed from the high purpose of philosophical inquiry. On the other hand, when moral philosophy does address real-world questions, the effect can quickly become partisan: the need to assume certain premises as starting points too often leads us to regard these premises as obvious or necessary grounds for all moral thinking. In the worst, but common, case, each camp or school of moral philosophy (Kantian, feminist, utilitarian, Christian, Aristotelian), sure that all the others lack intellectual and moral standing, addresses those who think differently in terms of derision and attack, or else avoids engaging them altogether. To the extent that this happens, the goal of illuminating everyday questions again is lost: it seems more "philosophical" to vindicate the truth and moral honor of a certain approach than to take seriously the arguments of those who disagree on first principles.

Of course, relevance can be overrated. Ethical argument need not (and no doubt cannot) be "relevant" in the sense of determining this evening's news. And there is something to the accusation that excessive demands for relevance can mask a failure to value scholarly analysis and reflection. But there remains the simple demand for a kind of inquiry that illuminates and guides us through the complex and clashing moral demands that engaged people cannot avoid in daily life. So, while I have been instructed and inspired by contemporary ethics and the intellectual quality of those who practice it, I have often found the mainstream of ethical study remote from the questions that genuinely puzzled me.

Besides the social issues just mentioned, most of these questions are political. While much political theory is "political" in name only—it really concerns *social* ethics, the question of how certain groups and individuals should "be treated" by unspecified moral actors—the questions that interest me are political in a narrower sense. These questions concern responsibility, loyalty, compromise, respect for voters, ideological consistency, and how to balance good policies with persuasive politics. These are the questions that most people think about when they find politicians praiseworthy or the opposite. This is not to say that most people have good answers: when addressing these questions average citizens fall into easy and dogmatic opinions. More often than not, their beliefs are contradictory, or at least in tension with one another, as when they call for politicians to stand firmly on principle while avoiding partisan squabbling. Through a great deal of reading and a little political experience I figured out part of the problem: political actors not only have different opinions but very different ideas of how people should go about asserting their opinions. They disagree not only on political outcomes but on what politics should be.

The differences are not random. Depending on how they view the political world, people interested in politics are drawn to pursue particular kinds of political actions and to join the particular groups that employ them. If they choose the wrong kind of group or action they find themselves out of place, ill-suited to what they are doing, and often end up making a change. As a result of this self-selection, the moral psychologies of political actors fall into fairly clear categories. Instinctive lovers of establishment politics display a salutary realism about the sources of power and the need for compromise. Their professional deformations are those of all hierarchs: uncritical devotion to those who hold power and unjustified contempt for those who lack it. Those who see politics in terms of moral causes (with various labels: I am a lover of principle; you have strong opinions; he is a fanatic) can hardly imagine such love of hierarchy. Their ingenuous belief in Right over Might provides their moral strength—while often causing them to forget that claims of Right involve their own kind of arrogance. Then there are those who see politics as the art of making sure that everyone's voice gets heard. Their love of the underdog is as infectious—and honestly valuable—as their unwillingness to recognize larger social goods and interests can be positively dangerous. There are other political types, but these are the ones that struck me. I researched and wrote this book as a way of understanding and evaluating these three types, which soon sorted themselves into narrower analytic categories: "senator," "moral activist," and "organizer."

In the process of doing this, I came to see ethics, too, in a different way. The mainstream of ethical theory regards people as having the duty to do the best thing in all circumstances, with respect to everyone, and all the time. The ideal is for each of us to be constantly open to ethical demands, rigorously universalist, and immune to moral weakness and compromises. Nobody expects real people to fulfill this ideal, but to the extent that we do not we are said to be doing something wrong, to be mistaking or neglecting our moral duties.

I came to think there were good reasons for not viewing ethics this way. Political life contains too many moral demands to weigh them all in every decision or even most of the time; political responsibility involves so much reliance on steady character that such weighing, with its constant opening to radical moral change, would not even be admirable. Politicians—the *best* politicians, the most morally and politically admirable—respond to this quite reasonably, if usually unconsciously: they latch on to a particular piece of the moral universe, a particular kind of praiseworthy action, and specialize in it. But ethics can still teach us how this specialization ought to go: which kinds of goods politics involves, which kinds of actions reflect those goods, which kind of universal constraints still bind everyone who would play the political game more or less fairly.

A concern for these questions provoked new respect for some old political theories. The classic defenses of liberal democracy have a poor reputation in political theory these days. Toleration is seen as a weak and stunted goal: both too easy to be very admirable and too selfish to be consistent with needed social change. Liberty fares hardly better: while "liberties" of various kinds are still prized, liberty as a general value—the right to be left alone—is seen as at best an antiquated illusion, and at worst a hindrance to government action and social solidarity. "Democracy" continues to be praised, but that depends on what the meaning of "democracy" is. Equal and universal voting rights, and the assumptions of political equality that underlie them, are regarded as showing too little respect for high-quality moral arguments and highly virtuous political activists. Democracy is respected when it means maximum moral deliberation, or maximum participation, but shunned if it means that politics should involve votes, where numbers matter.

By treating seriously the diversity of moral claims and actions in politics, I have gained a new appreciation of what liberal democracy is all about. Far from representing an obvious and easy answer to well-known philosophic questions, liberal democracy represents a desperate but recurrent attempt to reconcile apparent opposites: the need for political change and the requirement to respect individuals who dissent from the change; the ambitions of political actors and the interests of those who have little time for politics; devotion to moral principle and the pursuit of legitimate interests; a vigorous belief in democratic equality and the reality of a world in which not everyone can hold office at once. In this context, toleration means not moral weakness but an honest recognition that some of my fellow citizens regard all my core convictions with abiding hatred. Liberty represents not just a selfish desire to keep what is mine and deny the claims of others but an honorable reluctance to give any group of self-chosen elites authority over what I and others do. And democratic voting is not the reduction of politics to crass arithmetic but a reluctant recognition that, in the face of permanent disagreements and controversies, it is normally better that a few have their projects frustrated rather than many.

These claims are nothing new. They draw on the efforts of Madison and Tocqueville to reconcile political liberty and vigorous government; on Rousseau's loving study of moral and political independence and of the role of rhetoric in making government consistent with them; on Hume's skeptical yet sympathetic attitudes towards all parties and all moral claims; and on Locke's heartfelt (if perhaps doomed) attempt to base government on consent despite deep disagreement. But if few claims in morality and politics are absolutely new, some kinds of inquiry make clearer than others the meaning and value of old arguments, and illustrate better their application to new questions. By combining theoretical argument with the vividness of actual examples, I hope to have done a bit of both.

Form following substance, this book has benefited from both good people and helpful institutions.

To take the latter first, I am grateful to the National Science Foundation for awarding me a Graduate Research Fellowship, the Mellon Foundation for a dissertation completion fellowship, the Program in Ethics and the Professions at Harvard University for a Graduate Fellowship year during which I wrote the main body of this work, and Harvard's Program on Constitutional Government for a Postdoctoral Research Fellowship during which I revised it for publication. Needless to say, none of these institutions necessarily endorses my views.

This work began as a Ph.D. dissertation in the government department at Harvard. My dissertation committee—Harvey Mansfield, Dennis Thompson, and Peter Berkowitz—deserve endless thanks not only for the scope and quality of their advice but for their patience in looking at multiple drafts. Judith Shklar taught me only for a short time, and I missed having her advice on this work, but her spirit lights every page, especially those she would disagree with. My fellow graduate students, including Carla Bagnoli, Tal Brewer, Jim Ellis, Russ Muirhead, Sankar Muthu, Jennifer Pitts, Joe Reisert, and Tim Shah, provided intellectual fellowship as well as comments and criticism. Ben Berger, an intellectual "second self" during hundreds of hours and scores of late evenings, deserves to be singled out. Arthur Applbaum steered me well away from some early false paths. The MIT theory colloquium, especially Stuart White and Ralph Wedgwood, tore apart one chapter that needed it, and that is much better in reassembled form.

As the manuscript progressed past the dissertation stage, Randy Strahan provided important criticisms of chapter 4. Peter Euben, Sharon Krause, and Sankar Muthu very kindly read different versions of the whole manuscript and gave perfect suggestions. Ian Malcolm, my editor at Princeton University Press, has been both sympathetic and helpful throughout the process, and three anonymous reviewers gave critical assistance. My research assistants, Amy Carter and Karen Peterson, were meticulous and tireless in checking the text and notes. David Sedgwick provided excellent copy editing, and Shirley Kessel prepared a fine index.

Part of chapter 5 previously appeared in a different form in *Society* (vol. 36, no. 4, May/June 1999).

The most important influences are often more distant ones. The English and History teachers at Harvard School in North Hollywood, California, taught me how to write (no doubt not yet to their standards); my undergraduate teachers—Michael J. Sandel, Patrick Riley, and Bonnie Honig—taught me to love political theory.

What my wife Miriam has taught me is, always, most precious of all.

Los Angeles
May 2001

Ruling Passions

Introduction

THIS IS A book about how different kinds of politicians ought to act. By this I mean not which policies they should pursue or which interests they should further—in a democracy, the people decide that—but how they should pursue them.

The work is organized around the idea of a *political office*. My use of this phrase needs explaining, since its several everyday meanings contradict one another, and my own specialized use differs from all of them. In British usage, a public "officer" or "official" tends to mean a civil servant. In American usage, the word "official" tends on the contrary to mean an elected politician, and "officer" is mostly limited to military and police use. Michael Walzer's well-known treatment employs yet a third sense of the word: for him, an office is something one competes for, and attains, based on standards of merit or just entitlement.[1]

My usage is based on that of Cicero, whose book on "offices" (*De Officiis*) refers to recurring public duties or responsibilities.[2] A similar usage appears in the work of John Rawls, who uses "office" to mean any public role stemming from a morally justified social or political practice, including nonpolitical roles such as "promisor" and baseball player.[3] So understood, an office may be defined as a social or political position that embodies ethical value: a position, devoted to a characteristic kind of action, whose existence is judged to serve worthy purposes, and whose grounding in those purposes gives rise to particular duties and privileges that derive from the position. Like Rawls, I prefer "office" to terms like "role" and "function" because the usual sense of the latter words is descriptive and value-neutral, while talk of office retains a moral connotation. By an office, then, I mean a position, profession, occupation, or status that has both social and ethical meaning.

Political office means something narrower, of course. What counts as "political" is endlessly controversial: among plausible definitions are those so narrow that they include only formal occasions of state sover-

---

[1] Walzer (1983: chapter 5).

[2] Cicero (1991). As the translators point out, Cicero's *officium*, usually used in the plural, is a Latin rendering of the Greek *kathekon* (appropriate action). Cicero's usage gives the term Roman associations: Cicero discusses virtue "in terms of the obligations of role and relationships, obligations to other individuals or to the *res publica* as a whole" (xliv).

[3] Rawls (1999c: 23, 29, and esp. 33, 36–37, 39–40; 1999b: 47).

eignty and those so broad that all private choices count as political. My own usage is somewhere in between: a political action is one which attempts to influence others on matters that require common decision. In this case my definition does seem to track common intuitions. Surely few people would call civil rights marches or community organizing drives "nonpolitical" (whether one favors them or not); on the other hand, few would call a preference for zucchini over broccoli a political choice, except to be contrary.

To talk of office is to stress the moral character of political action. Each office, even when there are no written rules governing it, involves obligations and licenses different from those of ordinary citizens. The term "office," with its emphasis on a particular job or task, also stresses the *diversity* of political action and the variety of moral requirements associated with different kinds of action. One office is not like another: different modes of political action have different requirements and should be judged by different standards. This work will argue for an approach to ethics and politics that I call "governing pluralism," which attempts to do justice to this diversity in political action and to the ethical diversity that goes with it.

I shall address, and distinguish, the habits of governance proper to three offices. They are all taken from the politics of the United States, but with the hope that conclusions reached will apply to modern democracies more generally. One is formal, and elected: United States *senator*. Two are informal and unelected: the hortatory *moral activist*, articulator of high public principles, and the political or community *organizer*, builder of movements and assembler of pressure on the basis of interest. These are not the only political offices in the United States or a similar democracy, but focusing on them has both commonsense and scholarly advantages. Those who fill these offices address issues of fundamental importance in public life, do so with great fanfare and under great public scrutiny, and labor under the burden of great responsibilities. Such officers—as opposed to, say, campaign canvassers or city planners—are the kind of people we think of when we praise great "leaders" or castigate inept or irresponsible "politicians."[4]

The responsibilities of these offices have received comparatively little attention from ethicists and political theorists, who tend to stress the duties of executive, judicial, and administrative positions. The proper performance of these duties is of course very important. Yet an exclusive focus on such offices distorts our picture of what political life generally involves and what kinds of moral problems politicians most commonly

---

[4] One advantage of the phrase "political officer" is that it lacks the positive connotations of "leader" or "statesman" and the negative ones of "politician." It does not stack the deck.

face. In particular, it encourages the belief that the most important ethical questions in political life involve whether (and when) occupying an office gives people an excuse to do things that are simply unjust or immoral by everyday standards.

Administrative office involves keeping secrets for the sake of larger goods, denying justice in particular cases for the sake of smooth bureaucratic functioning, and implementing policies one regards as ill-advised, even unjust, but imposed through legitimate channels. Judicial office involves the adjudication of conflicting rights (and inevitably the denial of some rights that parties think they clearly and absolutely deserve), and judicial decisions invoke such distinctively moral arguments having to do with legitimacy, authority, liberty, and equal justice that the occasions for moral and immoral outcomes receive our full attention. Executive office involves, as Weber famously claimed, the authority to use legitimate force—less euphemistically, a license to kill.[5] On a more mundane level, it involves the responsibility of ordering *all* the administrative tasks that already arouse moral worries when taken individually. The potential immorality of all these roles is so striking that political ethics has become almost synonymous with the "dirty hands problem," the question of when politicians may do the wrong thing for good reasons, and how both politicians and the wider public should respond to their consciousness that it was indeed wrong.[6] Or else political ethics involves an insistent denial that such questions are relevant, either from a hard-nosed consequentialist perspective that denies that actions with good outcomes can be morally wrong or from a Kantian perspective that denies that either office or the prospect of good outcomes can justify violations of moral duties.[7]

If hard cases make bad law, easy cases of moral conflict make bad political philosophy. By focusing on cases in which politicians clearly violate (or are tempted to violate) commonsense moral duties, we guarantee drama at the cost of perspective. We portray day-to-day politics as worse than it is. More subtly, we may encourage the lesson that political ethics is only interesting when the prospect of evil-doing is acute. This, however, is very misleading. In a more or less stable democracy, after all, most political hands are sweaty with handshakes, not dirty with clear moral filth.[8] Everyday political morality involves questions of judgment and rhetoric in which our intuitions of good and bad are not clear. The

[5] Weber (1946).

[6] For treatments of the dirty hands problem, see Walzer (1973b); Thompson (1987); and Coady (1993).

[7] With some trepidation, I would attribute these positions respectively to Hare (1989) and Applbaum (1999).

[8] A similar point is made by Shugarman (1990).

morality of ordinary life does not tell us how to reconcile good policy and popular politics; which sorts of compromises on legislation and movement strategy are permissible (even required) and which involve selling out too much; how to make strong public appeals without offending people's prerogatives of disagreement, dissent, and simple self-assertion; how to persuade people that their true interests lie in collective action without denigrating the important private projects to which most people naturally devote their lives. Such decisions rarely involve clear "wrongs" by everyday standards. They result in neither death nor dismemberment; even their effects on property are slow and moderate, and take place through legitimate channels. They do not even involve clear lying and insincere manipulation nearly as often as people think, for such acts are remembered and hurt the offender later.

In fact, the kinds of collective reasoning and public appeals involved in legislative and citizen politics have few analogues in everyday life. Some of the nastier kinds of executive action do indeed look like ordinary butchery dressed up in nice words.[9] But the deliberation and bargaining of the legislator, the hortatory rhetoric of the activist, and the patient listening and persuasion of the community organizer are different: the everyday, "unofficial" analogues of these activities simply do not have moral bite. Speculating about policy, trying to convince others of a moral point in a philosophy study group, or trying to understand why two of one's friends dislike each other are not immoral acts. (One is tempted to say they are *never* immoral.) One reason that politics is interesting, and the ethics of political life counterintuitive, is that it transforms "cheap" talk and mundane virtues into vital questions involving democratic respect, the nature of democratic collective action, and the special responsibilities of those whose daily actions embody power. As Amy Gutmann has pointed out, there is a great moral difference between a mere discussion, which may yield interesting conclusions, and deliberation, which aims at "action-guiding decision."[10]

As a way to get at such questions, this work applies the concept of office to both institutional and noninstitutional politics, and seeks a common theoretical starting point for the political actions appropriate to both. This is not usual, and may be controversial. Neither the advocates of "citizen" or noninstitutional politics nor its opponents would normally describe those who practice it as holding an office or facing the respon-

---

[9] To claim that what the executioner of Paris performed during the Terror should be called "executions," rather than "brutal killings," is to substitute language for moral argument. As Arthur Applbaum has argued (1999: chapter 2), they were killings as well as executions, and the actions of the office can only be justified if the killings can be defended.

[10] Gutmann (1999: 233–34).

sibilities of office. Advocates would find the label demeaning: to call Martin Luther King or Gloria Steinem an "officer" is to associate them with the duplicity and corruptions of power that the holders of office are assumed to embody. Opponents would find the label too flattering: conservatives and others have often argued that protest politicians lack moral standing since "nobody elected them." Both responses, I think, start from the association of *office* with *authority*: elected officials have the authority to make law; elected and appointed officers have the authority to enforce it; and both kinds of authority stem from institutions that cannot easily be questioned or challenged. Those who distrust authority do not want citizen politics tainted by association with it. Those who value authority do not want formal politics debased by association with activities that have lesser dignity and that in fact seem to undermine authority.

Without denying the link between formal office and authority, a work focused on political action rather than the design of formal institutions has reason to place questions of authority to one side and focus instead on how power of all kinds may be responsibly exercised.[11] As I shall argue, the test for political officers is not only whether they cause the right outcomes but whether their actions stand to make democratic politics as a whole better or worse. So understood, the relevant question is not "Who has the authority to make and enforce law?" but "Who has the power to help or harm the democratic polity through his or her actions?" The latter question clearly involves broader issues than the former. To the extent that political ethics has focused on the actions of law-makers and law-enforcers, it has ignored not just an important set of theoretical questions but important kinds of political action that have serious implications for the quality of our public life. In my discussion of office I shall retain the everyday sense that an office involves difficult work and distinct moral responsibilities, while avoiding the natural but hasty assumption that only formal or institutionalized roles embody these qualities.

When we try to judge the behavior of politicians, or consider whether to take a more active role in supporting or opposing them, we immediately encounter problems. To judge politicians, we must balance democratic accountability against governing discretion. We must grapple with contradictory intuitions—that politics is at once a distinctively immoral business, that it is (or can be) somehow nobler than other ways of life, and that it is simply one kind of human action among many, subject to the same ethical rules. And we must decide what it is we fear most from

[11] In this context one might think of the distinction between citizen "power" and state "authority" stressed by Arendt (1961b, 1972b). I do not endorse Arendt's argument as a whole.

political action: fanaticism, selfish indifference, gridlock and inefficiency, baseness and ignobility, unthinking cruelty, incompetence.

At least three different fields of inquiry claim to be helpful on these issues: leadership studies, political ethics, and political theory.

Leadership studies, a branch of political science, is concerned with political success and failure. A good leader is one who succeeds in getting done what she wants to get done: she is good at using power.[12] Some leadership theorists argue that the things conducive to success and power are also conducive to "viable policy," meaning effective, durable policy.[13] Others, more confident in moral progress and more romantic in their picture of how leaders are linked to followers, call for "transformational" leadership: they hope for leaders who will empower the inchoate moral strivings of the electorate in opposition to the self-interested demands of bureaucrats and political hacks.[14] Both outlooks are forceful, as well as moral in their own terms, but neither is good enough. Constitutional, pluralistic government aims at limiting political power, not just promoting its effectiveness. Leadership studies, generally written as advice to princes, should always provoke the question about when we should root for princes to succeed and when we should cheer their failures. When it avoids talking about the ends and principles of governance, leadership studies stacks the deck in favor of the politicians it counsels. It is insensitive even to the claims of opposing politicians—let alone to the claims of ordinary citizens, who lack power and whose ability to control the top leaders may be more notional than real. To the extent that leadership theory claims to fill this moral gap by borrowing from psychology, or by making appeals to the needs of democracy, it does not (I shall argue in chapter 3) put forth well-supported theories of the psyche or of democracy to back these claims up. This weakness in theory is more or less fatal, and the current project will take only three things from leadership studies.

First, a concern with cases. To force clarity and avoid ambiguity, ethical statements about political action should cite concrete examples of when the rule has been broken, the office disgraced, as well as concrete examples of when the rule has been followed, the office done credit to. Second, a concern with character. As citizens, we must select which politicians to trust with power before we can judge actual actions in office.[15]

---

[12] See, for example, Neustadt (1990). By the way, in what follows I shall often use "she" as the generic pronoun. This departure from common usage represents a modest blow for gender equality that harms no one and makes for better style than common alternatives (such as using "he or she" or pretending that "their" is singular).

[13] Neustadt (1990: 153–56).

[14] Burns (1978).

[15] The United States political system, with its weak party discipline and entrepreneurial

To do this we need an idea of which qualities of character are conducive to acting well in office, and how to discern these qualities. Third, a wide definition of what an examination of office should concern itself with. Politicians can and do lie, solicit bribes or more subtle forms of influence, embezzle, abuse their offices, and break laws; we want to know when we should condemn them for such things. But in talking of "ethics," which Bernard Williams has rightly returned to its ancient and broad sense of "how one should live,"[16] we should consider not just what it means to act badly but what it means to act well. Political ethics must address the substance, as well as the form, of a political life. How politicians should aggregate interests, engage in complex policy negotiations, or make public appeals are *ethical* questions, not just pragmatic ones. Plain corruption is morally wrong but also morally simple: where we most need guidance is in judging more complex actions, which offend no formal law or ethics code but affect all our fortunes. I shall focus in this project on the *affirmative* duties and proper habits of political life, both because corruption has received more attention than these questions and because it is easier to recognize betrayal or malfeasance when one knows what one means by trust and good service. Leadership studies, then, asks many of the right questions about political life, though it often gives inadequate answers.

The relation of the present project to moral philosophy is more complex. In a sense, of course, all moral reasoning about politics and society (or at least all careful reasoning that makes serious arguments and rebuts objections) is moral philosophy. Yet the field of moral philosophy as currently constituted tends to embody not only a set of approaches but a characteristic set of premises. First, moral philosophy tends to be *universalist in scope*: the standards of morality are assumed not to vary among different spheres of life. Second, moral philosophy is *universalist in justification*: a moral action is one that can be justified from the standpoint of the rights and/or interests of the whole human race (and on some accounts animals as well); to favor some people's interests over others' is precisely the kind of selfish and narrow impulse that moral philosophers regard it as their duty to oppose. Third, in making exceptions to general rules, moral philosophy *prefers instrumental to intrinsic arguments*: even those philosophers who justify occasional violation of people's rights, or occasional preference for one group's interests over another's, find such actions justified only when carrying them out will ultimately serve the rights or interests of all. That certain special relationships or practices

---

political culture, makes this particularly necessary. Parties and movements in all countries, however, know that the character of their top leaders is crucial to their public appeal.

[16] Williams (1985: chapter 1).

might overrule universal rights and interests permanently and in principle is not seriously considered. Finally, moral philosophy *distrusts political compromise* as a response to moral diversity. Starting from the natural (but perhaps mistaken) assumption that only one moral position can really be best on a particular question, the moral philosopher tends to regard deep moral disagreement as a problem or a tragedy, and to regard most everyday compromises as potentially dangerous concessions to "simple human badness."[17]

I shall dissent from all these positions. I shall argue that politics involves special relations between politicians and the constituents or followers on whose behalf they act. These relations acquire particular moral force in democratic politics, where equal democratic respect for each citizen's opinions requires that politicians limit their reliance on their own personal, fallible judgment. I shall claim that politics rightly involves links between politicians and particular groups (constituencies, voluntary political associations, parties, local neighborhoods) and that in respecting these links politicians normally should give partisan and partial attention to the claims of those to whom they are connected. I shall defend these partial attachments on intrinsic grounds—having to do with democratic values and the special vulnerability of the unaffiliated citizen in the face of collective power—rather than claiming that they always lead to good consequences (though they may). Finally, I shall defend in principle, and not only as a second best, the goods of pluralistic, constitutional politics as "made for people of fundamentally differing views."[18] Once a moral position has proven persistently appealing and incapable of clear refutation, the only way to show respect to those who hold it is to accommodate them, and their views, into the democratic polity as much as possible—while looking for ways in which the pursuit of their views can be made maximally compatible with the legitimate claims of others. At some point in moral disputes, the highest moral imperative is not further moral remonstration but an effort to reach principled compromise.

All of these dissenting positions, to be sure, have vocal defenders from within moral philosophy, and I shall have cause to mention them. But these defenders are often seen by both themselves and their opponents as marginal or exotic, their works regarded as interesting and provocative japes at mainstream moral philosophy positions rather than threats to the ultimate status of these positions. Departures from austere moral universalism are taken seriously, by and large, only in the applied fields: professional ethics and political and constitutional theory. As I shall claim in

---

[17] Nagel (1991: 26). Nagel's use of this phrase is all the more striking because his work is much more pluralistic and nuanced than many.

[18] *Lochner v. New York*, 198 U.S. 45 (1905). Holmes, J., dissenting.

chapter 1, these fields should in fact be regarded not as poor or inexact cousins of "real" ethical theory but as containing their own independent and subtle insights, which respect the complexity of our moral experiences and political lives.

For such reasons, the study of political office turns naturally and all but inevitably to political theory, with its focus on more or less acceptable political orders and more or less salutary political actions. Political theory starts where the admittedly more ambitious aims of moral philosophy are left at an impasse. In the second chapter, I shall argue that a certain account of the relation between political office and the purposes of a democratic polity provides better answers to the ethical questions surrounding political action than do the simple and uncompromising theories of both ethical universalists and their particularist critics. I shall defend the merits of deriving the privileges and limits of a political office from an analysis of the purpose that office serves in a democratic and constitutional political arrangement.

This is not to claim that political theory solves these questions easily or immediately. For the clash between moral universalism and democratic particularism affects our political intuitions as well as our philosophic debates. Not just moral theorists but ordinary citizens want politicians to respect everyone's rights and interests equally—at the same time as we all want special attention paid to our own. A political-theory treatment of office, therefore, cannot start with "ordinary" opinions or a supposed consensus on political norms. Something more is needed if political theory is to avoid merely replicating the interminable disputes over principle that wrack political life—disputes between populists and elitists, fervent activists and determined insiders, instinctive purists and instinctive compromisers. As with the conflict between vocationalists and universalists in the sphere of ethics, this work will try to settle these political disputes in the political sphere through a third alternative that recognizes and accounts for the appeal of each perspective while finding well-grounded principles to settle unavoidable disputes between them. This does not mean bloodless compromise, but a new account that accommodates more concerns than either unmodified perspective yet captures some of the appeal of each.

What this means will be fleshed out in chapter 2 through a reading of three theories of the democratic political order: Aristotle's *Politics*; Hamilton, Madison, and Jay's *Federalist*, and Tocqueville's *Democracy in America*. The basic conclusion will be that political officers must in different ways embody, and promote in the populace, the half-virtue I shall call "democratic constancy," which resembles not so much ancient "virtue" as the effective pursuit of interest. Democratic officers' function is not to tell ordinary citizens how to live but to restrain us from overhasty and ill-advised methods of getting what we want, while prodding us to pursue difficult and farsighted projects whose worth we might not see on our own. Senators embody constancy directly in the course of governance, by responsibly listening to, evaluating, transforming, and enacting into good laws public passions and desires that already exist. Moral activists and organizers encourage constancy in the population by using the moral appeals and organizational structures that Tocqueville noted were so important for fighting individualistic and shortsighted tendencies in democratic life.

Thus, against current trends in democratic theory to define democracy in very demanding terms that stress deliberative rationality, human perfection, and/or universal participation, this work argues for a view of democracy grounded in competing interests. Aspects of this interest theory can be derived from the political philosophy of theorists like Madison and Tocqueville, from the old pluralist tradition in democratic theory and political science, and, in a different and more recent version, from certain sophisticated forms of rational choice theory. Interest theories are often criticized for being reductionist in their view of human nature and indifferent to questions of power and social justice in the portrait they paint of human affairs. This work seeks to address both criticisms by stressing a complex definition of human interest that incorporates Humean sympathy for others and Tocqueville's "self-interest properly understood," as well as a complex definition of democracy that stresses how citizen politics and social movements are needed to challenge the tendency of interest politics to favor the powerful and connected. The work seeks to generalize Madison's insights in *Federalist* No. 10: democratic politics, if it is to avoid tyranny and factional domination, needs not only the checks of representation and geographic diversity within formal governing structures but effective mechanisms for enabling moral critique and organized pressure from powerless people who stand outside those structures.[19]

In chapter 3, I shall address the objections of those who concede the link between political office ethics and larger theories of democratic politics, but whose accounts of democracy, and hence of office, differ from mine. My claim will be not that opposing accounts of democracy are incoherent or simply wrong, but that my account makes fewer controversial assumptions, is less time-bound in its judgments, and is more helpful for guiding practical assessments of political figures given people and democratic politics as they are. First, I shall examine the attempt of moral perfectionists to claim authority over office ethics, not (as some moral philosophers do) by claiming as an axiom that moral philosophy

---

[19] I am indebted to Peter Euben for this way of characterizing my project.

defines the only legitimate framework for practical ethics, but by claiming that a certain portrait of moral reasoning can best define what *democracy* needs, what true egalitarian political principles look like. I will argue that the proponents of this view cannot and do not consistently hold it. Once they examine actual political examples, it becomes clear that moral philosophers who seek to avoid political irrelevance (or worse) must acknowledge the importance of politics, must acknowledge that philosophic truth and moral perfection are not always the standards that motivate political argument. Once we realize this, moral philosophy ceases to have any special claim to distinctive expertise about political discussion (though it can give us useful starting points and questions for political inquiry). Second, I shall examine three works on leadership, which put forth explicitly or implicitly "functional" definitions of leadership success but whose notion of good democratic functioning differs from mine. I will argue that these theories combine, to a greater or lesser extent, dogmatic and time-bound theories of psychopathology with unexamined and utopian ideals of democracy, using arguments from one of these standpoints to cover up weaknesses in arguments derived from the other. Democratic constancy theory is more credible, more durable, and more honest. Finally, I shall examine "economic" theories of democracy that lay claim to a hardheaded understanding of the incentives that drive political action. While sophisticated versions of these theories do tell us much about how politicians and ordinary citizens can be expected to act and to respond to each other, and remind us not to make moral suggestions that contradict democratic realities (especially the need for politicians to maintain public support), they also leave room quite explicitly for considerations that they cannot themselves address. Within the bounds of electoral reality and voter preference, there remains room for ethical action, political judgment, and voter deliberation, and on these subjects economics provides less insight than political theory.

Three succeeding chapters will examine the three political roles I have selected for inquiry. As mentioned, one of these, the senator, holds formal office and has special obligations of governance; the other two, the moral activist and the organizer, do their work in civil society, that is, by rallying ordinary citizens outside formal institutional roles. This work will argue that the last two offices should be treated much like the first. They are political offices, no less real for being informal and voluntary. They are needed for the good functioning of the polity, and their occupants should be scrutinized with the same mix of hope and skepticism that we apply to elected politicians.

First I shall address the office of senator. The office obviously involves representation, often considered the most difficult single issue surrounding the discussion of political office. I will argue that an analysis of democratic and constitutional purposes provides a persuasive account of representation in the particular case of legislative representation (though other accounts may be better suited to other political and nonpolitical roles). Senators, in a constitutionalist analysis, contribute two distinct functions to the regime: deliberation and interest mediation. Deliberation requires that senators force a second look at proposals that are politically popular but perhaps unwise or badly formulated. Interest mediation requires that senators find some way to reconcile both the objective interests of their own states and the deeper fears and concerns of the states' voters (not necessarily the same thing, but both necessary for legitimacy and stability) with the interests of other states and the concerns of other voters. These might seem like two different functions, or three, but I will argue that the same process, or habit of action, serves all of them. Senators who act well will frustrate, as much as possible, unwise or evil public passions while seeking to articulate and address the legitimate concerns and fears that promote these passions. They will look for sets of policies that the electorate may not feel strongly about now nor even understand, but will accept in time (six years being a long time in politics) as conducive to their long-term aims. A bad senator will do the opposite: she will indulge constituents' most ill-advised passions and create new and more dangerous ones, will avoid opportunities to recast debates when demagoguery is easier, and will let an inordinate obsession with reelection overwhelm any concern for longer-term goods of a state or country. The difference is neither obscure nor partisan in nature, as I hope to show by a comparison of Everett Dirksen's senate career with that of Joseph McCarthy.

The moral activist and the organizer do not control the coercive power of the state. This gives them (in comparison to senators) more freedom to make the kinds of appeals we do not want our rulers to make. But it also gives them duties to improve the quality of public desires and demands in ways consistent with democracy, and to limit their ambitions for themselves and their offices lest they become new sources of coercive rule—"antidemocratic" officers in the double sense of unelected and acting contrary to democratic principles of freedom and moral diversity.

The moral activist seeks to achieve social reform primarily by making public appeals (spoken, written, or both) to widely shared public values. Having no direct power over law, the activist seeks to improve society by improving mores—the "habits of the heart" that shape our daily life and personal aspirations—and public opinion, the force that enforces mores. The difficulties and dangers of doing this can be seen from a reading of Rousseau, who claimed that mores could not be altered by force and could only be affected by enlisting those with social prestige on the side of change. The moral activist enlists the *prestige of numbers* in order to buttress a moral argument for changing mores. Combining the two roles that Rousseau called "minister" and "tribune," she uses her standing as a leader of a voluntary moral community to gain a hearing for her appeal to civic values. To combine the two roles requires a subtle understanding of democratic political theory—an ability to distinguish old or new versions of the City of God from the City of Man—and a great deal of personal restraint in keeping one's ministerial ambitions within the bounds of a moral association and one's political ambitions outside it. Martin Luther King Jr. exemplifies the best case. He is to be valued not only for his moral stature and rhetorical nobility but for his subtle perception of constitutional powers and limits, which his own soaring rhetoric often concealed. King not only combined the minister and tribune roles but used each to enrich the other. At the other extreme, however, activists are tempted to try at remaking society in the image of their religious ideals, and to deform the principles and wisdom of their religious and moral traditions out of political impatience with their restraints. Frances Willard, the prohibition activist and social reformer of the nineteenth century, will serve as an example of the harm that can be done to our liberty and our democratic structures when moral activism is done badly.

Finally, there is the office of organizer. The organizer, as distinct from the activist, displays little interest in the question of shared values and in the method of moral appeal. An organizer's function is to exert pressure on the political process (or on private organizations) in order to promote the interests and civic activity of a class, neighborhood, or social group. She does this by enlisting the allegiance and participation of that group. "Pressure" here means the attempt to force change through fear of political damage or economic losses. And the means of building organizations and adding pressure generally involve unabashed appeals to self-interest, pride and ambition, and constructive anger. Any interest theory of democracy must make room for this office, both because the free pursuit of interest allows it inevitably to arise, and because without organizers those who lack power would be treated unjustly and in ways that endangered the values and peace of the democratic order. Even though organizers must be allowed and encouraged to operate, however, the tactics of pressure, when effective, are crude and dangerous. Once again, an account of democratic constitutionalism provides ethical limits on action even in the absence of formal laws. A good organizer seeks to extend either the formal tools of democracy—voting and pursuit of interest—or the effective exercise of these tools, to groups who have previously seen little benefit from such mechanisms. The goal is full and equal integration into the life of the polity. Good organizers want those they are organizing to develop their civic capacities and improve their material opportunities (this does not require a narrow "bourgeois" attitude, though it is consistent with one). The degenerate organizer has no such goal. Driven by anger and pursuing hatred as an end in itself, he—for he is generally male—is accurately accused of "loving the ghetto," or slum, or sweatshop, for the hatred it fosters and the angry audience it provides for the organizer. Because the end is the glory of the organizer, not the civic development of the community, the intelligent interests of the community are soon abandoned as the organizer seeks out meaningless confrontation. Ella Baker, the unsung hero of civil rights organizing, provides a fine example of hardheaded organizing in the service of human ends; Black Power leader Stokely Carmichael demonstrates the danger of an organizer whose hatred led him to miss the difference between real progress and flamboyant self-promotion.

I shall close with two wider points about the project. First, a functional or purposive analysis of democratic office need not imply a quietist acceptance of the status quo or even the assumption that only minor changes are needed. The functionalist political analysis pursued here is distinct from the kind of functionalist *sociology* that sees society as an organic whole with well-designed and well-ordered parts contributing to the good of that whole. While it claims ethical neutrality, such sociology contains a tacit moral preference for keeping social structures the way they are: in a vulgar form of Hegel's "the actual is rational," we are supposed to accept the system, and the roles within it, as the best possible, or at least avoid fundamental criticisms lest the whole edifice come crashing down. To speak of function in political philosophy or legal theory, however, is only to suppose that political offices exist for *good reasons*, and that filling them well means acting according to, and with attention to, those reasons. A democratic constitutional order is a good thing, but it will not work well, or at all, unless the people who run it—including ordinary citizens—act, in some sense, decently.

The actions suggested by political ethics must, if they are to be taken seriously, be politically *possible*, but that does not mean that they are easy or that the habits supporting them are common. An office can be said to have an ethic appropriate to it even if few people currently appreciate this ethic or act according to it. In fact, it is very likely that political offices will be filled by the wrong people, and be performed rather badly, much or most of the time. All we can do is set forth the best possible arguments and examples as standards, so that we have something clear to look for in our officers and yardsticks to assess when they are falling short. In sum, this work shall try to abide by the first rule of good political theory: "be pessimistic."

Second, the animating spirit of the whole inquiry should be made clear. While it aims to provide useful insights to members of all democratic polities, this work frankly values the special genius of American political thought and practice, which I shall call *governing pluralism*. Americans insist, both in theory and in practice, on denying that any organ of government is sovereign.[20] Different state, county, local, and national levels of government have different duties and functions; within the federal government power is not concentrated in a parliament but dispersed among branches; and we expect the voluntary institutions of civil society to play a role in political affairs that in other countries would be monopolized by the state. This principled plurality of governing institutions implies a principled plurality of office ethics: since the functions of governing offices are diverse, so are the characters and habits that conduce to the good performance of each office. Our representative and voluntary institutions not only allow diversity of character, by letting citizens live various nonpolitical lives and not requiring citizens to subscribe to a single national ideology. They also *require* diversity of character even within the broad class of politician, since the good functioning of the polity demands diverse political officers who vary (systematically, not arbitrarily) in their outlooks, styles, and temperaments.

Doing justice to governing pluralism is more radical than it sounds, since many thinkers talk of pluralism without having this governing pluralism in mind. Theories of *moral* pluralism, in particular, can recognize a plurality of moral beliefs and ideologies in the population while still thinking of politicians as having a single function: to create order amid this Babel. (After all, one undeniable moral pluralist is Thomas Hobbes.) A concern with *cultural* pluralism is consistent with having nothing to say about the different modes of government. A theory of *interest-group* pluralism can lead to conclusions opposite to those of this project: while interest-group pluralists often claim that clashes among groups will lead to order, liberty, and approximate justice if left alone, this work denies this and claims that at least a certain attention to the principles and purposes of the whole polity must animate the actions of all political officers.

Finally, it is often thought that theories of *universal democratic participation or deliberation* by their nature do justice to all the different viewpoints present in the regime. But one can speak of democracy as a standard

[20] "To the Constitution of the United States the term sovereign, is totally unknown": *Chisholm v. Georgia*, (1793), 85 (opinion of Justice Wilson). Justice Wilson also notes that the framers could have proclaimed *themselves* sovereign in the name of the people, but avoided doing so. Compare the use of this conclusion, slightly misquoted, in Arendt (1972c: 100ff.). Of course, various forms of constitutional theory regard the people as sovereign in some ultimate sense, but constitutionalism of all kinds seems incompatible with their personally and continuously running the government.

while using this concept in a rigid way that denies governing pluralism. Kantian and deliberative ideals of democracy sometimes argue as if a modern democracy were, or should be, a single rational conversation among the whole citizen body.[21] I shall defend instead the mix of barter, persuasion, moral appeal, group power struggle, and limited rational deliberation that at its best gives modern democracies both vitality and stability—and is in any case the only way democracy is ever likely to be practiced. To engage in political life is not to join an austere Kantian or deliberative order, but to play one of several different positions in a loud, democratic contest where power and persuasion are hard to separate and rarely need to be separated. This is not to deny that the contest has rules, reasoned rules. What follows will aim to do justice to both the reasons behind the rules and the excitement of the game.

---

[21] Thus Sunstein (1984: 1732) calls for a "unitary theory of the constitution," which would explain all its provisions by reference to a single goal.

PART ONE

Theory

Political Offices:
Universalism, Partiality, and Compromise

IN THINKING ABOUT what politicians should do and the qualities of character that will help them do it, we have conflicting intuitions. Our populist worries that politicians will "sell out" their constituents for personal advantage or campaign contributions clash with our good-government worries that they will sell out the public good, or minority rights, in pandering to their constituencies.[1] We want politicians to be policy experts, but also to have the sympathy with popular beliefs that excessive expertise can obscure. We want politicians to represent our desires as well as our interests, but we know these sometimes clash. We believe that individuals are the best judges of their own interests, as long as the individuals involved are ourselves: we want politicians to listen to people like us while saving others from their obvious ignorance.

At the heart of the conflict is the question of partiality. While we want politicians to place the public good above their own greed or ambition, we do not want cold calculation of the public good to displace altogether a regard for particular opinions, needs, and fears. We want politicians to listen to our special and diverse concerns—both because this deepens and enriches their consideration of what is right and good[2] and because the listening is intrinsically valuable and shows respect for citizens' democratic aspirations and capacity for independent judgment. What Robert Post writes about lawyers also applies to politicians: they "bestride the following cultural contradiction: we both want and in some respects have a universal, common culture, and we simultaneously want that culture to be malleable and responsive to the particular and often incompatible interests of individual groups and citizens."[3]

The rest of this chapter defends this cultural contradiction on principle. Both conflicting intuitions, I claim, reflect something vitally important and worth preserving. Our views of political society should reflect the desirability of a workable and permanent compromise between the

---

[1] I am using "constituencies" broadly to include the nongeographic constituencies of a social movement, organization, or party as well as the local constituencies of a district-based representative system.

[2] See Benhabib (1992: chapter 5).

[3] Post (1987: 386).

two. While compromising with evil can be defended on grounds of necessity, I have in mind a more principled compromise: the kind that arises in philosophy when two or more legitimate but incommensurable values clash, and in politics when one respectable culture or social group regards as fundamental to its ethical life certain moral assumptions that another such culture finds offensive or appalling.[4] Compromise of this kind expresses not a lack of courage or moral principle but respect for a diversity of standpoints and moral assumptions.

As Martin Benjamin has pointed out, attachment to compromise need not mean indifference towards simply evil groups. "Nazis, professional murderers, racists" and so forth may have ways of life and moral assumptions, but we need not respect them. While we may have to tolerate their actions for pragmatic reasons, it is perfectly fine to hope for (and advocate) the ultimate extinction of their views and habits.[5] Even Aristotle, often viewed as an advocate of basing all politics on class compromise, did not advocate a politics that simply mixed all partial views together out of indifference or a love of color. He wanted to accommodate a range of political axioms for the sake of peace—a principled consideration— but also because he respected the partial truths that the prejudices of the many, the wealthy, and the virtuous brought to politics. The best political order, in his view, sought to accommodate the best features of each group's worldview while persuading each group to abandon (or at least give up on achieving in politics) those parts of its view that were without value or clearly unacceptable to others.[6] Some values and outlooks, then, deserve to provoke not compromise but moral opposition, and at most grudging toleration when necessity demands it.

Beyond this (and less often noted) lie two further considerations. The first involves the *costs* of compromise. Even when a position is not inherently evil and may be believed in good faith, uncompromising opposition to it may be justified if the costs of being wrong about it are very high. For instance, those who oppose a war may find the pro-war faction reasonable and even well-intentioned, but if the destruction caused by the war is great enough, the war's opponents may still be provoked to extreme measures—massive peaceful resistance at least, and armed revolt in the final case—in opposition to it. Similarly, much of the debate on abortion concerns not only the rights or wrongs of it but how direly the costs of being wrong should be portrayed. Those who see a "conflict of social values" between human life and individual autonomy draw very different

---

[4] Benjamin (1990: chapter 4).

[5] Benjamin (1990: 94).

[6] Aristotle (1984: II.9, 1270b21; III.13, 1283b27ff.; IV.9, 12–13 passim). See also Resnick (1979).

practical conclusions from those who focus on screaming fetuses or bloody coat hangers.

Second, compromise is not always possible in the real world: two proposals can be practically incompatible even when neither has much morally wrong with it. Consider two groups debating how to design a legislature: one group demands proportional representation so that the full diversity of citizens' views may be represented as much as possible; the other calls for a system of single-member districts as more likely to result in clear legislative majorities and hence coherent legislation. In this case, splitting the difference will have perverse results. An assembly elected half by one method and half by the other will tend towards neither a clear majority nor an accurate mirror of the electorate; adopting a bicameral legislature, with each house based on a different plan, will accommodate both views at the cost of inefficiency and continued dissension over which house has more legitimacy. Here both views are respectable, but a principled compromise is elusive: we can cobble together an agreement for the sake of peace, but in doing so we shall frustrate *both* the values involved. Rhetoric can sooth the problem politically—and is morally desirable to the extent that it expresses respect for the losers—but it cannot create a result that *really* embodies the best of what each party sought. Apart from constituent assemblies, the clearest example of such an issue is probably, once again, abortion.[7]

A case for principled compromise between two positions must therefore show that neither position is so evil that no compromise is possible, that the costs of compromise are manageable, and that a practical middle ground can be found. This will involve not just moral but social and political argument. What seem to be moral disagreements may reflect deeper quarrels about how the world works. On the other hand, a thorough look at political possibilities may make moral compromise seem more practical than it first appears.

The Moral Issue: Universalism and Vocationalism

In moral philosophy, the ordinary or default position is one of moral universalism: "actions are to be governed by principles that give equal consideration to all people who might be affected by an action."[8] This can be interpreted in a utilitarian way, following the maxim "each to count for one, none for more than one," or in a more Kantian way that

---

[7] The issue of compromise on abortion arouses almost as much disagreement as the substantive morality of abortion itself. For a range of views see Tribe (1992); Glendon (1987); Gutmann and Thompson (1996: chapter 2); and the articles by Alan Wertheimer and Robert P. George in Macedo (1999: chapters 12 and 13).

[8] Gomberg (1990: 144). See also Gewirth (1988: 283).

stresses the need to respect the rights and dignity of all autonomous persons even when utilitarian considerations would counsel ignoring such rights for the greater good.[9] For current purposes, the differences are less important than the common problems these two sorts of universalism pose for the defenders of vocation and particular commitment.

As Richard Wasserstrom has noted, both conventional moral relations (like that of parent to child) and professional duties (like that of lawyers to clients) can be hard to justify if we take universalism seriously. There is an inherent tension both between conventional practices and the more idealistic forms of conventional morality, and between professional ethics and universal moral theory. Particularly where "important needs and interests are at stake," moral theory tends to insist on "equality of consideration and treatment in quite a strong sense." Our personal and professional habits, however, involve giving some people much more consideration than others.[10]

A strongly universalist perspective can make particularism seem wrong on its face, even evil: it is precisely our selfishness, our tendency to prefer our own loved ones and associates to those who need our help more, that it is the purpose of ethics to combat. Universalists point out the dark side of particularism and the real harms at stake. The world contains starving people whom I ignore by spending money on my family; it contains victims of racism and colonialism whose prospects I harm when I hire "my own sort of people"; it contains, even in one's own country, truly needy candidates for charity who are forsaken when I spend my wealth on hospitality and generous tips.[11]

Such utilitarian, Marxist, and Christian versions of universalism may demand extraordinary activism or a crusading attitude towards social evils. But there is also a Kantian version of universalism that is less demanding, and for that reason all the more credible. Excessive devotion to roles, says this argument, can make people simply callous and prone to harm people in obvious ways: to lie, or humiliate truthful witnesses, in the name of serving legal clients; to obey administrative orders that of-

[9] See Dworkin (1978: xi–xii). The Kantian formulation is particularly prominent in legal reasoning, because of its attachment to protecting people's rights and treating cases equally regardless of consequences. Likewise, philosophers of the welfare state who view economic justice in terms of just entitlements often want to extend such entitlements to the poor regardless of their utilitarian effects. Many who support Kantianism in law, economics, and private life become utilitarians on policy matters, particularly when war or other crises are involved, when necessity can require that we let some be harmed to prevent pressing harm to others. See, for example, C. Fried, "The Lawyer as Friend" (1976: 1087n39); and Nagel (1979b). The case for being a utilitarian in the political realm but not necessarily in other areas of life is made by Goodin (1995) and Rawls (1999c). For a dissenting view, see Applbaum (1999).

[10] Wasserstrom (1983: 34).

[11] For classic arguments see Singer (1979); Gomberg (1990); and Lewis (1952: 68).

fend our core moral and political principles; even to kill innocent people if the name of our calling happens to be "executioner."[12] In private life, our roles or particular duties may not regularly inspire such dubious deeds, but even the role of friend or family member can motivate arguably unjust actions, such as gross nepotism. When particularists praise values like devotion to family, preference for associates over strangers, loyalty, attachment to cultural norms, suspicion of abstract right, and mutual aid based on personal acquaintance, universalists might reply that they have just described the Mafia. The problem with arguments from particular roles is that they shield from all criticism a huge range of morally wrong acts: we simply allow ourselves (and others) to do bad things with the question-begging excuse that our accustomed roles permit them.[13]

The accusation of badness, however, goes both ways. If universalism is the mainstream position in moral theory, particularism is the mainstream position in moral practice and, by extension, among "applied moralists."[14] From the perspective of our everyday practice, the austere maxims of universalism demand too much and too little: they ask that we spend excessive time and attention on the needs of strangers while neglecting the familial, professional, associative, and patriotic acts that lie at the heart of what most people mean by a good and moral life. A favorite example is that of Dickens's Mrs. Jellyby in *Bleak House*: absolutely devoted to African orphans, she neglects her own children, whom visitors find dirty and unfed.[15] This is perhaps a poor example—for one thing, Dickens stacks the deck by not showing us how the African children live and what Jellyby's acts might mean to them. Still, there remains something stern and scary about taking universalism too seriously. Are we really required to pursue social justice causes that are so controversial and ill-paid that we "parent" from jail and clothe our children from the charity bin?[16] Are we really required to help the world's needy if this means decimating the social and economic institutions of our own countries? At *some* point it seems mad not to respect a range of particular claims: that one should save one's mother from a plane crash before saving a famous surgeon, that one should, other things equal, fight for one's own country in a war, at least in one that threatens its whole way of life; that one should be entitled to pursue one's accustomed projects free from constant moral criticism of the resources devoted to them.[17]

Fairness and impartiality are very important goods, but even these

---

[12] Applbaum (1999).

[13] Wasserstrom (1983: 28).

[14] As claimed by Goodin (1985: 6).

[15] Dickens (1991), and see the reference thereto in Sandel (1996: 343).

[16] The example is a real one: for a chronicle and defense, see Berrigan (1996).

[17] See, respectively, Williams (1981: 1–17); MacIntyre (1984); and Nagel (1991).

goods have their limits. In breaking up a fight among nine-year-olds, perhaps *teachers* have a responsibility to ascertain the facts without bias, but *parents* are entitled to start from the premise that their own children are innocent. If they did not, their children would surely be right to regard them as bad parents, and bad people—though possibly good "judges," a role no one asked them to fill. As Virginia Held points out, it is very misleading to assume that "ordinary morality" is equivalent to universalist moral reasoning and that particularist or professional exceptions are exotic and hard to fathom. Ordinary people neither practice nor expect impartiality most of the time: they assume that people devote themselves to the moral tasks they know best, and in fact assume that moral reasoning should vary according to role and circumstance.[18] Some particularists accuse universalism of "thinness" and alienation, of failing to give us moral direction and to ground our lives in definable moral tasks and obligations.[19] But in fact, a more intuitive and widespread criticism is almost the opposite of this. Ordinary people, according to this criticism, do quite well at pursuing their everyday tasks as parents, friends, lovers, and so on, and do their best (with some professional advice) to perform difficult professional obligations as (say) lawyers, ministers, and doctors. Universalism tells us to abandon these manageable tasks in favor of universal crusades, but this risks—perhaps guarantees— that the crusade will lose while the tasks remain abandoned.[20] Universalism, on this account, is not culpably thin but culpably thick: it advocates utter devotion to controversial theories while failing to help us with our real ethical lives.

Things are not as bad as all this. The interminable rock-throwing between particularists and universalists naturally teaches us a certain modesty and pluralism in our moral evaluations. In deference to universal morality, we should, and generally do, reject the most immoralist, aristocratic, and Nietzschean forms of particularism. For the sake of a limited particularism grounded in the worth of certain personal relationships, we should reject in turn the most leveling and uncompromising forms of universalism. The concentration camp guard may not defend the camp by pleading his sense of vocation and his deep devotion to Hitler (or

---

[18] Held (1983).

[19] This is the main line of criticism assumed by Applbaum (1999: 47); he presumably has in mind the tack taken by Sandel (1982), inspired by Hegel (1991). The Hegelian defense of *Bestimmung*—properly translated as "role" or "vocation," but with the root meaning of "specification" or "determination"—does indeed appeal to arguments against the alleged thinness of Kantian morality. Sandel likewise makes much of John Rawls's (1971) perhaps unfortunate phrase "thin theory of the good."

[20] See Held (1983: 64).

fellow Aryans); the moral urgency of international famine relief does not excuse the head of the relief agency if he fails to ensure that his children go to school.

There remains an asymmetry involving theory and practice: universalism, probably never seen in practice anywhere, is easy to defend with simple reasoning, while particularism is common in practice but hard to justify theoretically in a form that allows for criticism and moral judgment. Defenses of particularism often seem to justify anything people do out of deep conviction or out of attachment to close friends or family. Especially in politics, this will not do: without making too many claims for public life, one thing it should surely do is disabuse people who think that they are entitled to everything they want and that everyone should bow to their personal projects. So if we want to articulate a compromise between universalism and vocationalism in political life, it is the latter that needs a theoretical defense. The kind of vocationalism we need to defend is not a heroic or violent sense of vocation that leads some to believe themselves destined (or chosen) to break all the rules, but a moderate sense of vocation: the kind of particularism that ordinary people can easily grant to others as well as themselves, and that universalists, uncomfortable with all moral exceptions and particular attachments, can at least regard as a position they can compromise with.

In what follows, I shall defend *one* kind of vocationalism: the kind that justifies certain types of action rooted in special relationships, and that defends those relationships on the basis of the need and vulnerability of those whom they involve. Such needs are, in a modern democratic polity, held by everyone: each of us is politically powerless on his or her own, and needs the assistance of politicians if our interests and opinions are to be heeded. The particular claims involved may not be universal*ist* in form, but they are universal in scope. Moreover, in a democratic polity, in which political offices do not stem from birth or force but are voluntarily sought and democratically responsible, such relationships will have particular moral force. For they will combine the special duty to protect the helpless or vulnerable with the special obligations and permissions that arise from choice and voluntary agreement.[21]

---

[21] The argument here therefore does not concern what Samuel Scheffler has called "associative" duties, which are often based on ascriptive membership (Scheffler mentions moral claims made by "families and clans . . . nations and states . . . races and religions . . . cultures and communities and classes" [1994: 18]). Scheffler (1999b) argues that any relationship we have reason to value gives rise to obligations whether or not it is voluntarily incurred; Hardimon (1994) makes the more limited claim that duties to the State and to family are of this category. The current work is agnostic on these questions. In any case, democratic political offices are clearly different from ascriptive roles: in a modern democracy, offices are voluntarily incurred, and those who do not choose to seek them do not incur the special

This kind of vocationalism takes us, at least in politics, fairly far. It serves to explain and justify political actions and roles that unsympathetic critics (and even inarticulate supporters) might defend on the basis of raw power, cynicism, or unalloyed self-interest. But if the vocationalism of democratic relationships is far-reaching in practice, it is sharply defined in theory. It is important to distinguish it from other defenses of vocationalism that claim to justify particular vocations on the grounds of moral integrity or high-level forms of universalism.

Vocationalism and Integrity

We all know people who claim their work is their life. We have at least read of people who would not consider life worth living if they could not do a certain kind of work. To the extent that we value people's lives, we are then required, according to a simple syllogism, to value the "ground projects" on which their leading meaningful lives depends. This is the well-known argument of Bernard Williams.[22] Martin Benjamin makes a milder but similar argument: we aim at moral compromise with others because we recognize that their adherence to a moral tradition different from our own is constitutive of their integrity, and we demand, in turn, that others not ask us to compromise so much that we endanger our own integrity.[23] From such arguments can follow a very strong defense of vocation, including political vocation.[24] To ask people whose lives are strongly grounded in vocation or moral projects to give up their grounding for universalist reasons is to ask them to sacrifice all that gives their life meaning.

Integrity arguments seem to rest on the premise that one's identity is unified and indissoluble, clear and transparent to oneself, and consistent over time—all of which may be doubted for skeptical reasons associated with Hume.[25] But the best responses to integrity-based defenses of vocation involve not philosophical skepticism about identity (which is admittedly technical, unsettled, and controversial) but everyday skepticism

---

obligations that go with them. Put another way: the relationships discussed here stem from what Scheffler calls "particular" or "discrete" interactions (1999b: 199), namely, the political interactions involved in seeking and granting office, and do not involve the unchosen "web of social relations" (1999b: 204) with which Scheffler is chiefly concerned.

[22] Williams (1991: 1–19).

[23] Benjamin (1990).

[24] The defense is not, as some critics maintain, absolute or crude. Williams (1991: 37) stresses that whether a person's ground projects benefit society or are valued by it matters a great deal, especially in politics where official actions clearly affect everyone. Likewise Benjamin stresses throughout his work that a principled defense of one's own integrity contains the moral requirement that one try to accommodate the jarring implications of others' claims to moral integrity as well.

[25] Hume (1978: 1.4.6, 251–63); see also Parfit (1984).

about whether our moral lives really work as portrayed. As David Luban has pointed out, it just does not seem true that abandoning ground projects is impossible or undesirable. People can, and do, become former communists (one might multiply examples: former Kantians, former Tories, former rock stars) without thereby rendering their whole lives untenable or without meaning. In fact, the rejection of former ground projects can lead to new sources of meaning. Nor is rejection of ground projects always undesirable. Passionate engagement in a project or way of life does not and should not rule out sometimes putting aside one's engagement when pressing moral or prudential considerations require this.[26]

In some cases, we might add, people *should* reject their projects to the extent that they find others more coherent, important, or morally worthy. Religious conversions and their secular equivalent (relatively quick and thorough transformations of one's whole moral outlook and character) are certainly rare, difficult, and potentially dangerous. We are right to regard them as uncommon and not to blame people for failing to convert to our views at a snap. But Benjamin's integrity argument seems to require the judgment that such conversions are *wrong*—ethically wrong, violations of integrity—and that they always involve a loss of moral coherence, even when people abandon a traditional but narrow and barely defensible worldview in favor of one that is more inclusive. While this kind of moral traditionalism is always attractive to many, the defense of moral rootedness against all comers is too controversial to base a social philosophy on: the Enlightenment tradition of moral criticism and ironic self-examination has too much to say on the other side. In any case, the traditionalist defense of vocation does not translate well to democratic politics. In a democracy, few people grow up and are educated in traditions that assume they are destined to gain political power. Those who are (perhaps communists, as well as scions of political families who expect to engage in public service), are themselves in some tension with democratic principles, by which power, even power over a social movement, is to come from popular selection. In a democracy, nobody should think of himself as to the office born.

Indirect Consequentialism

Given the problems with integrity arguments, most defenders of vocationalism try another tack. They argue that special duties and professional roles, taking the long view, promote universal values. The util-

[26] "I may find music a thing that makes life worth living and commit my life, my fortune, and my sacred honor to hearing, playing, and studying music. This does not prevent me from appreciating that music-making is of strictly limited importance, and I will join the bucket-brigade to stop Rome from burning even if I must give up a once-in-a-lifetime opportunity to hear Peter Nero" (Luban [1988: 144]).

itarian argument appeals to a division of labor in both the social and psychological senses. When people are devoted to their friends and to particular tasks, they gain the propensity and ability to benefit certain people; and this creates more happiness than would a diffuse and merely theoretical commitment to benefiting everyone at once. "If mothers had the propensity to care equally for all the children in the world, it is unlikely that children would be as well provided for even as they are. The dilution of the responsibility would weaken it out of existence."[27] A rights-based, more or less Kantian argument (though not Kant's, and Kant would probably oppose it) can be made along similar lines. In many circumstances, people's human rights can only be protected if a given group, including a particular political body or state, takes the lead in protecting them. Since a person cannot undertake such a defense either for herself or for all human beings at once, a call for defending everyone's rights and dignity equally but no one's dignity specifically all but guarantees that many people's rights and dignity will not be defended at all. An analogous argument justifies familial particularism: our sense of dignity and agency is enhanced when someone in particular puts us first. "Mutual concern and support" in loving relationships "enhance the partners' general abilities of agency."[28]

There are three problems with such arguments. First, they are uncertain. Like so many sophisticated consequentialist arguments, they are plausible but not even remotely provable. Arguments with opposite conclusions—for example, monastic or communist arguments for renouncing normal human ties and devoting our lives to the poor—are also plausible. If we defend our love for our own children on the basis that children as a whole need care, we might further our goals just as well by combating our selfish desire to procreate, devoting the money (and time?) saved to supporting orphanages for the parentless.

Second, while indirect consequentialism might justify *some* level of particular attachment to our own roles and vocations, it probably justifies nowhere near the *amount* of particularity we ordinarily think justified.[29]

---

[27] Hare (1981: 137). See also Sidgwick (1981: Book 4, chapter 3, 432–37).

[28] Both arguments appear in Gewirth (1988; quotation at 294). For a similar argument that proclaims itself broadly consistent with both Kantian and utilitarian viewpoints, see Goodin (1985). Note that these sorts of arguments might be called something like "rule-rights-based" arguments in analogy to so-called "rule-utilitarianism": such arguments justify a whole scheme of institutions and practices on the grounds that they best serve the cause of rights and human dignity. Thus they are not Kantian if this implies being deontological and stressing our duty to refrain from any individual act of dignity-violation. Applbaum (1999) is closer to orthodox Kantianism—at the cost (or benefit, depending on one's views) of granting very little leeway to claims based on roles.

[29] A similar point about lawyers' roles is made by Wasserstrom (1983: 36).

Utilitarianism might allow that parents buy two sets of warm clothes for their children when some children have none, and that judges spend time marginally improving their court systems even when some countries live in anarchy. But as Peter Singer has argued (approvingly),[30] pure utility would probably imply that we should spend some vast amount of our resources and those of our family on relief of the Third World poor. Similarly, the utilitarian case for professionals' devotion to clients cannot easily survive the question of *which* clients to serve: utilitarian doctors should probably leave their current practices and move to Bangladesh, and utilitarian judges volunteer for war-crimes tribunals in Rwanda. Consequentialist arguments that go beyond utility and try to maximize rights or dignity face similar problems. However useful in rebutting a stern abstract moralism under which nobody cares about anyone in particular, they still make our ordinary moral commitments seem inferior to a life of loving selflessness. This is another version of the orphanage objection: surely a person maximally concerned with seeing that *everyone* has sustaining relationships should engage in only a small amount of parenting and helping of friends as long as there are orphans in the world who live in great danger and are totally devoid of personal care. In terms of professional roles, the call for professionals to practice selfless crusading in countries devoid of law, medicine, or political peace once again seems unanswerable.[31]

Finally, two-level universalist arguments defend particular devotions for the wrong reasons. Some have claimed that even to question our particular duties makes us ethically worse. It is said that when we stop to think why we are permitted to rescue our spouses before strangers, or (we might add) why lawyers may favor their own clients over anonymous other claimants to their help, this is "one thought too many": the demand for justification demeans both the act and the moral status of the person for whom we are acting.[32] This is too strong. Even deep, unquestioned, and heartfelt moral impulses can be wrong, even hateful, and they are in any case subject to legitimate question.[33] The more accurate point

[30] Singer (1979: chapter 8).

[31] Goodin (1985: 154–69) admits that the "vulnerability" argument entails a duty of massive aid to poor countries, but does not seem to appreciate how deeply his universalized vulnerability argument would implicate our special duties to friends and families. The amount of foreign aid he regards as morally required would entail tremendous disruption of the lives and expectations of people in rich countries.

[32] Writing about someone facing a choice whether to save his wife or a random stranger in an emergency, Williams (1981: 18) attacks universalist reasons for preferring the former: "It might have been hoped by some (for instance, by his wife) that his motivating thought, fully spelled out, would be the thought that it was his wife, not that it was his wife and that in situations of this kind it is permissible to save one's wife."

[33] Gewirth (1988: 298).

is that we want our argument for special devotion to friends, family, and professional to be based on *intrinsic*, not *instrumental*, values: we do not want it to depend on whether the relationship survives a calculation of consequences for the world's happiness or for the promotion of equal and universal rights.[34]

This is not to deny that our attachment to certain relationships must be balanced against universal concerns. No one claims that one's attachment to a sibling would justify torturing innocent people to death merely because the sibling enjoyed watching. An intrinsic argument for special devotions, however, requires seeing conflicts between universal and particular duties as involving a balance between different sorts of value. Universal duties may in many cases clearly *outweigh* particular attachments without rendering the latter unimportant; in other cases, it may be particular attachments that provide sufficient weight to outweigh universal concerns. Taking seriously our relationships with friends, family, or clients does not entail doing all that they need (or want), but it does entail doing *some* things for them that we would not do for others, without having to justify these things by universal standards.

Intrinsic Political Relationships: the Politician as Friend

The most plausible defense of particularism in politics, then, will involve an account of the intrinsic goods that political relationships serve. The political ethics literature seems to contain no such account, but we can take as a starting point Charles Fried's famous argument in legal ethics: "The Lawyer as Friend." Fried's analogy between the lawyer-client relationship and the bond between friends has been mercilessly attacked on several grounds, and rightly so. I shall claim, however, that when we transfer the friendship analogy from law to politics we avoid all the criticisms. Politicians at their best *are* what Fried calls "special-purpose friends." They serve others in ways that ordinary lawyers cannot, and with far less harm to society than Fried's adversarial mercenaries are licensed to inflict.

Fried defends the lawyer's special concern for his or her own clients, even when this devotion to clients' interests fails to maximize, or even harms, the common good. Fried is skeptical of rule-utilitarian arguments for roles. For reasons similar to those cited above, he believes that an intrinsic argument for the lawyer-client relationship will be both more

---

[34] C. Fried (1976: 1068). Gewirth's use of "intrinsic" is somewhat different: he argues for particular attachments for non-utilitarian reasons, but his goal is apparently to maximize the actual promotion of universal human rights in the world. Gewirth is probably conflating "instrumental" with "utilitarian": an argument to the effect that acts are justified if they maximize rights in the long run is instrumental and consequentialist though not utilitarian.

credible than a consequentialist one and more likely to reflect the immediate, noncalculating attachment that we would like people involved in such relationships to cherish.[35]

Fried's argument has three main elements. First, he defends personhood and individuality as intrinsic goods that we are entitled to favor even at some cost to public utility. Second, he claims that certain close relationships affirm or respect personhood better than impersonal standards of justice do. Building upon several traditions in which love of one's friends is compared to a proper love of oneself, Fried writes: "The individualized relations of love and friendship (and perhaps also their opposites, hatred and enmity) have a different, more intense aspect than do the cooler, more abstract relations of love and service to humanity in general. . . . Justice is not all of morality; there remains a circle of intensity which through its emphasis on the particular and the concrete continues to reflect what I have identified as the source of all sense of value—our sense of self."[36] Finally, Fried argues that certain aspects of personhood can only be affirmed through a peculiar professional relationship—the lawyer as "limited-purpose friend" devoted to legal matters only. For only lawyers, and not people's everyday personal friends or family, can defend individuals' rights and personal integrity when they are confronted with a powerful and complex legal system that laypersons cannot master.[37]

The picture that emerges is one of human dignity under fire. While a legal system that did not allow for vigorous advocacy (an inquisitorial system, say, or one founded on administrative models) might effectively further utilitarian ends, it could do so only by operating over the heads of those it governed, making expert decisions that individuals could neither understand nor effectively challenge. In short, such a system would be manipulative, opaque, and unfair: "Without such an adviser, the law would impose constraints on the lay citizen (unequally at that) which it is not entitled to impose explicitly."[38] The precise actions justified by the advocate's role are of course relative to the content of the legal system, but the role itself derives from the nature of human dignity: systems that lack it are inferior, morally speaking, to those that recognize it.[39]

The general form of this argument is, I would argue, compelling. Only

---

[35] C. Fried (1976: 1067–1068).

[36] C. Fried (1976: 1070). Compare Aristotle (1985: 9.4.11.1–9.4.11.6, 1166a1–1170b8). Fried (1069n21) cites similarly the biblical injunction to love one's neighbor (or in Leviticus, "friend") as oneself, and Thomas Aquinas's gloss on this passage, which as usual in Aquinas's work synthesizes biblical charity and Aristotelian philosophy.

[37] C. Fried (1976: 1068–1073).

[38] C. Fried (1976: 1073).

[39] C. Fried (1976: 1066).

the crudest utilitarians would be likely to deny that respect for individual dignity is a good, that close human relationships are good in themselves (at least partly because they express this good), and that among the most honorable of such relationships are those in which people with special power or knowledge help the less powerful defend their rights and dignity as they would want their own defended. While one can put a Kantian gloss on this, none is required. We need only care that individuals be able to defend their own rights and reasonable claims, and recognize that they often need help in doing so.

My account of political office is modeled on Fried's account of legal advocacy. It starts with a conception of political dignity—rooted in the democratic idea that every citizen is equally entitled to judge his or her rights, opinions, and interests, and to put forth those judgments in the political arena. Democratic dignity is expressed most fully when all citizens have not only equal political rights but real and equal influence in the effective exercise of those rights. With Fried, I maintain that this dignity is best expressed in relationships: in this case, *political* relationships in which democratic dignity is not only allowed in the abstract but directly affirmed by political figures who identify with concrete citizens' actual claims. Finally, both the content of policy and the operation of the political system are, no less than the law and the legal system, frighteningly complex and opaque: ordinary citizens can hardly hope to articulate their claims effectively without the help of professional political advocates who make public life a vocation.

The politician-as-friend model avoids several criticisms that have dogged Fried's claims about lawyers. Fried's argument is more infamous than famous; it has been attacked at virtually every point. One can identify five separate lines of criticism. All of them have some bite against Fried's argument, but none carries over when we apply his analogy to politics.

The first criticism is that legal clients are not always as helpless as Fried implies. As David Luban has argued, *some* parties to legal cases would be truly forsaken without their lawyers—criminal defendants facing the power of the state come to mind—but other legal clients, such as large corporations in civil suits, may have much more power and information than their adversaries. They do not need the kind of befriending on which Fried bases his defense of legal zeal.[40]

Second, Fried is said to claim too much for friendship: even if we accept the analogy between lawyers and friends, there is a limit to what we may do for our friends. When defending actions that actively harm people (like humiliating witnesses one knows to be telling the truth, or

---

[40] Luban (1988: 8, and passim).

freeing one's client from a just lawsuit by pleading the statute of limitations), we cannot rely on friendship arguments.[41]

Third (and related to the previous argument), one might argue that omissions of duties to the common good, as well as harms against specific persons, can be hard to justify with friendship arguments. If a president or general deserts his post because his retired father would really like his company on a three-month fishing vacation, the desertion of public duty is culpable. Of course, no one is required to take on strenuous public duties, but in a study that focuses on those who have chosen such duties—politicians—this is no excuse. If a duty to serve the public good goes with the professional office, friendship cannot excuse people from this duty.

Fourth, the friendship argument can be generalized to absurdity, or at least to consequences few would endorse. Just as the consequentialist arguments mentioned above would seem to require giving succor not just to one's own children but to all the helpless children of the world, professionalism as limited-purpose friendship would seem to require assigning priority for legal aid to the people who are most helpless before the law. To accept the consequences of this we would have to revolutionize professional codes: no one could represent a well-off private client until all poor people were in fine shape.

Finally, it has been pointed out that a limited-purpose friend is a strange beast both conceptually and experientially. The lawyer-client relationship is, after all, mercenary: "While it is true that the lawyer and the client may be friends, like the butcher and the baker, what they do for each other for the sake of money are not offices of friendship."[42]

Now consider these arguments in the political realm. In politics, individual citizens really are helpless, without exception. As individuals, typical citizens know very little about politics. They cannot describe the stance of candidates or parties on important issues, or even name major politicians beyond the most prominent national officers. Nor is this surprising: following politics takes time and effort, and most people, even most competent and reflective people, have too much to do in their private lives. While Ronald Dworkin concludes from this that ordinary people's opinions should be given little weight in political decisions,[43] this conclusion

---

[41] Luban (1988: 84).

[42] Donagan (1983: 128). See also Goodin (1985: 96n80). Donagan excuses Fried from this argument by claiming that the friendship metaphor represents only a loose analogy for Fried and does not do essential work. This may or may not be true of Fried's own argument; in any case my current argument is unwilling to jettison the idea of a close parallel between politics and friendship.

[43] See the surprisingly blunt statement in Dworkin (1999: 106).

does not follow. For one thing, none of us would be considered competent if asked for opinions on *every* policy question; the difference in competence between one citizen and another is much smaller than that between even a well-informed lay citizen and a policy expert on a given issue. In any case, Dworkin's conclusion ignores an obvious alternative: if ordinary people are ignorant or inarticulate, we could, rather than ignoring them, encourage the activities of informed advocates who can speak for them. We respect people's dignity not only when we treat them fairly but when we try to improve their chances to articulate their own opinions of what is fair.[44] Finally, even if an individual were omnicompetent, isolated individuals would still be helpless when it comes to political action. As stressed by political scientists from Hobbes to Tocqueville and beyond, only by combining with others can a single individual ensure her physical safety, let alone some chance of achieving her ends. One can advocate (as I shall too) giving everyone as many associative skills as possible, but realistically speaking there will be specialized skills here too. Each of us, in pursuing political ends, needs the help of those who know how to form coalitions, mold movements, persuade skeptics, and otherwise help isolated individuals attain collective goals.

As for the harm argument, it is simply less relevant to politics than to law. For the kinds of nastiness we take for granted in lawyers is unlikely to succeed in a political argument, where every group has a choice of excellent advocates and today's adversaries might govern us tomorrow. Verbal browbeating is expected up to a point (this is culturally relative), but utterly humiliating a serious political opponent is rarely easy and would rarely be rewarded. One can mount a political campaign against a hostile group, but this is largely self-limiting in a stable democracy, since to arouse a group's hostility is to guarantee that group will support the other side in the future. When coalitions are fluid and groups can defend themselves, a reciprocity argument for civil conduct becomes good policy as well as good morality.[45] Many arguments for limiting the vigorous interplay of political opinions assume that many groups are "discrete and insular minorities," so despised that any coalition they tried to form would lose rather than gain by their presence.[46] In fact, such cases are *very* rare. Even the most despised groups often show a surprising ability to leverage political influence through astute strategy, especially when they take past political defeats as reasons for more activism rather than

---

[44] Compare the "dignity of autonomous beings" defense of legal representation in Donagan (1983: 129–133).

[45] Goodin (1992: chapter 5).

[46] See, for example, Gutmann (1999: 232); Ely (1980). The phrase is taken from *United States v. Carolene Products Co.*, 304 U.S. 144 (1938), footnote 4.

less. While we should strenuously preserve constitutional safeguards protecting the few groups that will be predictably disadvantaged, most actors in a democracy can stand up for themselves, or else gain much of what they value by threatening to do so.

The argument from the common good has much to be said for it, in politics as well as law, and should in large part be granted. The democratic-relationship justification of office is meant to justify not unlimited advocacy or partisanship but a balance between partisanship and larger political goods. But there are two reasons to suppose that the common-good argument is less dangerous to the professional-as-friend argument in politics than it is in law.

The first reason is mitigated skepticism. We cannot say that particularist relationships between politicians and their constituencies endanger the common good if those constituencies disagree deeply about what that good is. Granted, some political proposals would clearly harm almost everyone and should be rejected out of hand: advocates of nuclear war, or of converting jumbo jets to passenger cars, deserve to have their opinions somewhat neglected. But as Alan Donagan has pointed out in the case of legal advocacy, people with very different opinions who seek to live in mutual respect must at some point assume a bit of good faith.[47] A lawyer so sure of "the public interest" that he rejects any client whose views of a case he disagrees with seems moral to himself but arrogant and self-righteous to everyone else.[48]

A similar argument can be made for politicians. If political officers really regard their fellow citizens with respect, they will tend to assume that their disagreements with constituents or supporters reflect neither idiocy nor obvious vice but an honest difference of opinion about what should be done. Ordinary citizens may not know much about politics, but especially on moral or cultural issues, which do not turn on matters of complex fact or policy expertise, there is no procedure or formula by which a politician can be sure of improving on an ordinary citizen's opinions.[49] Using a similar argument, Jeremy Waldron has (somewhat controversially) defended the mundane democratic institution of voting. We settle controversial issues by votes not because we do not care about the outcome or doubt that any opinions are better than others but because

---

[47] "Holding an opinion to be mistaken is not the same as holding it to be indefensibly reached or not honestly held, and nobody who contrives to live in harmony with neighbors who think for themselves can fail to draw the distinction" (Donagan [1983: 130]).

[48] Donagan (1983: 132).

[49] Even on complex policy matters, democratic considerations would point towards making expertise more accessible to nonpoliticians rather than assuming, dubiously, that politicians are always and uniquely qualified to master all policy fields. Surely policy debate benefits when politicians do not have a monopoly on informed argument.

we have no systematic way of picking out an elite that will know in all cases which opinions are better. In the absence of an algorithm for achieving moral knowledge (more precisely, we have many such algorithms and people fight over which is best), a politics that respects our fellow citizens must give some weight to what most of them conclude.[50] Again, there are exceptions involving clear bias; again, these are rare and should not serve as models.

The second response to the common-good argument stresses that moral divisions of labor do something very different in politics from what they do in law. In law, moral role-playing narrows the range of views considered by each actor; in politics, it broadens them. Luban argues that excessive devotion to role morality involves the opposite of good moral reasoning: advocacy teaches us to think only of the client, while moral thinking requires "divid[ing] my perspective . . . thinking from the other's point of view."[51] The argument is excellent in certain legal contexts, in which people's sense of right and wrong is relatively strong and lawyerly tricks often involve purposely muddying the issue. In politics, however, the argument works the other way. Most people think that murder is wrong, and that a lawyer who gets a murderer off on a technicality has explaining to do. But anyone who believes that a live political issue is this simple is almost certainly wrong. A private political opinion is almost always half-baked: each of us is sure that his or her own political views (however inarticulate or inconsistent) are broadly correct, and has little incentive to explore the dizzying differences in religion, ideology, and social situation that bring others to see things differently. *Only* spirited exchanges among gifted advocates—people who are defending, as Mill put it, what they "actually believe,"[52] but more forcefully than the typical believer—force us to broaden our perspective. The higher someone is in a political hierarchy, the more likely it is that she will be insulated from dissenting opinions; the more certain an administrator is that she has taken "all possible" considerations into account, the less likely this is. A radical division of moral labor among lawyers resembles putting blindfolds on each of two prizefighters (which guarantees decreased craft without decreased risk); the division of moral labor in politics is more like giving each member of a search party a different area to look in. The search metaphor is again consonant with political and moral pluralism. Important values and claims might lie in several areas, and we are trying to find, and do justice to, as many as possible.

The fourth objection, which asks why we should not generalize from

---

[50] Waldron (1999). The argument is broadly similar to that of Dahl (1956, 1989).
[51] Luban (1988: 127).
[52] Mill (1975: 36).

care for some to care for all who need help, works only if we generalize along the wrong dimension. An argument for partiality towards some can be "universalized" in two senses: we can generalize the object, so that my partiality towards some must be extended to all others in the category, or we can generalize the subject, so that if I claim the prerogative to be partial towards my friends I must grant others the same privilege. Robert Goodin generalizes across the first dimension, thus arriving at radical conclusions, but Fried generalizes across the second: he is willing to endorse limited-purpose friendship for others on intrinsic grounds, even at prejudice to his own interests.[53] There is no general reason for preferring one dimension to the other. It all depends on whether we care more about our rights as the potential objects of policy or about our rights as agents, whether we define our rights and interests as something we want others to further or as something we want to claim for ourselves. This will vary according to temperament and circumstances, but most of us probably want both at once, even to the point of contradiction. In fact, the "cultural contradiction" mentioned above probably has this origin: we simultaneously want politicians to pay special attention to us and resent it when their special attention to others makes them biased against our fair claims. The demand for universalization leads not to absurdity but to one more argument for accommodation or compromise among values.

Finally, political relationships, unlike legal ones, are not mercenary, or not ordinarily so. For one thing, they are less limited-purpose than legal relationships: politicians help us with a wide range of concerns, much wider than our occasional interest in avoiding loss in a courtroom.[54] They are also more reciprocal than legal relationships. Politicians have more articulate opinions than ordinary citizens and more skill, but they are dependent for their power on constituents' opinions: in a democracy, their personal merit does not itself entitle them to political authority. Finally, full-time politicians are generally paid, but not directly by their particular constituents or those for whom they do favors. Payment from

[53] "My claim is that the kind of preference which an individual gives himself and concrete others is a preference which he would in exactly this universalizing spirit allow others to exhibit as well. It is not that I callously overlook the claim of the abstract individual, but indeed I would understand and approve were I myself to be prejudiced because some person to whom I stood in a similar situation of abstraction preferred his own concrete dimensions" (C. Fried [1976: 1070]).

[54] Exceptions occur in serious criminal and civil cases in which the client is in danger of having his whole life ruined. But in such cases, the lawyer-as-friend argument itself starts to seem more attractive: the legal relationship will be enduring, will last over time, and may involve real warmth and devotion. Moreover, the client in such cases really is vulnerable and in need of aid.

the latter sources is universally, and properly, regarded as illegal corruption.[55]

It is true that activists and organizers rely for money on those for whose interests they agitate (though in spite of populist theories to the contrary, they usually rely on outside support as well). But even here, the rewards are usually given for ongoing efforts and general political activity, not as a quid pro quo for particular services successfully rendered. Politicians certainly seek, and obtain, nonmonetary rewards from their constituents and supporters: the votes that keep them in office, adulation, the chance to achieve their own policy preferences, and the hope of lasting fame, as well as baser rewards like sexual attractiveness and the ability to strike fear in others. But these resemble the usual rewards for friendship and personal magnetism in everyday life as well. The respect and adoration to be won in politics are different in degree and character from those we gain from helping a friend or striking an emotional rapport, but not disconnected altogether from the relationship (as a monetary reward would be). Voting for politicians, marching when they call for a march, joining the organizations they are trying to form are ways in which we show something like personal approval for them. This is an unusual extension of everyday friendship, but not a perversion of it, and it is not corrupt.

To defend a set of roles and practices on intrinsic grounds is an uphill fight, particularly in a realm such as politics, where universalist values are generally regarded in moral theory (though not in everyday opinion) as at their strongest. Contemporary philosophy's endemic neglect of politics and political rights is an additional handicap. In recent philosophical and theoretical discussion, those who defend political rights as intrinsically valuable and worthy of theoretical attention are often caught between classical liberals, who stress private and legal rights, and social democrats, who see political rights as a transient way-station between laissez-faire liberalism and a new social order in which economic and social entitlements are the true badge of citizenship.[56] To demonstrate the intrinsic

---

[55] Public resistance to politicians who vote increases in their own salaries can be explained this way: the resistance is not to politicians' earning more but to their appearing to be pursuing office for mercenary ends. Similarly, cultures in which financial gain from public office is regarded as routine could be said to have precisely a mercenary model of politicians and political office: political officers are expected to reward an identifiable group of supporters in return for large fees.

[56] See Marshall's (1992) well-known articulation of the progression from legal to political to social rights. Current Anglo-American usage can be particularly confusing: "liberals" are often defenders of legal rights and social rights but not the political rights that historically developed between the two, while "democrats" often follow Dewey in downplaying individual claims altogether and defining democracy as a certain mode of mutual interaction and

importance of political rights one must go beyond philosophy and appeal to history, political science, the study of actual political rhetoric, and everyday opinion—all of which may bring to life important values and concerns that recent political philosophy neglects. A lot of the argument will inevitably be negative: an account of office that stresses democratic relationships will seem credible to the extent that existing theories of political life are seen to leave out too many things we value.

The above argument will not convince everyone. In fact no argument could completely dispel democratic citizens' nagging suspicion that the rhetoric and partisanship of political life is somehow dirty and gets in the way of true public service. But the task here has been only to prove that a certain kind of political partiality is respectable both in theory and as a partial guide to action: that some version of it has a legitimate place in political life as part of a balance or compromise. As argued above, the case for compromise must address practice as well as theory. It must show not only that the two values between which we are striking a compromise are genuine but that they can be accommodated in ways that respect both values rather than defeating both. With the universal and particular values served by political office, this is in fact the case.

There is a simple empirical argument for this: democratic politics in fact contains attachments to both values (the cultural contradiction stressed above), and does not fall apart. Old-fashioned politicians who talk of loyalty and standing up for "one's own" and reformers who are impatient with interest politics and long for a politics of the common good may think they are fighting to the death, but they are wrong. The fight between the two is interminable, and a reasonably decent politics does not require a victor.

One reason this accommodation is possible is because the extreme forms of the two positions have already lost.[57] Extreme proponents of partiality are limited in their ambitions by the rule of law, by a public ethos of fairness and procedural equality, and by established democratic

---

society-wide cooperative habits. Both find it hard to comprehend historical democratic movements, which placed the highest value on voting and other political rights such as association, petition, and dissent.

[57] Compare the argument of David Hume (1987: Part 2, Essays 12–14) regarding the possibilities of compromise in Great Britain between Whigs who accept monarchy in some form and Tories who accept liberties in some form. The argument is historical, not a priori: there was a time, Hume knows full well, when compromise was not possible and a series of revolutions could scarcely have been avoided. A similar point about the ability of constitutionalism to negotiate pluralism—because constitutionalism is "an institutional configuration that represents a reasonable way of balancing a diverse group of values under one set of conditions"—is made by Scheffler (1997: 205–6).

institutions that ensure that today's victories will be open to contestation tomorrow. Extreme proponents of impartiality are limited by the natural human desire to have one's special pleas heard, a desire that manifests itself every time revolutionaries find that citizens have too little public virtue for their taste. On the one hand, Rousseauians devoted to the general will *no longer* foster serious plans of banishing private and partial interests from politics altogether. On the other hand, Madison's defense of some sorts of faction, so striking and novel in his age, is *no longer* so sorely needed. In fact, few partisans of either universality or partiality are really as uncompromising as their own rhetoric would suggest: the opposing claims are too compelling, the need for balance too clear. There is in this way a sort of ethical party system: the proponents of universality and those of partiality coexist warily but permanently, dreaming of each other's demise but not really wishing it.

The politics of compromise among values is a story of constitutionalism. Both a Rousseauian democracy ruled by the general will and a fascist state ruled by one person who divines the public purpose require the assumption that all values are compatible or that one will always be clearly supreme. A polity in which all the actors know there are competing values (and know they are prone to forget this) is necessarily one in which people seek checks. Enabling restraints—constitutions, written or implicit; independent judiciaries; free public criticism; devolution of power—deliberately prevent political actors from pushing their moral premises too far, so that they can focus their minds on the vast range of political questions that the basic value compromises leave unsettled.[58]

This sort of constitutionalism, based not on a fixed view of natural rights but on a wise acceptance that no single end or human value should triumph outright, affects politics in deeper ways: it makes everyone a self-conscious partisan and balancer. Politicians who hope to succeed in a pluralistic polity and gain public respect must free themselves of illusions that they represent "the" public good, absolutely and without qualification. They must adapt to the constant tensions between the opinions of specific groups and a more general "public opinion." They must conform their own desires for fame to both the requirements of partisan politics and the judgment of a "history" that will try to discern what was best for the whole. They must try to bridge misunderstandings among people who disagree profoundly in their values, while realizing the limits to such an enterprise. Above all, they must avoid the arrogance of assuming their own moral superiority. Democratic constancy, the cardinal virtue of

[58] The idea of enabling restraints comes from Montesquieu; for a recent articulation see Holmes (1988).

democratic politicians, requires that they control their own urges to demonize opposition and sweep it away, and that they adapt their arguments not to the opinions, interests, and principles they think most
important but to those the public and their fellow politicians find
compelling.

ONE OFFICE OR MANY?

If the above argument is right, we should expect political office to embody a special kind of relationship between officeholder and ordinary
citizen. This should give rise to special moral duties for politicians that
differ from those of everyday life (while remaining bounded by a concern
for everyday moral consequences). But this book goes further: it seeks to
argue not only that politics is different from other pursuits in its ethical
aim but that different kinds of political action are different from one
another. The actions appropriate for an organizer are not appropriate for
a legislator; some qualities that would be virtues in a senator are vices in
a moral activist. There are several different ways of justifying this position. Some are better than others.

The first argument is a familiar one: it argues for a division of labor,
and a specialization of tasks. The most minimal version argues from time
and practicality. Even if all habits, skills, or modes of action would be in
principle available to everyone (assuming for the sake of argument that
people's characters are radically plastic or mutable), no one claims that
everyone can perfect every skill at once. A basketball star might have
been able to choose success in volleyball or swimming instead, but the
same person is unlikely to be the world's best in all three. Each requires
too much specialized practice. Once we admit that political offices involve skills, in the most prosaic sense, we must admit on pragmatic
grounds that politicians are likely to specialize.

A related argument, which assumes a greater fixity in human character,
stresses the advantages to be gained by doing what one does best. Plato's
hypothetical three-class society in the *Republic* represents an extreme example of this argument, but in more moderate form the claim is more
plausible. Cicero makes an analogy between politicians and actors—
specifically, actors who play (as we would say) "against type," portraying
characters whose emotions and manners are very different from their
own. Playing against type is not morally prohibited, but Cicero argues
that it is likely to be frustrating, and that the best actors pursue roles that
come more naturally. In the same way, those contemplating lives of action "must act in such a way that we attempt nothing contrary to universal nature; but while conserving that, let us follow our own nature, so

that even if other pursuits may be weightier and better, we should measure our own by the rule of our own nature. For it is appropriate neither to fight against nature nor to pursue anything that you cannot attain."[59]

While this argument is strong, the conclusions that follow are minimal. The argument is empirical, and its advice for likely success in action may not apply to everyone. The theater contains not just stars, with distinctive personalities, but also character actors, able to play the most diverse roles convincingly. Similarly, politics contains both strong and admirable characters who seem unable to bend with the wind (e.g., Churchill) and more subtle and shifting types who excel at playing both "the lion and the fox." Thoroughly protean characters, whose manner changed from hour to hour, would be less admired in politics than on the stage: a true "character" politician would arouse contempt, not admiration. But the reasons for this involve trust and public expectations, not mere impossibility: we judge shifty politicians harshly because we know that extreme shiftiness in political style and substance *is* possible.

If the previous argument reflects the classic justification for the division of labor, another argument starts from the idea, mentioned above, of a division of *moral* labor. An ordinary economic division of labor is justified to the extent that specialization increases both individual fulfillment and the social good (though there may be tension between the two). Similarly, the defenders of a division of moral labor—in which each individual is expected to focus on one value or set of values and one set of interests, while giving more cursory attention to others—claim that such a division better furthers both individual moral character and overall public attention to the whole range of values and interests than would an attempt to make everyone consider all values and everyone's interests at once.

The argument comes in several versions. A liberal version stresses our moral weakness: given that few of us are public-spirited enough to find personal fulfillment in pursuing the common good, the only liberal solution is specialization. The State will pursue public ends, supported by public willingness to pay taxes rather than attention, while private life remains the sphere of individual projects.[60] Another version, put forth by Virginia Held, stresses our *intellectual* weakness. It is very hard to comprehend the full complexity of moral considerations all at once. Given that no simple theory or set of rules will provide answers appropriate for all decisions and all domains, we ought "to divide the immense task of moral inquiry" into more manageable bits, and "experiment with different moral theories" and sets of actions in different domains. In both

---

[59] Cicero (1991: I:110, p. 43).
[60] Nagel (1991: chapter 6).

cases, the goal is not efficiency or greater skill, as with the economic division of labor, but increased overall moral attention and a greater tendency to make the right decision when things are complex: "If everyone in every role is obligated to take all moral considerations into account as completely as all others, there will be more of a tendency than otherwise for no one to take any moral considerations into account, and for responsibility to be even easier to evade than if different roles have more limited and specifiable obligations and expectations."[61]

Once again, both forms of the argument are strong, but prove less than their authors would like. They serve as correctives to theories that envision people thinking about every little action to make sure that it meets all possible moral tests. And they rightly point out certain truths of moral psychology: people are more likely to pay effective attention—the kind that results in action—when faced with a clash of vivid perspectives, each with its advocates, than when faced with a "conclusive" but bloodless account in which all things are considered.

Yet the metaphor goes too far. The opponents at which it aims are straw men: sophisticated utilitarians, and Kantians, already make allowances for human weakness and the limits of human intellect in their theories. They would often be quite willing to admit that moral criticism must attack one problem at a time while leaving much of everyday life temporarily undisturbed. To the extent that those who advocate a division of moral labor go further, their arguments are not fully convincing. While it may not be possible to think of all moral considerations at once, we regularly think of *several* at once. When we meet people who seem incapable of this, we find them frightening, not ordinary. Similarly, while considering all moral viewpoints or theories at once, or weighing them all impartially at the same time, is probably impossible, a willed blindness to all perspectives but one's own is (while not uncommon) neither necessary or desirable. Professional politicians in particular have obligations to think more broadly. Finally, politicians have a responsibility to take many views into account simply because their sphere of action is broader than that of other professionals. While political partiality is important, a client-centered view of politics only takes us so far. Since political decisions are binding on whole jurisdictions, even the most partisan politician must learn to compromise, and to make arguments that persuade across constituencies as well as within them.

So the argument I shall pursue will focus on a third justification, based on *stable expectations*. Different kinds of politicians should act according to more or less definite types, not primarily because they could not act in other ways nor because this is the most effective way to take moral con-

---

[61] Held (1983: 61, 64).

siderations into account, but because only a consistent character and a distinctive mode of action allow a person's constituency—the set of people who count on him for representation—to rely on him. Only when politicians have this kind of consistency can people hope to hold them to previous commitments and hope to successfully predict future actions from past performance.[62] There are intrinsic reasons for cultivating steadiness of character, some of them familiar from private morality. It can be plausibly claimed that only stable character ensures true moral responsibility and earns justified praise: when I say or do something good, I am pleased if my friends treat this as expected rather than random.[63] The reasons I have in mind, however, have to do less with personal fulfillment and self-concern than with the legitimate claims of others in democratic politics. Acting according to type is important because of what people need from their democratic institutions and from those who make them work.

What I have in mind might be called a division of *moral responsibility*: one reason to act in ways that others find reliable and fairly predictable (at least in terms of what one can be relied on *not* to do) is that it lets others do the same. The argument from division of moral responsibility stresses neither moral weakness nor intellectual limitations but the need for people in complex societies to be able to rely on one another. As Richard Wasserstrom argues, the moral requirement that generals weigh their own soldiers' lives more heavily than those of the enemy might seem puzzling at first—until we consider the whole range of roles in war, not just the role of general but that of ordinary soldier. The only thing that enables soldiers to do their duty, to follow orders and execute maneuvers even at clear risk to their own lives, is the knowledge that generals are thinking about their welfare and would never sacrifice their lives to no purpose.[64] One might add that when generals violate this expectation, when they seem incompetent or indifferent to loss of life, the usual result is a devastating loss in morale: decreased willingness to make sacrifices in the expectation that greater goods will follow. The category of morale may help us explain the costs of betraying political loyalties as well. A union leader who throws his support to a legislative candidate or a party, and enlists rank-and-file support for electioneering, does so with the understanding that the legislator or party will take unionists' interests into account in forming legislation. Legislators who violate this understanding act in accord with their formal rights, and sometimes doing so is

[62] A similar argument is implied in Goodin (1985: 46–7).
[63] Bradley (1988: Essay 1, p. 16).
[64] Wasserstrom (1983: 32).

morally necessary. But if they do this regularly, they cannot complain if the unionists melt away when their support is next needed.

Another way of making the same point stresses the tendencies political actors should resist, rather than the expectations they must validate. This "negative" approach is useful, both because most of us are more inclined to shirk our responsibilities than to follow them and because the offices discussed in this work are less formalized than those of general and soldier. Much more than war, democratic politics involves offices whose duties are controversial, whose interactions are complex and hard to define, and whose contours shift over time. But persistent starting points for democratic politics remain.

One of these fixed points is that democratic politics requires would-be politicians to show respect for others' opinions of them. Politicians who regard themselves as the only proper judges of their own characters, who complain that their critics are unfair and cannot know their true intentions, are aristocratic literally to a fault. As Cicero puts it: "We must exercise a respectfulness towards men, both towards the best of them and also towards the rest. To neglect what others think about oneself is the mark not only of arrogance *(non solum arrogantis est)*, but also of utter laxity. There is a difference between justice and shame when reasoning about humans. The part of justice is not to harm a man, that of a sense of shame not to outrage *(offendere)* him."[65] Moral philosophy has focused much more on what Cicero calls justice than on his "sense of shame." In political life, however, the "insolence of office" shines forth clearly as a vice,[66] and a concern for not giving offense is its corresponding virtue. Just as Cicero's warning against arrogance expresses democratic equality, a concern for persuasion and public opinion expresses democratic respect—a sign that one understands the full meaning of the doctrine that political power derives from public approval.

Democratic Constancy as Political Virtue

Cicero calls the politician who neglects others' opinions not only arrogant but "lax" or dissolute: every politician is tempted to such arrogance, but overcoming this temptation is the essence of laudable political self-control. This is part of Cicero's discussion of "constancy" *(constantia)*. The word means many things at once: consistency of character, consistent attachment to particular individuals, and dogged pursuit of what one

---

[65] Cicero (1991: I.99, p. 31).
[66] Walzer (1983: 155), following Bentham.

sees as the proper long-term end in the face of temptation.[67] These three things are not the same, but the above argument shows the link between them: consistent attachment to individuals reflects the worth of democratic relationships; consistency of character lets others count on one to do one's part in such relationships, and a focus on long-term consequences helps one keep in mind the value of such considerations when short-term temptations, in the form of pleasure, ambition, or the like, make this difficult.

Constancy in its various forms, a common theme of ancient Stoic thought, became something of a cliché in Enlightenment ethics, where it appears as a tendency to define liberty as the capacity to forbear from hasty decisions (Locke), "strength of mind" (Hume), "self-command" (Smith), "self-restraint" (Kant), or "self-conquest" (Mill).[68] Opposition to constancy, in turn, is a staple of anti-Enlightenment rhetoric, as various schools of postmodernism and critical theory take aim at "bourgeois" self-denial and call for liberation through erotic self-expression and protean reinventions of identity. The importance of the bourgeois virtues to politics, including radical politics, is probably greater than usually admitted.[69] But in any case, what I have in mind is not a defense of private, mercantile virtues (typically expressed as "industry, sobriety and thrift"), but a defense of a particular kind of constancy that is distinctively political, and even distinctively democratic.

The idea of constancy as a distinctively democratic (or "republican") quality is not common in Enlightenment thought (though we can see glimmers of it in the passion-based theories of Hume and Smith). Its virtues are best seen in Cicero, and specifically in his republican critique of a Stoic form of constancy that pays too little heed to politics.

Ciceronian constancy can be called democratic in three senses. First, it demands something close to what ordinary people can manage. Cicero takes moral duty very seriously, probably with more seriousness than the typical political leader or citizen can live up to. But in comparison to the chief philosophical moralists of his time, the Stoics, Cicero intended his account of duties to be tempered by experience and adapted to ordinary capacities. Cicero knew that the duties to country, friends, and fellow citizens that he talked about, and the virtues of justice, constancy, and

---

[67] See, respectively, Cicero (1991: I.110, p. 43, and I.114, pp. 44–45; I.112, p. 44; I.119, p. 46).

[68] Locke (1975); Hume (1983); Smith (1982); Kant (1983); and Mill (1986). For a summary and critique, see Taylor (1989: chapter 9); and Hirschman (1977). The current project is largely immune from Hirschman's criticism: unlike the optimistic Enlightenment theorists he cites, I do not claim that constancy or a sober pursuit of interest can eliminate political conflict.

[69] See Walzer (1965: 124, 306).

decorum he recommended as conducive to performing duties, fell short of the ideal of the Stoic sage. Stoic "right" was "complete and unconditional ... and it cannot belong to anyone except the wise man," but Cicero's virtues were "those that the Stoics call 'middle'. They are shared, and widely accessible."[70] Precisely because they were virtues that the Stoics would call "honourable in a second-rate way," they were "not appropriate to wise men only, but shared with the whole human race."[71] This modesty is a good thing: it makes ethical theory not only more likely to be taken seriously but more democratic. Democratic constancy does not require a political class of inordinate virtue, and does not counsel despair when we (as usual) lack such a class. We can try to find able people to fill offices, but government is no longer democratic if it requires its politicians to be so extraordinary that they scarcely seem human.

Second, democratic constancy is respectful. Unlike Shakespeare's (and Plutarch's) Coriolanus—who displayed many private virtues, especially courage, but whose contempt for the plebeian class made him both unlikely to be elected consul and unworthy of it—the Ciceronian politician avoids "arrogance." He displays the political virtue that consists in putting aside one's high opinion of oneself in the service of finding out why others' opinion might differ. This represents another dissent from Stoicism. Stoics traditionally hold the masses in contempt and uphold the virtue of the sage by contrasting it with the rabble who are swayed by fear and advantage.[72] Cicero's politician, like Cicero himself, is proud of his ability to make moral cases to others as well as himself. A more modern example appears in Richard Brookhiser's study of George Washington. While the first generation of American political leaders is often said to be influenced by Roman models of civic virtue, Washington could be a democratic leader (and not just a patriotic symbol) because he rejected the pure versions of those models. Where Joseph Addison's neo-Stoic 1713 play *Cato* portrayed its protagonist glowingly for executing soldiers afraid to fight in defense of Rome, Washington at Valley Forge turned to persuasion, not slaughter. Where Addison's heroes assumed their own sterling virtue and spoke in harangues—which became all the louder the less people listened—Washington earned wide popular respect by showing universal respect for others.[73]

[70] Cicero (1991: III.13–14, p. 105).

[71] Cicero (1991: III.15–16, p. 106).

[72] See, for example, Epictetus (1925: I.3.5–11, p. 17; I.2.12–20, p. 19; I.2.26–34, p. 23; I.2.34, p. 25; I.11.1–7, p. 79; I.29.29–35, p. 195; I.29.57–65, p. 203); and Seneca (1963: XI.1–XII.3, pp. 81–85; XIX.1–2, p. 103). See also the early modern neo-Stoic Guillaume Du Vair (1598: 33–34, 75, 199).

[73] Brookhiser (1996: 124–25, 136).

Finally, Ciceronian constancy is democratic to the extent that it requires democratic coalitional politics in order to work. One conventional model for checking democratic politics is essentially juristic: judges are supposed to strike down laws and practices that do not accord with moral requirements. This model requires an assumption of moral superiority: the judges know the moral principles and have the courage to uphold them, while ordinary people are too ignorant, self-seeking, or biased to do so. A political ethic of constancy can live with a lower standard in leaders because it has a complex and long-term view of how democracy enables groups to look after their own rights. As Goodin has pointed out, political self-restraint is motivated by the salutary effects of political uncertainty and shifting coalitional politics: to demand all that one wants, arrogantly and without regard for others' desires, is a recipe for long-term political failure. Even if those whose opinions and interests are trampled wantonly seem weak now, they will eventually form coalitions to place in power those more responsive to their concerns. Constitutional democracy in particular prevents enduring arrogance and promotes a salutary restraint: if the future rules of the game are hard to rig, those eager to dominate will be unable to prevent adverse coalitions in the long term.[74] One can say in turn that democratic politics *rewards* democratic constancy: respect for others is eventually paid back, while those who seem to profit from ruthless aggression will fall behind.

One element missing from Goodin's argument is a recognition that different kinds of politics are necessary if the arrogance of office is to be suitably checked. At least in a large, complex country, building alternative parties and political organizations takes great amounts of time, money, and political experience. The mere existence of groups that feel victimized or outraged does not guarantee effective opposition. Even if such opposition does arise, it may take a very long time, and its formation may require levels of outrage and bitterness that are by no means conducive to democratic cooperation and just, peaceful government.

"Protest" or citizen politics provides an essential missing ingredient here. Even when protest movements do not seek to govern, they are instrumental in restraining the passions and short-term ambitions of those who do. At the same time, the protesters themselves are restrained by the knowledge that they have no binding authority on their own: if they alienate too many people outside their own narrow group of supporters, they will lose whatever influence they have. There is good reason for a division of moral responsibility not only among officeholders but among different offices as such. Each officer's knowledge of other officers devoted to different tasks, and different people, keeps her ambi-

[74] Goodin (1992: chapters 4–5, esp. 109–11).

tions within proper bounds, while motivating her to concentrate energy on the difficult political tasks that may quite properly win her fame and influence.

Thus, the three aspects of the "middle" or modest virtue of constancy—consistency of character, consistent attention to certain political relationships, and long-termism in the pursuit of political goals—reinforce one another through the mechanisms of popular politics. Consistent character enables the trust that cements relationships; consistency in relationships places a check on political arrogance; long-termism both reflects and reinforces consistency of character, while giving constituents a reason to stay in a relationship of persuasion and trust rather than leaving it. All these virtues are admittedly semi-virtues: they do not guarantee that we will do the right thing but only prevent certain bad outcomes from becoming too likely.

These complex relationships—among different aspects of steady character, among different types of character and the offices through which they are expressed, and between office ethics and universalism—work through actual politics. They vary as political conventions, institutions, and expectations vary. The philosophical and ethical treatment of political office points beyond itself to a consideration of political institutions and roles, and of the actions that take place within them (or serve to challenge them). When thinking about politics, our philosophy must be political: attuned to the real goods, and real compromises, present in the democratic order. Fortunately, we do not need to start this from scratch. As we shall see in the next chapter, the relationship between democratic constancy and democratic institutions is a neglected theme running through the history of political thought.

CONSTITUTIONAL PURPOSES: ANOTHER MODEL OF POLITICAL OFFICE

For these reasons, I argue that the ethics of political office, the ethics of constancy, makes sense only if we pay attention to what we want, need, and expect from particular offices—in short, to an account of constitutional purposes. The holder of a formal or informal political office ought to do the kind of things, and be the kind of person, that will best fulfill the purpose of the office, the special contribution that the office makes to the effective and just functioning of a democratic political system.

This kind of argument is not new. We make it all the time in the context of discussing highly symbolic and authoritative offices—those of the president, or Supreme Court justices (though we are less used to applying the argument to the everyday activities of legislation, political organization, and public speech). When we argue about the president and the Court, we are used to starting with a political ideal or theory:

an account of how the political system will work most effectively, most peacefully, and with the least possible violence to as many cherished principles as possible. We then take from this theory both rules for acting—duties and permissions—and lists of character traits for determining good candidates for the office.

Consider Alexander Bickel's *The Least Dangerous Branch*, an influential work on judicial review. Bickel starts his analysis with the "counter-majoritarian" character of judicial review. Any doctrine of judicial activism, even activism in pursuit of principle, runs against the democratic principle of majority rule, and against the "policy-making power of representative institutions, born of the electoral process . . . the distinguishing characteristic of the [democratic] system."[75] Bickel does not conclude that judicial review is illegitimate, but rather that its defense requires a special search for the Court's distinctive function or purpose within a fundamentally democratic system and in accordance with its principles.[76] This function can be found in the ability of the Court to force the public (by striking down or recommitting measures) to think twice about constitutionally dubious measures, to force "the sober second thought": "Their insulation and the marvelous mystery of time give courts the capacity to appeal to men's better natures, to call forth their aspirations, which may have been forgotten in the moment's hue and cry."[77] From this function Bickel derives detailed advice to judges on how they should *act*. In particular, he tells judges they should learn how to delay laws or strike them down for sneaky reasons rather than taking the democratically drastic (though we might think intellectually honest) step of calling them unconstitutional as such. Counsels for action, and a doctrine of proper disposition—judicial restraint—are derived from a concern for the democratic order and an inquiry into the function of an office in that order.

Other theorists of judicial review counsel different actions and dispositions, but in doing so they invoke their own theory of the democratic order, and their own account of judicial function. For instance, egalitarian and judicial activist Ronald Dworkin believes that majority rule is subordinate to (and derives from) the principle of equality. He then at-

---

[75] Bickel (1986: 16–19).

[76] "The search must be for a function which might (indeed, must) involve the making of policy, yet which differs from the legislative and executive functions; which is peculiarly suited to the capabilities of the courts; which will not likely be performed elsewhere if the courts do not assume it; which can be so exercised as to be acceptable in a society that generally shares Judge Hand's satisfaction in a 'sense of common venture'; which will be effective when needed; and whose discharge by the courts will not lower the quality of the other departments' performance by denuding them of the dignity and burden of their own responsibility" (Bickel 1986: 24).

[77] Bickel (1986: 26). "The sober second thought" is a phrase of Justice Stone's, cited by Bickel from H. F. Stone, "The Common Law in the United States," 50 *Harvard Law Review* 4, 25 (1936).

tributes to judges a measure of impartiality, and willingness to use reason in pursuit of equality, superior to that of elected branches. Since this propensity to be impartial makes their judgments morally superior to those of other political actors, judges should not be afraid to act on this propensity in striking down laws as unjustifiable or biased.[78]

In both cases, considerations of proper judicial action quite rightly start by arguing from the ends of the democratic polity and the special purpose or role of the judiciary in pursuing those ends. The result is an account of an ethic peculiar to the office, an ethic calling for different qualities from those ordinary citizens should expect to employ in their day-to-day deliberations and decisions.

Or consider accounts of how American presidents should act. Clinton Rossiter, in his well-known work, begins with the "strictly constitutional burden of the President": "Chief of State, Chief Executive, Commander-in-Chief, Chief Diplomat, Chief Legislator." He then notes informal functions that people have come to expect of the president and that add to his power and responsibility, including party leader and "Voice of the People." These formal constitutional duties and informal democratic demands, claims Rossiter, justify a presidential office strong enough to fulfill the duties and meet the demands.[79] The American system needs certain things done that the people as a whole demand but that their geographically fragmented legislators cannot give them, the least controversial example (at least when Rossiter is writing) being national defense. Because defense under Cold War conditions requires strong and instant leadership that only the president is in an institutional position to provide, a president is entitled and required to act with strength and vigor in carrying out his duties and strengthening his institutional power.

This argument resembles Locke's derivation of the need for presidential "prerogative" from the needs of a constitutional democracy to preserve itself.[80] Unlike Locke, however, Rossiter defines *limits* on prerogative, what we might call a negative ethic with respect to the constitutional-democratic order. America's "*constitutional morality* into which this office fits" provides the ultimate restraint on presidential abuses. This constitutional morality makes itself felt in opposition parties, in Congress, and in public opinion. But its ultimate manifestation is in the presidential character as defined by his dispositions as well as his (generally accepted) ends:

> In the end, . . . the checks that hold the President in line are internal rather than external. His conscience and training, his sense of history and desire to be judged well by it, his awareness of the need to pace himself lest he collapse

[78] Dworkin (1985).
[79] Rossiter (1963: 19–21, and passim).
[80] Locke (1960: Second Treatise, Sections 159–68).

under the burden—all join to halt him far short of the kind of deed that destroys a President's "fame and power." . . . If he knows anything of history or politics or administration, he knows that he can do great things only within "the common range of expectation," that is to say, in ways that honor or at least do not outrage the accepted dictates of constitutionalism, democracy, personal liberty, and Christian morality.[81]

Thus Rossiter's claims concerning the presidency, like Bickel's concerning Supreme Court justices, involve an account of democracy and its principles, a corresponding account of desirable presidential actions or habits, and an idea of what kinds of disposition or character are conducive to a president's carrying out such actions.

Opponents of the strong presidency have adopted a formally similar argument, one starting with a different account of the purposes of the office and the nature of constitutional democracy. Thus Jeffrey Tulis, in criticizing the aggressive, rhetorical presidency of the "bully pulpit," talks of the "purposes behind the separation of powers," under which "different structures were designed to give each branch the special quality needed to secure its governmental objectives." The special qualities of the presidency were to be "energy and 'steady administration of law,'" with which qualities the bully pulpit is not easily compatible. Tulis claims, much as I will claim, that "governors and governed need a theoretical compass with which to position themselves to be able to assess appropriate and inappropriate exercises of power"—and argues that one of the inappropriate exercises is moralistic public rhetoric on controversial policy matters.[82]

There are accounts of presidential leadership and character that lack a well-developed account of American democracy and the president's place in it, but these accounts (I claim) seem capricious and ill-founded precisely because their starting-points seem partisan and arbitrary rather than grounded in deeper principles of democratic governance. When discussing these most formal of offices, we are used to moving from democratic theory to office theory to ethics. We justify certain actions and dispositions because they further the special purpose of that office in a constitutional democratic order. Indeed, this kind of inquiry is so common that I will not attempt to add anything to the various accounts of the judicial and presidential purposes that already exist.

Instead, I shall extend this kind of inquiry to the less constitutionally conspicuous offices of representative, moral activist, and organizer. In each case, I shall sketch the democratic purpose served by the office, the actions needed to fulfill that purpose, and the disposition or character conducive to such action. Unifying the inquiry is a bare-bones account of

---

[81] Rossiter (1963: 65–66).
[82] Tulis (1987: 42–43, 204, and passim).

democracy and human nature summarized by the doctrine of "democratic constancy" sketched in this chapter and the next. In later chapters I shall take on, explicitly and implicitly, competing accounts of what democracy should be and politicians should do. But I hope in any case to persuade the reader that some sort of inquiry like Bickel's and Dworkin's, Rossiter's and Tulis's—starting with an account of the democratic system before working down to rules and character tests—provides the most solid and widely plausible grounding for political ethics and the study of good leadership.

CONCLUSION: PHILOSOPHY, POLITICS, AND CONSTITUTIONALISM

Universalism and partiality are always with us. Philosophy cannot negate either the demand that all be treated equally or the demand that everyone's special perspective be heard. Both embody genuine values and are reflected in legitimate, if conflicting, intuitions about both politics and other forms of life. If neither of the two conceptions of political life can be eliminated or tamed, both must be preserved, accommodated, and given a recognized place in the political order. The reasons for seeking such a compromise are both political and philosophical.

The political reason is based on a hatred of tyranny, and is familiar to us from Isaiah Berlin and Judith Shklar. We should stop longing for societies based on single worldviews or unitary, sovereign decisions, say Shklar and Berlin, simply because the costs of imposing such unity are too high—tending toward totalitarianism.[83] This position seems correct (though strangely apolitical in failing to ask how this liberalism of "permanent minorities" can be made attractive to powerful and complacent majorities). This work will follow Shklar—as well as Aristotle, Hume, and others—in proposing a political doctrine of "semi-justice, in which several incompatible goals are allowed to live in compromise, even though logically they are mutually exclusive."[84] The result is a kind of liberalism, a liberalism more pluralistic than some recent formulations in its insistence that even the fundamental principles of our political institutions will be disputed endlessly, if for the most part peacefully.

This is not to say that philosophy is useless, or no different from pragmatic power-brokering (though the latter deserves a better reputation than it gets, given how often the alternative is bloodshed). Not everything should be negotiated; sometimes we should be ashamed to compromise. Only philosophy can show that this is not one of those times. We should retain our attachment to partiality in politics not because we

[83] Berlin (1969); Shklar (1986: esp. 64, 101–104, 122, 224).
[84] Shklar (1986: 122).

cannot defeat its defenders but because we appreciate the value of close human relationships, and recognize that impersonal institutions and rules cannot embody the goods these relationships represent. Politics teaches us when compromise is possible; philosophy, when it is good.

In the next chapter we shall explore the structured democratic compromises put forth theoretically by Aristotle—whose prescriptions for class-compromise were theoretically visionary but mocked in practice by impending foreign invasion—and by Madison and Tocqueville, whose modern experiences gave them hope that the worst extremes of politics could be durably avoided. The constitutional tradition has long recognized the problems of moral pluralism and of durable differences in worldview. It has sought to foster justice, free government, and political equality in ways that recognize this benign cacophony and seek to profit from it. The wisest forms of constitutional philosophy are pluralist, not in the political scientist's sense of endorsing interest-group competition whatever its outcome, but in the moral sense of recognizing that political life involves trade-offs, that few political setbacks lack redeeming virtues, and that few improvements come without costs.

CHAPTER TWO

Political Office and the Theory
of Democratic Constancy

IN THE PREVIOUS chapter, I discussed the conflict between two approaches to political office, one stressing ethical universalism and the other focusing on particularistic relationships. I argued that both approaches had merit, and that we should therefore try to resolve the clash between them through a principled compromise. Such a compromise was within reach, both because each approach in its most credible form made limited and negotiable claims, and because our current political institutions and ideas reflected a world in which extreme positions had already lost and the partisans of both universalism and particularism had been forced to agree to a grudging peace with each other. Finally, I sketched briefly the form that such a compromise takes: a division of moral responsibility in which the occupant of a political office ought to act in such a way that the purpose of the office is well served. In this way, the constituencies of each office are respected; ordinary citizens are able to place broad trust in politicians whom they can count on to act in more or less consistent ways; different and valuable modes of political action are allowed to operate, each in its own sphere—and all this particularity must pay homage to universalist concerns, since each office must justify itself in terms of the service it provides to the democratic polity as a whole.

This chapter will flesh out how this account of democratic office improves on simple or naïve accounts that stress universalism on the one hand or particularism on the other. As in the last chapter, the hard part of this is to justify particularism, to explain how apparently unprincipled concessions to partial, local, or partisan claims need not offend our attachment to the good of the whole. I shall in fact claim even more than this: common political goods are *best* safeguarded by people who take pride in their particular service to parties, constituencies, and particular political institutions and forms of politics, and who are responsive to the moral claims of these partial units as well as to more general ones. On the other hand, not every particular attachment deserves our respect. Democratic politics demands that particular claims respect democratic ends (equality and popular rule) and democratic means (accountability to public opinion, expressed ultimately in terms of numbers and the sentiments of popular majorities). Thus, those looking to the good of a whole democracy should pay attention to particular offices; those inspired to serve particular constituencies, parties, movements, or kinds of politics should pay attention to larger democratic principles that chasten these heady attachments; and students and critics concerned with ethics, leadership, and democratic theory should study the myriad, complex ways in which these two concerns interact.

For now, I shall set forth the basic theory. What characteristic actions, sentiments, or sorts of character are salutary in democratic life, and what kind of officers does a democratic polity need? The answer to both questions involves the democratic constancy discussed above with reference to Cicero: democratic politics needs this sort of constancy, and good democratic officers are those who systematically embody and promote it. Cicero's discussion of democratic character is republican and respectful of public opinion but still fundamentally elitist. He presupposes that only a few will be politically prominent, and since he assumes that those few will have time for philosophic and political reflection, he directs his theory to them. Mass, democratic politics requires adapting his advice to new circumstances. The *officii* of a modern democratic regime—its political offices and their attendant, socially based duties—involve not only formal offices whose holders embody steadiness of character, able to resist both their own self-indulgent passions and the transient passions of the public, but also informal practitioners of more popular kinds of politics, whose constancy is expressed through close relationships with ordinary citizens, and who personally encourage those citizens to more steadiness in considering their own interests and attachments.

Constancy is, as noted above, a "middle" virtue, involving not extremes of nobility or self-denial but the kind of steady attachments to goals, persons, and salutary habits of which most people are capable. A democratic politics based on constancy rejects the aristocratic impulse to seek ultimate human excellence and doubts the possibility of a wholesale transformation of values. In basing politics on constancy we seek to make possible the satisfaction of long-term interests and the more complete fulfillment of existing values. Democratic theory at its most persuasive acknowledges that human beings will never be motivated completely, or even most of the time, by altruism, solidarity, nobility, or heroism, or even aspire to be so motivated. (This is not to disparage democracy: the leaders, and citizens, of aristocracies, technocracies, and charismatic tyrannies are just as selfish, petty, and cruel as those of democracies— usually more so—and represent ethical nobility only in their own delusions.)

It is not that democracy has no ideals, or makes no demands on its citizens. But those demands are somewhat modest: democracies rely on institutions that give people what they value in the long term, rather than what they want in the short term. And they require of their citizens that quality of character that will make them patient when their wishes cannot be achieved and persistent in the face of obstacles to their considered projects. Democratic constancy in this way includes not simply the negative ability to refrain from acting in the face of temptation, but also the positive ability to continue to act as one has resolved in the face of dissuasion, opposition, or even hatred.

Authors in the history of political thought who have written of self-command and self-denial have rarely thought of it as exclusively private or directed to avoiding "sin," and have often stressed its active and political aspects. Rousseau regarded the ability to disobey inclination as the premiere social and political virtue (which he unfortunately did not have); Smith thought self-command was best displayed in political battles, where only rare characters were able to hold to their positions in the face of partisan pressures.[1] Even Freud, whose doctrine of "delayed gratification" has been so attacked by the Frankfurt school of philosophy as a capitalist ethic of too much saving and too little joy, believed that the highest rewards for erotic restraint lay in areas of life other than economics: science, love, art, the learning achieved through education, and creative work done for its own sake.[2] In political terms, far from being merely a repressive bourgeois construct, as is sometimes asserted, democratic constancy or self-discipline has been the ethic practiced by every successful movement for social change. The value is broad enough, neutral enough, and central enough to modern life to be advocated not only by Adam Smith but by Martin Luther King, who claimed "extraordinary discipline and courage" to be necessary for nonviolence.[3]

Though constancy is a much-discussed virtue in the history of political philosophy, in examining the role of constancy in a democratic order I shall turn to figures currently regarded as on the margins of that history. In what follows, I shall examine primarily the work of Aristotle, Madison and Hamilton, and Tocqueville, rather than that of Locke, Hume, Smith, Kant, or Mill (though these authors will appear occasionally).

This choice requires a bit of explanation, for it is the latter set of theorists who are more commonly invoked when moral and political theorists argue about justice, legitimacy, equality, and liberty. Aristotle, Publius, and Tocqueville are often likened to sociologists in their detailed treatment of group conflict and their close attention to empirical politics; conversely, philosophers often regard them as time-bound or dated, as

---

[1] Rousseau (1979: 96, 103 ["Sixth Walk"]); Smith (1982: 153).

[2] Freud (1958: 223–25; 1961: chapter 2).

[3] Martin Luther King, "The Social Organization of Nonviolence," in Washington (1991: 32).

eccentric observers of particular political phenomena rather than speakers of enduring moral truths. Moreover, Aristotle, Publius and Tocqueville are widely known for their ambivalence toward democracy, and, in the case of Aristotle, for unjust and antiegalitarian views on women and slaves. Leading Enlightenment theorists were antidemocratic too, and generally fell short of contemporary standards on questions of race, gender, and slavery as well.[4] But these "liberal" theorists tend to be forgiven precisely because they did not treat democracy as a major concern. It seems forgivable if a book about freedom of conscience, opposition to the Catholic Church, and individual development contains incidental slights against equality and democracy. But to write about democracy in ways that question its virtues directly (as Aristotle, Madison, and Tocqueville sometimes did) strikes contemporary democrats as a culpable choice, which renders suspect whatever points the theorist makes.

As a determined democrat, I shall argue that this suspicion is misguided. These acute, partly aristocratic critics of democracy help us think through issues that the more canonical Enlightenment theorists did not even address and that contemporary political theorists' celebrations of democracy also tend to slight.

The first of these is a concern with democratic *stability*. In American political philosophy it is sometimes considered a sign of conservatism (or worse) to worry about the preconditions for democratic institutions and the possibility that such institutions might be undermined. This prejudice is somewhat provincial. It is not shared by comparative political scientists, nor by scholars of political thought from other countries who have impeccable democratic and even socialist credentials. Those who focus their attention on Weimar Germany, interwar Republican Spain, Northern Ireland, Chile, or Brazil realize that democracy is not self-sustaining. If civil war or oligarchic takeover are to be avoided, the institutionalized political conflict that democrats rightly hold dear must embody certain practices of compromise and restraint. It must be supported by social and cultural conditions. And it presupposes certain qualities of political character, both elite and popular. A concern with democratic weakness or breakdown does not entail worshipping the State, adopting a conservative horror of all political change, or supposing a mystical collective being that stands above individuals and has moral claims that trump theirs. The reasons for caring about democratic stability are liberal, concrete, and pragmatic, and based on a down-to-earth human sympathy: when democracies fall to anarchy, oligarchic coup, or foreign conquest, many ordinary people get imprisoned, maimed, tortured, and killed. As

[4] Laski (1997); MacPherson (1962); Dahl (1989: chapter 9).

Stephen Holmes has put it, "The largest and most reliable human rights organization is the liberal state."[5]

The more widely read Enlightenment philosophers tend to neglect such questions. This is only natural. Anxious to establish the right to overthrow old institutions, or to defend unfamiliar principles for founding new ones, they did not always attend sufficiently to the problem of maintaining institutions once founded. If the most attractive philosophers are those who imagine the light of human freedom, the "social" theorists of democracy are the ones who think through the power supply. Madison and Hamilton hoped to apply Enlightenment philosophy to the study of practical political action and the founding of good institutions; Tocqueville sought to explain the cultural and social preconditions for democracy's ultimate success, for its ability to fight off new Napoleons. Finally, even Aristotle, with his hopes for an ideal regime that excluded women and gave all unpleasant labor to noncitizen slaves, was in much of the *Politics* a canny, even cynical political scientist willing to give advice to democracies, even though he believed that democracy in its purer forms gave too much power to the many and too little to the rich and the virtuous.[6] Without ignoring or minimizing Aristotle's antidemocratic and inegalitarian tendencies, we can take what he regarded a science of the second best and use it to explore the requirements of democracy, which is our own most cherished ideal.

Second, the classical democratic regime theorists represent a salutary *pessimism* about human nature. By this I do not mean a sense of paralysis or futility—it was Hamilton who talked about founding good government on "reflection and choice" rather than "accident and force"[7]—but a demand that expansive claims about democracy's virtues be supported by evidence, experience, and solid arguments that address potential critics. Democracy has great advantages: it is more just, more fair, and more equal than any other political order. But we must all admit that particular democracies can be unjust, inefficient, weak, or otherwise unable to sustain their promise. The classic democratic regime theorists are often more honest about this than are those democratic theorists who take the sweeping progressive hopes of the Enlightenment and pin all those hopes on democracy *sans phrase*. Moreover, Aristotle, the federalists, and Tocqueville—like the high Enlightenment in this regard but unlike many

---

[5] Holmes (1997: 33).

[6] It should be noted that Aristotle also had disdain for oligarchies. His comments about idle oligarchs who mistake their wealth for virtue tend to exceed in sarcasm his comments about democrats who quite reasonably try to give everyone a piece of the political action.

[7] Hamilton et al., *The Federalist Papers* (1992: No. 1). Henceforth simply *Federalist*.

contemporary democratic theorists—have a salutary skepticism toward the possibilities of democratic leadership: "Enlightened statesmen will not always be at the helm."[8] This does not mean that we should abandon politics or give up hope of finding good leaders, but it does mean that the arts of popularity by which democratic leaders get chosen should not be confused with the merits of character that will gain them more lasting fame. As we shall see, some enthusiastic democrats end up longing for charismatic, almost magical forms of leadership that place dangerous reliance on leaders' images and their self-proclaimed virtues. Democrats' proper attitude toward politics should be mitigated hope combined with skepticism. As modern Madisonian Arthur Schlesinger Jr. explained the "moral and rationale" of democracy, "The people as a whole are not perfect; but no special group of the people is more perfect."[9]

Finally, the classic democratic regime theorists preserve a sense of *agency*: they realize that individual actions matter. Many Enlightenment philosophers exaggerated the virtues of formal institutions, attributing to them an ability to weather the most deficient and despicable actions by individual politicians. Many contemporary democratic liberals follow them in this. This again is understandable: the Enlightenment's main concern was to establish the legitimacy of new institutions, and its writers sought to defend representative and constitutional government against all accusations. As a result, they did not always want to admit that democratic institutions could work badly if people made the wrong choices. But of course they can. It may be fine for the average person, with little political power or knowledge, to believe falsely that his or her political system takes care of itself. It may also be salutary for revolutionary movements to stress only the virtues of the institutions they aim to establish, ignoring their possible vices. But those who have chosen a life of politics, and who either found institutions or act within existing institutions, should take note of their political system's characteristic tensions, blind spots, and gaps, and of the need for intelligent political action to keep democracy safe and make it better.[10]

This is far from a counsel of despair. On the contrary, it leads logically to a greater focus on what should and must be done if democracy is to fulfill the aspirations that we have for it. An excessive focus on institutions, on the regular and scientific laws of change, blinds us to the importance of creative and intelligent action, not just by the formal leaders of

[8] *Federalist*: No. 10.

[9] Schlesinger (1988: 170).

[10] Hirschman (1977: 18) has noted that even Mandeville, normally thought of as believing that self-interest would solve all problems, thought that turning "private vices" into "publick benefits" would require "Skilful Management of the Dextrous Politician." But as Hirschman points out, Mandeville did not spell out what this would entail.

the legislative, executive and judicial branches but by ordinary citizens. We sometimes think of democracy's greatest virtue as the extension of formal rights to the greatest number. The more sociological political theorists teach us something different: democracy depends on the radical notion that everyone has an equal right to demand and fight for his or her political interests and opinions—and thereby to incur the responsibilities, formerly known only to the great, that fall on those who engage in such fights.

Thus Aristotle's pre-Enlightenment skepticism about progress, Hamilton and Madison's practical-political suspicion of "parchment barriers," and Tocqueville's non-Enlightenment, eccentric liberalism provide essential correctives to our tendency to attribute automatic goodness to democratic institutions and to place too much faith in the inevitability of progress. To the extent that they are friendly critics of democracy, they force us to address the tensions and difficulties all democracies face. Even at their most extreme and antidemocratic, they educate us about the dangers posed to democracy when plausible criticisms of its goodness or workability go unanswered. For even when democracy seems most secure, there are always powerful discontented groups who seek to short-circuit or circumvent democratic decisions they regard as inattentive to their concerns.

A decent democratic polity requires that political actors regularly display the ancient middle virtue, or semi-virtue, of constancy—which is not too different from the modern virtue-substitute called enlightened pursuit of interest. The proper function of democratic politicians is to pursue the persistent values and long-term wishes of democratic citizens. Some must find ways to transform (or in certain cases, simply resist) short-term demands whose enactment citizens would regret. Others must persuade citizens to accede to political changes whose unsettling effects they tend to resist. Aristotle gives us a brief but persuasive account of why democracies need this semi-virtue, and why they should not seek perfection or full human virtue. Fleshing out this account, Publius and Tocqueville teach us that steady policy in government requires some steadiness of character in ordinary citizens. Governors who embody constancy will devote themselves to cherished long-term projects; and a citizenry that tolerates such governance and contributes long-term projects of its own will be a citizenry that sees the need for enterprises that transcend short-term and individual pleasures. Such a citizenry will be willing both to support long-term projects for the public good and to engage in long-term opposition to political measures that cannot be justified.

The opposition between universalism and particularism, so clear in theory, is often less clear in practice. In fact, good democratic politicians act on the knowledge that no policy can be durable if its only backers are disinterested experts. Good government requires not only good decision but also politicians who know how ordinary citizens feel and can persuade them of the right course. This persuasive relationship goes both ways: in a democracy, those who think themselves experts must sometimes admit that they have left out an important consideration, and change course. Not every democratic relationship leads to good outcomes, but disdain for such relationships is a guarantee of bad ones.

ARISTOTLE's ROLE ETHICS: THE POLITICS OF RESTRAINT

To begin an ethical study of political roles or offices with Aristotle raises a simple problem: to the extent that ethics for him means the study of the virtues and of good character, the special or partial requirements of role morality seem to have no place at all. Political science, on Aristotle's account, pursues the end of action and of human life in general—"the good," which is happiness—not some good specific to politics or to particular political offices.[11] In this context and in others, Aristotle speaks of "*the* human good," not of distinct goods that are in principle available to some humans and not to others.[12] While it is true that particular figures deliberate *(bouleuesthai)* about what pertains to their given ends (health for doctors, good order [*eunomia*] for politicians),[13] this does not excuse the wise deliberator from questioning and examining the nature of those ends, and judging the qualities of lives according to the single standard of happiness.[14]

This claim from Aristotle's *Ethics* carries through into the *Politics*. There, the aim of the best regime is happiness, defined as "the actualization and complete practice of virtue, and this not on the basis of a presupposition but unqualifiedly." By "unqualifiedly" Aristotle means with the fewest concessions to necessity, and nobly.[15] The good regime is characterized by its citizens' "being excellent": "What is most choiceworthy for each individual is the highest it is possible for him to achieve," with

[11] Aristotle, *Nicomachean Ethics* (1985: 1094b7, 1095a18–19). Henceforth this volume will be referred to as *NE*.

[12] *NE*: 1094b7, 1102a13–15. Aristotle hardly claims that everyone is equally able to achieve the good (see, for example, Aristotle, *Politics* [1984]: 1331b39ff; henceforth this volume will be referred to as *Politics*). But a proper role ethic seems to require not this simple admission but the stronger claim that the goal everyone ought to *pursue* differs from person to person and role to role.

[13] *NE*: 1112b12–15.

[14] Kraut (1989: 160–61, and passim). Even if Kraut is wrong on the general point, it is clear that a politician who seeks the general goal of good order—which is probably identical to public happiness—is pursuing an abstract, general end. That is, he is not pursuing an end for which the constraints of his role are immediately salient.

[15] *Politics*: 1332a8ff.

lower actions always for the sake of higher, that is, more virtuous ones.[16] Where could careful attention to a particular role, let alone to the ordinary practices of democratic citizens and politicians, possibly fit in this uncompromising, high-minded scheme?

In fact, role ethics does not fit in *this* scheme, but in another. The above statements all concern the *best* regime, not actual regimes, and our concern is with the latter. Aristotle speculated about a regime in which all citizens would be virtuous and the goal of politics would be happiness, or at least the highest forms of happiness that politics can achieve. But he was not stupid. He recognized that no achievable political order would have citizens like that or goals like that, and spent most of the *Politics* examining more down-to-earth cases. Since actual political orders do not make any claim to pursue ultimate human happiness or the best possible human association, governance consistent with these orders will involve "virtues" that are not directed at happiness, that facilitate the more modest goals that typical human beings pursue. These will be the "virtues" of democratic office, and in Aristotelian terms they will not be true virtues at all but rather semi-virtues or substitutes for virtue. These are states of character worth pursuing because the nature of the political system makes pursuit of the second-best the best we can do. Aristotle, though dreaming of aristocracy, does not imagine or advocate aristocratic virtues for citizens situated as we are: democratic, skeptical, aware of our own faults and those of our neighbors, devoted to freedom rather than some search for the most noble possible character.

Jon Elster has described (and endorsed) an "Aristotelian" view of human nature in which human weaknesses of character can be cured by education in individual cases but cannot be avoided on a society-wide basis.[17] This is broadly correct, and Aristotle's ancient solution will turn out to be very similar to the well-known recent analysis by political economists like Elster and Thomas Schelling. This analysis claims that we should (and in fact do) arrange and support political institutions, as well as more informal social practices, that help us achieve our long-term desires in the face of short-term temptations. Elster and Schelling mention in this respect various procedures and institutions: independent central banks and other bureaucratic bodies; stable constitutions that enforce the rule of law; second readings of bills; and public notice and debate requirements.[18] "The chief mechanism," notes Schelling, "seems to be

---

[16] *Politics*: 1332a32–36, 1333a20–30.

[17] Elster (1984: 37, and Part 2 passim). Elster contrasts this view of human nature with an existentialist view in which moral self-transformation is universally possible, even common; I share his skepticism regarding the latter view.

[18] Central banks: Elster (1984: 89–90). Other bureaucratic bodies, such as the Foreign Office and BBC: Elster (1984: 90). Constitutions: Elster (1984: 93ff.). Second readings and notice requirements: Schelling (1984: 97).

mandatory delay."[19] While endorsing this mechanism, I shall place equal stress on two mechanisms mentioned by Elster and Schelling but not often pursued by scholars with an economic bent. The first is the mechanism of representation and election, which Elster describes as an electorate's way of "binding itself and of protecting itself against its own impulsiveness," especially when dissolution of the legislature between elections is not possible.[20] The second is the mechanism of voluntary association and voluntary self-binding, involving social but not penal sanctions, in the sphere of civil society. Schelling notes that promises made to oneself ("vows") have no standing in law, but can receive "social and institutional support" if recognized by a church or fraternal organization collectively devoted to enabling such voluntarily chosen moral projects.[21]

As we shall see, these pieces of contemporary analysis recapitulate, broadly speaking, the respective thought of the *Federalist Papers* and of *Democracy in America*, and represent two important directions of practical thinking about the formal and informal offices that democracy requires. But the most careful theoretical treatment remains Aristotle's, and before rushing to practical judgments we should study his account of why such devices are needed in the first place.

For Aristotle, good political offices do not embody absolute virtue but rather the relative purposes held by those who make the decisions in a given political system. Consider the well-known passage in book 3, chapter 4 of the *Politics*, in which the virtue of the good man is contrasted with that of the excellent citizen. In this passage, Aristotle still maintains that the "most precise account" of citizens' virtue is "that peculiar to each sort individually"[22]—which I take to mean assessment of each human being as a human being, abstracting from considerations of role or political purpose. However, the "common account" that fits all is an account relative to the common work of preserving the polity.[23] This "work" (*ergon*, usually translated as "function" in the ethical works) of preservation is not the work proper to a human being as such, which is "the soul's activity that expresses virtue."[24] The ideal regime pursues virtue, but actual polities pursue a mix of oligarchic goals (wealth) and democratic ones (freedom and equality).

So Aristotle resorts to the concept of citizen virtue not to correct or enhance his account of ethical virtue but to explain how the citizens of a

[19] Schelling (1984: 97).
[20] Elster (1984: 90).
[21] Schelling (1984: 99).
[22] *Politics*: 1276b24–25.
[23] *Politics*: 1276b25–30.
[24] *NE*: 1098a15–16.

typical city, who will not have what he regards as true or full virtue, can still be called good or bad citizens. Citizens can be relatively virtuous insofar as preserving an existing political society is a relatively good thing. As ends of life go, political security is a distant second best to happiness, but is far better than, say, an unalloyed devotion to power, or sybaritic pleasure. In contemporary terms, unchecked, selfish pursuit of the latter sorts of things leaves everyone worse off.

Thus Aristotle's theory of civic virtue embodies a measured response to pessimism about what most people and societies are likely to pursue. "The virtue of the excellent citizen must exist in all, for it is necessarily in this way that the city is excellent, but this is impossible in the case of the virtue of the good man, unless all the citizens of an excellent city are necessarily good men."[25] There are a few people of sterling character, and we can imagine a city made up only of them, but such speculations should not influence our practical study of what ordinary citizens are capable of. In late chapters of the *Politics*, Aristotle pursues this latter possibility (an excellent city made up of good men, in which all have the virtues both of citizens and of men). But his discussion there is not, we must stress, directly relevant to the discussion of actual regimes. It is in the imperfect city, one containing citizens of widely varying personal virtue, that the virtue of citizenship, distinct from that of ideally good human beings, becomes relevant.[26]

This implies that politics is an imperfect business, and that we should not expect good politicians to embody ideals of absolute virtue and perfect goodness. (This "modern," skeptical belief about politics was in fact Aristotle's as well: one reason his works are still relevant to modern democrats.) But good democratic politicians, concedes Aristotle the partisan of aristocracy, still can have something praiseworthy in their characters and pursue praiseworthy ends. They can have constancy, and can pursue what we would call the public interest (as well as their own interest, in the uneasy but productive tension that modern political science ceaselessly explores).

This comes out in Aristotle's discussion of education. There, Aristotle names "virtue and justice of the sort that is relative to (*pros*) the regime" as one of three qualities necessary in those holding authoritative offices.[27] The other two qualities are ability to do the relevant work and affection for the established regime. It might appear that these qualities of loyalty

---

[25] *Politics*: 1277a1–4. In many places the use of the English man/men can be attributed to sexist translations, but here Aristotle actually uses the word *anêr/andròs* (adult male), rather than *ánthropos* (human being). However, while Aristotle certainly had sexist beliefs, his argument here does not entail them.

[26] *Politics*: 1277a5ff.

[27] *Politics*: 1309a33–38.

and competence are enough to assure good officeholders, but Aristotle believes they are not. He puts his reason in the form of a rhetorical question vital to our inquiry: "Is it because it is possible for those who possess these two things to lack self-control *(akrateis einai)*, so that just as they do not serve themselves by knowing *(eidotes)* and being friendly to *(philountes)* themselves, there is nothing to prevent some persons from being in this condition with respect to the community?"[28] This passage, taken seriously, explains how a role ethic can provide standards for officeholders without being a guide to full virtue or the highest political or human goods. The word translated here as "lacking self-control" *(akrateis)* is the word in the *Ethics* traditionally translated as "incontinent,"[29] and we can identify it with lack of constancy. Someone with this lack "knows that his [*sic*] actions are base, but does them because of his feelings."[30] Inconstancy involves a kind of ignorance analogous to being drunk: people who lack constancy have proper practical knowledge in a way, but in a way also lack it. They are like actors speaking lines without fully taking them to heart, or like cities that vote for the right decrees and laws but do not apply them.[31] Because they are not vicious and recognize the right first principle of action "in theory" (as we might say, though Aristotle would call such reasoning practical), people who are weak are not completely bad—which means in particular that they regret their actions, know they must improve, and can therefore be taught.[32] But in the meantime, they lack the virtue of *phronesis* (practical wisdom).[33] They deliberate in a way but do so badly, and while their character is not fundamentally unjust, they act unjustly since they are overcome by emotion or pleasure.

If virtue and justice with a view to the regime are remedies for a lack of political constancy, we have some clue to their function. These kinds of virtue and justice are modest guidelines for people who believe, as almost all of us in fact now believe, that they do not have perfect practi-

---

[28] *Politics*: 1309b12–14.

[29] *NE*: 1145b9ff. Contemporary moral philosophers generally leave "lack of constancy" untranslated and use the Greek *akrasia*. They often associate *akrasia* with weakness of will (knowing that one ought to do something but being unable to do it). But since Aristotle claims that lack of constancy corrupts our very reasoning, it would seem *not* to be equivalent to the modern idea of weakness of will in this sense. Some commentators regard Aristotle's "Socratic" position on this issue, his conviction that one can always act properly if one possesses a certain kind of knowledge, as a weakness (thus Ross [1953: 224]), though I would regard it, properly understood, as a strength. The question is very complicated and controversial. For two sophisticated positions, see Norman O. Dahl (1984: 139–218); and Kenny (1979: esp. 155–66). None of what follows rests on this debate.

[30] *NE*: 1145b13.

[31] *NE*: 1147a15–20, 1152a20.

[32] *NE*: 1150–1151.

[33] *NE*: 1152a10ff.

cal knowledge and need help in acting well. Constancy is not full or complete virtue of the kind Aristotle seeks. If we were fully virtuous, we would possess the virtue of temperance, which means not even having bad desires.[34] Constancy involves an ability to abide by one's "calculation" (*logismos*) in spite of *not* being virtuous. The word "calculation" instead of "reason" (*logos*) here is deliberate: constancy is important to the extent that people do not have the sagelike ability to find the right thing to do by reason alone.[35] For the intellectual ability to find this right thing— again, what Aristotle called *phronesis*, or practical wisdom—depends on having virtue, and specifically temperance. Absent temperance, desires will "corrupt" one's assessment of what is worth pursuing in the first place.[36] (This will be true even if that person is also constant and can suppress current desires for the sake of future plans.)[37] Constancy, then, is the ability to suppress short-term desires for the sake of plans aiming at long-term desires or one's long-term advantage. One can have it even if one neither has nor wants the ability to engage in deeper reflections about what is really worth striving for. It is, in other words, something very like the ability to act in one's long-run *interest*.

A certain lack of virtue is characteristic of all political orders except the

[34] *NE*: 1146a10–17. There is an important distinction to be made here between the kind of rational decision that occurs when we would not even dream of doing what is not to our advantage, and the kind of decision that occurs when we are tempted to act unwisely but manage to refrain from doing so. Contemporary ethics as well as economics might call both of these decisions "rational," and say that neither involves weakness of will. For example, Elster (1984: 111) defines what it is to be rational as "deliberately sacrificing present gratification for future gratification." This would seem to involve constancy. Elster seems to claim that Aristotelian education is aimed at producing this kind of rationality (52), but if so he is not quite right: Aristotelian education aims to promote the temperance of character that makes unwise things not even gratifying. Perhaps Elster is referring to *political* education.

[35] In the *Rhetoric* (1991: 1389a32–35, 1389b35), Aristotle says that "calculation concerns the advantageous, virtue the honorable" (*kalos*), and that "the advantageous is good for the individual, the fine (*kalos*) absolutely."

[36] *NE*: 1140b12–23, 1144a29–36. Aristotle does not tell us exactly what this means, but presumably someone who has, say, excessively gluttonous, lustful, or power-hungry desires will, in deliberation, overestimate the degree to which a wisely led life should involve pursuit of food, sex, or political power.

[37] This discussion has deliberately omitted some difficulties. In particular, it is not obvious exactly how the constant but not temperate person is to arrive at the calculation of the right action, given that intemperate people are supposed to have the starting-points of their ethical reasoning corrupted by bad desires. Perhaps Aristotle's distinction between the constant person, who abides in the face of base desires but is easily persuaded "whenever it is appropriate," and the simply stubborn person (*NE*: 1151b8–13) provides some clue: the constant person can be *persuaded by others* to follow decent ends even if his independent reasoning would be corrupted. This is consistent with the argument of this work: as democratic citizens we need others to remind us of what is good, though we might tend to slip into imprudent action on our own.

best, but the use of constancy to compensate for this lack could be considered a *democratic* device, because it leaves intact the ability to live as one likes with no distinction between better and worse lives. Democratic politics retains, as far as distinctions of virtue and character are concerned, only the distinction between people restrained enough to get what they happen to like and those who end up not getting their desires because they pursue them foolishly or without proper forethought. Aristotle's guides for *democratic* action are in this way not "Aristotelian" in the sense the word is usually used in ethics: they are *not teleological*; they do not involve a concern with the human end, human functions, or the pursuit of human happiness *(eudaimonia)*. Aristotle's political science is mostly pragmatic: it does not depend on his speculations about the proper human end and the best human life. The standard of democratic constancy is not for officeholders with full virtue; such officeholders would likely make bad democratic officers and end up despising the political order. The kind of officials who have need of constancy are those who like the political system and their fellow citizens, and have the proper skills to pursue that affection, but whose emotions, passions, or love of power tempts them not to use their skills to benefit the polity.

Office ethics, then, are a guide to those aware of their own weakness. A society of people with perfect characters would not need to take ethical guidance from their political relationships and political institutions. They would just know what to do by thinking, and would have the character to act on it. The rest of us must be inspired by more accessible semi-virtues if we are to act as well in politics as our affection for democracy and our fellow citizens makes us want to act.

Aristotle's comments on political regimes immediately following the passage discussed support this reading. Aristotle discusses the desires that tend to lead astray oligarchs and democrats, respectively, and proposes an educative remedy for each. Or rather, he proposes not exactly a positive remedy but a negative counsel: each political order should *not* do the things it predictably tends to do (and later to regret). The advice to would-be oligarchs does not concern us, but the advice to democratic rulers and citizens is highly relevant.

This advice is essentially a warning not to love freedom and equality too much. Freedom and equality are what democracy is all about, but fanatical pursuit of either undermines both. Aristotle notes that democratic justice consists in equality, and that equality can imply two things: "{1} that whatever the multitude resolves is authoritative, and {2} freedom and equality involve doing whatever one wants." The former criterion is no more than deciding matters by votes in which all count equally, and a political system that calls itself a democracy could hardly discard it altogether. But to adopt the latter perspective is to "define freedom badly. . . . In democracies of this sort everyone lives as he wants and 'toward whatever [end he happens] to crave.'"[38] This sort of democratic life, however, is "a poor thing" in terms of the democratic end of (democratic) preservation itself: "To live with a view to the regime should not be supposed to be slavery, but preservation."[39]

Integrating this comment into our scheme: democrats wish to preserve the political system and know that certain radically licentious ways of life endanger it. As Aristotle notes elsewhere, excessive demands for consumption can lead the rich to fear for their property; or excessive hatred of class distinctions can lead them to fear for their persons; or, if popular zeal causes demagogic leaders to be given too much power, these leaders can set themselves up as tyrants.[40] Living in a stable democracy, less concerned than Aristotle with the political effects of an oligarchic class that demands special privileges and immunities, we might stress different requirements for democracy: attachment to compromise, toleration, sympathy with fellow citizens who may seem very different from oneself. Even democracies require a certain inequality, in limited but important senses: orderly lives must normally be preferred to criminal ones; bringing up children must be rewarded and abandoning them punished; the decisions of government agencies and officials must sometimes be obeyed, rather than contested by every citizen all the time. Officeholders are few and the governed many, which may be why Aristotle says that oligarchs may hope to rule oligarchically *(oligarchein)* while democrats should seek merely to "have a political system that is run democratically" *(demokrateisthai)*.[41] But egalitarian emotions, especially a tendency to regard all political authority as "slavery,"[42] get the better of democrats, who, in their weak state, forget their planned restraint.

It is the task of democratic officeholders, able persons who love democracy, not to deceive the people or even to alter their plans systematically, but to remind them to act with the restraint that they intended to begin with, while acting with such restraint themselves rather than pursuing the ill-advised objects that democratic power makes so tempt-

---

[38] *Politics*: 1310a28–35; interpolations in curly brackets are mine; those in square brackets are the translator's.

[39] *Politics*: 1310a34–7.

[40] *Politics*: 1304b19–1305a27.

[41] The verb for running oligarchies is in the active voice; the one for running democracies is in the so-called middle voice, which carries a sense between the active and passive and can mean, as likely here, "have something done for one." It can also mean "do something to oneself," and the word could therefore be translated "govern themselves democratically."

[42] "Where the multitude of middling persons predominates either over both of the extremities together or over one alone, there a lasting polity is capable of existing. For there is not reason to fear that the wealthy and the poor will come to an agreement against them: *neither will want to be the slaves of the other*, and if they seek a regime in which they will have more in common, they will find none other than this. They would not put up with ruling in turn on account of their distrust toward one another" (*Politics*: 1296b38).

ing (including the demand for unlimited power). These tasks stem from concerns internal to democratic values, not alien to them. No matter how devoted to equality and democracy we are, we should note that a frenzied and uncompromising ardor for equality is a way to doom equality through civil strife, oligarchic reaction, or demagogic tyranny.

All this, however, gives rise to two natural questions. First, how can we expect people to choose good rulers and abide by their decisions if they indeed lack perfect decision-making powers? Put another way, what makes a people decent and constant over time? After all, Aristotle, in the passage explored above, exhorts democracies to seek restrained and non-licentious government because he thinks they have a tendency to do the opposite.

Second, why should we expect those who seek and are elected to office to serve relatively well themselves? What is the incentive for rulers to preserve the political order, if "affection" for it is not enough to resist temptation? This problem is especially acute since the rulers in a democracy do not have freedom of action and are constantly subject to popular demands. Full virtue for Aristotle is literally its own reward—one who has perfect virtue is happy, or as happy as possible given fortune—but what is the reward for constancy, a half-virtue which consists in restraining oneself for the sake of purposes that seem a bit arbitrary?

The government of all political orders is, we should remember, a matter of the morally imperfect ruling the morally imperfect.[43] But if a democracy wants to remain peaceful, stable, and able to retain its egalitarian political principles, its leaders and ordinary citizens must at least be semi-virtuous or constant. Aristotle does not tell us how to ensure this, an omission that can be attributed to his disdain for democracy as a poor second-best, combined with his unmodern inability to imagine a sphere of culture and society separate from politics and political education. This is where Madison and Hamilton (who I believe are similar enough on these matters to be called by the collective "Publius") and Tocqueville come in. Publius tells us that the reward for politicians who are constant is democratic fame; Tocqueville tells us that the guarantors of constant citizenship are organizational life and a proper use of "religion" in the broadest sense.

The FEDERALIST Papers: Constancy in Government

"Liberty may be endangered," writes Madison in *Federalist* No. 63, "by the abuses of liberty as well as by the abuses of power." Publius' doctrine

---

[43] That is why democracies are democracies; if they were based on ideal virtue, according to Aristotle, they would be his dreamed-of utopian aristocracies, and the nonvirtuous would not be citizens. See, for example, *Politics*: 1308b32ff.

of governance teaches us how to get good rulers who will check such abuses. Institutional structures encourage in politicians the stability of character we have called democratic constancy, and love of fame provides the incentive to continue in constant habits.

In *Federalist* No. 49, Madison puts forth the well known formula: "It is the reason of the public alone that ought to controul and regulate the government. The passions ought to be controuled and regulated by the government." While a scholar of ancient constitutions might read this as endorsing a mixed order, one in which aristocrats with superior virtue rule and a less virtuous public is content to judge,[44] this is not what Publius means. The *Federalist* explicitly rejects the ideal of the mixed order, defending "unmixed and extensive republics."[45] Publius suspects that passionate and imprudent behavior will characterize the rulers as well as the ruled, and lacking some of Aristotle's biases, he does not limit this suspicion to particular (democratic) orders. He speaks of the "passions of men" as needing constraint, not only those of democrats.[46] Consistent with this, Publius refuses to attribute to "national rulers" more than a "common share of prudence" (though he insists on allowing them that much).[47] We are dealing here with a "democratic" theory in the double sense of being a theory aimed at designing a democracy and one embodying democratic assumptions about the equality—equal virtue or equal vice—of most if not all human characters.[48]

But if governors are not ethically much better than the governed, what makes government better than lack of government, representation better than direct democracy, deliberate decision better than factional strife? One could answer with a Hobbesian appeal to order for its own sake, or a technocratic hope that politicians will have greater expertise on the subjects of policy than the average citizen does. The *Federalist* makes gestures toward each of these positions: Hamilton proclaims the need for

---

[44] Compare, for example, *Politics*: 1308b32ff.

[45] *Federalist*: No. 14. The *Federalist* repeatedly stresses the principle that all authority emanates from the people—see Nos. 22, 28, 43, 46, 58, 78, and esp. 39, 49, 51.

[46] *Federalist*: No. 15. And in No. 51, Madison opposes the creation of a separate, aristocratic body in the government, on the grounds that an aristocracy may not oppose popular majorities, or may oppose both majorities and wronged minorities. Unlike Aristotle, he does not take seriously the thesis that aristocrats may have a prudence or discernment that makes their deliberations different in kind from those of interested or passionate publics.

[47] *Federalist*: No. 27; see also Nos. 55, 73, 75.

[48] The authors of the Federalists were not themselves democrats (Madison assumed property qualifications for voting and bitterly opposed their later erosion), but it is remarkable how few oligarchic arguments and biases in favor of property are contained in the *Federalist*. Political arguments do not always mirror personal opinions: Madison thought "the people" were best represented by the propertied, but in his public writings for the citizens of New York he did not say so. The theory as written is potentially fully democratic.

a "uniform rule of civil justice" to regulate the "endless diversities in the opinions of men";[49] and Madison writes of representatives' knowledge and experience.[50] If these were the only considerations, the conclusions to be drawn would be edifying but boring, since few politicians run for office on a platform of anarchy or incompetence, or espouse these as guiding principles once in office. Constitutional government would then be valued for the horrible states of government it prevented—anarchy, rule by lot—rather than for any positive qualities. And under such a theory an account of democratic institutions could not provide clear guidelines for selecting and judging political officers or guiding their deliberations.

But this is not all there is to it. Madison is not willing to suppose legislators are virtuous, but he is willing to suppose that the "senatorial trust" requires "stability of character."[51] Stability of character is not the ancient virtue of prudence, nor does it imply lack of passionate temptation. But it does imply an ability to resist momentary excitement and to suppress passions. It supposes, in other words, constancy. I will read *Federalist* Nos. 63 and 71–72[52] as modern discourses on the modern semi-virtue of constancy, and as guides to distinguishing good from bad office-holders (even when, as good democrats, we are reluctant to distinguish good people from bad in our personal ethical judgment).

Madison thought that the most important characteristic of an upper

---

[49] *Federalist*: No. 22.

[50] *Federalist*: Nos. 52, 62.

[51] *Federalist*: No. 62.

[52] The first paper is on the Senate, and the last two on the presidency. I will concentrate on these papers because I assume, and not only for the sake of argument, that the House of Representatives is supposed to reflect the immediate passions of the people and that the ethic appropriate to that body is one of obedience to the views of the majority of constituents in each district, where such views exist. It may not even be wrong for representatives to be passionate and immoderate when their constituents are—this will remind the other branches both of the people's will and of their own responsibilities. This is in fact what Madison (*Federalist*: No. 63) sometimes supposes, or at least fears: "Many of the defects, as we have seen, which can only be supplied by a senatorial institution, are common to a numerous assembly frequently elected by the people, and to the people themselves." This is why Madison in No. 51 emphasizes that the two branches of the Congress have "different modes of election and *different principles of action*," and are "as little connected with each other as the nature of their society will admit" (emphasis added)—precisely so that the Senate can check the House. (As Wills [1981: 122–23] persuasively argues, the "checks" considered in the *Federalist* mean primarily checks *within* the legislative branch, the Senate as a check on the House, not checks of one branch by another.) In the same paper, Madison contemplates, as a modification of the Constitution as it stands, a mode of checking the House which will combine "this weaker department" [the presidency] and the "weaker branch of the stronger department" [Senate]. It seems plausible to think that, at least with respect to their role in lawmaking, Madison expected the Senate and president to be animated by a similar spirit. Wills (123–24) implies a similar reading.

house was length of tenure. Criticizing in a letter Jefferson's draft constitution for Virginia, Madison argued that an upper house must have a term of at least six years. One advantage of this was the greater "knowledge and experience" that a senate could thereby achieve in comparison to a popular branch. But beyond this, Madison stressed the dispositions of character and modes of decision that a long term made possible: the members could "derive a firmness from the tenure of their places" that would ensure "that system and steadiness in public affairs without which no Government can prosper or be respectable." The purpose of this institution was not to repress popular government but to sustain it: "By correcting the infirmities of popular Government, it [such a senate] will prevent that disgust against that form which may otherwise produce a sudden transition to some very different one."[53] This short passage summarizes the reasons for the Senate contained in the *Federalist*: friendly to popular government but pessimistic. about human character, Madison sought to place a bias towards constancy and careful decision-making not just in "parchment" laws but in a body of specific individuals bound by interest and ambition to do what the people would ultimately want them to do.

The *Federalist* No. 63 defends the institution of a senate for what might seem an unexpected reason: the senate ensures "national character." The emphasis here is not on "nation" (Publius sometimes lauds the special advantages of America or Americans, but rarely, and not here) but on "character," in the sense of a consistent tendency to act in a certain way. In particular, Madison thinks that democracy's penchant for "variable" policy can be tempered by a senate. Variability is bad partly because of diplomatic appearances: why should other countries regard American policy as thoroughly "wise and honorable" if we are so dissatisfied as to change it all the time? But this is not merely a matter of appearance, since the regard of other countries parallels our actual merits: "Where the national councils may be warped by some strong passion or momentary interest, the presumed or known opinion of the impartial world may be the best guide that can be followed."

Here, as almost everywhere else in the *Federalist*, the argument for resisting passions speaks of "strong" or "momentary" passions.[54] There is

---

[53] James Madison, "Remarks on Mr. Jefferson's Draught of a Constitution," letter to John Brown (ca. 15 October 1788), in Meyers (1981: 34–35). I thank John Wright for first drawing my attention to this letter.

[54] "*Momentary passions* and immediate interests have a more active and imperious controul over human conduct than general or remote considerations of policy, utility or justice" (Hamilton, *Federalist*: No. 6; emphasis added).

"Those occasional ill humors, or temporary prejudices and propensities . . . beget injustice and oppression of a part of the community, and engender schemes which, though they

no such thing as a long-term passion. Or rather, long-term passions are called by another name (perhaps "public opinion," "utility," or the "public happiness"). And "impartial" does not connote absolute objectivity, which would be a high standard for judgment indeed; it retains instead its original sense of "nonpartisan, not a party to the dispute," a standard that domestic officers are to aspire to, if they cannot hope to reach. Senators are to aim at decisions which would gain the approval not of some hypothetical judge or of "the Universe" but of foreign nations; informed foreigners are presumably fallible in judgment but are unbiased in relation to American disputes, therefore dispassionate and measured in judgment. The advantages of such deliberation will be most felt on issues requiring not immediate and conspicuous action but "a succession of well-chosen and well-connected measures, which have a gradual and perhaps unobserved operation." By deciding on such measures and pursuing them over time, senators will further "the collective and permanent welfare" of this country or any other. This, not some supposed *Volksgeist*, is what is at stake in "national character."

The next section of the essay is often considered elitist or aristocratic but in fact advocates a standard of good democratic rule unaccompanied (to the regret of aristocrats) by nondemocratic principles. Madison argues that an institution like the Senate

> may be sometimes necessary as a defense to the people against their own temporary errors and delusions. As the cool and deliberate sense of the community ought, in all governments, and actually will, in all free governments, ultimately prevail over the views of its rulers; so there are particular moments in public affairs when the people, stimulated by some irregular passion, or some illicit advantage, or misled by the artful misrepresentations of interested men, may call for measures which *they themselves* will afterwards be the most ready to lament and condemn. In these critical moments, how salutary will be the interference of some temperate and respectable body of citizens, in order to check the misguided career, and to *suspend* the blow meditated by the people against themselves, until reason, justice, and truth can regain their authority over the

gratify a *momentary inclination* or desire, terminate in general distress, dissatisfaction, and disgust" (Hamilton, No. 27; emphasis added).

"sudden breeze of passion, or . . . *transient* impulse" (Hamilton, No. 71; emphasis added. See discussion below).

". . . that fundamental principle of republican government, which admits the right of the people to alter or abolish the established Constitution, whenever they find it inconsistent with their happiness, yet it is not to be inferred from this principle, that the representatives of the people, whenever a *momentary inclination* happens to lay hold of a majority of their constituents, incompatible with the provisions in the existing Constitution, would, on that account, be justifiable in a violation of those provisions . . ." (Hamilton, No. 78; emphasis added).

public mind? What bitter anguish would not the people of Athens have often escaped if their government had contained so provident a safeguard against the tyranny of their own passions? Popular liberty might then have escaped the indelible reproach of decreeing to the same citizens the hemlock on one day and statues on the next.[55]

Note what this passage does and does not say. It speaks of blows "meditated by the people against themselves," not of oppression of the few by the many. It speaks of the "tyranny of [the people's] own passions," but these passions are "irregular," and do not involve the people's being consistently wrong. The final standard for judging the irregularity is, in fact, the people's own subsequent and more sober judgment; there are no standards for judging the people's conduct besides popular ones. And Athenian democracy is reproached for its *inconsistency* in imposing death sentences it will itself immediately regret, not, as in Socrates' and Aristotle's criticisms, for being *unjust* in executing or exiling prominent citizens.

In other words, the advantage of a deliberative senate is not that it decides better than the people would in the long term, but that it enables the people to get to the "long term" before they make decisions they would reject *by their own standards.* An argument Madison uses a few sentences later, in arguing for a senate, confirms this reason: he claims not that republics without senates are ignoble or unwise, but that they have a "fugitive and turbulent existence," and are never "long-lived."[56] Democracies need deliberative senators if they are to preserve the principles of government they themselves hold dear. The Senate exists in order to blend "stability" with liberty, *not* in order to add to liberty nobility, wisdom, or a view to the good life.

This is a liberal, democratic theory, and the Senate is not an aristocratic branch. To be sure, it contributes to liberal democracy not by giving the people absolutely everything they want but by adding to policy decisions the forbearance required to preserve liberty and the opportunity to satisfy future wants. In response to accusations that the Senate will become a "tyrannical aristocracy," Madison replies that "liberty may be endangered by the abuses of liberty as well as by the abuses of power. . . . The former, rather than the latter, are apparently most to be apprehended by the United States." This assessment is not based on mere "conservative" bias, but on attention to the whole form of the political order including its guarantees in favor of democracy: if the Senate ever tends toward an aristocratic revolution, "the House of Representatives, with the people on their side, will at all times be able to bring back

[55] *Federalist*: No. 63; emphasis added.
[56] Ibid.

the Constitution to its primitive form and principles [i.e., republic, and republican]. Against the force of the immediate representatives of the people nothing will be able to maintain even the constitutional authority of the Senate, but such a display of enlightened policy, and attachment to the public good, as will divide with that branch of the legislature the affections and support of the entire body of the people themselves."[57]

I take this to mean that while a body representing the immediate, short-term passions of the people will always preserve its power and authority, the only way a deliberative branch intended to check such passions can survive in a democracy is by demonstrating its devotion to the people, and to democracy, in substance rather than form. "Enlightened policy" and "attachment to the public good," taken together and in the context, should be interpreted not as high, rationalist goals but as a disposition to preserve what the public would choose upon reflection, combined with the strength of character to force such reflection. A Senate directly elected by the people, as we have now, can be expected to have somewhat greater "natural" democratic legitimacy than the former Senate (elected by state legislatures), at the cost perhaps of a lesser tendency to deliberation and reflection. But to the extent that the senators' length of term and the size of their constituencies let them keep some of their intended role, the two parts of their constitutional ethic remain clear: senators exist, in accordance with a democracy's need for government, in order to deny the people what they now want to the extent that they would regret their passions later. And senators preserve themselves, in accordance with democratic principles, to the extent that they persuade the people that they do this out of love of the people rather than oligarchic bias, moral corruption, or pure mulishness.

Such mechanisms neither transform democratic citizens and their governors into embodiments of virtue and wisdom nor change democracy's essential nature. If, in spite of delay and persuasion, the public decides to adopt unwise or dangerous policies, there is not much that Publius can consistently say. The standards internal to democracy do not allow considerations of wisdom or virtue to trump those of freedom and majority rule: "The cool and deliberate sense of the community ought in all governments, and actually will in all free governments, ultimately prevail."[58] If that deliberate sense is itself mistaken due to lack of wisdom or deficiencies of character, there is nothing for senators to do, especially since (once again) they themselves are unlikely to have perfect practical judgment.

This conclusion may be too bleak to win much admiration as a gov-

[57] Ibid.
[58] Ibid.

erning principle. Fortunately, other, more informal offices exist whose function is to give us a better public so that senators may give us a better policy.

Similar conclusions may be drawn from Hamilton's defense of the presidency. While this book will not discuss the presidential office as such, it will take inspiration from Hamilton's papers on the subject, especially since I shall claim that his arguments closely parallel Madison's claims about the Senate. In *Federalist* No. 71, Hamilton defends the president's lengthy term as conducive not only to "stability" but to "energy" in the executive. But energy turns out to be linked to stability, for it involves not a sort of restless dynamism but, on the contrary, willingness to pursue projects requiring time and determination. Like Madison's defense of the Senate, Hamilton's defense of the executive is based not on a simple opposition of governmental reason to public passion but on the distinction between the "*deliberate* sense of the community"—which should indeed "govern the conduct" of those who hold office—and "every *sudden* breeze of passion, . . . every *transient* impulse which the people may receive from the arts of men, who flatter their prejudices to betray their interests" (emphases added). (Earlier in the paper, Hamilton also calls the recurrent "ill-humours" of the public "transient.") The executive should serve the people's considered, deliberate public assessment of interest rather their short-term passions: "When occasions present themselves in which the interests of the people are at variance with their inclinations, it is the duty of the persons whom they have appointed to be the guardians of those interests to *withstand the temporary delusion in order to give them time and opportunity for more cool and sedate reflection.*" Political leaders with the "courage and magnanimity" to do this earn, Hamilton claims, "lasting monuments" of public gratitude.[59]

This mention of "courage and magnanimity" should not deceive us. There is no indication that courage is the Aristotelian mean between overboldness and cowardice, knowing when to fight. (Elsewhere in the paper, Hamilton attributes to the president only a "tolerable portion of fortitude," not even a large one.) Nor is magnanimity the Aristotelian virtue of acting with knowledge of one's virtue and the actions appropriate to it: that virtue goes together with relative political inactivity,[60] not with Hamilton's presidential virtues of secrecy, energy, and dispatch. For Hamilton, magnanimity and courage apparently mean a reasoned resistance to some public opinion, some of the time. If the president does not have virtue in the ancient sense, perhaps he does have fewer "prejudices"

[59] Hamilton, *Federalist*: No. 71.
[60] Aristotle, *NE*: 1124b.

to be "flattered" than the average citizen: his virtue is a kind of wise stubbornness, or again, a kind of constancy. A president is not as easily swayed as the public or its representatives in a "popular assembly, [who] seem sometimes to fancy that they are the people themselves, and betray strong symptoms of impatience and disgust at the least sign of opposition from any other quarter."[61] So the president may take the action he thinks will win him monuments for magnanimity in the long term. Again, these monuments are democratic monuments and depend ultimately on persuading the people that one's measures have served what they see as their interests. When a president is voted out of office, "the person substituted is warranted in supposing that the dismission [*sic*] of his predecessor has proceeded from a dislike to his measures."[62]

This is relevant to a long-running debate over whether the arguments for the Constitution in the *Federalist* ultimately appeal to interest or whether they presuppose in addition a kind of virtue in the rulers, the ruled, or both. In fact, a central goal of the *Federalist* is to unify virtue and interest: to define virtue narrowly, so as not to require radical self-abnegation, and to define interest broadly, so as to include public spirit and praiseworthy, noble aspirations. When virtue is mentioned in the *Federalist*, it is sometimes to deny that we should expect it in rulers.[63] But

---

[61] Hamilton, *Federalist*: No. 71. The mention of "representatives in a popular assembly" implies that Hamilton's well-known criticism of legislatures is meant to apply primarily to the House, not the Senate. At least, that is the most charitable interpretation, unless we think Madison's arguments for why the Senate will act differently are altogether meaningless or badly thought out.

[62] Ibid.

[63] Since temptations to corruption under the Articles of Confederation may prove too powerful to be overcome by "any but minds animated and guided by superior virtue," we may expect that at least a third of the Congress might be corrupted by a foreign power (Hamilton, *Federalist*: No. 22). The Senate is disposed to punish those of its members corrupted by executive influence because it will be offended by the "abuse of their confidence" and fearful for its authority: "We may thus far count upon their pride, if not upon their virtue" (Hamilton, No. 66). Hamilton argues that the "stern virtue" that would be necessary for a president to resist congressional threats to cut off his salary is "the growth of few soils; and in the main it will be found that a power over a man's support is a power over his will. If it were necessary to confirm so plain a truth by facts, examples would not be wanting, even in this country, of the intimidation or seduction of the Executive by the terrors or allurements of the pecuniary arrangements of the legislative body" (No. 73). He makes a similar claim about temptation by foreign powers in No. 75: "The history of human conduct *does not warrant that exalted opinion of human virtue* which would make it wise in a nation to commit interests of so delicate and momentous a kind, as those which concern its intercourse with the rest of the world, to the sole disposal of a magistrate created and circumstanced as would be a President of the United States" (emphasis added). Finally, Hamilton denies in *Federalist* No. 73 that he supports the veto power on the grounds that the president will have "superior wisdom or virtue" to the wisdom and virtue of the legislature: the veto only allows for more time for deliberation and makes hasty or factional decisions less likely to become final.

in those papers where we are told to expect some virtue in the public or its governors, virtue is used as a synonym for everyday faith with democratic government and lack of inclination to treachery and treason.[64] (It therefore resembles the "affection" part of Aristotle's three standards for rulers, not the "virtue" part; in no passage do either Hamilton or Madison suggest that rulers' "virtue" provides them with extraordinary characters conducive to great acts or exceptional fortitude.) Rulers governed by virtue, then, are more or less those who will not sell their office and their country for money or for offers of power under a foreign government. This is not what "civic republican" advocates of virtue-based government usually have in mind. To the extent that they do have such limited virtues in mind, this only shows that the noble language of civic republicanism comes down to a call for acts that are really quite ordinary.

Nor does "interest" always mean a selfish interest in power or office. "Interest" is often synonymous with "private faction," but such phrases as "public interest" are often, for Publius, synonymous with "public good."[65] To be sure, if the argument made above is correct, this represents not so much an ennobling of interest as a humble view of the public good: the

---

[64] Virtuous officeholders are contrasted to those inclined to "tyranny" in *Federalist* No. 53 (Madison), and to those "disposed to form and pursue a scheme of tyranny or treachery" in No. 55 (Madison). Madison argues for elections as the method of keeping rulers virtuous in No. 57, which must surely mean keeping them from betraying the public, not keeping them of sterling character, for which mere elections would presumably be either superfluous or ineffective. Jay, if his papers count, apparently links "abilities and virtue" respectively to "those who best understand our national interests, whether considered in relation to the several States or to foreign nations, who are best able to promote those interests," and those "whose reputation for integrity inspires and merits confidence" (No. 64). Hamilton contrasts the president's likely "ability and virtue" with the "talents for low intrigue, and the little arts of popularity" that "may alone suffice to elevate a man to the first honors in a single State" (No. 68), which clearly distinguishes virtue from mere glibness or cunning but does not define it as anything grander. In No. 73, Hamilton's "stern virtue" means the president's (unlikely) ability to do his duty by resisting bribes or threats from Congress with regard to the president's salary. In No. 76, the famous passage urging us to "view human nature as it is, without either flattering its virtues or exaggerating its vices" refers to Hamilton's belief that the majority at least of the Senate would retain "integrity," "probity," and "independence" in the face of executive attempts "to corrupt or seduce a majority of its members" through direct offers of political office. Apparently feeling that even this belief is too strong, Hamilton goes on to deny that "the integrity of the Senate [is] the only reliance"—there are also direct constitutional safeguards against the practice. For No. 72, see text.

[65] Faction is defined as what is against the "permanent and aggregate interests of the community" (No. 10). Hamilton speaks of "the OBJECTS of federal administration, or in other words, . . . the management of our NATIONAL INTERESTS" (No. 23). Hamilton argues that learned professions can transcend "the rivalships between the different branches of industry, [and are] likely to prove an impartial arbiter between them, ready to promote either, so far as it shall appear to him conducive to the general interests of the society" (No. 35). And in No. 71, the people's "interests" are apparently identical to the "PUBLIC GOOD."

public good is whatever the people upon reflection think is in their interest. But we should still not interpret interest in terms of venality or immediate desires. Just as Hume's civil magistrates have an "immediate interest in every execution of justice" because they are satisfied with their position and have no reason to do injustice,[66] and Hamilton echoes this link between interest and duty in talking of the federal government as particularly "interested" in guarding public safety,[67] the officers described in the *Federalist* have an interest not only in power or office but in an able performance of their jobs and the successful completion of their particular projects. As Garry Wills points out, the well-known claim that "ambition must be made to counteract ambition" in No. 51 is followed by an explanation that "the interest of the man must be connected with the constitutional rights of the place." In Wills's gloss: "It is the ambition expressed in *office* that Madison calls a combination of personal motive and constitutional means. Those in office identify their own reputation with that of the institution, and do not like to see it diminished."[68]

If this interpretation seems speculative, consider how *Federalist* Nos. 71 and 72 give two different accounts of the reasons for presidential attention to the duties of office. One is in the language of virtue, one of interest. Given what virtue and interest mean, however, one can read both in terms of the semi-virtue/enlightened interest that can be associated with democratic constancy.

In No. 71, Hamilton argues that presidents calculate the extent of their interest in their power according to a "general principle of human nature," and in much the same way that ordinary people calculate their interest in their property. Interest in property, however, means for Hamilton not an expectation of pleasure or gain from it but a regard for the preservation and cultivation of the property itself:

> It is a general principle of human nature that a man will be interested in whatever he possesses, in proportion to the firmness or precariousness of the tenure by which he holds it; will be less attached to what he holds by a momentary or uncertain title, than to what he enjoys by a durable or certain title; and, of course, will be willing to risk more for the sake of the one than for the sake of the other. This remark is not less applicable to a political privilege, or honor or trust, than to any article of ordinary property. The inference from it is that a man acting in the capacity of chief magistrate, under a consciousness that in a

---

[66] Hume (1978: 537, 552).

[67] "Who is so likely to make suitable provisions for the public defense as that body to which the guardianship of the public safety is confided; which, as the center of information, will best understand the extent and urgency of the dangers that threaten; as the representatives of the WHOLE, will feel itself most deeply interested in the preservation of every part; which, from the responsibility implied in the duty assigned to it, will be most sensibly impressed with the necessity of proper exertions . . . ?" (Hamilton, *Federalist*: No. 23).

[68] Wills (1981: 124).

very short time he *must* lay down his office, will be apt to feel himself *too little interested in it* to hazard any material censure or perplexity from the independent exertion of his powers, or from encountering the ill-humors, however transient, which may happen to prevail, either in a considerable part of the society itself, or even in a predominant faction in the legislative body.[69]

The mention of "privilege, honor, or trust" in the same breath as property shows us that "honor" for Hamilton is not, or not consistently, a spirited motive divorced from sober calculation. An honor for Hamilton is a resource to be cherished and developed; when securely held, it is not an end in itself but a spur to "independent exertion of [one's] powers." And it is on this interest, an immediate interest in the use of the powers one has, that the ability to resist "ill-humors, however transient, which may happen to prevail" in the public or legislature is based. The duration of the executive provides an interest in the office: Hamilton thinks the president will have determination in carrying on his official duties simply because the office is (durably) *his*. This, of course, assumes that a president sought office in the first place out of a desire to accomplish something substantial, and not out of mere hunger for power. Whether this is the case is what would-be candidates must ask themselves, and what we must ask them.

So read, interest in office sounds a lot like pride. In fact, the next paper continues the same argument in the language of pride. Hamilton mentions "the love of fame, the ruling passion of the noblest minds" in the context of *denying* that this passion would motivate an executive with a limited term. For such an executive would rationally foresee that he would not have time to finish what he had started and hence *earn* fame, which apparently means future adulation based on real achievement:

> Even the love of fame, the ruling passion of the noblest minds, *which would prompt a man to plan and undertake extensive and arduous enterprises for the public benefit, requiring considerable time to mature and perfect them, if he could flatter himself with the prospect of being allowed to finish what he had begun, would, on the contrary, deter him from the undertaking, when he foresaw that he must quit the scene before he could accomplish the work*, and must commit that, together with his own reputation, to hands which might be unequal or unfriendly to the task. The most to be expected from the generality of men, in such a situation, is the negative merit of not doing harm, instead of the positive merit of doing good."[70]

Love of fame, therefore, is not a wild or irrational impulse, any more than a regard for honors and privileges is.[71] In order to operate, each

---

[69] *Federalist*: No. 71; first emphasis Hamilton's, second emphasis added.

[70] *Federalist*: No. 72; emphasis added.

[71] The best single consideration of the theme of fame in the American founding era remains Adair (1974). As Adair's essay makes clear, the question of which achievements

requires an assurance that real accomplishments are possible. We can expect constancy in the president because the institution is designed to allow such accomplishments. This alone counterbalances the temptation to surrender to transient public inclinations.

Conversely, we may evaluate the president on the extent to which he performs the kind of "arduous enterprises for the public benefit" that the institution is designed to give him an interest in. According to republican principles, the president is supposed to carry out not just any projects, but those that are likely to win public approval. Hamilton makes explicit the link between the president's interest in vocation and the public's judgment according to its view of its own good:

> With a positive duration of considerable extent, I connect the circumstance of re-eligibility. The first is necessary to give to the officer himself the inclination and the resolution to act his part well, and to the community time and leisure to observe the tendency of his measures, and thence to form an experimental estimate of their merits. The last is necessary to enable the people, when they see reason to approve of his conduct, to continue him in his station, in order to prolong the utility of his talents and virtues, and to secure to the government the advantage of permanency in a wise system of administration.[72]

The "utility of [the president's] talents and virtues" means nothing more, or less, than our judgment that he has done his part to ensure a "wise system of administration." In the first phrase, utility and virtue are clearly and nobly joined; the proper (humble) virtues of the office are judged by the standards of public good, and the public good is furthered when the president has what might be called a fame-interest in resisting public pressures for the sake of carrying out determined projects.[73]

Madison makes a similar argument about the Senate. It embodies responsibility (itself a word first used in the political sense by Hamilton and Madison)[74] not merely because senators must stand for reelection by state legislatures but because senators are both few enough in number and persist in office long enough for the success or failure of projects to be attributed to them.[75] Speaking of those objects of government that

---

were most deserving of lasting fame was an important and recurring one in both Enlightenment thought and the ancient sources on which it drew.

[72] *Federalist*: No. 72.

[73] For a fuller consideration see Flaumenhaft (1992: esp. 116–17 and 285n5). While Flaumenhaft's interpretations are generally excellent, his larger theoretical outlook, and therefore the conclusions he draws, differs from mine. Walling (1999) is more measured in his judgments but does not treat in much detail the topics stressed in this work.

[74] Flaumenhaft (1992: 285–86n6).

[75] The question of whether senators are truly few and prominent enough to gain fame for projects well pursued may have divided Hamilton and Madison and certainly divides con-

require "a succession of well-chosen and well-connected measures," Madison argues that

> an assembly elected for so short a term as to be unable to provide more than one or two links in a chain of measures, on which the general welfare may essentially depend, ought not to be answerable for the final result any more than a steward or tenant, engaged for one year, could be justly made to answer for places or improvements which could not be accomplished in less than half a dozen years. . . .
>
> The proper remedy for this defect must be an additional body in the legislative department, which, having sufficient permanency to provide for such objects as require a continued attention, and a train of measures, may be justly and effectually answerable for the attainment of those objects.[76]

The quality expected in rulers who love fame is not merely ambition and desire for reelection, but a desire to be recognized for actual achievement of projects long-planned and carefully executed—to be recognized, that is, for a quality like constancy.

Thus Hamilton's and Madison's arguments about fame, however brash their tone may sound, do not in fact reject the Aristotelian concern with second-best virtues in favor of some more heroic (or cynical) standard. They envision flawed yet restrained political officers who mirror in their own characters the importance of constant action in the republic as a whole. Whether one calls it constancy or attention to interest, what governs the actions of responsible leaders is the ability to put aside present

---

temporary commentators. Walling (1999: 120–21) articulates what he calls "'Hamilton's rule' of responsible government: individuals will take responsibility for important and risky measures in proportion to their ability to understand what needs to be done and to pursue their objectives consistently over time, and to the degree to which they will be held personally accountable for failure or success. Responsibility is generally directly proportional to the amount of time a representative has to accomplish a task, and inversely proportional to the number of representatives who can share blame or take credit for the task." Walling argues, however, that Hamilton hoped that the senators involved in a particular policy would be few enough (and their terms in office long enough) that their interest in the success of long-term policies, and sense of responsibility for their decisions, would resemble to some extent that of the president. Flaumenhaft (285n5) quotes a letter of 1780 in which Hamilton insists that responsibility will exist only where it is not "shared" with anyone at all. But Hamilton may have been wrong. More charitably, his conclusions may have been based on circumstances that no longer obtain: for instance, the long delays in promulgating political information, and the American experience with British royal government, which taught people to look to the monarch as the unchallenged symbol of national policy. Hamilton might not have foreseen the day in which we refer to bills by the names of their legislative sponsors: "Bradley-Gephardt" tax reform, "Gramm-Rudman" mechanisms for cutting spending, "Humphrey-Hawkins" plans for Keynesian economic management, the "Helms amendment" on Cuba trade policy.

[76] *Federalist*: No. 63.

fears and pressures and to remember the goals that they entered office in order to further. This is not to claim that Madison and Hamilton had the same theory of human nature as Aristotle did, only that they came, through different theories, to similar understandings of the nature and limits of democratic rule. The main such limit, to repeat, is that the fundamental priority of freedom and majority rule cannot be challenged. However stabilized or chastened by constant rulers, the ultimate democratic value is choice itself, individual or collective, not some idealized, correct choice of a good, happy, or noble life.

What does this imply for the ethic of office? For senators, the proper ethic involved is one of slow work: instruction, persuasion, deliberation, attention to the little-known details and difficulties that lie behind the heated issues of public debate. This ethic requires standing somewhat apart from the people, realizing that while long-term or ultimate public opinion is binding and must be respected, transient public or constituency passions are not binding on representatives but exactly what representatives are supposed to resist or turn in a more constructive direction. This kind of action need not lack brilliance; no one knew better than Hamilton how scarce were those with the perseverance and intelligence to formulate and carry through long-term endeavors of government.[77] The authors of the *Federalist* were not joking when they wrote that we (eventually) build monuments to people who govern this way. On the other hand, senators bring nothing but disgrace on themselves if they seek power and reelection through a superficial charm that masks weakness of character, inattention to policy, and a desire to exploit the most ill-thought-out passions of the electorate. "Unstable," power-hungry characters earn infamy, not fame.

TOCQUEVILLE: THE HOPE FOR A CONSTANT PEOPLE

Of the two problems of democratic constancy noted above, I have argued that Publius addressed one of them: officeholders' incentive for constancy can be derived from interest in the office or love of a (merited) fame—and these amount to much the same thing. The remaining question is why democratic citizens can be expected to tolerate such a constitutional scheme when the desire to get one's way immediately is so strong.

Some liberals have denied that liberal, constitutional democracies need virtue of any kind. Stephen Holmes's claim is representative. He claims

---

[77] See also Adams (1973), who in a little-known passage (*Discourses* No. 10, quoting an unnamed "great writer" who sounds like Hobbes) praises the anonymous, industrious folk who actually run government over the ambitious and flamboyant graspers who gain office through wealth, birth, and charm.

that we should value good political institutions because they do not rely on virtue: a reliance on civic virtue requires "character standardization" and "deprive[s] society of an extrapolitical variety of selves." This is why "liberal framers ... reject virtue-based politics for a looser, less all-engaging, more procedural and discussion-stimulating sort of common framework."[78]

Liberals are right to reject a civic republican common good founded on a demanding (and boring) common virtue, and right to call for a politics that is based on procedure and discussion and promotes a diversity of lives. But Holmes ignores both the need and the possibility for an in-between ground, a minimalist virtue that sustains procedures and makes discussion possible. After all, no institution or procedure can be sustained if the majority of people have extreme dispositions: if people are utterly immoderate, utterly unwilling to compromise, debate, and rethink their aims, they will resort to obstruction or violence in pursuit of their ends, and will thereby make democratic politics impossible. Institutions require a popular willingness to work within the institutions, or contest them peacefully, rather than overthrowing them whenever they get in the way. One way to define democratic constancy is the willingness to abide by procedures and work through institutions, even when the time wasted is frustrating and the final outcome is not guaranteed to be in one's favor. This is a minimalist disposition of character—it does not require uniform personalities and is perfectly consistent with almost all ways of (private) life—but an important one. However, *pace* crude functionalist social theories, the fact that a disposition would be useful does not make it possible. What concrete practices or institutions can we expect to sustain democratic constancy? How can a society preserve a love of diversity and full freedom to pursue individual ends and still prevent the arrogant selfishness and insatiable greed that endanger both politics and liberty?

This is of course the question addressed by Tocqueville. While agreeing with Madison and Hamilton on the merits of constitutional offices, he did not think Federalist institutions were enough to prevent democracy from being undermined by its own vices. He sought in the "social state" of the United States resources for taming democratic pleasure-seeking, selfishness, and impatience with constraint. If interest and fame are Publius' incentives for constancy in governors, religion and association are Tocqueville's guarantors of constancy in the governed. Tocqueville's talk of virtue and mores will turn out in the end to mean a quest not for perfection but for the more modest dispositions that safeguard democracy.

When it comes to the proper function of senators and the president,

---

[78] Holmes (1988: 238).

Tocqueville follows the Federalist line, as far as it goes. Like Aristotle, he argues that the "natural vice" of democracy is a tendency for the people to arrogate all power for its own immediate execution.[79] Tocqueville believes that Hamilton tried to correct this vice by setting up the presidency as one of several constitutional "authorities which, though not entirely independent of it [the people], nevertheless enjoyed within their sphere a fairly wide degree of freedom; by this means, though forced to obey the *permanent directions* of the majority, they could still struggle against its caprices and refuse to be the tools of its dangerous exigencies."[80]

In addition, Tocqueville not only endorses but quotes at length Madison's and Hamilton's fears of the mutability of lawmaking, a problem endemic to democracy and exacerbated by the "feverish activity" of frequent elections. Tocqueville endorses the Federalist remedy of making elections less frequent (while sounding amazed that democrats ever thought to adopt it).[81] In claiming that the "mass of the citizens very sincerely desires the country's good" but lacks the "skill to judge the means to attain this sincerely desired end," Tocqueville sounds like Hamilton in *Federalist* No. 71, even to the extent of blaming elites for being more corrupt and corrupting than the masses.[82] He echoes Hamilton on the danger that legislatures will usurp the whole power of government in the name of the people.[83]

But Tocqueville seems to add to Federalist reasoning a non-Federalist concern with substantive virtue and character, which often leads him to use non-Federalist rhetoric. Concerning the election of senators, he is less concerned with the length of term and the usefulness of giving representation to the states through their legislatures (Madison's main arguments) than with the practice of indirect election, which enables the Senate to represent the popular will "in nobler and more beautiful shape. . . . Thus the men elected always represent exactly the ruling majority of the nation, but they represent only the lofty thoughts current there."[84] In

[79] Alexis de Tocqueville, *Democracy in America* (1969: I.1.8, p. 137). Henceforth this will be referred to as *DIA*.

[80] Ibid.; emphasis added.

[81] *DIA*: I.2.5, p. 202.

[82] *DIA*: I.2.5, pp. 197–98. The full quotation is this: "I freely admit that the mass of the citizens very sincerely desires the country's good; I would go further and say that lower classes of society generally confuse their personal interests with this desire less than the upper classes do; but that they always lack to some extent is skill to judge the means to attain this sincerely desired end."

[83] *DIA*: I.1.8, p. 122.

[84] *DIA*: I.2.5, p. 201. Of course, Madison in No. 10 hopes that legislators under the federal system will be "a chosen body of citizens, whose wisdom may best discern the true interest of their country and whose patriotism and love of justice will be least likely to sacrifice it to temporary or partial considerations." Tocqueville may have thought he was

addition to good democratic laws, he thinks the "instincts of democracy" require a "corrective" from "enlightenment, and above all mores." The shining example of this corrective is found in New England.[85] Tocqueville maintains that the executive power is not well designed in itself but too weak; indeed, it can only survive being as weak as it is (notwithstanding Hamiltonian claims about its "energy") because "the geographical position, laws, habits, mores, and opinions of the nation" happen to conduce to its survival.[86] Tocqueville doubts the ability of the president to delay popular designs for long, arguing for an ultimate reliance on "the good sense and virtue of the citizens . . . reason and mores."[87] ("Mores" here cannot merely mean "integrity"—which would not ensure a lack of folly in pursuing desires—but must mean a certain sobriety of character and goodness of judgment.) He does not believe a president eligible for re-election will be able to ignore or tame popular passions as he should, given that "political morality is growing lax and men of great character are vanishing from the scene."[88]

These mentions of "political morality" and "men of great character"—not Federalist terminology—illustrate a consistent difference in emphasis between Tocqueville and Publius. Where Publius uses a theory of interest to explain why those in government will tend to maintain constant, reasoned government in the face of public passions, Tocqueville uses a doctrine of interest to explain how public passions themselves might be moderated, and constitutional government be safeguarded, from the bottom up. Where the authors of the *Federalist* hoped that sound institutional structures based on interest and a minimal constancy could preserve republican government from democratic tendencies, Tocqueville despairs of a stable republican order unless it can find decently virtuous and self-denying citizens. Tocqueville wants to make the public's "sense," or its "habits of the heart," as good as possible.

However, given the substance of what he says about this sense and these habits, it is clear that Tocqueville does not expect full virtue from a democratic public, only a kind of constancy, "self-interest properly understood." Some of the vices inherent to democracy that Tocqueville

---

expressing similar sentiments, but in fact he has moved from the language of interest, and of honest "virtues" in the service of democratic constancy, to the aristocratic language of nobility and loftiness.

[85] *DIA*: I.2.5, p. 200.

[86] *DIA*: I.1.8, p. 128. For reasons unclear to me, Tocqueville does not expand on how American habits, mores, and opinions make a weak executive viable; he goes on to speak only of geography. Perhaps the passage on New England mores, just cited and explained further below, is an answer.

[87] *DIA*: I.1.8, p. 122.

[88] *DIA*: I.1.8, p. 138; see also p. 135.

notes are beyond the scope of this work, either because they do not threaten the existence of the polity as such, or because they can hardly be prevented by the actions of politicians.[89] Leaving these aside, let us consider the danger to the polity that politics can prevent: individualism.

Equality, writes Tocqueville, "tends to isolate men from each other so that each thinks only of himself." This is directly conducive to despotism, since a despot is cheered by public indifference and lack of interest in public affairs, and "will lightly forgive his subjects for not loving him, provided they do not love one another."[90] This individualism, we may note, is not the same as apathy and is compatible with political desires that lack moderation and constancy: a passionate individualist wants politicians to satisfy his or her *selfish* wants immediately,[91] and is willing to turn to a despot who promises to do so, perhaps by liquidating the rich.[92] (A more public-spirited citizen would realize that other citizens also had desires and that satisfying as many of them as possible required long-range policies, and patience on the part of the public.)

Tocqueville mentions three counterweights to individualism, leaving us to figure out how they relate to one another. The first is religion, which "imposes on each man some obligations toward mankind, to be performed in common with the rest of mankind, and so draws him away, from time to time, from thinking about himself."[93] The second is association in the broadest sense—commercial and social as well as political.[94] The third is the "doctrine of self-interest properly understood." In accordance with this doctrine, "American moralists do not pretend that one must sacrifice himself for his fellow because it is a fine thing to do so. But they boldly assert that such sacrifice is as necessary for the man who makes it as for the beneficiaries."[95]

Now, "self-interest properly understood" is a doctrine of constancy. It does not judge what is in our long-term interest—what it is to live a good life—but merely tells us how to achieve our long-term interests by sacrificing, or appearing to sacrifice, short-term ones. It "cannot make a

[89] In the first category comes the whole range of concerns about baseness and social uniformity in society (*DIA*: II.1.5, p. 448; II.2.10–11, pp. 530ff; and passim.) In the second category comes the anomie and moral doubt characteristic of a people without social and political authorities (*DIA*: II.1.5, p. 444), which according to Tocqueville requires religion for its solution, but not a religion with directly political doctrines or direct backing from the State (445–49).

[90] *DIA*: II.2. 2, p. 506; II.2.4, pp. 509–10.

[91] *DIA*: II.3.21, p. 639.

[92] Plato (1991: 564e–566d); Aristotle, *Politics*: 1305a8–30. Tocqueville had such arguments always in mind; see *DIA*: I.2.7, pp. 259–61.

[93] *DIA*: II.1.5, pp. 444–45.

[94] *DIA*: II.2.4–7, pp. 509–524.

[95] *DIA*: II.2.8, p. 525.

man virtuous," though it can shape habits that ultimately tend toward virtue; and if it were universally adopted, "extraordinary virtues would be rarer," though "gross depravity would also be less common." Significantly, Americans who practice and preach this doctrine do not claim to have virtue, and in fact seem rather ashamed of virtue. They explicitly deny that they act out of noble "impulses" or "emotions": "They prefer to give the credit to their philosophy rather than to themselves."[96] And Tocqueville does not necessarily think they are wrong to denigrate their own spontaneous virtue in this way. With unquestioned belief and spontaneous feelings growing weaker, "personal interest . . . provides the only stable point in the human heart," on which all salutary doctrines of citizenship, and in particular the proper "use of political rights," must be based.[97] For such reasons, Tocqueville considers the doctrine of self-interest properly understood "the best suited of all philosophical theories to the wants of men in our time" (note that he says "wants," not "good" or "happiness"), and calls the doctrine "their strongest remaining *guarantee against themselves*. Contemporary moralists, therefore, should give most of their attention to it. Though they may well think it incomplete, they must nonetheless adopt it as necessary."[98]

Tocqueville, then, seeks to combat individualism both through social structures and through a moral doctrine of (long-term) interest. There is no contradiction here. Tocqueville is seeking the social conditions that will foster a polity based on the wisest possible interest doctrine.

We may regard Tocqueville as solving a problem with democracy that Aristotle implies but does not address: democracy needs constancy from its leadership, but the tendencies internal to democracy makes them likely to resent such leadership out of impatience. For this reason, Aristotle's favorite kind of democracy is one made up of rural citizens who can get together for political action only infrequently: he hopes that the worst effects of democratic impatience and passion can be prevented by circumstance if not by good character. (This is why the rural democracy seems vaguely associated with a democracy based on secure laws, not often changed.)[99] But Tocqueville, who saw the rise of a truly mass public opinion and recognized the effects of communication organs like newspapers, could no longer hope to rely on mere geographic dispersion as the condition of constancy, and sought instead new social and cultural conditions for habituating citizens in the democratic virtues.

---

[96] *DIA*: II.2.8, pp. 526–27. Again, we are reminded that constancy does not imply virtue, and in particular does not imply the virtue of temperance, the state of having good rather than bad desires to begin with.

[97] *DIA*: I.2.6, p. 239.

[98] *DIA*: II.2.8, p. 527; emphasis added.

[99] Aristotle, *Politics*: Book 4, chapter 6 passim.

One example of such conditions is the civil condition of New England, where "morality," "religion," "maxims" and "belief" combine to form a proper condition of "enlightenment, and above all mores" so that "the people are accustomed to respect intellectual and moral superiority and to submit thereto without displeasure."[100] This social condition is so perfect, however, that it is little help to us: it seems that the people of New England have solved the problem of democratic constancy by not having very egalitarian, democratic, or licentious mores to begin with. If they submit to authority "without displeasure," they might even be said to be temperate rather than constant, and if their rulers are really superior, their form of government is at least as close to aristocracy as to democracy.[101] It is highly unlikely the mores of government and governed in New England were as virtuous in Tocqueville's day as he claims. In any case, because Tocqueville portrays his New Englanders as so virtuous, his theory ends up seeming quite irrelevant to more humble democracies in which an allegedly well-ordered political hierarchy and the shining virtues that sustain it are not to be found.

Fortunately, we are not left at a loss, for Tocqueville did not expect the details of New England morals and habits to be sustained over time, and thought of other social remedies. This is where religion and association come in.

Religion, as noted, makes citizens constant: it combats the "inordinate love of material pleasure" characteristic of democracy, and "imposes on each man some obligations toward mankind. . . . Thus religious peoples are naturally strong just at the point where democratic peoples are weak."[102] Religion serves as a perfect counterweight to the excessive desire to do what one likes, to submit to no one and nothing, that Aristotle thought characteristic of democracy. While Americans, notes Tocqueville, have no great generals, philosophers, or writers to instruct them (to this day Americans respect only the first), a preacher could "stand up in front of a free people and gain universal applause" for a "fine definition of freedom" that contrasted "a *liberty* of corrupt nature, which is affected by *men* and *beasts* to do what they list" to "a civil, a moral, a federal *liberty*, which is the proper end and object of *authority*."[103] "For my part," Tocqueville writes, "I doubt whether man can support complete religious independence and entire political liberty at the same time. I am led to

---

[100] *DIA*: I.2.5, p. 200.

[101] For an account of New England "ordered liberty" that emphasizes its hierarchical aspect, see Fischer (1989: 200–205).

[102] *DIA*: II.1.5, p. 444. "Man" (*homme*) in this sentence is meant to be inclusive of women. In fact Tocqueville, following common prejudices, assumes that women will be more religious than men and will serve as the preservers of proper mores.

[103] *DIA*: I.1.2, p. 46; emphases in sermon as quoted by Tocqueville.

think that if he has no faith he must obey, and if he is free he must believe."[104] And Tocqueville asks elsewhere, "How could society escape destruction if, when political ties are relaxed, moral ties are not tightened? And what can be done with a people master of itself if it is not subject to God?"[105]

This rhetoric has its limits. Tocqueville's citizen, "subject to God," does not adopt godly behavior to the exclusion of worldly pursuits. Indeed, nothing could be more self-defeating, more destructive of religious belief, than for a minister to strive for such complete authority over moral life. American clergy realize this: "They try to improve their contemporaries but do not quit fellowship with them."[106] In this way the clergy avoid alienating public opinion and indeed keep that great force on their side. "Religion in America is a world apart in which the clergyman is supreme, but one which he is careful never to leave; within its limits he guides men's minds, while outside them he *leaves men to themselves, to the freedom and instability natural to themselves and to the times they live in.*"[107] To accept freedom and instability as natural to democratic citizens and democratic times is to be content with constancy rather than temperance, with the best democratic ideal rather than the best (probably impossible) human ideal. Unlike an aristocracy, which Tocqueville describes as "master of itself" and "not subject to transitory impulses," democracy is subject to such impulses and must learn how to deal with them.[108] In a democracy, religion cannot hope to destroy individualism, but only to tame it: "The main business of religions is to purify, control, and restrain that excessive and exclusive taste for well-being which men acquire in times of equality, *but I think it would be a mistake for them to attempt to conquer it entirely and abolish it.* They will never succeed in preventing men from loving wealth, but they may be able to induce them to use only honest means to enrich themselves."[109]

This might seem less than relevant to political office. For if Tocqueville's attachment to religion is well known, so is his desire to keep it separate from government. Tocqueville stresses repeatedly that religions should not rely on political authority, lest they be burdened by the "animosity" roused against particular governments and become reliant on the very "ephemeral" and "fragile" foundations on which governments can

---

[104] *DIA*: II.1.5, p. 444.

[105] *DIA*: I.2.9, p. 294.

[106] *DIA*: II.1.5, p. 449.

[107] *DIA*: II.1.5, p. 448; emphasis added.

[108] *DIA*: I.2.6, p. 232. Tocqueville does not idealize aristocracy here; he admits that aristocracy concentrates wealth and power in a few hands and that while its measures are efficient they are unlikely to be directed toward the public good.

[109] *DIA*: II.1.5, p. 448; emphasis added.

barely rely themselves.[110] And while admiring the Puritans in many respects, Tocqueville heaps scorn on the "ridiculous and tyrannical laws" by which fornication, cursing, smoking, and nonattendance at church were forbidden under threat of high public penalties.[111] So in Tocqueville's favored democratic scheme, governing officers play no direct role in promoting religion: it might seem that religion is purely private or social, not political.

As I shall sketch later, the United States has addressed this problem of religion and politics by developing a special political role—so ingrained as to reach the status of an "office," albeit an informal one.[112] This office uses religion without establishing it, thus squaring the circle of a polity that wants religion (or quasi-religious bodies of moral and spiritual uplift) for political purposes, but refuses to link religion with political authority. This is the moral activist, public speaker of jeremiads, which I will call, for short, the "activist." The activist preaches against individualism, indulgence, and brute, narrow forms of majority rule, and in favor of charity, mutual sacrifice, and higher moral purposes. Though not a *formal* officeholder him- or herself (this is one of the few political roles that Americans have been willing for at least a century to allow to women as well as men), the activist does not scorn the tools of public power, and preaches at officeholders and citizens alike to use those tools for high purposes: solidarity, rights, and justice.

At their best, moral activists combat the vices of democracy without contesting its fundamental principles; they respect Tocqueville's distinction between improving selfish, individualist, and democratic tendencies and seeking to abolish them. But activists are rarely at their best, and are constantly tempted to ignore this distinction. A dislike for the base politics of selfish interest easily becomes a dislike for democratic politics itself, and culminates in a tendency to curse people—and if necessary, the whole people—for not living up to the same moral standards that activ-

---

[110] *DIA*: I.2.9, pp. 297–98.

[111] "The framers of these penal codes were especially concerned with the maintenance of good behavior and sound mores in society, so they constantly invaded the sphere of conscience, and there was hardly a sin not subject to the magistrate's censure" (*DIA*: I.1.2, pp. 42–43).

[112] This role might seem less prevalent in other countries, but I would argue that most Western democracies fill the gap by making "movement" politics, particularly labor and environmental politics, more moralistic than it is in the United States, and endowing movement leaders with more moral authority and social prestige. (Consider the role of the *engagé* intellectual in France, whose status can best be explained in religious terms.) Michael Walzer's (1970) description of citizen allegiance to socialist and revolutionary movements, an allegiance that rivals (and constrains) attachment to the state, resembles uncannily Stephen Carter's (1998) more traditionally "American" portrayal of the allegiance owed to religion.

ists believe themselves to exemplify. Excessively high ethical standards are, to the core, nondemocratic. When activists start to believe that the demands of religion and morality rule out all appeals to democratic interest as unacceptably corrupt, they will soon become disillusioned with democracy—and democrats should feel free to be disillusioned with them.

In addition to religion, Tocqueville seeks a remedy for democratic individualism, and a social support for the proper understanding of self-interest, in association. If religion is directed against a tendency to take interest too far, association is directed against a tendency to regard interest too narrowly. To this end, association combats individualism partly by supplementing interest with pride and partly by reminding us that not all interests can be pursued individually.

These methods are not distinct. Association is necessary because democracy produces no aristocrats able to act vigorously by the nature of their position: "Among democratic peoples all the citizens are independent and weak. They can do hardly anything for themselves, and none of them is in a position to force his fellows to help him. They would all therefore find themselves helpless if they did not learn to help each other voluntarily."[113]

In this way associations combat individualism, in the sense of political passivity and acceptance of despotism, by making government less necessary. "At the head of any new undertaking where in France you would find the government or in England some territorial magnate, in the United States you are sure to find an association."[114] It is fortunate for "the morals and intelligence of a democratic people," not only for its commerce, that it can rely on its own resources, and not on a public authority, for organizing the mass of its commercial, moral, and social affairs. Association therefore keeps people from living as they like in the short term but furthers their aspiration to living as they like in the long term, to accomplish singly or with others the things they need in order to make money and enjoy it at home.

Association operates not merely by transmuting interest but also by transmuting pride. Oligarchic pride, the desire of the rich to stand apart from the people and help them condescendingly from noblesse oblige, is something the rich must sacrifice: "They could ruin themselves in that fashion without warming their neighbors' hearts. What is wanted is not the sacrifice of their money but of their pride."[115] But not all pride is

[113] *DIA*: II.2.5, p. 514.
[114] *DIA*: II.2.5, p. 513.
[115] *DIA*: II.2.4, p. 512.

antidemocratic. There is a kind of pride that is paradoxically built into democracy, or at least a democracy with elective local civil and social bodies. This is a pride—and ambition—founded on the esteem of others, which in turn is founded on usefulness. "Love of fame" in Hamilton's sense thus filters down to the local level: "When the public governs, all men feel the value of public goodwill and all try to win it by gaining the esteem and affection of those among whom they must live. . . . It thus happens that ambition makes a man care for his fellows, and, in a sense, he often finds his self-interest in forgetting about himself."[116] Nor is this ambition furthered by flamboyant one-time expressions of "care," any more than Hamilton's "love of fame" encourages flamboyant actions in national office. In fact, local affairs, in which one's fellow-citizens get to know one over time, provide less opportunity than national affairs to further one's ambition, except through determined, constant action over time. Local reputation comes only from "a long succession of little services rendered and of obscure good deeds."[117] In this way, interest and the love of fame are united to give local notables and politicians a passion for liberty rather than servility. Because of associations and local self-government, despots can neither claim their usurpations are required nor hope that they will lack prideful opposition.

Community organizers, properly understood, do no more than build on such associations. In the classic model that I shall set forth, they are quick to build on local religious, civic, and political leadership; suspicious of crusading attempts to sweep away these intermediate institutions in the interests of justice; and eager for citizens to take more interest in public affairs than they do. Such efforts are particularly noticed among the poor, because the poor through lack of civic association have often become servile vis-à-vis the nonpoor, and their political activity is sudden and conspicuous. But the ideal community organizer has no objection to the institutions of allegedly bourgeois respectability, and indeed wishes there were more of them among the poor so that their ambition and resources might be drawn upon. The organizer characteristically appeals simultaneously to pride and self-interest, and we can see why this apparent paradox makes perfect sense. The search for "natural leaders" among the poor is based on pride, but aspiring leaders will fulfill their ambitions by providing real improvements in the daily lives of themselves and their neighbors. (And no one can tell the difference between real improvement and sham claims better than one who has nothing.)

Once again, of course, the ideal is unlikely to sustain itself. The vices of democracy, so frustrating to activists, can also be frustrating to orga-

[116] *DIA*: II.2.4, p. 510.
[117] *DIA*: II.2.4, p. 511.

nizers, especially to the extent that local civic institutions atrophy and achieving real change through the actions of a few individuals among their neighbors becomes very difficult. Organizers degenerate when the link between pride and interest is severed. When that happens, organizers who cannot point to tangible gains from local action are tempted to reject the quest for esteem stemming from real achievement, and to aim instead at a "pride" based on anger and violent urges. At the extreme, the organizer starts to hate democracy for not allowing himself or his protégés to gain what they want as soon as they want it, and pride is then used as an excuse for destruction. This process represents no more than the vices of democracy run wild, but its culmination could only be the destruction of democracy as a stable polity that respects the interests and opinions of all.

CONCLUSION

This chapter has made a tacit assumption: that officeholders should indeed have "affection" for the democratic polity, should wish for it to be preserved and to remain in the best state possible. It does not follow that political officers should be the best human beings possible: affection for the polity requires officials who embody and foster the half-virtue of constancy rather than the nobler virtues of high-mindedness, perfect justice, or ideal wisdom.

A certain impatience with such constraints is natural. A moral activist or community organizer, no less than a president or senator, is likely to bridle when told that politics should stick to the rhetoric of individual interests and should assume that citizens will conform reluctantly (if at all) to noble plans for their betterment. But that is democratic politics. Those who seek to make all citizens love one another, to fix public attention on nothing but noble goals, or to deny the primacy of private concerns in a democratic polity should either become principled rebels against the whole polity or leave politics altogether and pursue their goals through other means. If many, if not most, politicians persist in trying to foist nondemocratic aims and methods on democracy, that testifies not to democracy's faults but to their own lack of constancy. When they do so, they prove themselves unable to restrain their immoderate desires—for glory, and for the intoxicating feeling of moral superiority.

CHAPTER THREE

Office and the Democratic Order: Alternative Views

IN THE PREVIOUS chapter I argued that the best way of doing political ethics is to ask what a democratic political order most needs. More substantively, I claimed that a democratic polity demanded of its politicians and officeholders an ethic of democratic constancy. The argument was based on a conception of democratic politics rooted in Aristotle, Madison, and Tocqueville, and in particular on these thinkers' insight that democracy presupposes an attachment to freedom, enlightened self-interest, and an equal distribution of political authority, rather than to the pursuit of absolute well-being or perfection.

Critics might agree that political office ethics must start with an account of the democratic order, but disagree with the account of democracy given above. In this chapter, I shall address two possible criticisms of this kind by discussing accounts of democratic politics that implicitly or explicitly entail office ethics different from mine. First, I shall explore the *ethical perfectionist* thesis that liberal democracy sets its sights too low: that political officers should embody the highest and best qualities of moral and political judgment, and that political action generally should strive directly for the fullest or most perfect development of all citizens. Judging politics by perfectionist standards goes with denying that individual choice and equality of political power are fundamental values that politics should pursue and with criticizing democratic politics to the extent that it does not follow higher standards of good human functioning. Taking Martha Nussbaum as the clearest and most influential recent exemplar of perfectionism in political theory, I shall argue that a perfectionist politics that takes human flourishing as its standard lacks an empirically and ethically convincing account of democratic politics. When it credibly addresses concrete political concerns, it does so only by departing from its own philosophic framework.

Second, I shall touch on the genre of leadership studies, which often presupposes a psychological model of politics that Harold Lasswell called *social psychiatry*. To the extent that leadership studies relies on psychiatric models of politics, I argue, its theories of democratic character become arbitrary and time-bound, and its account of what a polity needs to count as democratic becomes excessive and utopian. Compared to psychiatric models, democratic constancy will provide a more credible account of both individual action and its relation to democratic politics.

Finally, I shall explore an account of the regime that offers more support to my own than might be thought. The *economic conception* of democracy and the pursuit of office, which is often regarded as ruling out all ethical considerations except those based on self-interest, will be shown on the contrary to allow and even require something like the ethics of constancy and fame presented here.

HUMAN FLOURISHING VS. DEMOCRATIC POLITICS

The link I have drawn between office ethics and the demands of a democratic order seems perverse from a certain tradition of political philosophy, one in which ethical theory is "prior" to political philosophy in the two senses used by Michael Sandel.[1] Moral philosophy is supposed to be prior to political philosophy in that it provides the moral framework without which political questions, including political ethics, can hardly be discussed.[2] And it is allegedly prior in another sense: that political institutions are legitimate, and political obligations binding on individuals, only to the extent that they can be defended from the standpoint of moral philosophy. Philosophy is supposed to lay down rules for politics according to its own standards: that an institution or practice may embody the best available compromise among values, or may represent a legitimate concession to what democratic publics can be persuaded to accept, is not supposed to count. Martha Nussbaum is a prominent exemplar of this position, and an instructive one. For her perfectionist ethics brings out clearly the conflict between certain uncompromising forms of moral philosophy on the one hand and an ethics that pays attention to the real possibilities of democracy on the other. Nussbaum is forthright in defending full human flourishing as a standard for society (and ethical perfection as a standard for political action), steadfast in refusing to make concessions to the demands of imperfect human nature and to stubbornly persistent opinions and practices. Her work demonstrates both the real attractions of moral vision in politics and the serious limits of such vision as a guide to judging both political officers and ordinary democratic citizens.

The disagreement between Nussbaum's account and the one presented in the current work is clear. I have claimed that liberal democracy is

---

[1] Here I follow more or less the distinction between epistemological and moral or "lexical" priority made by Sandel (1982: 2–3). Unlike Sandel, however, I am not here attacking the priority of the right to the good found in the philosophy of John Rawls.

[2] See, for example, Kant (1957: Appendix 1, 35–46 [Ak. 371–80]); and more recently Thompson (1987: 2).

devoted primarily to liberty and the equal political power of all citizens as such, and to the ethical practices, involving democratic relationships and respect for ordinary opinions, that both flow from and further buttress these political principles.[3] Nussbaum takes the grounds of all good politics to be something higher or more ambitious: the human good as such, in the form of an account of good human functioning.

Nussbaum's approach fails sufficiently to address matters of democratic ethics. It fails to ask whether actual democratic regimes could be based on pursuit of the principles it proposes without becoming illiberal, or antidemocratic. Insufficiently attentive to democratic ethics, it is also insufficiently respectful of democratic politics. For the case she herself cites when explaining the application of her theory brings up questions of democratic feasibility for which her framework has no theoretical room, and at the same time highlights democratic political resources (involving the persuasive use of self-interest) that her theory is prone to ignore. The current work addresses explicitly questions of political action and institutions that Nussbaum treats more casually, and without sufficiently acknowledging their implications.

Nussbaum's account of human functioning seeks to judge regimes and public policies according to whether they give as many people as possible the goods and capabilities required to live a good human life.[4] She makes reference to John Rawls's "thin theory" of the good, which seeks to do justice to diverse conceptions of what a good life is by putting forth only

---

[3] As Robert A. Dahl has argued (1989: 164, and passim), democracy should itself be seen as embodying a kind of distributive justice. The good to be distributed is political power, and the most just distribution is taken to be an equal one. Indeed this form of procedural justice is perhaps the highest form of justice, and by no means necessarily inferior to distributive justice of a substantive (social or economic) kind. While I would not go as far as Dahl does in letting democracy override other values, the general point is well taken.

[4] The key texts are Martha Nussbaum, "Aristotelian Social Democracy" (1990a; henceforth referred to as ASD); "Human Functioning and Social Justice: In Defense of Aristotelian Essentialism" (1992; henceforth "Essentialism"); and "Nature, Function and Capability: Aristotle on Political Distribution" (1988; henceforth NFC). Nussbaum's later work often cites these texts as examples of what her conception of human flourishing entails in social or political terms. Other works by Nussbaum (Nussbaum 1986, 1990b, 1993, 1994, 1995; Nussbaum and Sen 1989) will also be cited briefly as relevant.

As this book was in production, I was made aware of the symposium on Nussbaum's work in *Ethics* 111, No. 1 (October 2000). Some of the articles in that symposium, particularly those by Richard Arneson and Richard Mulgan, develop arguments similar to those of the current text, though with very different emphases. Nussbaum's article in reply does not, I think, decisively refute any of my points, and in fact confirms the tension between her views and a democratic perspective that stresses equality of political power. I do accept one correction: it is now clear that Nussbaum's "Scandinavian" model of social democracy was meant to refer to Finland, not Sweden.

minimal criteria for what is required for a plan of life to be "rational," and then addressing the conditions necessary for all citizens to pursue the ends they have.[5] Nussbaum rejects Rawls's treatment in favor of a "thick vague" theory that says a great deal about the proper *content* of the ends, about the capabilities and experiences that are good for humans qua humans. (It is "vague" in that it allows the specification of the capabilities and experiences to vary widely within and across cultures.) Nussbaum claims that Aristotelian thought contains "a conception of political rule, which involves full support for these functionings ('no citizen should be lacking in sustenance') and insists that this support is to be done in such a way as to treat citizens as free and equal."[6]

Nussbaum accordingly uses an account of good human functioning to criticize various forms of political rule that fail to promote it universally. These include many liberal regimes on the one hand, and exploitative third-world polities and societies (and their Western relativist defenders) on the other. To both of these she prefers a political arrangement devoted to making sure that everyone has the goods and capabilities of a good human life. These include a life of normal length; health, food, and shelter; "opportunities for sexual satisfaction"; mobility; absence of pain and presence of pleasure; opportunity to use one's senses and to think and reason; ability "to love, grieve, to feel longing and gratitude"; ability to reflect on the good; the chance for family and social interaction; attachment to nature; the capacity for laughter and play; and various forms of individual differentiation.[7] "The idea is that the entire structure of the polity will be designed with a view to these functions."[8] This is not to say that Nussbaum envisions government arrangement of such goods as sexual satisfaction (though perhaps for consistency she should, and she concedes that Aristotle did).[9] She believes, however, that the entire structure of labor, property, political participation, and education should be designed with a view to the human goods. Nussbaum advocates Scandinavian social democracy as the closest approximation to such an arrange-

---

[5] Rawls (1971: 395–433, 446–49, 567–75).

[6] ASD: 205. The internal quotation is from Aristotle, *Politics* (1984: 1330a3), and the "free and equal" phrase refers to *Politics*: 1255b20.

[7] ASD: 225.

[8] ASD: 230. Nussbaum's use of the phrase "entire structure" is serious and deliberate: she means "not only programs of allocation, but also the division of land, the arrangement for forms of ownership, the structure of labor relations, institutional support for forms of family and social affiliation, ecological policy and policy toward animals, institutions of political participation, and education" (ibid.).

[9] ASD: 239. Nussbaum assumes that the proper forms of love relations and sexual desire are "political" in the sense of being proper subjects for communal attention and political action (Nussbaum [1994: 140–91]; and even more explicitly [1994: 504])—but stops short of endorsing coercive regulation.

ment, since she believes that not only its practices but its basic principles approximate her Aristotelian account.[10]

Since Nussbaum calls her account "Aristotelian" and repeatedly cites Aristotle for support, the first thing to be noted is that, according to Aristotle, devotion to the best possible human functioning, the maximum human flourishing or happiness, is precisely *not* a *democratic* end. The quotations Nussbaum cites in support of her Aristotelian view of politics—that the regime should ensure sustenance for all to the extent of keeping half the land in common, that the quality of air and water should be a matter of political planning—are both from book 7 of Aristotle's *Politics*: the account of the *best* regime, the ideal, aristocratic regime where all productive labor is done by serfs.[11] While Nussbaum distinguishes the "ideal" theory of book 7 from what she calls the "empirical" theory of books 4–6, she calls both part of a "single project."[12] It is not clear in what sense she means this, but it is in any case misleading to call the middle books of the *Politics* merely "empirical." They involve not a value-free discussion of political regimes but an ethically laden discussion of political forms in terms of their respective assumptions or principles. This discussion does not favor Nussbaum's argument, because Aristotle denies that the democratic regime is concerned with human flourishing at all. The concern with human flourishing in general is a concern of the best regime (and of the aristocratic types present in any regime), but democracy is devoted, as noted above, specifically *not* to happiness but to freedom and majority rule.[13] The "justice that is characteristically popular" is equal political power, which implies majority rule: "Where justice is of this sort, the multitude must necessarily have authority, and what is resolved by the majority must be final and must be justice.... This, then, is one mark of freedom, and it is regarded by those of the popular sort as the defining principle of the regime. Another is to live as one

[10] This is not to say that even social democracy fulfills all the conditions Nussbaum would like. Nussbaum's remarks about work tend to cite the early Marx, and the Scandinavian countries would seem to tolerate too much alienation. (Nussbaum [1995: 119] endorses Marx's view that physical comfort as such amounts to "mere 'grazing,' merely animal hearing and seeing.") But Nussbaum repeatedly cites her article on social democracy as embodying her social and political program more generally (see, for example, Nussbaum [1990: 102, 201n15]).

[11] *Politics*: 1324a23–5, 1330b11, 1329b39ff.; cited in NFC: 146–50, and ASD: 203ff.

[12] NFC: 159n18. Elsewhere Nussbaum briefly describes books 4–6 (and implicitly dismisses them as ethically uninteresting) as "discuss[ing] strategies for achieving stability in situations where different classes have different ends" (1994: 60n37). Her corpus contains almost no discussion of these distinctively political portions of Aristotle's work.

[13] *Politics*: 1294a8, 1291b30ff., 1310a28, 1317a40ff.

wants. For this is, they assert, the work of freedom, since not living as one wants is characteristic of a person who is enslaved."[14]

Happiness or human flourishing (Nussbaum's preferred translation of Aristotle's *eudaimonia*, literally "goodness of spirit") is the end of ethics, and the end of the best regime, but it is not the end of democracy. Democrats do not want to live well; they want to live as they like.

I would stress my large degree of agreement with Nussbaum's account of human functioning. There are indeed good reasons to reject a casual relativism that claims that the desire for clean water is culturally relative, or that female genital mutilation should be regarded as just if "local culture" condones it. But Nussbaum's work does not stop at these questions of social ethics; it seeks to lay down imperatives for political practice. And democratic political theory, unlike moral philosophy, should not ask merely what principles people ideally ought to live by, but what principles we can persuade people to adopt (just as importantly, *how* this persuasion is to occur) and what states of character are realistically accessible, to enough people, to be appropriate as a standard that we expect the average citizen to meet. There are of course methods of "applying" moral ideals without regard to questions of accessibility and persuasive force. These include Platonic guardianship, imperialism, and Mandarin-style bureaucratic elitism.[15] Those who reject such methods, as Nussbaum certainly does, must supplement the conclusions they take from moral philosophy with a concern for whether these conclusions fit with democratic principles and democratic ethics. This is where Nussbaum falls short. Whatever the merits of Nussbaum's account as Aristotelian *ethical* theory, it fails as Aristotelian *democratic* theory.

This is not just a point of interpretation concerning Aristotle. The tension between Aristotelian human flourishing as a political goal—which goes with perfectionism as a political philosophy—and liberal democracy as a political arrangement is not a fanciful or artificial issue but a central theme of modern political thought. Two obvious issues arise at once. First, it is doubtful whether Aristotle's ideal of citizen flourishing can be achieved without relegating an unlucky set of noncitizens to serfdom and drudgery.[16] Nussbaum, troubled on this question, is finally

[14] *Politics*: 1317b1ff.

[15] The grouping is neither arbitrary nor completely unfair: at one stage, British colonial administrators in India were encouraged to take the account of guardians in Plato's *Republic* as a model, and Benjamin Jowett, the famous *Republic* translator, chaired the committee that designed the process for selecting them. See Mason (1964).

[16] Nussbaum's (1994: 490) description of the philosophic life makes clear that it would require so much leisure, reflection, and cultivation of philosophic community as to be difficult to combine with ordinary working life, even if working hours were reduced.

forced to admit that at least in poor countries there will be no alternative to most people's getting less than is optimal for full human flourishing.[17] She does not, however, grapple with the implication: that her theory is less than useful as a guide to making tough choices under conditions of scarcity. Second, one might take seriously the part of Aristotle's ethical account that Nussbaum leaves out: that true human flourishing requires *virtue*, and that in fact the regime whose ethical qualities Nussbaum cites is explicitly an aristocracy of the virtuous. Without virtue, the "capacities" guaranteed by social institutions will not lead to good human functioning as Nussbaum hopes: a well-paid person with meaningful work and a fine education can still ruin her life through drinking.[18] Aristotle's elaborate regulation of private life—in the best regime, marriage ages would be set by the government and pregnant women required to exercise daily—is not accidental, as Nussbaum claims,[19] but essential to a regime that aims to ensure happiness itself, and not merely the pursuit of happiness.[20]

How this relates to political office may seem unclear, especially since Nussbaum admits that her main concern is not so much with politics or

---

[17] NFC: 172. Nussbaum argues that in rich countries this problem can be solved by moderating "Aristotle's extreme requirement of leisure," and by adopting "some form of redistribution, together with a strong subsidized programme of subsidized education" (ibid.). But Aristotle's extreme requirement of leisure is necessary, in his imagined regime directed towards full human happiness, precisely because such happiness would require more virtue and more constant, conscious attention to the individual and collective cultivation of character than any modern democratic regime would find either possible or desirable.

[18] Nussbaum (1990b: 204) seems to recognize this problem in the case of education: One can be educated "without being intelligent," or an educated intelligence can be wasted if one has the wrong passions. Nussbaum's conclusion, however, is that the obligation to offer everyone education, combined with (it seems—Nussbaum is not clear) a social expectation that all must avail themselves of education in order to be fully human, is "hardly a sufficient step. . . . But it is, in this world, something." This seems not quite adequate. The additional step required to transform the potential *conditions* for human flourishing into its continual *existence* would be coercion and indoctrination on a massive scale. Absent a willingness to enforce these, we may certainly offer health and education to everyone on other grounds, but should not expect the availability of these to make Aristotelian ethical perfection universal or even widespread.

[19] ASD: 239.

[20] Nussbaum shows a lack of concern on this point in the course of arguing for a democratic reformulation of Aristotle's ideal regime. Criticizing Aristotle's idea that a regime could be "the best" one even if only a few inhabitants had the status of citizens, Nussbaum claims that this would render Aristotle's account incoherent—for then a regime that included only one tyrant as citizen could be the best (NFC: 157). This is to misunderstand the reasons Aristotle finds tyranny an inherently bad regime: Aristotle denies a tyrant could be happy *precisely* because he would have external goods but no virtue, and therefore could not pursue true happiness (*Politics*: 1313a34–1315b10).

political philosophy as with the effects of social and political institutions on the "inner world" or individual psyche.[21] But Nussbaum's own brief accounts of citizen agency and political leadership make the connection clear: her attachment to perfectionist political standards leads her, as we might expect, to reject the democratic theory of office presented above.

What we must demand of a "good leader," writes Nussbaum, is not "technical intellect" but "a different, and more Aristotelian kind of reasoning." This means "development of the imagination, . . . a vigorous sense of concrete reality, and even . . . a rather Athenian level of passionate engagement with life."[22] Citing Henry James, Nussbaum calls the ideal Aristotelian agent "finely aware and richly responsible," not tempted by evasions, simplifications or abstractions when approaching decisions: in short, "a person whom we could trust to describe a complex situation with full concreteness of detail and emotional shading, missing nothing of practical relevance."[23]

As an ideal for the best imaginable political actor, this has obvious attractions. But as a practical standard for judging democratic politicians it faces some immediate objections. First, and most obvious, it sets our sights too high. We do not always get the candidates for high office whom we would prefer. It is not clear from Nussbaum's theory what we might do in the likely case that our choices are not as finely aware as Nussbaum's ideal requires. Of course, there is nothing wrong in general with striving for better choices than now exist, but in the case of democratic politics the demand for ideal leaders has a long and unhappy history. It can lead and has led to Weber's temptation: to disdain actual democratic politics as the realm of hack personalities and interest-brokering decisions, and to search for a charismatic personality whose leadership will sweep this unpleasantness aside. Second, it is not clear how Nussbaum's standards could be applied in practice: we would seem to lack rough rules of thumb, let alone a more reliable method. The most richly perceptive person is not always the one who brags about his or her subtlety or sensitivity, nor even the one who seems to display these qualities on striking occasions (the latter could be acting, or coached). There is something to the Enlightenment counsel not to try looking into the souls of others. The search for richness and authenticity can prove more difficult than anticipated.[24]

[21] Nussbaum (1994: 12). Nussbaum (1990b: 207), however, uses "ethical" and "political" agency interchangeably.

[22] Nussbaum (1990b: 101). Nussbaum contrasts this ideal with an ideal of technical intellect that she apparently believes to be common in political leaders and commonly valued by political commentators.

[23] Nussbaum (1990b: 84).

[24] Frankfurt (1988).

Finally, the consequences of incomplete perception are greater in politics than in other spheres of life. Even the most gifted novelist describes only part of the world—the "omniscient" narrator is a conceit, not a fact—and not even the most gifted critic interprets or explains every word of an epic, every stroke of a painting. In aesthetic judgment this is fine: the selection and choice involved only make aesthetic judgment keener, the personality expressed in art or criticism more vivid. In private moral judgment as well, the inevitable partiality involved in attempts to judge fully and deeply is generally a good thing. In private life, coldness, insensitivity, and a tendency to judge people by abstract rules may be, as Nussbaum suggests, the things to be feared most. And the problem of incompleteness is in some ways not serious: we want our family and friends to deeply appreciate *our* side, to appreciate the claims of our enemies only reluctantly and with a gaze colored by a desire to help us. But in politics, as I have suggested, things are more complex. Political judgment in a democracy is not impartial and should not try to be; universal claims must be balanced against sympathy for the claims of those most affected. But if impartiality is not everything, it is *something*: to be *merely* sensitive to the claims of those whose claims strike one most vividly is to leave oneself and others open to the bias and shortsightedness that good political institutions should try to check. The search for fine awareness in politics has fundamental and not just practical limits: since even the most perfect judgment only sees part of a situation, we should look for ways of making politics less reliant on what even the most perfect judgment can see.

Put together, these three considerations explain why liberals and democrats do not expect those in power to have perfect character. They therefore justify the political value of liberal-democratic checks (including the central democratic check: making officers responsible to their constituents). Since we cannot know who the finely aware politicians are, might not be able to place them in power if we did know them, and would soon recognize the limits of even the finest awareness if such people were in power, it is wiser when designing institutions and assessing leaders to rely on qualities of character that are easier to find, judge, and rely on.

Nussbaum's perfectionism does not stop at leaders but applies to ordinary citizens as well. On her account, even when it comes to ordinary, citizen-level decisions (we might think of voting, though voting does not appear in Nussbaum's examples of politics), government at all levels should ideally be "based on perception": its constituent unit should be a "citizen perceiver."[25] Nussbaum freely describes her view of politics and

[25] Nussbaum (1990b: 102).

society as perfectionist: "not all human lives are equally complete, equally flourishing," and "among the conditions of *eudaimonia* and practical wisdom" are not just "material" but "educational necessary conditions."[26] This argument leads Nussbaum to call for radical expansion in educational opportunities. But the logic of the argument seems to require going further. If Nussbaum is right, those who lack educational opportunities, or who do not use them, or who receive higher education but fail to take to heart its humanistic lessons, lack what they need to earn respect as political agents. For if higher education is "a necessity for a fully human development of the faculties of citizen perception,"[27] those who do not receive its benefits must apparently and by "necessity" be inferior citizens and inferior human beings. Nussbaum rejects the temptation to assimilate moral judgment to aesthetic taste, and consistently opposes ascriptive or hereditary aristocracy.[28] But her stress on "rich perception" (Greek *aisthesis*) as the prerequisite of political judgment allows us to call her ideal regime less a democracy than an "aesthetocracy."

This aesthetocracy has at least two concrete implications. First, Nussbaum's account of human flourishing leads her to a fairly radical rejection of free choice in the economic sphere.[29] In facing the accusation that social democracy plans too much and restricts the scope of individual choice, she shifts from Aristotle to Marx to argue that true choice is in fact enhanced by economic planning that provides the conditions for "a more naturalistic and worldly conception of choice": "In Aristotelian social democracy, citizens . . . in every area of life, given the material provisions of the plan, . . . become capable of choosing to function well in that sphere (or not to, should they choose that)."[30] What the latter point means is this: "The person who is given a clean public water supply can always put pollutants into the water she drinks. The person who has received an education is free, later on, to waste it. The person who has good recreational facilities may fail to take advantage of them. The government aims at capabilities, and leaves the rest to the citizens."[31] This argument may not be consistent with a theory that elsewhere aims at

---

[26] Nussbaum (1990b: 201).

[27] Nussbaum (1990b: 102).

[28] Nussbaum (1990b: 84, 201).

[29] In contrast, Nussbaum's arguments for preserving various privacy rights, political liberties, and guarantees of personal differentiation and separateness are fairly down-to-earth and persuasively consistent with liberal doctrines on this score (ASD: 238–39). Whether they are consistent with Aristotle is another matter: while Aristotle claimed that our physical separateness was scientifically important, for instance, he never gave this fact moral significance as a guarantee of bodily rights, as Nussbaum does.

[30] ASD: 238.

[31] ASD, 214.

human flourishing as such (and not merely the right to choose to flourish or not). More to the point, it distorts the anticipated objection. Consider this "person," who lives in a social democracy yet does not feel as strongly about the environment, or enjoy education, as much as the "plan" does (Nussbaum's word).[32] When this person complains about government policies, she does not covet the chance to simply spoil the public goods she has. She wants the money now spent on those goods *refunded* to her so that she may do something with it that she prefers. This objection does not require the philosophical libertarian's argument that the state is morally wrong to tax for the sake of public goods. It is enough to make the empirical point that many democratic citizens would prefer fewer public goods (especially in the luxury areas of recreation, higher education, and very stringent environmental protection) than Nussbaum would have the state provide.

This desire may not simply represent one's narrow horizons under liberal capitalism, as Nussbaum claims, but can on the contrary represent a long-brewing frustration with social democracy. This frustration can be effectively and legitimately allayed through democratic persuasion and coalition-building, but Nussbaum does not acknowledge the need for this. In denigrating the basic desire for choice as mere false consciousness, Nussbaum is "antidemocratic" in the *empirical* sense: she does not make sufficient effort to inquire what the citizens of liberal democracies want.[33] She therefore can advise officials how to plan good human lives, but not how to make plans that the liberal democratic public will accept. This might not concern Nussbaum. She talks casually of the "revolutionary implications" of Aristotle's work, and dismisses as irrelevant the concerns of "entire communities that teach, and deeply believe, false values

[32] ASD, 238. References to political and social planning are common in Nussbaum. In addition to the citations above, see Nussbaum (1986: 352) on "legislation and political planning"; Nussbaum (1990b: 58n11) on "political planning" as a planning of society's values; Nussbaum (1994: 60) on "social planning"; and Nussbaum (1994: 100) on how the "radical and far-reaching task" is "the design of a society" that does not value money, honor, war, or empire.

[33] One can of course make an argument that democratic regimes require universal economic welfare rights as preconditions for truly universal political opportunities; see, for example, Gutmann (1983: 25–50). This argument is not persuasive if taken completely literally, for it makes dubious empirical assumptions about how much wealth and education are necessary for effective citizenship or political leadership. Beyond freedom from slaughter, a minimum of daily calories, and water, there are probably no socioeconomic preconditions for citizenship that are not culturally relative; see Walzer (1983: chapter 3). To be sure, the argument is persuasive if interpreted in a broader or looser sense that takes account of what Walzer calls "socially recognized" needs, but Nussbaum cannot easily appeal to such an argument. For in its willingness to let citizens choose their own ends, the liberal argument for welfare is "thinner," more individualist and choice-based, than Nussbaum's position allows.

that are inimical to true human flourishing."[34] But if we believe that the wishes of existing communities must be respected and to some degree accommodated, this kind of disdain should concern us.

This leads into a second flaw with Nussbaum's account: its political naïveté. Nussbaum writes as if Swedish social democracy had sprung full-grown from the head of moral philosophers. But its actual preconditions were not so much abstract theories of human functioning as powerful combinations of interests. The Swedish Social Democratic party has a deep base among trade unions (themselves among the most powerful in the world) civil servants, working women attracted by generous child care and other feminist programs, pensioners, and so on. Where there is no similar coalition, there is no social-democratic state. Nor does social democracy require (or normally command) universal acknowledgment of the conditions of human flourishing. Sufficient as well as necessary is the power of numbers: a majority of citizens who believe in social democratic principles, or merely in a certain set of interests, trumps a minority that does not. The point is not that political ideas and programs do not matter, but that social democratic politics will arise, and persist, as long as a majority of voters support it, even if various elements of that majority support social democracy for very different reasons. Even people who seem ideologically similar (who express strong support for "socialism," for instance) often have very different philosophical reasons underlying their common political program. And regardless of coalitions, nowhere does a majority join Nussbaum in rejecting in principle the Aristotelian vice of *pleonexia* (the vice of always wanting more material goods).[35] In every society, a majority of human beings (known in a democracy as voters or constituents) believe that more wealth is always better.

When economic conditions grow less prosperous, social democracy conveniently begins to seem a less attractive account of human flourishing. Shortly after Nussbaum's main defense of Scandinavian social democracy appeared, Sweden experienced a deep, multiyear recession. In response voters threw out the Social Democrats and elected a (relatively)

---

[34] NFC: 176, 184. See also NFC: 154, summarizing Aristotle: "He stresses throughout his ethical and political writings that many people are badly educated and therefore want the wrong things, or in the wrong amount. . . . The fact, for example (repeatedly noted by Aristotle), that people in many societies have a very strong desire for money, and feel frustrated when they cannot heap it up indefinitely, should not influence the lawgiver's decisions regarding money." Unfortunately, Nussbaum does not specify what kind of lawgiver Aristotle is talking about here. Certainly no one would call this an account of *democratic* lawgiving, least of all Aristotle. His defense of Solon, whom he numbers among the truly great legislators, stresses the latter's middle-class origins and the moderate rather than radical nature of his constitutional reforms (*Politics*: 1273b34ff., 1296a16ff.).

[35] ASD: 209–210; see also Nussbaum (1994).

conservative government. As of this writing, a few years later, the Social Democrats are back in power, reflecting voter opposition to cuts in programs that benefited them. Even so, more recent Social Democratic governments have had to scale back the welfare state a bit and reform various government policies: the conception of human flourishing has not changed, but economic circumstances have. This is democratic politics. It is based on shifting coalitions, responses (or failure to respond) to political competitors, changes in the economic roles of the population and in the interests corresponding to these roles, and astute, or less astute, political leadership.[36] Actual political officers take account of these things: they seek to persuade a majority of voters to support them. They are reluctant to talk of human flourishing, primarily because such talk is unlikely to win public support. It is perfectly natural for those who have devoted their lives to moral and political philosophy to believe that politics can be (or already is) based on the kind of sophisticated theories we ourselves favor. But the temptation to believe this should be resisted. One can reasonably expect the average citizen of a democracy to endorse simple principles like liberty and equality, but not to have knowledge of, or even interest in, the question of what constitutes a full and complete human life.[37]

Nussbaum's favorite example of concrete political action is more attuned to political practice than her theory is, and has theoretical implications she does not recognize. Nussbaum describes a group of development activists who visited a Bangladeshi village to improve the literacy of women there. The aid workers first tried a "liberal" approach: "They handed out to the women of the village ample adult literacy materials, taking no stand on whether they should choose to use them." But given the inequalities and cultural expectations they labored under, few local women made use of the materials. They failed to see how literacy was relevant to their needs, and feared its effect on their existing roles.[38] The liberal approach, giving people a capacity to pursue whatever preferences or desires they currently had, failed (claims Nussbaum) because "the development people made no attempt to perceive the women's lives in a

[36] For an analysis along these lines of the differential success of Social Democratic parties in Europe, see Kitschelt (1994).

[37] Even if one wants to analyze the success of Sweden's welfare state in ideological terms, it has been persuasively argued that its main ideological basis is the goal of expanding citizens' choice and autonomy, not moral perfectionism or the pursuit of the good. See Rothstein (1998: chapter 7). Rothstein stresses that while some Swedish elites have conceived the purposes of the welfare state in paternalist and perfectionist terms, public support for the welfare state has rested on less demanding and more egalitarian foundations.

[38] "Essentialism": 235–36; ASD: 215–16.

broad or deep way or to ask what role literacy might play in those lives and what strategies of education were most suited for their particular case. Perhaps even more important, they did not ask the women to tell their own story."[39]

Nussbaum portrays the next step as a turn from liberal preference-mongering to Aristotelian dialectical encounter. Having learnt from their mistakes, the development theorists began to engage in a "searching participatory dialogue concerning the whole form of life in the village." The local women told the aid workers about the "special impediments to education that their traditions had given them," while the aid workers "discussed with the women the role that literacy was currently playing in the lives of women elsewhere, showing concrete examples of transformations in empowerment and self-respect."[40] The result was a philosophical triumph, a dialogue about what is good for human beings, resulting in shared conclusions about the action to be taken to ensure greater *eudaimonia*:

> The very structure of the dialogue presupposed the recognition of common humanity, and it was only with this basis securely established that they could fruitfully explore the concrete circumstances in which they were trying, in the one case, to live and in the other case, to promote, flourishing human lives.[41]

> Without such an inquiry into the *goodness and full humanness of various functionings*, and into the special obstacles faced by deprived groups, the most valuable sort of social change could not have begun. Simply making enough things available was not enough. But to do more we need a *conception of the good*.[42]

A skeptic might think this story too philosophical to be true (of everyday politics). Did aid workers and Bangladeshi women really use their cooperative education sessions to consider human flourishing and refine their conceptions of the good? In fact, Nussbaum's source for her account—Martha Alter Chen's *Quiet Revolution: Women in Transition in Rural Bangladesh*—makes it clear that they did not. The approach that caused real results in a political setting was not Aristotelian dialogue about human flourishing but political organization on the basis of self-interest.[43]

---

[39] "Essentialism": 236.

[40] Ibid.

[41] Ibid.

[42] ASD: 216; emphasis added.

[43] As this work was going to press, I learned that Chen is actually very familiar with Nussbaum's work and has not taken notable exception to it. Nevertheless, I stand by my claim in the text that Chen's account is incompatible in crucial respects with Nussbaum's gloss on it. The relevant passages seem to require this conclusion; readers may judge.

Chen is explicit about what her group BRAC (Bangladesh Rural Advancement Committee) now believes, based on its experience:

- that the village is made up of groups with differing and conflicting interests
- that these groups can be mobilized around issues perceived to be in their self-interest
- that the rural poor do not participate adequately in or control their environment because they are sociopolitically and economically powerless
- that the poor through the power gained in collective economic and social action can more fully participate in and control their environment.
- *people generally act on the basis of self-interest*
- the poor can, *if they perceive it to be in their self-interest*, be organized into groups.[44]

The political approach that followed from such conclusions was a shift from a focus on credit cooperatives to a structure of "organized groups of poor ... around which all activities are to be organized and through which resources and power are to be mobilized." The key activities became "reorganizing and mobilizing the poor and disadvantaged sector of the population," with the more specific goal being "to organize women, at least initially, around immediate and tangible economic activities."[45] In fact, the projects fostered by the development workers and debated by the village women were primarily *money-making* projects: the villagers regarded literacy as a means not to human flourishing but to success within the market and the power that went with that. Moreover, like all good organizers (I shall argue), the BRAC organizers were concerned as a first step with the *numbers* that were organized.[46] (Nussbaum does not mention this criterion and could not adequately explain it with her theory.)[47] Finally, the BRAC members grew to understand the organizer's concern with identifying pride and status feelings—"love of fame," in different language—among leaders, potential leaders, and conspicuous

---

Perhaps, since Chen is not primarily a political theorist, she has focused on the many substantive goals the two share, without particularly noting the ways in which Nussbaum has obscured Chen's stress on the role of self-interest in organizing for development.

[44] Chen (1983: 13, 92; emphasis added). The portrayal of a village as made up of people with conflicting interests contradicts the strongly communitarian assumptions of Nussbaum and Sen (1989: 317), for whom human beings are explicitly "seen essentially as social creatures whose deep aim is to live in a community with others and to share with others a conception of value."

[45] Chen (1983: 13, 92).

[46] Chen (1983: 153–54).

[47] Nussbaum and Sen (1989: 307) contains a surprisingly quick and derisive dismissal of the idea that numbers could be relevant for judging the worth of political decisions. To be sure, the context of this dismissal is a bit unclear, and on 318 it appears that the authors may have situations of striking cultural diversity in mind.

opponents, and with making sure these were channeled in the direction of public good rather than narrow and petty attempts to sabotage common projects.[48] Nussbaum does not acknowledge the legitimate place of fame and status elements in human nature and political life.[49]

All this is not to deny that BRAC changed, and intended to change, the capabilities and confidence of the women they worked with. The political intervention made them more eager, and more able, to pursue better lives for themselves. But the method used to do this was not that of Aristotelian philosophical dialogue (itself to be distinguished from an Aristotelian *political* decision, which takes interests into account). The philosophical elements were overshadowed by, and situated in, political activity: political organizing based on human pride and on self-interest properly understood.

Nussbaum's theory is not a political theory: it pays little attention to politics, politicians, or democratic citizenship. Its talk of "political arrangements" abstracts from what democratic citizens want, and what democratic politicians must do to stay in power.[50] Accordingly, it misses the extraordinary range of political options that are usually available. It implies that we must either accept existing desires and opinions as they are—leaving unjust or flawed institutions unexamined—or engage in a kind of uncompromising philosophical examination that regards existing social opinions as utterly without worth.[51] Her own examples, however,

---

[48] Chen (1983: 155–65).

[49] An exception is Nussbaum (1994: 236–37), which apparently endorses Lucretius' yearning for "fame for good activity, and for helping others who need help." But this endorsement concerns literary and philosophic fame. Nussbaum never applies this insight to politics, possibly because she assumes without citing many examples that existing politicians' desire for distinction is pathological and based on an undue fear of death (103, 198, 218–20, 261–64, 501–2).

[50] Nussbaum (1990b: 215) conflates "persuasion" with "writing and reading," and implicitly reduces politics (in the form of resistance to "reaction") to "political ideas."

[51] In addition to the citations above, see Nussbaum (1990b: 63): "Aristotle does not think that the bare fact that someone prefers something gives us any reason at all for ranking it as preferable"; see similarly the disparagement of existing social preferences as deeply pathological or deformed in Nussbaum (1994: 26, 31, 77, 96, 103, 206n, 234–35, 249, 488ff., 501).

It may be noted that in discussing preferences Nussbaum repeatedly stresses the problem of *adaptive* preferences: the so-called sour-grapes tendency to stop desiring what one cannot imagine ever having (ASD: 213; "Essentialism": 230; Nussbaum 1990b: 62; 1994: 20–21, 27). While adaptive preferences are real, and their existence should cast doubt on the mechanical calculations of some crude welfare economists, an excessive focus on them may make one prone to antidemocratic temptations: it justifies ignoring the actual opinions of those one is trying to help. Such a focus may also not be true to political phenomena: it would appear from Chen's work, for instance, that people who are shown practical alternatives (ways to obtain, say, more food and income) rapidly adjust their preferences accordingly, without subjecting their psyches to deep philosophic or psychoanalytic examination.

reveal a third alternative: political persuasion, which starts from the interests people currently recognize, and respects citizens' natural reluctance to regard a stranger as an expert on their souls.

We may take from Nussbaum's experience in turning from philosophy to an account of democratic politics a lesson about how philosophy must be transformed in the political realm. Philosophical arguments, including certain accounts of the good life, can certainly be made in the political realm, but in that realm neither their effectiveness nor their legitimacy depends on their philosophical soundness. As Michael Walzer reminds us, a democrat may believe that the public should pay attention to philosophical arguments in considering binding decisions, but not that these philosophically grounded positions are justified or required *whether or not* anyone can be persuaded to accept them: "It is not at all obvious that a policy's rightness is the right reason for implementing it. It may only be the right reason for hoping that it will be implemented and so for defending it in the assembly."[52] The philosopher who covets relevance to democratic politics must trade lofty distance for democratic engagement. Aristotle distinguished between the truths of ethical philosophy and those of rhetoric, on the grounds that each had its own rules in its own sphere. Contemporary theorists of the just and the good would do well to do the same.

Political Psychiatry: Love of Fame as a Pathology

The discussion of democracy and political character in the last chapter was based on a reading of certain classics in political theory. This is not, of course, the only source of speculation on the subject. One very popular alternative starts from a radicalized version of Freud (though not from Freud himself, a partisan of constancy and the work ethic) and attempts to use psychoanalysis in its strict or loose forms to analyze the health or pathology of political regimes and political leaders. Harold Lasswell's work represents a pure example of this approach. But most well-known works on "leadership studies," of which I will focus on those by James David Barber and Bruce Miroff, share a modified form of its basic premises: (1) political leaders are to be studied with a view to their mental health or sickness, (2) "health" in this context means a healthy tendency to love democracy (defined rather radically) or "people" (defined rather idealistically), and (3) scholars must be prepared to warn us of maladjusted leaders before their antidemocratic neuroses can wreak destruction on the body (or mind) politic. Lasswell explicitly called for a

---

[52] Walzer (1981: 386, and 379–99 passim).

new science called "social psychiatry."[53] Though the phrase sounds immoderate, the sentiment behind it is implicit in any effort to study leadership issues in terms of "ego" or "psychological development." A good leader, says this school, is a mentally healthy leader, and mental health, politically speaking, means having a character attuned to the needs of democratic politics.[54]

Before criticizing this argument, I would stress its many virtues. It reminds us that the character of politicians affects how democracy works—a fact that theorists influenced by sociology are determined to deny and that economic theories of politics (as we will see) admit as a possibility but do not flesh out in either descriptive or ethical terms. It seeks standards for good character in objective assessments of the health of the polity, in a laudable effort to avoid biased or personal evaluations. And it respects historical reality in its search for evidence, treating political actions quite literally as its "case" studies.[55]

But the social psychiatrists fall short in three ways. First, the psychological theories involved are arbitrary: they rely on scanty evidence, tend to be hopelessly vague, and are easily affected by political fashions. Second, the underlying misanthropy is too selective: while willing to trace the pathologies of politicians to disappointing childhood and family experiences, the social psychiatrists assume the public, though reared in similar ways, is quite healthy and even innocent. This is related to a third flaw: social psychiatry assumes without argument a partisan, controversial standard for what it means for a democratic system or particular political outcome to be successful: either a radical or "civic" democratic standard, in which participation is assumed to be more important (and more imperiled) than stability, good government, or individual liberty; or a cosmopolitan-humanistic standard under which democracy is inadequate unless it involves benevolent feelings for all mankind. The social psychiatrists are *weak in theory*: weak in psychological theory, weak in social

---

[53] Lasswell (1948: 118ff.).

[54] Such Freudian and psychological theories of leadership were remarkably and persistently popular in the United States shortly before World War II and several decades afterwards. The great prestige of Freudian theory in all circles of mainstream and left-wing thought made psychoanalysis of politicians seem a scientific enterprise, and assumptions that we might now regard as ridiculous about the roots of adult actions in childhood experience seemed like no more than common sense. For a short history of psychoanalytic theories of leadership, see Greenberg (1999). Jackman (1993: 279) claims that Lasswell's "psychopathology of politics" approach, which stresses the subconscious basis of decision making, had a "monumental" impact in political science. The field is not yet exhausted. For a recent attempt at psychiatric assessment of political candidates, quite respectful of Lasswell and his Freudian approach though not uncritical, see Renshon (1996).

[55] I am indebted to Russ Muirhead for discussion on these virtues.

theory, weak in political theory. In each of these areas, democratic constancy can provide something better.

First, consider the underlying theory of child development, healthy social interaction, and moral maturity. These are difficult, controversial topics, but the studies of leadership character adopt, explicitly or by implication, very simple accounts of them. Lasswell, a Freudian, traces the orientation of a particularly bureaucratic and detail-obsessed judge to overstringent toilet training;[56] he attributes another judge's fascist leanings to "exhibitionistic and homosexual trends" (full red lips, limp wrists, flamboyant dress, fondness for youth groups).[57] "If we are to understand the growth of democratic personality," he avers, such facts as the following are needed: "Is the image of the good mother smoothly projected upon the mother country, if the country is presented as a woman symbol? Is the image of a bad mother (or father) extended to the country when it is symbolized as the fatherland? . . . Do the names of political parties, racial and religious groups, nations and other collective symbols of identification become defined as extensions of a good or bad father, grandfather, mother, grandmother, older or younger sibling figure?"[58]

Barber's models of character, while less time-bound in their terminology, are simplistic in other ways. Barber considers the most dangerous type of presidential character to be the "active-negative," who seeks endless power for its own sake. He traces the origins of such a character to "severe deprivations of self-esteem in childhood[;] the person develops a deep attachment to *achievement* as a way to wring from his environment a sense that he is worthy; progressively, this driving force is translated into a search for independent *power* over others, pursued with intense dedication, and justified idealistically. Whatever style brings success in domination is adopted and rigorously adhered to; but success does not produce joy—the person is frequently depressed—and therefore ever more striving is required."[59]

In principle, Barber believes that "character has its *main* development in childhood"[60] but he focuses his analysis on "style in the period of first independent political success" because it is easier to get evidence on this than on details of childhood.[61] Leaving aside the biases involved in treat-

---

[56] Lasswell (1948: 69).

[57] Lasswell (1948: 80–84).

[58] Lasswell (1948: 157).

[59] Barber (1992: 85). The account is very close to Lasswell's (1948: 37–44), which in turn has echoes of Freud.

[60] Barber (1992: 7; emphasis in original).

[61] Barber (1992: 85). The move recalls the so-called drunkard's dilemma, the story about

ing only early successes and not early failures, Barber's method leads him to place great weight on experiences presidents had as adolescents, generally in college politics. The resulting anecdotes are amusing.[62] But Barber's stories are just as easily explained by a "rational" or "pure ambition" theory of politics as by deeper, psychoanalytic speculation. Nor do they convince as predictions of the future: such late-adolescent traits as the boisterous socializing of Lyndon Johnson and the prep-school Anglophilia of Woodrow Wilson are common college tendencies that we normally and rightly expect to disappear in more mature years. When Barber does examine early childhood, his conclusions convince even less: one doubts that recurrent battles with a barnyard gander at the age of four really did much, as Barber claims, to form the mature political character of Dwight Eisenhower.[63]

Bruce Miroff spends less time on accounts of childhood, but compensates for this by greater use of fashionable but underargued psychological theories. Drawing heavily on difference feminism, for example, he characterizes leaders as "feminine" to the extent that they listen well and take different views into account. Comparing Miroff's treatment of Lincoln with Lasswell's, we will get a sense of just how arbitrary and time-bound psychiatric theories of politics can turn out to be.[64]

Lasswell, living in an age that valorizes strong sex roles and masculine vigor, finds Lincoln's slow, consultational style of decision too weak and suggestive of unmanliness: "Those who came in closer contact with Lincoln saw that he was overgentle and lacking in firmness in intimate relationships. They saw how incapable he was of disciplining his own children, and how overindulgent he was of his exigent wife."[65]

Thus Lasswell seeks to link Lincoln's lack of decisiveness to his (slightly excessive) gentleness in dealing with his family. Lasswell finds that failure to chastise his wife and children was not Lincoln's only unmanly characteristic: like the fascist judge discussed in a later book, Las-

---

the person who loses a watch at one place but looks for it fifty yards away because "the light's better over here."

[62] Lyndon Johnson at Southwest Texas State Teachers College ended up opposing the popular Black Stars campus society after being blackballed from it by a jealous romantic rival; Woodrow Wilson at Princeton started a debating club with himself as secretary, but set down a rule that said office depended on British-style votes of confidence (Barber [1992: 117, 97]).

[63] Barber (1992: 185–86).

[64] Barber (1992: 266) writes that "a close study of what subsequent Presidents have admired about Abraham Lincoln . . . would provide an image drawn at least as much from the admirer's mind as from Lincoln's, a kind of Presidential Rorschach test." The same test may be performed on scholars.

[65] Lasswell (1936: 184–85).

swell's Lincoln preferred "maternal women who were usually older than himself" and had trouble with what Lasswell considers more normal relationships.[66] Seeking to explain such traits, Lasswell speculates (without evidence) that someone like Lincoln was likely overindulged in nursing, remained orally fixated, and tended to regress to immaturity in times of stress.[67] The consequent leadership style was somewhat too conciliatory for normal times but ideally suited to get Lincoln elected by a politically uncertain North unnerved by the radical Seward: "The chances are that Lincoln would not have found his way to the top if the North had been a united rather than a divided people. Certainly the Southern leadership contained few figures of the Lincoln stamp."[68] Thus Lincoln's femininity was not "healthy" for the regime: it would have been completely nonfunctional had the Northern polity not displayed schizoid qualities of its own.

For Miroff, on the other hand, Lincoln's lack of consistent masculinity was his best quality, one that all democratic leaders should display all of the time. Much impressed by Carol Gilligan's distinction between a masculine "ethic of rights" and a feminine "ethic of care" (a distinction, by the way, held in much higher regard among political theorists who read only Gilligan than among those who have assessed Gilligan's evidence),[69] Miroff finds in Lincoln's "compassionate and nurturing practices" signs of a "masculine/feminine quality of democratic leadership."[70] He calls the ability to grant pardons "therapeutic for Lincoln." (In the evidence cited, Lincoln merely calls it restful.)[71] While some leaders seek only to "represent and educate the people as a collectivity," Lincoln also sought to "care for the dignity and needs of the individual."[72] According to Miroff, Lincoln rightly thought this feminine care necessary for democratic governance: "He recognized that the democratic perspective of leaders requires an openness to citizens' views and a sensitivity to their needs." That good government might require accepting some citizens' views while criticizing others, or delaying the satisfaction of some people's needs in order to safeguard their long-term interests, does not seem to be a possibility worth considering. Perhaps this would be too "masculine."

---

[66] Lasswell (1936: 190–91). Lasswell does not suggest that Lincoln was a homosexual like the judge, though there have been recent attempts to claim just that.

[67] Lasswell (1936: 192).

[68] Lasswell (1936: 189).

[69] For evidence, see "On *In a Different Voice*" (1986: 301–33); Faludi (1991: 327–32); Tavris (1992: 79–90); and Pollitt (1994).

[70] Miroff (1993: 104–5).

[71] Miroff (1993: 106).

[72] Miroff (1993: 111).

Both Lasswell's model and Miroff's are dubious on their own. Juxtaposed, however, they teach us something more: social psychiatry is too dependent on the conventional psychological wisdom of the day. Given an orthodox-Freudian belief in strong sex distinctions, one kind of presidential character will look "democratic" or healthy; given a contemporary tendency to laud androgyny, another kind seems exactly what is called for. The problem here is not in the facts—both authors agree as to Lincoln's gentleness—but in the theory. As the culture-bound semiscience that it is, developmental psychology cannot provide a lasting basis for judgments of political character.

The second problem with social psychiatry is that it applies its theories to only one group in society—potentially "pathological" leaders—even though most citizens were brought up in much the same ways that are supposed to produce destructive pathologies in politicians. In associating the "political" desire to gain affection through power with infantile urges to avoid deprivation through extreme acting-out, Lasswell must admit that political pathologies seem ubiquitous in infancy: "*It is not too far fetched to say that everyone is born a politician, and most of us outgrow it.* In a society where extreme deprivations are provoked or used by no one, the outgrowing would be complete."[73]

In speaking of extreme deprivations, however, Lasswell generally means nothing more than experiencing one stern or distant parent, or strict toilet training, or simply the double bind of the middle-class schoolboy (Lasswell assumes politicians will be male) who is supposed to "stand up for himself" in fights against bullies, while remaining a "nice boy" who does not fight.[74] Above all, he means sexual repression, even of a mild sort. If this is the kind of thing that causes destructive, pathological political action—"juvenile delinquency on a colossal scale," as Lasswell describes totalitarianism[75]—then we should expect most people, or at least most one-time juvenile delinquents, to show the pathologies of political tyranny. Lasswell states that "men are not born slaves but have slavery thrust upon them through interference with healthy sexual development."[76] But given his narrow concept of the healthy, we should expect most of us to want to enslave somebody. In fact, that is what Lasswell thinks in the end: after making some feeble gestures toward populism, he ends up advocating, in effect, that everyone undergo large amounts of therapy.[77]

---

[73] Lasswell (1948: 160).

[74] Lasswell (1948: 49).

[75] Lasswell (1948: 166).

[76] Lasswell (1948: 167).

[77] Lasswell (1948: 196–201). Lasswell does not cut corners on this point. He proposes the

Barber's psychological notions likewise end up describing as patholog-ical leadership habits and ways of acting that many people would con-sider signs of mature, courageous character. Barber claims that the leaders he calls "active-negative" (overly rigid in internal personality and deci-sion-making style) show signs that they were brought up dangerously. The signs of this upbringing, says Barber, are that they believe in strict moral codes that distinguish right from wrong; see life in terms of duty, often tragic duty; make efforts to suppress immediate appetites for larger purposes; prefer dogged hard work to verbal manipulation and glad-handing; and like to feel that they can resist the easy and tempting path.[78] In other words, what Barber considers dangerous rigidity is precisely what many uninstructed people would consider good character. Con-versely, what Barber considers a healthy, "active-positive" style of leader-ship—a detached, ironic attitude towards consequences, an attachment to change and excitement for their own sake, an eagerness and ability to please, great flexibility in playing roles and trying on new styles[79]—is what an earlier age would have called corruption. (In psychological terms, it could even be called "narcissism," and attributed to its own characteristic insecurity, as people unsure of their ability to do anything substantive seek reassurance in manipulating their image in the eyes of others.)[80]

Consistent with this, what we have called democratic constancy Barber sees as repressed machismo. The so-called active-negative president has a tendency to cover up inner insecurities by engaging in military adven-tures where obedience is the rule and masculinity may be expressed. "Short of that," however,

> the active-negative character may show his colors not in some aggressive cru-sade but in a defensive refusal—as Hoover did in his adamant stand against direct relief. Although such a stand may undermine his immediate popularity, it, too, resonates with the culture's piety of effort. *Paradoxically, the same public which may turn against a President's policy may respect him for resisting their de-mands.* . . . Particularly now that the President is restricted to two terms, in that

---

use of government films followed by analysis of audience members "to prod the audience-member into more and clearer self-knowledge," and says, "We must not overlook the possi-ble use of narco- and hypnoanalytic aids to the general reduction of tension in the commu-nity." Lasswell seeks to accomplish "mass therapy of destructive prejudices" by giving each person a cartoon image, such as Donald Duck, that he can call upon to deal with his own self-control problems "when he reaches the quacking point" (Lasswell [1948: 200–1]).

[78] Barber (1992: 52–53, 82, 81, 107, 160).
[79] Barber (1992: 267–68).
[80] Lasch (1978).

second term the temptation to clean up one's *integrity and long-term reputation* with some unpopular heroism may be very strong indeed.[81]

What does Barber mean by this rejection of constancy and the love of fame? Apparently, that resisting the public's demands is never the right thing to do; that a pursuit of "long-term reputation" is a sign of a sick personality; that taking a position and sticking to it is always a mistake, even if it proves popular in the short or long term.

This may not be fully fair to Barber's views. It is, however, difficult to know, since Barber does not argue against this style of political action directly or explicitly. He merely pronounces it guilty by association with a personality type that he has previously tarred as warped and narrow. And he argues from results: the policies that active-negative presidents pursue are so self-evidently wrong (Hoover's opposition to relief, Johnson's escalation in Vietnam) that the processes and habits by which they arrived at them *must* be wrong. Lasswell does something similar. That the homosexual judge is ill suited to his office is clear from his lack of a "well-thought-out attitude toward industrial concentration or government control of business,"[82] and lawyers in general have biases "of the utmost danger for democracy" because their belief in adversary justice resembles a belief in the economic Invisible Hand.[83] Take away Barber's antiwar sentiments and support for New Deal economics, and Lasswell's assumption that Keynesian government is absolutely necessary (beliefs for which I have some sympathy but which should not be taken as obvious or axiomatic), and there remains no actual argument concerning the relationship between psychological types and democratic institutions as such. On the contrary: Lasswell and Barber seem afraid that what they consider pathological leadership will in fact be popular, in accord with public morality, and perfectly sustainable over time. But then, that only shows (in a reluctant but inevitable conclusion) that the people are sick as well.

This brings up the third problem with social psychiatry: its analysis of which leadership characters are consistent with democracy is based not on analysis of institutions, principles, or political outcomes but on rigid humanitarian or civic-democratic ideologies. For Miroff and Barber mean something special and very stringent by "democracy." In talking of Hamilton, Miroff comments without argument that his desire to "tame the democratic passions of the American masses" stood in clear opposi-

---

[81] Barber (1992: 486; emphasis added).
[82] Lasswell (1948: 79).
[83] Lasswell (1948: 136).

tion to a "civic spirit of republican virtue."[84] Miroff prefers "the novel kind of greatness promised by the American Revolution—of republican citizens who refused to be molded and manipulated by authority because they insisted that they could govern themselves with wisdom and dignity."[85] Unwilling to put forth radical, spontaneous democracy—and opposition to democratic constancy—as his own ideological preference, Miroff professes that a "radical democratic thrust" is "*the* conventional idiom of American political discourse."[86]

Barber captures this idiom in his approving account of Franklin Roosevelt's governing style: "Another type of President, new to the office, might have surveyed the chaos of the country and decided to study the problem. Roosevelt acted. In the flurry of his first hundred days he could hardly send legislative recommendations to Congress fast enough or keep track of their passage amid shouts of "Vote! Vote!" . . . Hoover's gray government was overthrown in a burst of colorful, crusading rhetoric followed by a display of political fireworks such as the nation had not seen since Wilson's first term."[87] From its contempt for reasoned deliberation, to its cult of novelty, to its preference for color and flash over substance, this passage is a caricature of democratic excess. (One can support the policies of the first New Deal and still feel ashamed of the reckless spirit in which some of them were first enacted, and of the dangerously vague and contradictory laws that resulted.) Barber's model of democratic leadership is based, a bit incongruously, on this go-getter ideal of democracy: the president must listen to the people's desires so as to take immediate action, with a view to an immediately pleasing response. (Miroff is at least consistent: his radical-democratic biases lead him to be suspicious of leadership as such.) Barber professes to find the presidential role vital to democratic governance, but it is not clear why government by lot would not do the job as well.

Lasswell's definition of democracy has more to do with world-humanitarian sentiments than with flash and spontaneous approval: for Lasswell, a democratic ideology requires belief in the attainability of

---

[84] Miroff (1993: 5). Not all kinds of civic republicanism, of course, require a model of leadership that insists on deference to the public. As John Gerring has pointed out (1994: 759–60), Whig theories of republican virtue sustained a "Sir Galahad" picture of leadership under which leaders such as Jackson and Cleveland were revered for their stern aloofness, for having common origins and values but an uncommon ability to express virtue in defiance of public passions. This is in accord with democratic constancy theory and perhaps with forms of republican or Jeffersonian ideology actually present in the public. But social psychiatry is not satisfied with this.

[85] Miroff (1993: 30).

[86] Miroff (1993: 357; emphasis added).

[87] Barber (1992: 287).

universal, democratic world-government.[88] But like Miroff and Barber, Lasswell assumes that democratic interactions must involve no un- pleasantness, resistance, or diplomatic reticence: "Our conception of de- mocracy is that of a network of congenial and creative interpersonal rela- tions. Whatever deviates from this pattern is both antidemocratic and destructive."[89]

This picture of democracy is doubtful in itself. It requires democratic leaders to prefer momentary popularity to considered judgment. It as- sumes an impossible standard of popular virtue. In its insistence that every good "democrat" believe what few democrats believe or want to believe, it is both arbitrary and illiberal. It seeks to portray as undesir- able, and presumptively subversive, conceptions of democracy that stress the need for strong, stubborn individuals who resist popular ideas.[90] But most to the point, it calls "democratic" an ideology that is not required for democracy to function and that in fact makes democracy impossible. Democratic interactions involve conflict, and to approach them with childlike joy is, as Barber must admit, a bit fanciful.[91] Democratic move- ments can make errors or endanger rights, and to regard them solely as things for officeholders to "empower" is foolish. Democratic governance, like all governance, requires thought, and time, and to think democratic decisions are made best when made most quickly is itself "antidemocratic and destructive."

On all three counts, democratic constancy theory is less subject to attack. First, it makes no claims about "healthy" human development save that everyone should learn enough self-control as to be able to make and abide by long-term plans—an account of good moral decision that even John Rawls, deeply determined not to judge among conceptions of the good life, considers minimal and uncontroversial.[92] As long as citizens display constancy and political officers both display and encourage it, we should not care which psychological mechanisms are responsible for their doing so, or displayed in the doing (whether Judge Z has a limp wrist, or whether Woodrow Wilson played too much baseball in college). Second, democratic constancy theory applies the same standards of excel-

---

[88] "The principal expectation contained in democratic ideology is that it is possible to attain universal democracy by bringing into existence on a global scale the equilibrium that has repeatedly been achieved in more parochial communities" (Lasswell [1948: 108]).

[89] Lasswell (1948: 110).

[90] The outspoken "genius" praised by J. S. Mill (1975: chapter 3), and the humane, chas- tened misanthropes praised by Judith Shklar (1984: 214–21) come to mind.

[91] Barber (1992: 9) notes that the active-positive "may fail to take account of the irrational in politics. Not everyone he deals with sees things his way and he may find it hard to understand why."

[92] Rawls (1971: section 61).

lence to leaders and citizens, judging that a public culture and family structure that creates a lot of mediocre or dangerous leaders is likely to do the same to ordinary citizens (and vice versa). The constancy theorist expects leaders to be a bit more focused and ambitious than ordinary citizens, but to embody neither perfect virtue nor extraordinary evil. Finally, democratic constancy is an account of democratic functioning that concentrates on what democracies actually need to function well by their own principles. The social psychiatrists use the concept of democratic functioning in the service of personal programs without which democracy can, in fact, function quite well.

ECONOMIC THEORIES OF DEMOCRACY: WHOSE INTERESTS? WHICH STRATEGY?

This chapter so far has criticized theories that demand more from democratic reasoning, democratic citizens, and democratic officeholders than the principles and structures of democracy demand or can easily bear. I have called for a "constancy" theory that starts with democracy as an existing political structure—a method of selecting governments and creating associations on the basis of free choice and the power of numbers—and with democratic citizens as real people, with personal and limited interests, rather than as ideal participants in utopian philosophical, dialogical, or radical-democratic projects.

Some might criticize this view as too close to "economic" or "rational choice" theories of politics, which presuppose an electorate struggling for base and selfish interests, and a political class striving for reelection by appealing to those interests. The resulting picture of politics may seem base and cynical, which is why other models are more popular among political theorists and philosophers.[93]

Constancy theory is indeed similar to economic theories, but only because the latter do not have to be as base as they are portrayed (even self-

---

[93] The interest theory, however, has been credibly portrayed as hegemonic among both political scientists and politicians. See, for example, Mansbridge (1986: 159–61). I should note that the most well-known recent criticism of rational choice theory (Green and Shapiro, 1994) is for the most part not relevant, positively or negatively, to this work. For one thing, Green and Shapiro focus their attention mostly on the more uncompromising forms of rational choice theory, those which describe political actors as self-interested in the most narrow sense. These are not the theories that I find credible, either empirically or ethically. Second, Green and Shapiro's major criticism assumes the standpoint of the positive political scientist: they claim that rational choice theory yields no firm and testable predictions—or else predictions that are demonstrably false. I am not concerned with making predictions; as stated below, I regard the relative "looseness" and non-lawlike character of rational choice theory as a strength, not a weakness, in terms of its usefulness for the ethics of office.

portrayed). Though some of the economic theorists seem to revel in portraying both voters and politicians, in the most reductionist terms possible, as purely venal, the most refined exponents of the school analyze both voter interests and the quest for office in ways that leave room for some nobility and much ethical reflection. They merely assume that citizens have certain aims, that politicians have goals that require their staying in office, and that democracy is a process of reconciling these two realities. In Schumpeter's famous formulation, democracy is "that institutional arrangement for arriving at political decisions in which individuals acquire the power to decide by means of a competitive struggle for the people's vote."[94] Schumpeter may have intended a base view of the motives involved, but the formula itself does not. It entails no claim that the voters' motives are grasping, selfish, or shortsighted, nor that politicians must abandon sincere belief in their programs and projects, a sense of the dignity of office, or ethical considerations. The theory demands merely that each voter recognize that her interests and preferences differ from those of others—that democracy involves conflict among coalitions, not a single view of what is desirable—and that politicians pursue their projects, not quixotically or with antidemocratic contempt for public attitudes, but with a rational view to what will preserve their reputation in the minds of their constituents. A reading of classic rational choice works, including those of Anthony Downs, Morris Fiorina, and William Riker, as well as those of rational choice's critics, reveals that there remains room for self-interest properly understood, and for love of fame.

Take self-interest. Schumpeter's view of the electorate was base, and his contempt for the public has tarnished the reputation of economic theories ever since.[95] (Rational choice theory, writes Peter Euben, views a voter as "a consumer in drag.")[96] Most economic theories, however, posit that popular preferences may be as noble as one wishes, and that voters can take a sober, long-term perspective in trying to get those preferences enacted as policies. When the economic theorists do assert that voters are self-interested in a strict sense (caring about their own welfare as opposed to everyone else's), they generally present this as a simplifying

---

[94] Schumpeter (1950: 269). See similarly Aristotle, *Politics* (1984: 1308b34ff.).

[95] "Party and machine politicians are simply the response to the fact that the electoral mass is incapable of action other than a stampede, and they constitute an attempt to regulate political competition exactly similar to the corresponding practices of a trade association" (Schumpeter [1950: 283]). Interestingly, this view is base in a sense opposite to that usually assumed by opponents of rational choice. While most critics accuse the economic theories of portraying voters as money-grubbing consumers focused on personal gain and incapable of being swayed by noble appeals, Schumpeter portrays them as ambivalent lemmings who are all too easily moved by irrational appeals.

[96] Euben (1997: 180).

assumption which (they admit) is rarely a precise description of reality.[97] More usual, and perhaps more consistent with economic theories' larger goals, is a tendency to define self-interest so broadly that it includes a lot of actions that we would consider principled—as long as citizens are fighting to further their own principles rather than other people's. To borrow a distinction from a recent (critical) book, rational choice theory in principle is committed only to "thin" rationality—the assumption that people's political actions are instrumentally related to their preferences and goals—rather than the "thick" idea that their goals are self-interested.[98] Downs explicitly "leaves room for altruism," notes that "self-denying charity is often a great source of benefits for oneself," and argues that "utility" and "self-interest" can certainly include the pleasure one gets in being taxed to feed starving Chinese.[99] This broad definition of self-interest—so broad that simply "interest" might render the concept better—is also endorsed by such rational-choice stalwarts as Morris Fiorina and William Riker.[100]

When we combine the broad definition of self-interest with the tradi-

---

[97] "Whenever we speak of rational behavior, we always mean rational behavior directed primarily towards selfish ends.

"In reality, men are not always selfish, even in politics. They frequently do what appears to be individually irrational because they believe it is socially rational—i.e., it benefits others even though it harms them personally. . . . In every field, no account of human behavior is complete without mention of such altruism; its possessors are among the heroes men rightly admire.

"Nevertheless, *general theories of social action* always rely heavily on the self-interest axiom. [Adam Smith's] reasoning applies equally well to politics. Therefore we accept the self-interest axiom as a cornerstone of our analysis" (Downs [1957: 27–28, emphasis added; see also 7, 34]).

[98] The distinction is made by Green and Shapiro (1994: 17–19).

[99] Downs (1957: 37).

[100] "I assume that most people most of the time act in their own self-interest. This is not to say that human beings seek only to amass tangible wealth but rather to say that human beings seek to achieve their own ends—tangible and intangible—rather than the ends of their fellow men." Fiorina (1989: 37; see also 102). Compare Riker (1990: 172–73). This might appear tautological, since it seems that even altruism counts as self-interest, but there are distinctions to be made. The person who contributes to charity because it makes her feel good will do something else if her desires change; one who does so because she doubts her right to make decisions about her own money and so defers to social prejudice will not change her behavior unless she changes her whole worldview. (For this reason Sen [1977: 326] agrees that action based on fellow-feeling or sympathy is "in an important sense egoistic," and agrees there is real substantive content to the [rational-choice-type] claim that only sympathy, rather than moral "commitment," drives action. He then contests this claim.) Nor does any definition of self-interest include the motivations of someone who wishes to submerge her sense of self within a Rousseauian majority opinion or "general will"—who says, as Rousseau does (1978: 111), that I should follow the general will if it contradicts my personal opinion because the latter was not really "what I wanted." Riker (1990: 173–74) gives a somewhat different answer to the tautology problem.

tional social-science concession (unfortunately less common among recent rational choice theory than it once was) that "economic" theories are not perfect but merely better than prominent alternatives,[101] the accusation that rational choice assumes universal selfishness or a consumer attitude to politics starts to look like a mistake. At most, it seems to be accurate when applied to some doctrinaire rational choice theorists (particularly "public choice" economists of the so-called Virginia School) but unfair when applied to those with more sense and subtlety.[102] Granted, rational choice theorists often forget their own caveats: after granting the possibility that voters might get utility by feeding the hungry, they assume in practice that everyone is chasing madly after power and lucre. But if these theorists are held to the logic of their concessions, their description of politics should retain room for self-interest properly or broadly understood.

If economic theory does not require that voters be venal, it also does not require that they be imprudent or shortsighted. To be sure, it tends to regard voters' policy preferences, in good economic style, as "exogenous": difficult to change through anything politicians or the political process can do in the short term. But the long term is a different story: over time, voters' preferences can "change radically" (Downs).[103] From this it follows that the task of altering preferences cannot be entrusted to *elected* politicians who are trying to retain a majority in the next vote.[104] But the unelected positions of activists and organizers—whose long-term viability does depend on public support but whose short-term salaries and organizational positions are generally guaranteed from independent sources—are not so constrained by short-term considerations. The support these informal officers need in order to stay in office and continue

---

[101] "I only claim that political and economic theories which presume self-interested behavior will prove to be more widely applicable than those which build on more altruistic assumptions" (Fiorina [1989: 37; see also 104]).

[102] Some who attack rational choice theory from the standpoint of ethics or democratic theory are, I believe, attacking the crudest versions of the theory rather than the most sophisticated. I would say this of Petracca (1991) and Scalia (1991).

[103] "In essence, we are assuming that citizens' political tastes are fixed. Even though these tastes often change radically in the long run, we believe our assumption is plausible in the short run, barring wars or other social upheavals" (Downs [1957: 47]). I share the economists' skepticism about politicians' ability to take unpopular positions and then change voters' preferences through persuasion in time to get reelected. There is a reason why elected officials usually resist idealists' appeals to take on such an "educative" role: it does not often work. Downs suggests that "wars or other social upheavals" lead to more volatile voter desires and more room for political education. This seems right, too.

[104] This does not mean that politicians *never* bring it off, particularly on marginal issues about which their constituents have no strong opinions.

with the task of persuasion does not amount to *majority* support, and just how much support is needed is hard to predict.[105]

Voters may not only change their preferences over time but also take nuanced, wise, and long-term views of what their interest entails. For one thing, citizens have "in common a desire to see democracy work"—a concern for the good functioning of the polity as a whole—and out of this desire they will tend to vote, even if the self-interested gains from an individual vote seem to be outweighed by the costs. Downs in effect describes the act of voting itself as self-interest properly understood.[106] In a more substantive matter, Downs stresses the effects of "future-oriented voting": "A voter may support a party that today is hopeless in the belief that his support will enable it to grow and someday become a likely winner—thus giving him a wider range of selection in the future. Also, he may temporarily support a hopeless party as a warning to some other party to change its platform if it wants his support. Both actions are rational for people who prefer better choice-alternatives in the future to present participation in the selection of a government."[107] The economists thus do not deny the possibility of an enlightened electorate that will forego short-term interests for long-term ones and that can engage in slow, frustrating formation of voluntary organizations (including parties) to this end. (This is not, of course, much comfort to current elected officials who have a winning coalition already: to them, the formation of currently hopeless third parties will indeed look purely "destructive." But voters have different interests.) Given that doing this is empirically possi-

---

[105] The economic theories of democracy work best as electoral theories: the rational theorists would be hard pressed to deny that various citizen leaders advocate positions that are very unpopular in the short term. Of course, they have to show their supporters some concrete results from membership, and this is a problem (see Chong [1991]; Olson [1971]; Mansbridge [1986]), but it is not the same problem faced by majoritarian politicians.

[106] Downs (1957: 268). The rational choice literature is thick with attempts to explain why anyone votes. It is interesting that Downs, unlike some of his more dogmatic followers, has no qualms about appealing to a Tocquevillean argument that is based on interest, but understands interest in a less rigid and more civic sense than contemporary exponents are comfortable with. Downs makes a very similar argument with respect to party attempts to stay in office by fudging their programs: "If any party believes it can increase its chances of gaining office by discouraging voters from being rational, its own rational course is to do so. The only exception to this rule occurs when voter irrationality is likely to destroy the political system. *Since parties have a stake in the system, they are irrational if they encourage anything which might wreck it*" (Downs [1957: 138]). Downs has more recently restated and developed the idea that a democratic system based largely on interest and self-interest requires, in order to sustain it, more general values (we might call them all "Tocquevillean" or related to democratic constancy) like liberty, equality, citizen participation, self-reliance, limitation of power, willingness to compromise, attachment to law, and tolerance (Downs, 1991).

[107] Downs (1957: 49).

ble, even common, under sophisticated rational choice models, there is no argument from "realism" against our ethical claim that people ought to do more of it. To the extent that recent rational choice work studies strategies for encouraging association, it even does this ethical inquiry a service.[108]

Now consider love of fame. I have glossed this as a desire to stay in office and gain long-term reputation by doing good policy work toward ends that the public will come to approve of. All our examples of economic theorists (save Schumpeter, it turns out) leave room for officeholders to pursue fame as long as they also pay attention to reelection. Two of them turn out to *presuppose* something like fame as an empirical prerequisite for democratic stability, just as we have assumed it as an *ethical* duty for those who *value* such stability.

The self-interest theorists suppose that politicians want to stay in office. Why would they want this? The usual attractions of political office are mentioned: at the very least (and most venal) these are power, prestige, income, and the thrill of the political game. Downs, following Schumpeter, stops here, denying that politicians are motivated by a desire to pursue substantive policies.[109] But this is an extreme position even within the economic school. (Note that it fails immediately to explain why a second-term president, or any politician who has announced she will not seek reelection, would engage in any political activity at all.) The addition made by David Mayhew (a borderline rational-choice theorist), based on actual experience as a congressional staffer, is more helpful: politicians seek not only reelection but also "achieving influence within Congress and making 'good public policy'"—though they cannot pursue, much less achieve, the latter two goals unless they get reelected.[110]

The question then is whether the need to seek reelection leaves much room for fame in practice. The most astute economistic theories believe that it does. For one thing, politicians do not know exactly what voters want. This uncertainty leaves politicians a great deal of discretion: "much room for skill" in assembling coalitions and taking positions on issues.[111] There is even, explicitly, room for ethics: given uncertainty, no political

[108] See the citations of Chong and Mansbridge in note 105 above.

[109] Downs (1957: 28).

[110] "The electoral goal has an attractive universality to it. It has to be the *proximate* goal of everyone, the goal that must be achieved over and over if other ends are to be entertained" (Mayhew [1974: 16; emphasis in original]. Internal quotation in text above is from Fenno [1973: 1]). Thus, even a politician concerned with fame must have enough ambition to get reelected. Mayhew is not a self-proclaimed partisan of rational choice, but his approach is sufficiently consistent with rational choice for present purposes. And his argument is cited and endorsed by Fiorina (1989: 37).

[111] Downs (1957: 135; see also 159).

action is "rigidly determined by a vote function." Therefore political parties can listen to policy advice and be swayed by it; voters are "open to suggestions" and "normative recommendations are by no means futile."[112]

Base assumptions about the motives for behavior do not rule out noble conclusions about political possibilities, since even the need to safeguard base rewards (like power) can, if one takes a broad view, motivate farsighted acts. Fiorina, for instance, thinks that members of Congress are engaging in outrageously excessive amounts of constituent service in order to stay in office in districts where their politics are unpopular or controversial. But since this self-interested pursuit has made being a representative such an unpleasant and base-seeming job—because it contradicts, we might say, love of fame—Congress may decide the benefits of office are not worth the price, and plump for reform.[113] The long-term pursuit of political self-interest, it seems, may require noble acts of reform. For Downs, the relation is a little different but not unfavorable to fame: it turns out that what officeholders will do out of self-interest becomes *indistinguishable* from what we would predict them to do out of fame. Self-interest may "take such forms as competition for the best reputation for service, or striving for professional status by means of excellent work. . . . its forms may even be highly beneficial to society. All we ask is that the role of self-interest be illumined so that government may come down from more ethereal—and less realistic—realms and take its place in economic theories as a human agency."[114]

This last point is the distinctive contribution, and plea, of the economic theorists. To adopt an economic theory of politics is not to be cold-hearted, indifferent to ethics, hostile to political reform (however understood), or politically conservative. Fiorina thinks the pluralist thinkers "ill-advisedly" discarded the concept of the public interest.[115] Mayhew thinks that as a description of how legislators ought to act, John Rawls's egalitarian "difference principle" does better than economists' models of efficiency; he argues that the United States spends much too little on transfer payments to the poor.[116]

The economic theory of democracy was not developed to discredit those noble actions that do occur, nor to legitimate a dogmatically libertarian view of political and economic life. It was motivated instead by

---

[112] Downs (1957: 293). Fiorina (1989: 103) makes the point more cynically: "Not every decision [members of Congress] make has electoral consequences; on such electorally insignificant decisions they are free to seek other ends, including the public interest."

[113] Fiorina (1989: 78–80).

[114] Downs (1957: 292).

[115] Fiorina (1989: 106).

[116] Mayhew (1974: 7; for the comments on transfers, see 137–41). As Fiorina notes, calling Mayhew "right-wing" is, given comments like this, not quite accurate.

opposition to three tendencies of political thought that are still prevalent and that should still be questioned. First, the theory took aim at empty moralism in favor of realism, or, better put, moralism in a context of realism. It is all very well to attack political officers for not doing the right thing. But as we have emphasized, politicians should not be expected to pursue ideal ethics at the cost of the political prudence that makes possible their continued existence (and later ethical acts they might perform). If a politician could not adopt the "right" policy without being repudiated at the polls, our edifying instructions could be described as lacking both practical force and political legitimacy. (Such instructions are suspect in terms of democratic ethics as well: unalloyed contempt for the average voter is not a democratic virtue.) In a democracy, the reform impulse—which is strong in the work of many rational choice theorists—must take account of what politicians must do to stay in office. If their incentives are wrong, we must try to change the incentives rather than railing against politicians who respond to them most of the time.[117]

Second, the economists were attacking Rousseauian theories of democracy that assume that only an enactment of a common or general will counts as democratic.[118] Liberal political theorists have long criticized the Rousseauian position as having totalitarian tendencies. But we tend to forget this criticism when turning away from Rousseau himself to other contexts. We still have a residual notion that democracy must somehow be illegitimate, excessively "private," if it consists in the clash of interests among people and groups, all of whom have different agendas and different prejudices in viewing the world. Even when they go too far, the economistic theorists of democracy remind us that most people use democracy to chase interests rather than cogitate on a common good. And there is nothing more offensive in political life, more corrosive of egali-

---

[117] "[Economists] make policy prescriptions which assume governments should maximize welfare. But there is little point in advising governments to do so, or forming recommendations of action based on the supposition that they might, unless there is some reason to believe that they will. Otherwise the economists' advice may very well be as useless as telling a profit-maximizing monopolist to sell his product at marginal cost so as to benefit society" (Downs [1957: 283]). (The argument applies to many philosophers, as well as to economists.) The corollary of this argument is that breaking up or regulating self-interested political practices that hurt the common good (oligarchic campaign finance, excessive district staff doing "constituent service" to prop up members of Congress who would be unpopular on more substantive issues) is completely justified as a matter of law, and indeed precisely what the law should be doing—in analogy to antitrust enforcement.

[118] Schumpeter's theory of democracy is in fact called "Another Theory of Democracy," in contrast to the "classical doctrine" under which democracy "realizes the common good by making the people itself decide issues through the election of individuals who are to assemble in order to carry out its will" (Schumpeter [1950: 250]).

tarian, democratic respect, than hearing a claim to embody the common good made by a politician with whom one fundamentally disagrees. Politicians may claim to be pursuing the common good, but those who honestly disagree with the policies put forth in the name of common good quite rightly find these claims offensive if taken too seriously. The reductive view of ideology as "a means of getting votes" (Downs) should not be understood as denying the possible merit of normative claims. It represents instead a way in which dissenters legitimately gloss their opponents (and vindicate their right to disagree) when those in power make moralistic pleas for consensus and claim that their own positions uniquely track what goodness demands.

This brings up a final point: the economistic view of democracy is a theory of democratic accountability.[119] A politician who aims at getting votes will support a set of policies that she thinks a majority of voters in her district, or party, or national or group constituency, also support.[120] Those who call this immoral, and urge politicians to pursue a different goal, have a large burden from the standpoint of democratic legitimacy. And they have an even bigger burden from the standpoint of stability: what might we expect citizens to do if their leaders constantly promised to abide by their wishes and then proceeded to pursue the difference principle, or Aristotelian socialism, or world-humanitarian government, regardless of popular opinion? Elected politicians act democratically primarily to the extent that they respect the mode of choosing officers under democracy: election, with each citizen holding one vote. This is not to deny that there are better and worse ways of seeking reelection. And, as I have noted above and will discuss later, nonelected officials can and should seek to change the way people think, so that what politicians must do to please the voters may become less base, and more just.

Rational or economic theories of democracy, then, leave room for a subtle, humane, even somewhat noble account of political office and rea-

---

[119] Mayhew (1974: 6).

[120] As William Riker (1982) has stressed, the use of "majority" here is rough: a huge amount depends on how majority preferences are aggregated and how agendas are set. But for present purposes this makes surprisingly little difference. Like the populists, Riker endorses "a kind of equality[:] Equal chances to restrain, to reject, and to veto" (1982: 246). And he concedes that democratic responsiveness in a loose sense continues to function: "By reason of regular elections . . . officials may be rejected. In their efforts to avoid rejection they usually act in some rough way as agents of the electorate, at least attempting to avoid giving offense to some future majority. Since this future majority cannot at any moment be clearly specified, officials seeking to placate it in advance must anticipate several kinds of potential majorities, the union of which is often most of the electorate. By reason of this anticipation of the next election, officials are, even in the liberal view, subject to electoral discipline as the agents of democratic self-control" (1982: 11; see also 216, 242).

soned citizenship. The problem is that they rarely proceed to give the kind of account that they say is needed. As shown, economic theorists admit that credible accounts of politics must explain (1) which issues are so prominent that politicians must follow constituent wishes or risk defeat, and which allow politicians more leeway; (2) which normative positions politicians themselves hold, since this affects which of many plausible coalitions they are likely to pursue; (3) which politicians are skillful and which are not, and what the former are likely to do with their skill; (4) the use and limits of ethical appeals in those many cases when politicians have room for maneuver; (5) the reasons politicians have for wanting to be in politics, and when frustration stemming from such reasons will challenge or override their desire for reelection; (6) the kind of things that people value besides money, including things like nobility and a feeling of service; and (7) how these values are likely to change over time as a result of economic and social events as well as deliberate political persuasion. For the most part, economic theories ignore all these matters (except sometimes the first). Even leaving aside distinctively moral or normative issues, it appears that an adequate economic theory of democracy and office must treat history, society, and ethics with great subtlety, must look more like Aristotle or Hume than like a decision tree. As Peter Ordeshook has conceded, the uncertainties and complexities of rational choice predictions, and their dependence on a host of simplifying assumptions, mean that applying rational choice theories to real political situations would resemble an art rather than a science, engineering rather than physics.[121] The fact that economic theories so often resemble the decision tree should make us suspect how seriously their most prominent exponents really take their own caveats. The assurances of economic theorists that they take a range of human subtleties into account are often trotted out *only* when they are engaging in preemptive strikes against critics who accuse them of reductionism. This accomplished, the economic theorists then proceed to practice . . . reductionism.[122] I have

---

[121] Ordeshook (1993).

[122] For a particularly clear example see Rosenthal (1998). He puts forth a simple model that explains French and British political development as the result of bargaining between kings and nobles over the appropriation of funds to fight wars, a game based on who stood to profit most (or at all) from the potential success of such wars. He then admits (90) that profitability is not the whole story: "ethical" concerns—including the small matter of religious belief—had a substantial effect on political behavior in these countries in the seventeenth and eighteenth centuries. While religious factors might not be enough to determine political results absolutely (calculations of interest sometimes submerged them), they certainly had substantial complicating effects (92–93). However, the author notes, "In cases in which ethics matters, the policy space has two dimensions (profits and ethics), and this characteristic may complicate the political process greatly. Though the tension in policy would remain, equilibria could be difficult to attain within the model" (1998: 90n28).

said that economic theories "leave room" for inquiries like the present one. One might add: the room is presently poorly furnished.

Conclusion

The tone of this chapter has been primarily critical. This does not mean, however, that the alternative theories discussed should simply be discarded. Each has something valuable to contribute to an ethical account of political office.

Theories of human flourishing teach us to ask what democracy should be for, what it looks like when it is working well. They err in having too high a standard of "working well" (or justly): where Aristotle studied actual politics with a view to knowing when and how it most approaches the ideal, humanitarians who currently appeal to Aristotle reject actual politics completely on the grounds of its being too low.

The social psychiatrists teach us to look at political character, and remind us that a lot of submerged passion, self-delusion, and just plain quirkiness take place in the name of "rational" decision-making. And they are right to look for standards of good political character in the needs of the polity, what it needs to stay "healthy." But in their lack of modesty they propose standards of personality adjustment and democratic health that lack credibility and that follow transient psychological and political fashions rather than minimalist and uncontroversial accounts of what democracy actually requires. When theories of democracy speak of the needs of democracy, they should mean *needs*, not utopian aspirations. Democratic constancy theory attempts to respect this warning.

Finally, the economic theorists remind us that most people most of the time pursue their interests as they see them, that we should not expect democracy to consist in collective public deliberation about the good life (or about much else, for that matter). And in stressing that politicians have ambition before (literally) they display any other quality in office, they teach us an old lesson that contemporary political theory has all but forgotten. But their theories of political action, complex and nuanced as they are, only highlight the need to go beyond "parsimony" and reductionism, to pursue truly convincing accounts of politics, so that ethical inquiry may be as informed as possible.

Translated, this apparently means that the theory that accurately describes how people acted should be rejected because the equations needed to describe it would be too hard to solve.

The principles of democracy are freedom and the equal power of all citizens. Politicians who seek reelection by appealing to popular preferences respect both, and are therefore in one sense democratic—though they must aim higher, within these democratic constraints, if they are to make democracy as fair, as decent, and as stable as possible. Calls for politicians to seek ideal economic and social states without regard to public preferences may be antidemocratic; more likely, they are tacitly democratic, allowing democratic bargaining and empirical concerns for regime stability to enter through the back door. On the other hand, psychological schools of leadership are neither reflective friends of democratic processes nor reflective critics of them. They casually and without argument assume an account of democracy that no one much believes in and that has been met by no regime in history. And as a result, they resort to comical theories of developmental psychology to discredit politicians whose acts they cannot impugn on more principled grounds.

The previous chapter put forth Aristotle's view that affection and capacity for work are not enough for democratic officers. Such officers also need the half-virtue of constancy that is appropriate to democracy. Perhaps some theories of office lack even affection. Suspicious of the processes of actual democratic regimes, they seek to abandon the regime, imagining higher and better regimes so that the officers who serve them may exercise more virtue (perhaps a modern, egalitarian virtue). As Aristotle warned, they propose a change in democratic structures that seems innocent because it occurs in steps, and without proper thought.

PART TWO

Applications

THE PREVIOUS THREE chapters criticized prevalent theories of political office and began to argue for an alternative. The first chapter argued that universalist and particularist theories of office (and of ethics more generally) rely on plausible but conflicting assumptions. Compromise was called for, if possible, though only an examination of politics could show the forms in which it might be possible. Making this turn to politics, I defended a way of looking at office, familiar from studies of courts and the presidency, that relates the ethics of office to an account of what each office contributes to the well-being of democracy. The second chapter put forth such a functionalist theory, starting from Aristotle's insight that democracies' great need is not for full human virtue (the pursuit of which is even antidemocratic in principle) but for a certain restraint or "democratic constancy." The third chapter argued that democratic constancy theory is better than alternative accounts of the link between vocation and the general good: more realistic and democratic than liberal-humanitarian theory, clearer and more consistent in its account of human nature than leadership theory, and more aware of its uses and limits than rational choice theory.

All this was meant to show that a synthesis of theoretical positions would be desirable and is in principle plausible. It does not follow that the synthesis is in fact viable, or yields useful judgments about actual politicians. A theory that claims to be grounded and practical, a useful aid to actual judgments, must proceed from general claims to more detailed standards for judging political actions and political character. These standards should be conceptually clear, psychologically plausible, truly practical (in that politicians could actually adopt them and still be effective politicians), and respectful of both citizens' democratic aspiration to popular control of their government and conscientious politicians' aspiration to do good political work worthy of fame.

There therefore follow three chapters that will flesh out the theory and apply it to the three particular offices studied here: United States senator,[1] moral activist, and community organizer. As implied in chapter 2 above, the senator's ethic will start from the Madisonian principle that the people's transient and passionate plans should be resisted until the "cool and deliberate sense of the community" may prevail; the activist's

[1] Democratic constancy theory implies an ethic that in principle applies to legislators in general, but in practice is only available to legislators in this or other countries (or state and local government) who, like senators, have fairly lengthy terms. This conclusion will be justified in the next chapter when the senatorial ethic is discussed.

ethic will start from Tocqueville's insight about the need for religious institutions or their secular analogue to chasten the individualism endemic to democracies and awaken the mind to larger moral concerns; and the organizer's ethic will be grounded in another Tocquevillean insight into the role of informal business, voluntary, and political associations in challenging the power of the state and reconciling the ambitious striving of local leaders with larger democratic purposes. These canonical sources, however, are sketchy on concrete questions of political ethics (which are not, after, all, those authors' main concern), and were written in a particular polemical context that may mislead us on present-day questions. The way to respect classic authors is not to follow them slavishly but to creatively pursue the "new political science" that both Tocqueville and Publius hoped would become a practice, not a dogma.[2]

To this end, each of the next three chapters will begin with short theoretical accounts of a particular office. In keeping with the pluralist premises of this work, these accounts will draw on various theoretical sources and will not be treated merely as casual illustrations of a single theory that explains the whole world. Still, the chapters to follow do resemble one another in both method and substance.

In terms of method, each chapter will start with a piece of *democratic regime theory*, an account of a characteristic problem or tension in democratic polities, and an argument that a given office serves its purpose when it deals adequately with this problem or tension. From this will follow an account of the *principles of action* (for the most part less rigid and specific than "rules") that the officer in question must generally abide by in order for the purpose of the office to be fulfilled. Finally, there will come an account of the *dispositions of character* that people need if they are to act in these ways. Different offices will require different dispositions. This is one place where the "ethics" of office really are plural, and pluralist: many offices, many ethics.

The several ethics are unified by democratic constancy—which, as the name implies, is a theory of both regimes and character.

On the level of regimes, democratic constancy warns us not to expect too much of democratic governance: to respect the modest aims of a regime based on assumptions of equality rather than aspirations to perfection. We must choose between democracy, which accepts people's characters more or less as they are, and moral perfectionism, which tries to make the average person more and more ethical over time. Democratic governance, "disposed to view human nature as it is, without either

---

[2] Alexis de Tocqueville, *Democracy in America* (1969: Vol. 1, Introduction, p. 12; henceforth *DIA*). See also Hamilton et al., *The Federalist Papers* (1992: Nos. 37, 47, and 66, and esp. No. 9; henceforth *Federalist*).

flattering its virtues or exaggerating its vices,"[3] assumes the possibility of ordinary decency and application but tends to reject as dangerous and covertly aristocratic the goal of moral progress, of improvement towards ideals of altruism or heroic self-sacrifice.

A vital corollary is that moral discussion and debate, far from being the normal state of democratic society, is something that democratic citizens, with their attachment to living as they please, normally avoid. Outside the academy, good manners require that one *not* discuss "religion and politics." The enthusiastic promoters of public moral discussion have neglected the insight—discovered by Socrates, endorsed equally by Locke, and admitted more ruefully by Mill and more recently by Thomas Nagel—that ordinary people do not take kindly to having their customs, ways of life, and prejudiced beliefs questioned.[4]

Put another way: Thomas Scanlon has described his own moral motivations as rooted in "the desire to be able to justify one's actions to others on grounds they could not reasonably reject." This formulation is accepted by many Anglo-American moral philosophers, and many, including John Rawls, go so far as to propose this "principle of motivation" as a basis for political argument in a democracy.[5] Unlike moral philosophers, however, most people in a democracy do not in fact have a desire to justify themselves to others. As Nancy Rosenblum has noted, liberalism embodies a "general principle of unaccountability, whereby people do not have to give reasons for acting the way they do."[6] (It would make even more sense to attribute this principle to *democracy*: as Rosenblum writes, its concrete embodiment is the secret ballot.) Random demands for justification are normally regarded as offensive, and tend to arouse the question "Who do you think you are?" Most people feel entitled to believe what they already believe and act as they and their neighbors are accustomed, without needing to justify their beliefs and actions through moral argument. This is what separates them from moral philosophers.

---

[3] *Federalist*: No. 76.

[4] See Locke (1975: 659–60): toleration of diversity is desirable, since most people are not willing to abandon their opinions in the face of our criticism even when those opinions are wrong; Locke (1983: 34): "no man complains of the ill management of his Neighbour's Affairs" except in matters of religion, and we should extend this habit of forbearance to religion as well. Less optimistically, see Mill (1975: 72), complaining that while we ought to be able to correct others' faults without being considered "unmannerly or presuming, . . . the common notions of politeness at present" do not allow this; and Nagel (1979a: xii–xiii): moral arguments are "notably ineffective" when powerful interests are involved, and ethical theory is not normally useful as a "form of public service."

[5] Scanlon (1982: 116). See also Rawls (1993: 49n2); and Gutmann and Thompson (1996: 53ff. and 373n1). Rorty (1991: 184n) endorses Scanlon's formulation as "a sociological description of the inhabitants of contemporary liberal democracies."

[6] Rosenblum (1987: 61).

To be sure, every political office requires a certain degree of moral persuasion, often a very high degree. No conservative, I deny that ingrained systems of moral habits either are or should be immune to attempts at reform. Persuasion based on such reform is not only possible but mandatory if the practices involved are public, harm identifiable people, and cannot be defended according to democratic principles.[7] But the privilege of engaging in this persuasion must be earned through rhetoric. Before political officers seek to modify the political beliefs of the public, they must prove that they have a right to engage in such effrontery: that democratic citizens should take moral lessons from politicians when they are not normally inclined to take them from one another. How this is done depends on the office. Senators can argue from electoral legitimacy, agreed-on constitutional principles, and the need for compromise; activists can argue that the moral principles they speak for are already believed in by their audience; organizers can establish their bona fides through personal conversation, culminating in the trust that arises between people who know one another well. But in each case, moral persuasion is among the "just powers" accruing to office that must be based upon the "consent of the governed."

On the level of actions, democratic constancy denies that democratic office requires, or can rely on, the highest practical human virtue: the practical reason required to act well in all respects. Political action in a given office involves learning an imperfect reflection of a *part* of human virtue: learning how to perform a particular set of actions that the office calls for. Thinking abstractly about what would be required if one had powers and responsibilities that were very different from what they currently are is the luxury and the duty not of politicians but of democratic citizens and independent theorists, who must ultimately choose the occupants of all political offices but themselves serve in none of them.

On the level of disposition, democratic constancy starts from its roots in Aristotle and Cicero. It assumes that good (or second-best) character consists of good habits, acquired deliberately, with thought, and over time, and maintained in the face of temptation. This will provide one more reason why ethics must start anew with each office: the necessary dispositions for a given office are not only things not everyone has, but also things not everyone values and aims at. We will do well to find people whose native dispositions (imperfectly tutored, as all our dispositions initially are) fit well with those required in a particular office. To

---

[7] Contrast, for instance, the position of Jim Crow apologists who held that the Southern way of life should be allowed to continue "naturally" or organically and could not be changed by law (Woodward [1966: 108–9, 139]). As the succeeding chapters should make clear, no similar conclusion follows from the present work.

wish for someone who would be suited to all offices is to wish for more than a naturally flawed and imperfectly educated body of political aspirants—i.e., a body of normal, human candidates—can provide.

Starting with democratic regime theory does not mean starting with a dry or abstract account of how different institutions might look to a social scientist constructing a model. Instead, the starting-points are ethical in Bernard Williams's sense: they involve from the outset a concern with how a given type of politician ought to live. The need to unify particular attachments with universal responsibilities, the public good with fame and democratic responsiveness, implies that the ethics of office must describe not just a set of abstract principles for politicians, nor aesthetic criteria for institutions, but the proper functioning of an ethical relationship between politicians and the wider public. Senators *represent* people with interests, but in the context of a larger polity. The ethic appropriate to them resembles a certain view of the attorney's ethic: senators must consider how to represent their constituents' interests within the bounds of constitutional principle and a concern with the broader good. The moral activist's function requires her to *mobilize* supporters while *shaming* a larger public and spurring it to action; she must therefore combine the roles of "minister" and "tribune," voluntarily chosen moral scold and public proclaimer of constitutional principles. The community organizer exists to *challenge the state* and the industrial aristocracy by building, and building on, the power, pride, and self-interest of civil institutions and community leaders; she must avoid on the one hand striking out on her own and abandoning the local institutions that ground her power, and on the other hand worshipping local virtues too much, thus losing her capacity to judge between those local aspirations that are legitimate and democratic and those that represent merely ambition, hatred, or fanaticism. While what follows will not use the word "relationship" very often, it should be clear that a concern with human relationships—rather than with institutions abstracted from direct concern with human action— pervades the treatment.

These claims, once outlined in theory, will be backed up by biographical examples of political figures who have filled these formal and informal offices well or badly. (There will be no attempt to follow Weber's method closely, but speaking loosely, an "ideal type" in each case is followed by historical examples viewed in the context of that type.) These examples are not meant to break new historical or biographical ground, and rely mostly on secondary sources. Nor are the examples meant as a political scientist's case studies, which aim to prove an empirical generalization; they were not selected with this in mind and contain too little data to support such claims. Rather, the aim is to gain *ethical* insights from the good and bad actions and character traits displayed by the politicians studied. The method is a discourse on known events, which sharpens analysis by adding to philosophical speculation the discipline of historical research. And in a departure from common "case" methods in practical ethics, the units studied are not individual decisions but biographical characters and whole political careers. This is natural if political ethics seeks to illuminate not just action but the practice of political office over substantial amounts of time, and seeks to describe not just rules for decision or methods for dealing with ethical conundrums but the proper functioning of a lasting relationship between politician and public.

By looking at actual politicians and their actions, we can give the argument not only conceptual but also moral discipline: ethical ideals that are grounded in examples must not only be clearer and more concrete than those that are not but must also limit their moralizing to standards that actual politicians and citizens evaluating them could realistically hope to achieve. Beyond this: biographical and historical research should do more than provide examples of theoretical truths derived a priori. It should itself inspire us to recognize truths about politics that are more subtle and unexpected than deductive philosophy allows. Conventions of argument require that theoretical assertions precede their historical support, but actual thought often travels in the opposite direction. Many of the claims in the chapters to follow began as historical observations and yielded to theory after a hard struggle.

CHAPTER FOUR

The Senator and the Politics of Fame

"I am not a moralist. I am a legislator."
—Everett Dirksen.[1]

"Men often mistake notoriety for fame, and would rather be remarked for their vices and follies than not be noticed at all."
—Harry S. Truman, on Joseph McCarthy.[2]

I HAVE ARGUED that the proper ethic of a political office is rooted in the relationship between politician and public embodied in that office. The relevant relationship in the case of legislative office is one of *representation*. In this chapter I shall discuss the tensions between love of fame and democratic responsiveness that are inherent in legislative office. To understand the ethics of legislative office we must go beyond the usual normative theories of representation, which I shall call "populist" and "deliberative." An alternative approach, I shall argue, is more help in evaluating legislators and their actions. As in the rest of this work, the analysis starts by asking what purpose is served by the senatorial office— what it does for a democratic political order. From the answer to this question will follow a set of characteristic actions that a senator must engage in if the polity is to be as good as possible, and a set of character dispositions that senators should have in order to carry out these actions consistently. From such considerations we can derive a set of nontrivial principles for action. These will not be Kantian principles providing "oughts" for everyone, but political principles describing the proper starting-points for action.

To force concreteness, I shall not discuss legislation (and legislators) in the abstract but shall focus on the dispositions and actions appropriate to a United States senator, a political office as much reviled in practice as it is praised in theory. To flesh out the theory I shall then look at two senators—Everett Dirksen and Joseph McCarthy—whose careers are

---

[1] Quoted by MacNeil (1970: 1).

[2] Harry S. Truman to Alben Barkley, 21 June 1950, cited in R. Fried (1976: 155). Truman makes this observation in reference to an Aesop fable regarding a vicious dog whose master puts a bell on his neck to shame him. The dog misses the point and prances around in pride because the bell is so imposing.

widely regarded as models, respectively, of senatorial statesmanship and senatorial irresponsibility. The discussion below, while endorsing these assessments, will seek to explain them systematically. Dirksen embodied the senatorial ethic, and McCarthy flouted it, in ways that are clear and easy to document and for reasons that illustrate the account of political character I am giving. As usual, the hope is that theory and practice will each inform and clarify the other.

The choice of senators does not reflect a claim that the American case, or the American Senate as opposed to other institutions, operates under ethical requirements peculiar to one country and one institution. The distinctive quality of the Senate is simply the lengthy term of its members. I shall argue that legislators should not follow mechanically the wishes of those they depend on for reelection—i.e., parties, contributors, and most centrally, voters—but should engage in difficult and creative lawmaking and hope to persuade their constituents over the long term that their activities have been worthwhile. This activity is much easier to bring off if there is a long time between elections for education and information to sink in and for momentary passions to be forgotten. (In chapter 2, I noted that the *Federalist* defends the Senate for just this reason.) Therefore, while members of the House may ideally be bound by the same legislative ethic as senators, in practice—given two-year terms—they will have much less scope to act on it.[3] On the other hand, this implies that almost everything said here should apply to state senators, as well as to members of legislative bodies in other countries in which terms are fairly long. (Compared to the terms of lower houses in other countries, the two-year term of our House members is exceptionally short.[4] And many other countries have upper houses with long terms.) In turn, the arguments made in this chapter have prescriptive implications for institutions: every legislative system should have at least one chamber in which terms are long; and there is a good reason for the common opinion that members of upper houses with long terms should be expected to display more dignity or deliberation than those of lower houses with short ones. In any case, in what follows I shall use the terms "legislator" and "senator" interchangeably in theoretical discussion, and

[3] The line is not sharp, and some accounts of congressional representation imply that members of the House have more leeway than one might think (and more than uncompromising populists who want representatives to be mere "delegates" of the popular will might like).

[4] See A. King (1997: 30–31). I endorse many of King's individual observations but find his conclusions theoretically unpersuasive. For instance, while King stresses that having one branch of government frequently elected and close to the people is bad for policy making, he fails to see how good it might be for democratic legitimacy.

"senator" exclusively when talking about occupants of the particular American institution.

CONSTANCY AND THE THEORY OF REPRESENTATION: BEYOND POPULISM AND DELIBERATION

Above I argued that democratic constancy for legislators takes the form of "love of fame"—the determination to engage in "extensive and arduous enterprises for the public good" that will win long-term adulation for the politician involved, if not short-term popularity.[5] In a democracy, of course, love of fame—a kind of political vocation—is not enough. A legislator must be devoted not only to the public good and her own glory but also to carrying out the wishes and projects of constituents: this is the essence of the democratic principle of popular control of government. The task of the legislator is to balance her interests in fame, in good performance that will achieve worthy and well-praised long-term goals, with the satisfaction of constituents' interests. In the best case, the legislative role serves democratic responsiveness, constitutional stability, and good government at the same time as it serves the politician's career.

This formulation is admittedly rather vague. It enables us neither to choose among the theoretical positions of sophisticated representation theorists nor to judge the practical decisions that legislators face and the dispositions they display in facing them. What it does tell us is that two schools of thought that have sought to grapple with legislative ethics are flawed in principle to the extent that they consider either the public good or the popular will in isolation from other values. Sophisticated populists and sophisticated elitists often end up as practical compromisers whose compromises render their theories moot. It is often conceded that legislative ethics is an art involving a creative balance between responsiveness and courageous pursuit of the public good. But without an account that does justice to both sides of the relationship between voter and legislator, the desire to balance seems practically wise but theoretically unmotivated. If either a rationally defined public good or a popularly defined public will is *the* fundamental value to be furthered by representation, extreme prescriptions seem more logical than moderate ones. Nor do ad hoc, untheorized concessions to actual practice give us much help in exploring or defining the complex art of balancing people's concerns, determining what kind of politicians are likely to possess this art, or judging

---

[5] Hamilton applied the argument when justifying a fairly long and renewable term for presidents, but I argued that his argument resembles Madison's defense of long terms for senators. In any case, the logic of the argument seems to apply broadly rather than narrowly.

when the art is being practiced properly—precisely the sort of questions that the student of political ethics or of leadership needs to answer.

Two basic theories of representation are current in both academic debate and popular discourse: one "populist," the other "deliberative."[6] Populist theories (their partisans call them simply "democratic") argue that legislators should enact the wishes of the people who elect them. Populists regard this as required both by democratic principles—equality of interests, antielitism, and responsiveness to popular wishes—and by democratic skepticism or relativism regarding claims to superior insight about the good life.[7] The second, a "deliberative" theory (its proponents, again, call it deliberative *democracy*), argues that legislators should ignore constituent wishes when they conflict with the public good, or at least that the arguments made for pursuing particular goods should appeal to reason or principle or "the merits" rather than power and interest.[8] (Here I

[6] Here again, I avoid Pitkin's (1967: 127–35) opposition between "delegate" and "trustee" theories for three reasons. First, the terms I have chosen remind us of the *political* differences that underlie our disagreements about representation. "Populist" and "deliberative" (or "Burkean") are recognizable political viewpoints. "Delegate" and "trustee" are nonpolitical analogies, and Pitkin herself finally acknowledges (221) that they are less than useful when dealing with political representation (see also Thompson [1987: 99–102]). Second, the terminology can be misleading in that Jeremy Bentham, the leading theorist of populist democracy, used "delegate" and "trustee" interchangeably. Compare Bentham (1962: 63, 106) with Bentham (1926: 221). Finally, "populist" is the most natural name for a *democratic interest theory* of representation; and a name that reveals the principled roots of such a theory. Theorists of deliberation—not, to be sure, Pitkin herself—sometimes attribute to interest theories crude economistic and egoistic theories of interest that few defenders of interest politics (and, as noted in chapter 3, few sophisticated rational-choice theorists) endorse. The true populist view elevates not individual selfishness but civic suspicion: it is based on the fear that politicians will betray the public interest if they start thinking of themselves as free deliberators rather than agents of public desires (Bentham [1962]). Such a theory is much more appealing and serious, both intellectually and politically, than reductionist claims that voting is like buying a hair dryer and that there is no public interest.

[7] See, for example, Dahl (1989: 70–74, 100–5); and Pitkin (1967: 159–62, 234). It is worth noting that Pitkin's account of Burkean (deliberative) representation theory is cited ubiquitously and widely endorsed, while the fact that she *rejected* this theory in favor of a more skeptical and populist stance is all but forgotten.

[8] The adjective "deliberative," and the phrase "deliberative democracy," can mean many things. As originally coined by Joseph Bessette (1980) and expanded on in his recent book (1994), it meant something very close to the Madisonian analysis pursued (independently) in this work: Bessette thought that popular interests and the popular will played important parts in representation, but that they should do so by providing a check on representatives rather than a mandate for representatives. As Bessette originally argued, constituents are less knowledgeable than their representatives and lack the "time, inclination, or setting" for proper policy deliberation—but this does not imply a difference in virtue between constituents and representatives or a qualitative distinction between the moral preferences of ordi-

treat John Rawls's "public reason" standard as a kind of deliberative theory, without denying that he has serious differences with deliberative democrats on various issues.) The first view tends to deny in principle that legislators should criticize their constituents' interests or transcend them in the name of a public good; the second tends to deny in principle that legislators should heed voters' desires or self-perceived interests at all if they conflict with objectively higher goals or involve rationally impermissible claims.[9]

---

nary citizens and those of legislators (1980: 105). Bessette explicitly defines democracy in fairly conventional terms as action according to the "will of the majority," and denies that representation pursues antidemocratic goals. I largely agree with Bessette's theory, though not with his opinion that true deliberation takes place only in representative bodies. Some of Jane Mansbridge's work on deliberation also views it as a way of refining and making more sophisticated the policy preferences of a majority of voters, rather than replacing these preferences with something higher or purely "rational."

More prevalent in recent debates, however, is a rationalist sense of "deliberative," under which a deliberative democracy is one which pays no heed to majority preferences as such but instead puts into practice the results of a philosophic argument in which all are theoretically allowed an equal voice. A trail of citations reveals many direct and indirect references to Bessette's article but more or less universal departures from his central thesis. See Sunstein (1985: 45n72, citing Bessette); and Cohen (1989: 17n1, citing Sunstein's citation).

The meaning of "deliberate" in the *Federalist* resembles the first view much more closely. There, "deliberate" (and the cognate "deliberation"), when not used as a simple synonym for "consider," means to engage in *slow* and *careful*, rather than rushed, consideration: it does not describe some special kind of reasoning that takes account of only principle rather than interest. Similarly, the adjective "deliberate," when it does not mean "on purpose," also means "slow" or "careful." See *Federalist* No. 22 (unanimity rules "substitute the pleasure, caprice, or artifices of an insignificant, turbulent, or corrupt junto, to [*sic*] the regular deliberations and decisions of a respectable majority"); No. 37 ("fullest and most mature deliberation"); No. 63 ("cool and deliberate sense of the community" opposed to "particular moments" animated by "irregular passion"); No. 78 ("ill humors" quickly give way to "better and more information, and more deliberate reflection," but cause oppression of minorities and harmful innovations "in the meantime"); No. 83 (some legal cases requiring "long, deliberate, and critical investigation as would be impracticable to men called from their occupations, and obliged to decide before they were permitted to return to them"); and especially No. 70 ("In the legislature, *promptitude of decision* is oftener an evil than a benefit. The differences of opinion, and the jarrings of parties in that department of the government, though they may sometimes obstruct salutary plans, yet often promote *deliberation and circumspection*, and serve to *check excesses in the majority*" [emphasis added]). Theorists of deliberative democracy who allude to these papers without direct quotation, or out of context—e.g., without making clear that a synonym for "deliberation" is "circumspection"—present a somewhat misleading picture. Deliberation in the *Federalist* is directed toward ensuring that people get what they do want in the long term—not what they would want under some hypothetical and ideal form of moral philosophizing.

[9] Cohen (1989); Sunstein (1984, 1985); Rawls (1993: 190); Thompson (1995: 20–22, concerning "independence" and deciding on the merits). I am not claiming that deliberative democrats think senators are in principle better able to deliberate than ordinary people; in more thoroughly democratic versions of the theory, everyone is supposed to deliberate on

These are ideal theories. Their sophisticated partisans generally acknowledge their limits as standards for actual politics or legislative actions. The populists recognize that ordinary people rarely have detailed knowledge of legislative questions and settled preferences about how to resolve them.[10] Even if there were such preferences, social choice theory reminds us that who the "majority" is on an issue depends on how the matter is framed and which alternatives are available, making it impossible to tell what the real "populist" solution would be.[11] Finally, Robert Dahl, though mostly a populist, would chasten the principle of majority rule itself: he denies that we should "maximize" majority control to the exclusion of "leisure, privacy, consensus, stability, income, security, progress, status, and probably many other goals we are prepared to forego for an additional increment of political equality."[12]

As a result, populists end up rejecting the standard of majority rule in its strong sense: they accept that the most that can be expected of legislators is broad responsiveness to public views. Thus Dahl abandons ideal popular democracy in favor of "polyarchy": a system with a "relatively high degree" of majority decision (more accurately, decision involving the influence of many minorities), popular access to agenda-setting, and democratic control over administration. And Pitkin speaks up for a subtle bilateral relation between legislators and constituents in which the goal is not perfect representation of popular wishes but "systematic responsiveness" to "public interest and opinion," public opinion has many and unpredictable sources, and "interest" is something that the legislator often knows better than her constituents, at least initially.[13] Politics, says Pitkin, takes place in an "intermediate range" between deliberation and a clash among arbitrary interests; it is a "combination of bargaining and compromise . . . and common deliberation." A real legislator must take into account a wide range of constituent interests that are often vague and conflicting, *and* his party, institutions, and special interests, *and* his own views and opinions, which "may be shaped by those around him."[14] The resulting picture is subtle and rhetorically persuasive—but not useful as a

---

the public good rather than giving in to existing majority desires. The key point is that even here, *existing majority opinions or preferences are supposed to count for nothing* in making legislative decisions. Senators are supposed to ignore popular opinion, just as the populace itself is supposed to ignore its own desires if these cannot be supported by arguments of the proper kind, those that could be accepted by everyone who approaches the debate with the proper moral orientation. For an unusually explicit statement, see Gutmann (1999).

[10] Pitkin (1967: 217–20). For empirical discussions of this fact, see Converse (1964).

[11] Dahl (1956: 41–44); Riker (1982).

[12] Dahl (1956: 51).

[13] Pitkin (1967: 234, and 218–40 passim); see also Dahl (1956: 84, and 63–85 passim).

[14] Pitkin (1967: 212, 220).

guide to how legislators ought to go about balancing these claims, which is what we need.

From the other side, deliberative democrats realize the difference between an ideal theory of interest-free deliberation and the reality of a legislative process in which interests play a large role.[15] But deliberative democrats' prescriptions for dealing with this fact are sometimes a bit more utopian than they realize, or a bit less detailed than one might hope. Thus Dennis Thompson allows that legislators are not required to consider every piece of legislation on the merits, but says they may only "logroll" votes on one issue "in order to win passage of legislation they think more important," and then only if the general result of doing this is "consistent with a legislative process that generally considers legislation on the merits."[16] What to do in an actual legislative system, in which the merits *as such* are rarely the goal aimed at, is still an outstanding issue. And Cass Sunstein argues that courts must take a much more active role than they now do in striking down legislative outcomes that are not "deliberative," in matters ranging from economic regulation to welfare to commerce, but tells us little about what should be done in the real world, where judicial activism is on the wane and judges (reasonably) fear for their future institutional power if they go against public preferences too often.[17]

On some crucial questions, deliberativists, like populists, can only say that decisions are difficult and depend on circumstances. Discussing the conflict between the public interest and obligations to constituents, Thompson writes: "To find the balance between these obligations, even

[15] Thompson (1987: 113; 1995: 65–71); Sunstein (1984: 1692; and esp. 1985: 48).

[16] Thompson (1987: 113).

[17] Sunstein (1984: 1731–32, and passim; 1985: 57–58, and passim). Sunstein (1985: 71–72) mentions that some might question the courts' competence and objectivity in these matters, but does not proceed to answer this objection. In general, he does not address institutional arguments against judicial activism seriously, though he sometimes retreats from, or at least shades, his radically judicial-activist position when such considerations come up (1985: 58, 77). But judicial activism, based on the view that the court should not respect existing balances of political interests, remains Sunstein's main position (1985: 79, 85; 1984: 1729, 1731, and esp. 1714 and 1716, attacking the Court for its "awkwardness" in "attributing an impermissible motivation to a coordinate branch of government," calling for a requirement that congressional acts be based on "public values," and denying that "separation-of-powers objections to such a judicial role" are a sufficient basis "for refusal to implement the constitutionally mandated prohibition of naked preferences"). In *The Partial Constitution* (1993: 145–53), Sunstein seems to endorse some traditional arguments for judicial restraint, but the only specific issues to which he applies a restraint doctrine turn out to be those in which the Court might be prone to strike down legislative measures that Sunstein supports. Various later works are even less supportive of judicial activism (perhaps for similar reasons), though I know of none in which Sunstein explains why his earlier positions were flawed.

to decide whether they conflict, the legislator must consider the particular political circumstances at the time. Whether, for example, single-issue representation should be condemned depends on what the cause is, how many legislators are promoting it, and what its effect is on the conduct of legislative business. Ethical obligations of these kinds are contingent on what is going on in the legislative process as a whole and may differ for different members and vary over time for all members."[18]

Such observations, while wise to acknowledge complexity where it exists, should inspire a look for more explicit guidelines.

Both schools reach unsatisfying conclusions because their path from theory to practice is that of reluctant concessions to a base reality, reluctant departures from clear and unambiguous principle. Since their departures from their respective principles are matters of prudence rather than principle, both populists and deliberativists have trouble articulating just when (and why) concessions to political reality are acceptable and when they betray principle "too much." This is in marked contrast to our everyday intuitions, which see these matters in terms of *conflicting* principles. We tend to believe, in an uneasy and contradictory way, that politicians ought to follow the voters' wishes *and* that they should go against the popular tide, even sacrifice their careers, for the sake of principle. The populists, even as amended, are hard pressed to explain how it could ever be noble, or even allowable, for legislators to take stands that are markedly unpopular at the moment. The deliberativists are hard pressed to explain why we bother to let ordinary people vote—or regard voter preferences as salient for legislative decision—given that few people deliberate rationally in the way the theory ideally demands.[19] In more ev-

---

[18] Thompson (1995: 70–71).

[19] Joshua Cohen (1996: 107) has argued that we should value equal voting rights not because they produce a politics of democratic bargaining but primarily because equality of voting rights, "by reducing inequalities of power, . . . reduces the temptation to shift from deliberative politics to a politics of bargaining." An almost identical argument is made by Sunstein (1984: 1706; emphasis added) in a different context (discrimination by one state against out-of-state interests who have no votes in that state): "The underlying notion is that when a group of citizens enacts a measure of which they are the sole beneficiaries, there is a peculiar likelihood that raw political power is at work. *The absence of representation is undesirable not for its own sake, but because it increases the likelihood that the legislature is acting on the basis of a naked preference.*" This argument hardly describes why people actually vote or what they are likely to do with their vote. No voting majority would stop influencing policy as soon as its power were sufficient to balance precisely unscrupulous interests on the other side; majorities want to influence policy affirmatively. Moreover, the argument seems to imply that *once* voting occurs and legislators are chosen, those legislators should have no obligation to do anything the voters want if these wants conflict with what their ideal deliberation would conclude—a very radical notion.

More recently, Jon Elster (1998: 14) has pointed to "internal heterogeneity" among groups as a reason for allowing one-person–one-vote even if one is a deliberativist. The

eryday terms, deliberative democrats' perfect legislators would seem to embody a noble calling but not to respect the desires and interests of ordinary people (something most people expect from democracy), while the populists cannot explain why politics strikes at least some people as more important or honorable an activity than selling garden implements on late-night television.

Instead let us assume that representative democracy embodies a positive synthesis of competing values, and seeks to do justice to both democratic responsiveness and conscientious deliberation. In a well-functioning democracy, the love of fame characteristic of the best politicians serves the people's desire to achieve their political preferences—giving us politicians who act from conviction *and* are responsive, who serve democratic ends in difficult and demanding ways that do credit to their character.

Representative democracy is democratic, *and* it gives much of the work of legislating to representatives who have constitutional distance from those they represent (i.e., long terms of office). From these two facts will follow five democratic or public-interest-oriented principles for action, and two vocational or fame-oriented ones. From these in turn will follow two kinds of character traits that senators should have—broadly speaking, sympathy and pride—and one that they should lack: a Kantian attachment to practical reason and moral law.

SENATORIAL PRINCIPLES

Democratic citizens believe in equality. This means both equal claims to political control, and the assumption that ordinary people's decision-making powers and ethical character are approximately of equal quality. Above I have discussed this aspect of democracy in terms taken from Aristotle and Tocqueville, but many contemporary democratic theorists agree that the central principle of democracy is (or ought to be) "equal power to each citizen" (Jane Mansbridge) or the "right [of citizens] to have their preferences weighed equally in the conduct of the govern-

---

argument is not spelled out, but apparently requires the assumption that each of over a hundred million voters has a well-thought-out position, distinct from that of everyone else, on the issues, *and* that there is some meaningful sense in which the legislative process could take account of each position. This is doubtful. Every individual may have a different interest, but only a finite number of opinions, far less than the number of voters, can be fully considered in political debate—as Hannah Arendt noted in a different context (1965: 226–27, 268–69). Finally, the recent debate between Jeremy Waldron (1999) and Amy Gutmann (1999) makes the issues very clear: the former defends voting out of skepticism about deliberation, which cannot overcome conflict and disagreement; the latter, a strong defender of deliberation, explicitly denies that democracy has much to do with voting.

ment," due to their "roughly equal qualification" to make collective decisions (Robert Dahl).[20]

At the same time, those seeking political power aim to put themselves in a position of *inequality*—political superiority—with respect to their fellow citizens. We can strive to make influence on policy relatively equal among citizens, but decision-making authority is inherently unequal, and the privilege of those who have made a special effort to obtain it. The ethos of senators, and other legislators who have the authority to make rules binding on others, must therefore unite the democratic belief that citizens should have equal rights to influence decisions with the institutional necessity that some have disproportionate power and responsibility for using power. How should these two imperatives, democracy and institutional power, be reconciled?

1. Equal political influence is the fundamental value of democracy, and senatorial attachment to democracy requires, at its core, *constant opposition to the influence of big money in legislative campaigns and legislators' decisions.* This should be seen not as an extraordinary policy suggestion in an otherwise mostly formal theory, but as a fundamental consequence of attachment to democratic principles. If elections and decisions are determined by wealth more than by the influence of ordinary voters, the regime is an oligarchy rather than a democracy.

The reasoning here is not that "money should be kept out of politics," nor that every citizen must have *exactly* equal influence on the political order. As Nancy Rosenblum has argued, we should reject this conclusion if we value free speech, free association, and the right of citizens to differ in their attachment to politics.[21] Unlike Rosenblum, however, I would maintain the distinction between businesses and other interests' having an *influence* on politics (through forming associations or agitating on issues) and their giving direct donations to specific legislators. If businesses or wealthy individuals wish to influence politics, they should be forced to pay democratic respect to citizens by letting citizens form their own opinions on what businesses say. The road between money and political power should be forced to make a detour through public opinion. Direct

---

[20] Mansbridge (1986: 26); Dahl (1971: 2; 1989: 97 and passim). This is not to say that democratic principles require any particular method of aggregating majority preferences, much less the first-past-the-post (single-member district with plurality election) method that United States citizens are used to. But all democratic representation methods, including proportional ones, ultimately result in an assembly where decisions are taken by majority vote. For decisions to require a supermajority is more characteristically liberal (and antidemocratic) than democratic, and such supermajority requirements are generally limited to issues of individual rights or group prerogatives that are explicitly intended to be immune to democratic amendment.

[21] Rosenblum (1998: 229–38).

donations go beyond this: they efface the link between legislators' positions and the support of a majority of their constituents. Even if one wishes to deny that a big campaign chest can "buy an election," or scare off viable competitors, the fact that senators *think* these things happen is enough to make them listen to wealth more than to numbers. This corrupts the relationship between legislators and their constituents: a relationship that should be based on legislators' respecting all voters equally, and showing this equal respect by pursuing a majority of their votes. To the extent that voters who lack the funds to make donations feel permanently deprived of serious political influence, the office of senator itself could come to seem unjust. It could become subject to what Samuel Scheffler has called the "distributive objection" to those social relationships that help one particular group at the cost of exacerbating the plight of another, weaker group that has persistently less access to powerful contacts.[22] Thus, for a senator to owe his election to campaign cash rather than voting strength, or to be swayed after elections by influence based on money, is always wrong according to democratic principles, and the more a legislator's electoral success depends on the influence of great wealth, other things equal, the worse at performing his office he is.[23]

The caveat "other things equal" is crucial: given the current dependence of politicians on private campaign money, no particular legislator can be condemned for not giving up unilaterally either her own cash or

[22] Scheffler (1999a: 88ff.; see also 1994, 1997, 1999b). When resources are permanently maldistributed, this "distributive objection" can serve as a more general reproach to what I have called the division of moral responsibility: "If the inhabitants of Chad or Bangladesh are told that the citizens of affluent Western societies have little responsibility to assist them, they are unlikely to take much comfort from the assurance that they may rely all the more heavily on one another or from the reflection that they may pursue their own projects unburdened by excessive concern for the welfare of affluent Westerners" (1999a: 96). Democratic political relationships avoid such objections only because, and to the extent that, they are truly *democratic* relationships. That is, the resource requirements required to enter them (a vote, a right to speak and petition) must be equally distributed, or capable of becoming so, for instance through organizing. To be sure, economic and social factors can make a mockery of this (political) equality, and often do. But to the extent that this happens, the relationship to be attacked as unethical is the one between political officers and social/economic groups—as with campaign finance—not the one between officers and constituents. The latter creates no systematic inequality and cannot be blamed for any.

[23] Though in what follows I shall often cite the work of Richard Fenno, this is one instance in which the institutional and systemic perspective taken here differs from Fenno's "soak-and-poke" approach, which follows around individual senators and attempts to sympathize with their goals rather than critique them (Fenno [1991b: vii]). Fenno (1991b: 152, 158) notes that Senator Arlen Specter in 1986 greatly outspent his Democratic challengers in a reelection race, with significant effects on the outcome. Indeed, he raised so much money that potentially strong challengers were scared off altogether. Fenno does not seem to find this particularly troubling. We should.

the corrupt legislative behavior (granting of access and the willingness to keep issues off the agenda, as well as simple votes) necessary to keep getting it. The democratic principle against the influence of wealth in campaigns provides not so much a way of evaluating current legislators as a reason to make future ones better: we will never have properly democratic legislators without public financing or some other method of allowing legislators who flout the interests of wealthy individuals and companies to at least compete reasonably for the popular vote.[24] Senators are required to fight for some such mechanism for making an increasingly oligarchic regime democratic again.

Strangely, neither populist nor deliberative theory does a good job of explaining why this should be so. Populist interest theory, as realistically corrected, has tended to take the form of a "pluralist" theory of political influence. Under such a theory, moneyed interests are just one more "group" whose "resources" happen to consist of cash rather than membership lists, propaganda assistance, or volunteers. The influence of moneyed pressure groups is regarded as ethically unproblematic.[25] At the other extreme, deliberative democrats have trouble distinguishing between legitimate pressure through popular votes and illegitimate pressure through campaign money: both are unjust as reasons for legislators to act, since they involve preferences, desires, or interests rather than principle.[26] Deliberative democrats have trouble explaining why financial in-

---

[24] I have changed my earlier opinion, common in democratic theory, of assuming that democracy requires strict equality: a voucher system in which every voter is able to contribute a certain amount of money and no more (Cohen [1996: 109–10, citing articles by Bruce Ackerman and Edward Foley that I have not read]). Burt Neuborne in personal conversation has convinced me that the practical objections to this (e.g., the likely black market in vouchers) are fatal. In addition, the idea that political influence can be *simply* bought with money now strikes me as too simple.

[25] Truman (1951: esp. 33–44, 310–14). To be sure, pluralist theory has hardly escaped criticism for overstating the extent to which influence as part of a "group" is available to all; after a close examination of evidence, E. E. Schattschneider (1960: 34–35) concluded in a famous formulation that "the flaw in the pluralist heaven is that the heavenly chorus sings with a strong upper-class accent. Probably about 90 per cent of the people cannot get into the pressure system." But while Schattschneider's proposed solution—the strengthening of political parties—has many adherents among empirical political scientists, political theorists tend to shrink from it, since party pressure seems to them insufficiently rational, closed to the force of the best argument. The present work follows Schlozman (1984) in aspiring towards an "unbiased pressure system," which would necessarily look very different from the current one. The ideal, which Schlozman agrees cannot easily be attained and must be balanced against strong liberty concerns, is "the application of the principle of one-person one-vote to the realm of nonelectoral political activity" (1984: 1008–9).

[26] Sunstein claims the "task of the legislator is not to respond to private pressures *but* to deliberate on and to select values" (1985: 52). Similarly, Thompson (1987: 115) explicitly opposes the influence of big contributors on campaigns, but *not* because it threatens the

fluence through campaign contributions are illegitimate but attempts by *voters* to influence legislators by making their preferences known are not.[27] Popular opinion, of course, sees a clear difference; opposition to "special interests" in no way implies opposition to the *majority's* getting what it votes for. The democratic theory developed above gives a simple reason for this distinction: the fundamental principle of democracy is equality of political power, and this equality is consistent with majority voting but not with any system that gives the rich more influence than the poor. Michael Walzer summarized the argument well:

> Each citizen is entitled to one vote simply because he is a citizen. Men and women who are ambitious to exercise greater power must collect votes, but they can't do that by purchasing them; we don't want votes to be traded in the marketplace, though virtually everything else is traded there, and so we have made it a criminal offense to offer bribes to voters. The only right way to collect votes is to campaign for them, that is, to be persuasive, stimulating, encouraging, and so on. Great inequalities in political power are acceptable only if they result from a political process of a certain kind, open to argument, closed to bribery and coercion. The freely given support of one's fellow citizens is the appropriate criteria [*sic*] for exercising political power and, once again, it is not enough, or it shouldn't be, to be physically powerful, or well-born, or even ideologically correct.[28]

The next three principles of action follow from the democratic belief that everyone's ethical character and way of life is roughly comparable, in

---

Schattschneider's "pluralist ideal of equal influence for all interests. The objection [instead] is that legislation is substantially affected by a factor that bears little if any relation to the *merits* of legislation. In the imperfect markets of modern America, no one has yet demonstrated that wealth corresponds to *intensity of desire, let alone deliberateness of thought*" (emphasis added). But if *only* the merits or public values are what is at issue, equal influence exercised through *voting* may distract from this as much as campaign contributions do. Even public financing of campaigns—Thompson's solution here—would guarantee that political influence would be equal among all voters, those who know about the merits and those who do not alike. There is no reason to expect "deliberateness of thought" in the rationalist sense to be distributed equally, as voting power is, or even nearly equally. The fact that such deliberation is much rarer than it should be presumably animates the whole deliberative project. Hence what I regard as the correct conclusion—public financing is required for democracy—seems not quite to coordinate with the justification that deliberative democrats give.

[27] Joshua Cohen's defense of voting (1996; see note 18 above) does not mention pressure activities by voters (such as letter-writing campaigns) *between* elections. I do not see how deliberative democrats could defend such activities or a legislator who responded to them. No doubt they would argue that legislators should respond to one letter containing a good argument rather than the ten thousand letters on the other side containing only detailed and credible political threats.

[28] Walzer (1973: 404).

terms of political standing and assumed powers of judgment, to everyone else's. Even if this belief is not completely true, it limits the kind of reasons legislators may give for opposing the popular will.

2. Legislators must not act as if they and their fellows had extraordinary virtue; neither Aristotelian "greatness of soul" nor former President George H. W. Bush's boastful "prudence" is a democratic virtue. In a democracy, an opinion held by a fair number of constituents always has a claim to be heard: one characteristic sign of democracy is that the people hold themselves to be capable of ruling virtue (though they may lack some of the *skills* of political leaders) and to be entitled to political authority on the basis of their own majority decision as free citizens.[29] Senators should not therefore regard voter opinions as "raw feels" or consumer preferences, but rather as commonsense beliefs, rooted in dispositions that are reasonably useful in people's living of their decent daily lives.[30]

To be sure, senators have a duty to go against constituent wishes when the *result* would endanger constitutional principles. (This is not limited to rights but also includes changes that senators believe would seriously worsen the constitutional structure.) This has a warrant in democratic principles themselves: stable democracy requires limits on the short-term wishes of the voters—and just as important, the vast majority of voters accept that it does. But a senator is not entitled to ignore constituent wishes simply on the suspicion that the *motive* or *reason* a certain wish reflects fails to meet standards of deliberative reasoning. Democratic equality means that voters are not required to defend their ethical reasons except when they have consented to do so. Thus even suspect motives, like other constituent wishes, provide good democratic reasons for the legislator to act, and democratic restraints on how she may act.

This is a serious claim, and gives rise to a serious problem. On some issues, voter preferences are both very clear and very disagreeable to any high-minded legislator. Issues like race, abortion, and religion are both those on which public attitudes tend to be hardest to budge (compared to complex economic and foreign policy questions)[31] and those on which philosophers are likely to regard prevalent public attitudes as narrow and immoral. A great deal of philosophy as well as moral intuition says that in these cases government policy should take *no* account of popular

---

[29] Aristotle, *Politics* (1984: 1291b5–8, 33–38).
[30] See again Waldron (1999).
[31] Converse and Markus (1979: 32–49).

prejudices that violate basic principles of constitutionalism and moral equality.[32]

I must reluctantly contest this. Even the ugliest prejudices quite legitimately have some influence on legislation. (This is not the same as determining power. As mentioned above and developed further below, one can never tell what will determine legislative outcomes given the need for negotiation.) There are four reasons for this.

First, a skeptical reason: people's reasons for believing things may not be as prejudiced as we think. If we assume that they are, we may ignore powerful criticisms of our positions. For example, public attachment to certain forms of "workfare" and welfare reform is sometimes attributed to unfair stereotypes about "the poor in general and poor women in particular"; Sunstein thinks (or once thought) that courts should strike down various welfare reform proposals on this basis.[33] But cutting off benefits to recipients who refuse to take an offered job is also the policy in Sweden, a highly feminist society with no significant racial stereotyping of welfare recipients. Fair application of this policy may require a degree of cultural homogeneity and agreement on social values that the United States probably does not have, but there is a legitimate argument to be joined. It might be *possible* for a deliberative senator to listen to such arguments—after all, the "Swedish" argument for work requirements might have good reasons behind it of the kind a deliberativist could accept. But as a matter of practice or habit, it is *unlikely* that a senator will be eager to learn new moral arguments from constituents if he starts from the premise that his job is to ignore the many opinions that are morally worthless in favor of the few that are not.

Second, voter preferences must be given some weight as a matter of personal respect—in the sense of democratic, slightly relativist, rather than Kantian respect—in the legislator-constituent relationship. If people feel strongly about something, to ignore their views on that subject altogether is deliberately to cause them pain and to say that their preferences do not matter. This sacrifice may not seem like much to those whose sentiments have an easy time gaining respect, but for the socially

[32] See Sunstein (1984: 1728). This demand to "critically examine" (i.e., ignore if immoral) voter preferences seems a characteristic of Kantian and deliberative theories in general, and reveals their common rationalist roots. See also John Rawls's claim (1971: 226; also 31, 261, 425, 450) that parties must ignore "private demands" that are not "argued for openly by reference to a conception of the public good," and endorsements of similar views by Cohen (1989: 18) and Dworkin (1985: 68). Brian Barry (1990: 38–41) describes the central distinction as one between "want-regarding" and "ideal-regarding" principles. The current work endorses want-regarding politics but does so for ideal-regarding reasons.

[33] Sunstein (1985: 72–73).

marginal to be told that their legislators do not and should not care about their opinions can be galling, even intolerable.[34] For a senator to do this to constituents represents the most fundamental denial of equality in the representative relationship, even if it hides behind an alleged respect for the moral actions that people would potentially be capable of engaging in were they not so depraved.

Third, there follows from these considerations the pragmatic one that the people in a democracy can make their views felt in the long term. Politicians who support prominent and unpopular policies will likely be voted out of office, and judges who do so will give fuel to politicians who promise to remake the judiciary. Fame considerations require that politicians get things done; they also require that they try within limits to stay in office so that they can get things done. The desire to be reelected is not *merely* selfish, but reflects an understanding of the ultimate basis of all power in a democracy: the opinions of the people.

Fourth, a senator who respects popular wishes builds a particular bond of democratic sympathy. Hume notes that when admirers praise us we tend to embrace their opinions "both from *sympathy*, which renders all their sentiments intimately present to us; and from *reasoning*, which makes us regard their judgment, as a kind of argument for what they affirm. These two principles of authority and sympathy influence almost all our opinions; but must have a peculiar influence, when we judge of our own worth and character."[35] This argument can be applied to both parties in the legislator-constituent relationship. Citizens who are praised by their legislators will gain confidence in their own abilities and will find confirmation of their confidence in the authority of the one who praises. (Voters vote for a senator because they think he or she has good judgment; the senator's willingness to praise the voters demonstrates, as far as they are concerned, that the senator *does* have good judgment.) Conversely, consider what would have to be true of a senator who did not care what his constituents thought. Such a senator would have to be indifferent to social norms that encourage agreement with one's fellows. Moreover, such a senator would have to be indifferent to others' powers of judgment: a majority of his constituents would form a serious judgment on an issue they had strong views about, and the senator simply would not care. Such behavior, if repeated regularly, would prove that a senator did not consider himself in the same category as his constituents: not content with their loving him, he would be demanding that they *defer* to him as a superior creature empowered to think in their place. This is not a democratic position. When it comes to legislators, Richard Fenno

---

[34] For a criticism of Rawlsian "public reason" along these lines, see Wolin (1996).
[35] Hume (1978: 320–21).

draws the right lesson from Congressional lore: "'If your conscience and your district disagree too often,' members [of Congress] like to say, 'you're in the wrong business.'"[36]

3. Senators must engage in *deep and detailed listening* to constituent views. Respecting the ordinary moral sentiments of constituents means something more than listening to those sentiments that are obvious and conspicuous. Legislators have a duty not only to consult public opinion but to consult it in a certain *way*: one that gives them the most subtle information possible not just about superficial policy preferences but about the underlying values, concerns, and fears that underlie them. Fenno calls this "a complex and discriminating set of perceptions" of voter views.[37] The politician who consults a poll can use the information only for the slavish purpose of pleasing voters who may be relatively uninformed or uncaring about the issues they were asked about. But more can be gained—in the service of real democratic responsiveness *and* legislation in the public good—by talking personally and at length to constituents. This is an activity unjustly reviled by critics of Congress who wish legislators would stay in Washington doing legislative work, and who assume the only purpose of home visits is constituent service on trivial matters.[38] The legislator who talks at length with constituents can find out what is truly important to their lives, thus gaining more leeway to go against popular pressures on some matters if she follows them on more deeply felt ones.[39] And she can find out about the legitimate fears that are often expressed on the surface as resentment towards the position of racial minorities, immigrants, women, and so on.

Paradoxically, a politician who does not understand the local practices and ways of life of particular local and ethnic groups must often make *more* concessions to their naked prejudices than a politician who takes the time to mix and to understand. As Samuel Popkin has argued, voters with little time to spend on politics use politicians' understanding of constituent customs and habits as an "information shortcut" showing that politicians may be trusted on bigger issues. When Gerald Ford in the 1976 campaign showed that he did not know how to eat a tamale (one removes the corn husk before eating the meat and corn), this hurt his standing among Mexican-Americans, who (rightly) concluded that Ford had little knowledge of their culture. Cultural sympathy lets politicians keep sup-

[36] Fenno (1978: 142).

[37] Fenno (1978: 233).

[38] For example, Fiorina (1989: 32–34).

[39] Fenno (1978: 340) stresses how such "extrapolicy behavior" can win for members of Congress the trust from their constituents that lets them go against public sentiment when they feel they must.

port without making foolish policy commitments. Those who lack such sympathy often end up pandering to each group in ham-handed ways that end up alienating just about everyone.[40] A politician who intends to follow constituents blindly on policy matters does not need sympathy. But one who intends to pursue objectively justified policies that might irk many constituents at first must gain a license to do so through sympathetic personal interactions.

The "focus group," a long, structured discussion between a political consultant and a group of voters, is another much-reviled technique that should be better appreciated.[41] Used in the right spirit, it can give a legislator both flexibility in responding to public anger and the courage to do so.

Consider perhaps the most famous focus group in history (central to at least two influential books),[42] in which the Democratic Party hired pollster/political scientist Stanley Greenberg to interview white "Reagan Democrats" in Macomb County, Michigan, after the 1984 election. The county is a suburb of Detroit made up largely of current and former auto workers, including many white "ethnics," who have fled urban ills. It voted heavily for Kennedy in 1960, just as heavily for Reagan in 1984, and heavily for George Wallace (66 percent of the vote in the 1972 Democratic primary) in between. The last fact might have caused some to suspect the presence of racial resentment, but the results of the focus group were more extreme than anyone expected:

> These white defectors from the Democratic party expressed a profound distaste for black Americans, a sentiment that pervaded almost everything they

[40] Popkin (1994: 1–3).

[41] A similar technique, the "deliberative opinion poll," has been promoted by Fishkin (1991). Fishkin is a deliberative democrat in the older, Madisonian rather than the newer, rationalist sense. He neither requires nor assumes that participants in a long-running deliberative argument abandon a self-interested perspective in favor of Kantian or public good–oriented moral reasoning. On the contrary, he endorses Robert Dahl's doctrine of "enlightened understanding," under which a voter should be allowed the time and resources "to *express his or her preferences* accurately, . . . discovering and validating, in the time permitted by the need for a decision, *what his or her preferences are* on the matter to be decided" (Dahl [1979: 105–7], cited approvingly in Fishkin [1991: 36]). Fishkin specifically allows for and accepts the possibility that after hearing all relevant opinions and information, people will "finally decide in terms of their personal interests or values" (37).

[42] Edsall and Edsall (1992); Greenberg (1995). Greenberg conducted the original focus group, and his book is the most informative on the focus group itself. Edsall and Edsall give more on the wider social and political context of the race issue and its corrosive effect on economic and civil-liberties debates. It should not be necessary to stress that so-called Reagan Democrats are no more worthy of respect than other, competing groups whose views and aspirations also deserve detailed attention from politicians. The example is purely illustrative.

thought about government and politics. Blacks constituted the explanation for their vulnerability and for almost everything that had gone wrong in their lives; not being black was what constituted being middle class; not living with blacks was what made a neighborhood a decent place to live. . . .

These suburban voters felt nothing in common with Detroit and its people and rejected out of hand the social-justice claims of black Americans.[43]

How could a legislator use the results of such a study? He could conclude that the way to win working- to middle-class, formerly Democratic areas such as Macomb County is to make racist appeals, and proceed to make such appeals. Or he could probe more deeply and find that while Macomb County whites expressed racial fears, the driving force behind those fears was the voters' feeling that their middle-class goals were being taken from them—by taxes, crime, and economic change—in spite of their own good intentions and hard work.[44] The same voters who responded so readily to a racial message might respond just as readily to a nonracial message promising, say, a middle-class tax cut, welfare reform, a tough stance on crime, and federal action on education and industrial policy. President Clinton, running on such a platform (with Greenberg as his pollster),[45] did not win Macomb County in 1992, but he was competitive enough there to be able to win Michigan as a whole. Significantly, he in no way ran against civil rights laws or their enforcement—and his subsequent popularity among black voters is legendary—but he did make several symbolic gestures calculated (it is generally thought) to show that blacks as a constituency group—as opposed to civil rights principles—did not control him.[46] Walter Mondale, running before the focus group was conducted, had no idea what concerned these voters, tried to run on a traditional Democratic message of unionism, civil rights, and higher taxes and spending, and suffered humiliating defeat. Clinton may not have had better principles than Mondale, but he had better and more

[43] Greenberg (1995: 39).
[44] Greenberg (1995: 151–80).
[45] For an insider account, see Greenberg (1995: 181–214).
[46] Another successful politician from Macomb County is Representative David Bonior, the House majority whip who is widely regarded as an extreme liberal but is in fact a sort of populist (in the party-political sense—he is probably a constitutionalist according to the scheme put forth here) who takes flamboyantly antiestablishment stands against free trade in particular. (This is not to say that Bonior thinks opposition to free trade is only a sop to the electorate: he seems to oppose trade agreements quite sincerely, even bitterly. The point is that no strong supporter of free trade would be likely to stay in office as the representative in his district.) Here again, Bonior is free to be a serious progressive—to support more or less all the principles of Rawlsian social justice or deliberative social democracy—*only* because he has mastered the local idiom and is able to respond to strong local feelings on a few questions. See Kerson (1998: 20–22).

useful knowledge of the democratic electorate. For a legislator in a democratic polity, this is a virtue.

4. Respect for the character of ordinary people means that *senators cannot expect under normal circumstances to "educate the electorate"* on moral issues that are dear to their heart—and should expect to become reviled and retired if they try. Such education is generally both insulting and ineffective. People do not elect representatives to serve as their moral tutors, and are disinclined to listen to those who arrogate to themselves this role. Legislators have above-average commitment to policymaking and above-average familiarity with political issues. Voters are quite willing to listen to a legislator who seeks to inform them on this basis, as a roofer might inform them about Spanish tile. But they are no more willing to hear politicians tell them they are selfish, materialistic, or insufficiently tolerant than they would be to hear such preaching from a roofer. (They are not willing to hear too much of this even from preachers—as Tocqueville noted in commenting on ministers' accommodation to democratic principles.) In fact, as William Mayer has pointed out, the role of elected politicians *prevents* them from being effective advocates on policy issues because they are more self-interested and partisan than the average citizen:

> As aspirants for public office, they are likely to be seen as highly self-interested issue advocates and therefore prone to distortion or misrepresentation. As the officially-endorsed standard-bearer of a major political party, a Democratic or Republican candidate in the general election may have greater cachet with the 30–40 percent of the population that identifies with his own party. But for precisely the same reason, that candidate is likely to be viewed with increased skepticism by members of the opposition party.[47]

Legislators cause even more outrage when they try to educate than when they go against the popular mood on a legislative issue. The latter act can at least be seen as a matter of individual opinion to which everyone (even, grudgingly, politicians) is entitled; the former involves the offensive assertion that legislators are regularly superior in virtue to those they govern.

Those unconvinced by this analysis might heed the prudential argument that education rarely works. Even on pressing social issues like race, change in public sentiment from all causes is so slow that no individual's campaign of a few months or a few years is likely to make much difference.[48] Of course, social movements may last for decades and may

---

[47] Mayer (1998: 11).
[48] Mayer (1998: 10), citing his own findings and those of Benjamin I. Page and Robert Y. Shapiro.

indeed lead to substantial change during such a time. But this implies that moral tutoring is less effective when done by *legislators*, who must face reelection regularly, than when done by *social activists*, who can afford to wait and who have learned how to finesse the moral demands of social equality and the political problem of democratic offense.

5. Good senators must bargain, and in particular must be willing to *bargain even on matters of principle*. The premises of democracy, in which numbers provide moral authority, obtain within legislative chambers as well as outside them, since a majority of legislators is taken roughly to represent the majority of popular opinions. Roll-call votes are won by the majority of voices, not by the voice with the purest argument. This, once again, is consistent with respect for diversity of opinions, sentiments, mores, and dispositions among constituencies. As the saying goes among legislators, "Where you stand depends on where you sit."

Good legislators therefore bargain, and bargain with principles and opinions as well as interests. They realize that opinions will vary among legislators because of diversity in constituencies, party, and ideology, without anyone's necessarily being irrational or insincere. Responsible senators—in theory and in actual practice—neither demonize opponents' positions as false, unjust, or stupid, nor expect their opponents ever to be fully persuaded by argument, given that they have distinctive local interests and ideals to uphold. Since laws must be made and coalitions formed in spite of conflicts of viewpoint, the proper response to this diversity is the utilitarian, reductionist one: to regard these viewpoints primarily as preferences, and bargain with them. To paraphrase what Hume said about the assumption of egoism in human nature: the conflation of viewpoints with preferences may not be true in fact, but it is true in politics.[49]

To make this conflation goes against a strong moral requirement of personal relationships, in which to regard someone else's principled stance as a mere feeling or preference is to treat her with great disrespect. But among legislators themselves, this habit of mind is accepted because it is necessary. As Neustadt has pointed out, only bargaining and persuasion, rather than moralistic appeals to duty, take seriously the fact that people honestly *disagree* on matters of duty—partly because duties vary among offices, constituencies, and the temperament and goals of the person feeling the duty.[50] Everett Dirksen was often reviled for acting on

---

[49] David Hume, "Of the Independency of Parliament," in Hume (1987: 42–43).

[50] What Neustadt (1990: 40) says about presidential persuasion would apply just as well to senators: "The essence of a President's persuasive task, with congressmen and everybody else, is *to induce them to believe that what he wants of them is what their own appraisal of their own responsibilities requires them to do in their interest, not his.* Because men [*sic*] may differ in

such premises; treating opinions about constitutional rights as items to be traded made him seem unprincipled. But it was only his willingness to bargain away bits of principle that let him force favorable votes on Civil Rights and Fair Housing legislation. (Endless argument on the merit of issues is not a virtue in the Senate, where it is called a filibuster.) In this respect the virtues of a good legislator are not, once again, simply those of a good person. They are, rather, relative to the governing body in which legislators must act and the democratic relationships from which they draw their authority.

These five principles reflect democratic attachments to majority rule and equality of moral character. But they do not reflect representative government's concern with *who* rules in the majority's name. People who choose a life in politics ought to do so because they think that they are better able than others to act in the public interest and accomplish difficult tasks of governance. Democratic constituencies always exist, and a particular candidate's claim to office cannot rest merely on the goodness of the voters (though it must start there). In chapter 2, I have explained Hamilton's "love of fame" as an attachment to long-term projects in the public interest, and a strength of character ("ruling passion") to pursue those projects in spite of short-term pressures to abandon them. Applied to legislative activity, this implies two representative "fame" principles to go with the democratic "interest" principles already named:

6. A good legislator *cares about results*, about achieving long-term projects rather than merely talking about them. Anything that increases a senator's ability to achieve results counts as a virtue (though a contingent one, since the ends must also be in the public interest and in tune with long-term public opinion). This includes substantive policy expertise (and a capacity for the hard work needed to acquire it); patience to do the legwork of following the details of bills; parliamentary cleverness; knowledge of, and determination in using, arguments of political interest; personal charisma, however irrational its source (voice quality, appearance, physical presence); and persuasive skill. This also means that a legislator's background or past achievements may themselves be virtues if they affect the policies she is able to pursue, even if they do not affect the

---

their views on public policy, because differences in outlook stem from differences in duty—duty to one's office, one's constituents, oneself—that task is bound to be more like collective bargaining than like a reasoned argument among philosopher kings. Overtly or implicitly, hard bargaining has characterized all illustrations offered up to now. This is the reason why: Persuasion deals in the coin of self-interest with men who have some freedom to reject what they find counterfeit." I would endorse all of this except the term "self-interest": as Neustadt has emphasized elsewhere, interest need not mean self-interest, and the desire to help others can be a genuine motive force even in politics.

policies she wants to pursue or has the intelligence to implement. ("Only Nixon could go to China.")

Partial attachments, even apparently irrational ones, are virtues for a senator. A senator's attachment to his state's traditional mores, or his party's traditions, or the Senate as an institution, might not be justified as a matter of impartial evaluation. In practice, however, such attachments may be necessary elements in the process of ennobling ambition into fame and keeping the trust of the voters when specific policy positions are too hard or too many for the average person to understand. This is where regional and cultural pluralism in local mores, sentiments, habits, and interests comes into political ethics. Cultural pluralism has nothing to do with the core principles of democratic politics, but its existence creates principles of prudence for legislators. For they must get things done in a context where regional and tribal loyalties are *held* to count for something, no doubt more than would be ideal.[51]

That a "work horse" is better than a "show horse"—in more scholarly terms, that mere rhetorical "position taking" is less desirable than real legislative accomplishment[52]—is a commonplace both among senators and among students of the legislative branch. Neither the ideal nor the practice of results-orientated legislating seems to have died, despite repeated predictions that media pressures, political competition, or the demise of parties would kill them.[53] This ideal has, however, been too often

---

[51] Localist defenders of regional idiosyncrasies often speak as if the Constitution had obliterated such particularistic distinctions, but a quick glance at the personalities and viewpoints represented in national political debate should disabuse us of this view. Thus Sheldon Wolin (1989: 88) quotes wistfully George Mason's picture of representation attuned to local interests: "It ought to know & sympathize with every part of the community; and ought therefore to be taken not only from the different parts of the republic, but also from different districts of the larger members of it, which had ... different interests and views arising from difference of produce, habits, etc. . . . We ought to attend to the rights of every class of the people" (ellipses Wolin's). But Wolin does not sufficiently dwell on the context of the quotation: Mason is not referring to plans for some wildly decentralized confederation of localities but to his vision of the United States House of Representatives. Even the modern Senate, let alone the House, can hardly be said to lack richness in its representation of local interests and views. Nor is Mason endorsing the Articles of Confederation or other forms of wild democratic pluralism. The second ellipsis in the above quotation concerns Mason's admission *"that we had been too democratic* but [that he] was afraid we [should] incautiously run into the opposite extreme" (in Madison [1987: 39]; emphasis and interpolation added).

[52] Mayhew (1974: 179–80).

[53] Fenno (1991b: 33) calls the distinction between policy-expert "work horses" and publicity-seeking "show horses" "[p]erhaps the oldest and most basic of all the distinctions of the communitarian Senate." He cites a *Wall Street Journal* article that attributes the metaphor to former House Speaker Sam Rayburn (1991b: 140), but the idea seems to go back further. Donald Matthews (in a 1960 work cited in Harris [1993: 112–13]), in the course of

ignored by philosophers who think only about the ends politicians pursue and the reasons they have for pursuing them.[54] To a citizen concerned about the health of a democratic polity, a politician who cannot accomplish good things is just as useless as one who does not want to accomplish good things. (The former is not even "harmless," for he can discredit a cause by making it seem laughable and impractical.) Not for nothing did Aristotle list a "very great capacity for the work involved in rule" as the second virtue of a politician, just behind affection for the regime and ahead of (regime-relative) virtue and justice.[55] This capacity is a virtue in the epic rather than the moral sense: it is an "excellence" that lets a good legislator fulfill her function.

7. Not unrelated to this is the principle that a legislator *must be creative* in crafting policy and political solutions. Such creativity is another fame-virtue whose opposite would be slavish accommodation to whichever public opinion is read from a poll. Legislators need not be flashy or "entrepreneurial," still less aristocratically contemptuous of public wishes. But they must be capable of nonobvious insights that lead to long-term solutions. Legislative action in accord with democratic constancy means seeking a policy that the people would approve of, given time and information, and a set of policies that they will in fact approve of at the next election. The indefinite articles on both points are deliberate. Democratic preferences provide *one* reason among others for action, but the "fame interest" of legislators provides another reason to act for the public good whether or not it will be popular, and even to run some risk of electoral defeat if the issue is important enough. Moreover, since constituents' preferences on most issues are only loosely defined, any given democratic policy or set of policies will be only one of many that might have won popular approval—depending on the presentation of the policy, the available modes of persuasion, action by the opposition, and the ability to mix unpopular opinions on one policy with more popular

---

describing the norm in the 1950s, writes that Carl Hayden, then a senator, had been taught it years before when *he* entered the Senate.

Fenno speculates that changes in interest-group organization, increases in staff, and other factors have undermined the work-horse ethic and other long-time institutional norms of the Senate (1991b: xi). But he admits that such norms retain their power over time (xii), and his book on Senator Specter chronicles in detail the costs incurred by senators who fail to observe them. The norm persists in the Senate (see Senator Howell Heflin's comments in Berke [1991: 40]). If there has been a change, it might be to the advantage of work horses: as issues become more nationalized and the media more sophisticated, many senators have argued that being *both* a work horse and a show horse is possible and even necessary (Harris [1993: 113], citing Senators Warren Rudman and Orrin Hatch).

[54] An exception is Thompson (1987: 110), though his grounds for attacking position-taking do not concern effectiveness.

[55] Aristotle (1984: 1309a33–34).

opinions on others. Advice on these matters must therefore be "indeterminate" because it depends on the factual circumstances—but not because our ethical reasoning is fuzzy.

The resulting ethic is one of creative, sophisticated responsiveness. It is a poor (and one-term) senator who sees herself as so intellectually and morally superior to her constituents that she does not care what they think or is sure that she is justified in acting without reference to them. (Here I disagree with Pitkin, who seems to regard such an attitude or "personality" as one of many legitimate ones).[56] But it is also a poor senator who cannot find ways to respond creatively to popular demands rather than merely following them; in fact, given the need to get other legislators to agree on legislation, such stubborn following of constituent demands, even if a legislator wanted it, would be literally impossible. Robert Putnam has called the result a "two-level game" in which a legislator or other negotiator keeps one eye on his negotiating position with other legislators, and another eye on winning at least grudging support from those he is responsible to.[57] What is missing from this account is love of fame—recognition for difficult long-term achievements—which gives the legislator an interest not only in "winning" the game but in the substance of the result. Democratic officeholders, who *govern* yet rely on voters for their right to govern, must find ways to act both well and democratically.

Legislators may not ignore constituent opinions on matters of principle; they cannot and should not regularly stand on their own principles if the majority of their constituents are strongly against them. They can and should, however, find ways to sell pieces of their principles as dearly as possible. Senators can often defuse voter resentment through rhetoric, make up for unpopular stances against mass prejudice by taking popular stances on other issues, or simply wait out a mood of prejudice that is fleeting or based on a conspicuous crisis. This will often not be possible, however, and in that case the art of legislation consists in making small concessions to prejudice to forestall larger ones. As the discussion below shall show, Senator Dirksen made precisely such small concessions to racism in passing the 1968 Fair Housing titles, thus winning the necessary votes and preserving his own and several colleagues' political viability. He was right to do so. The legislator's function involves, then, as much room for nobility as the circumstances allow and the legislator's own talents win for him.

[56] Pitkin (1967: 214).
[57] Putnam (1988: 427–60).

SENATORIAL DISPOSITIONS: WEBERIAN PRIDE, DEMOCRATIC SYMPATHY, LEGISLATIVE DEVOTION

These principles lay out starting points, basic ethical considerations, for legislative action. But acting according to good starting-points, good "principles" in the original sense, requires good dispositions. In the case of senators, three main dispositions seem relevant.

First, a salutary *pride* in one's vocation, which is equivalent to love of fame but takes a different aspect when relations to other people (rather than to one's own work) are at issue. Pride gives legislators a resistance to being dependent on powerful interests; a healthy disdain for the small obstacles and insults endemic to politics; and the intellectual honesty that goes with knowledge of difficult technical details. Senatorial pride resembles an aristocratic virtue, and certainly the best senators are not known for underestimating their own importance. But this virtue can have salutary democratic consequences: for instance, it can make senators impatient with corrupt political practices that interfere with the ability to make good policy (though Max Weber's near-dictatorial impatience with political machines is not a democratic instinct).[58] Most important, it renders legislators willing to continue in their job in spite of its requiring moral sacrifices. Weber's famous politician of vocation has no illusions about the compromises, pettiness, bureaucratic annoyances, and indignities involved in the political life, but still manages to keep a sense of nobility: "Here I stand; I can do no other."[59] It is this "sober" yet noble "ethic of responsibility" that motivates politicians to do the work involved, what Weber called the "strong and slow boring of hard boards."[60]

Weber was right in one more way: an excessive attachment to justice is positively detrimental to legislative life. Excessive moralism inhibits the ability to listen to constituents; limits creativity by restricting the kind of argument that legislators will take seriously; offends the public by its shrillness and assumption of superiority; and inhibits the easy tolerance of opposing views that makes it possible to build alliances among other legislators who have their own pride. Not least, it gives legislators a tendency to focus on "clearly moral" issues and neglect the matters of commerce, taxes, regulation, and spending whose moral content is less obvious but whose debate and resolution take up nine-tenths of all legislative business. The problem with excessive moralism is not so much that

---

[58] Once again, the point is formally similar to one made by Fiorina, who at the end of his book on Congress (1989: 78) pins hopes for reform of the political system not on narrowly self-interested behavior by voters or representatives but on a frustrated backlash from representatives who find that a job based on constant huckstering is not worth the effort.

[59] Weber (1946: 127).

[60] Weber (1946: 128). For a contemporary treatment, see Dietz (1994).

it lessens (or, paradoxically, increases) our willingness to use violence, which was Weber's main concern, but that it makes us less able to deal with the prosaic moral complexities and imperfections of ordinary legislative action and the sentiments that drive it.

Second, a senator must have *democratic sympathy*. Like other legislators, he or she should feel discomfort, even pain, when his constituents do. (Nonpolitical sympathy is not required: legislators do not have special duties toward romantic partners or friends, and there is no evidence that extraordinary sentiments in these spheres translate positively into political dispositions.) To "know and sympathise with every part of the community" is a well-known virtue of democratic legislators as described by George Mason,[61] but it is not only politicians who put sympathy first as the sentiment of democratic legislators. Hume used "sympathy" interchangeably with "humanity" and "benevolence" for good reason: the sentiment of sympathy is at least as good an assurance of attachment to the public good as rational commitment to universal principles is. A democratic legislator, disinclined to place herself morally above constituents, does not want to hurt constituents' interests, or even to hurt their feelings by criticizing their deeply held beliefs. An inclination to democratic sympathy is what makes legislators respect popular preferences, listen in a deep and detailed way to popular grievances, and refrain from lecturing or educating the citizens on matters—like most cultural matters—on which senators lack particular expertise. These are all hard tasks that can stick in the craw of politicians who think well of themselves, and the disposition for democratic sympathy should not be underrated as a difficult virtue, deserving of our respect.

A formal "equal respect" for citizens as abstract citizens or moral actors can go along with great contempt for them as concrete individuals with histories, beliefs, and projects of their own. Democratic sympathy rules out such contempt. Democratic sympathy requires that legislators associate their moral beliefs and virtues with those prevalent in a particular polity and social order. Legislators may hope to embody popular values more richly or with greater intelligence than the average person does, but a politician who seeks democratic legitimacy is not entitled to live by his own set of values and look down on those of the public.

Third, senators must display *associational sympathy*, attachment to moral communities that lie between individual love of fame and the "will of the people," and that mediate between them. Few human beings could constantly negotiate and renegotiate the tensions between their fame-based projects and the unstructured opinions of hundreds of thousands of individual constituents; fewer still could do so if they had to add to these

[61] Madison (1987: 39).

claims the capricious demands of ninety-nine senators also walking on eggshells. What enables senators to find their way through these tensions are intermediate allegiances: attachments to the units of state constituency, political party, and senatorial institution that transcend the agendas of individual senators yet ultimately sustain their ability to pursue those agendas. Attachment to local mores, as in Popkin's tamale example, gives senators a feel for their constituents' opinions without their having to talk to each voter. Service to a party links each senator's own deeply felt political goals with those of peers, predecessors, and successors over time, as well as to the general public, who may not understand the specific history of a given legislator. And devotion to the Senate as an institution allows a senator to ignore the din of individual senators' claims and focus on cultivating the enduring qualities that have proven to earn senators respect as a general rule. Devotion to locality, party, and institution make a senator both more likely to be reelected and more likely to be worthy of being re-elected.

Some of the preceding principles are self-explanatory, if far from self-executing, but some will seem vague and compromising, and deserve an initially skeptical response. Can senators really pursue long-term fame and public service if they feel duty-bound always to take voter preferences into account? Is it safe to praise legislators for making minimal concessions to public prejudices, or will this only make them more likely to make larger ones? Is effectiveness really a virtue, especially when it clashes with other virtues?

Addressing these skeptical questions requires examining real politicians and judging real political decisions.

Everett Dirksen: Fame, Ambition, and How to Bargain with Principles

Everett Dirksen, Republican leader of the U.S. Senate from 1959 to his death in 1969, is widely considered one of the greatest legislators of the twentieth century. His qualities were not the public virtues of flamboyant charisma or conspicuous moral righteousness, but the "insider" virtues of hard work, tireless effort, legislative draftsmanship, willingness to compromise, and respect for the values of his state, his party, and the Senate. These legislator's virtues underlay his ability to pursue reformist goals when ideological zeal was not enough: Dirksen's personal efforts among conservative Republicans won for the Civil Rights Act of 1964 and the Open Housing act of 1968 the two-thirds majorities required to end Senate debate.

While Dirksen borrowed from Martin Luther King the line that civil rights was "an idea whose time has come," he could not afford the moral activist's faith that ideas alone win votes. Through bargaining, personal appeals, partial and particularist language, and a dollop of political manipulation, Dirksen won over the conservative senators who were not convinced by principle alone (or who thought the principle of equality was outweighed by the principle of states' rights). Nor were Dirksen's own motivations wholly idealistic: he was motivated by, and freely admitted to, a mixture of principle and political calculation. Insofar as we remember his contribution at all, we tend to eulogize his moral stances. But this gets it precisely wrong: it was in large degree his moral *flexibility*, his ability to know what his own and others' moral positions could be traded for, that won him respect among his peers and may in the end win him fame.

Dirksen's Dispositions and the Senatorial Ethic

PRIDE

The first question asked of all candidates is "Why do you want to be a senator?" (or president, or mayor). This question searches for those who lack Weberian vocation, who would like the office but have no plans for what to achieve in it. But answers to the question can be rhetorical rather than heartfelt: as with all qualities of character, Weberian pride is easy to feign. In Dirksen's case, however, hindsight helps us see his true sense of vocation, by drawing a contrast with his fellow senator Lyndon Johnson. Dirksen complained that Johnson cared about reaching compromises but not about the substance of the bills thus passed. Dirksen, on the other hand, "studied the bills, the committee hearings, and the committee reports, and he knew in detail the matters coming before the Senate." But this did not keep Dirksen from being a master coalition-builder who worked through quiet persuasion where Johnson mostly bullied.[62] No senator outdid Dirksen in hours spent on minutiae and "homework" *and* on the persuasion of fellow senators. Dirksen was devoted to both the tedious process of passing laws one senator at a time and the high art of drafting a country's laws. This is the essence of senatorial pride.

DEMOCRATIC SYMPATHY

Democratic sympathy, like pride in vocation, is a difficult quality to evaluate because every politician claims to have it. (No democratic politician starts a speech by saying, "I am superior to you": even Edmund Burke's famous speech to the electors at Bristol begins with his flattering the electors and professing his deep affection for them.) But in Dirksen's

---

[62] MacNeil (1970: 173–74).

case, the quality is particularly easy to see. Dirksen deliberately cultivated a rumpled appearance and invited cartoonists to draw him as a clown.[63] He made a point of telling homespun stories and jokes adapted to humble audiences, addressing a hardware dealers' convention on the history of tools.[64] Attacked on the campaign trail as a "storyteller" who lacked the dignity to be a senator, he reminded the crowd that it had once sent another storyteller to Congress: Abraham Lincoln.[65] The virtues he prized were the "homely virtues" he had been brought up in: to be "trustworthy, loyal, helpful, friendly, courteous, kind, obedient, cheerful, thrifty, brave, clean, and reverent."[66] Dirksen's biographer describes this philosophy as "lived" rather than something he consciously chose: "He assumed that hard work and diligence would bring any man success, and he never shrank throughout his life from the drudgery of painstaking labor to achieve what he wanted."[67] Dirksen on the campaign trail "carefully shunned the mannerisms of the statesman and even those lesser stylistic gambits of that other aloof creature, the self-satisfied politician": he proudly relied on the same atrocious jokes for decades at a time,[68] and ceaselessly "mouthed the homilies of mid-America."[69] The results were evident in Dirksen's speeches, which embodied a patriotism that some found stirring and others (or often the same people) described as "Steamboat Gothic," "banality," the style of a "cornball actor."[70] Many found Dirksen's style intolerable, but nobody called it arrogant or overweening, because it was not. Dirksen had true democratic sympathy: he wanted to see himself as embodying the values of the common American. If those values were clichés, he was willing to follow.

ASSOCIATIONAL SYMPATHY

Dirksen's motivations were not only democratic but particularistic: they reflected localism,[71] not universalism. Dirksen's work in the Senate was always intelligent, but his motivations were not intellectual. He was

---

[63] MacNeil (1970: 5).

[64] MacNeil (1970: 33; see also 11).

[65] MacNeil (1970: 44). Those who admire Lincoln should note that in his own lifetime he was known not only for the high language of his speeches but for the "low," frontier language of his jokes and anecdotes.

[66] MacNeil (1970: 35). The biographer is quoting the Boy Scout Code.

[67] MacNeil (1970: 39).

[68] MacNeil (1970: 91).

[69] MacNeil (1970: 310).

[70] MacNeil (an admirer of Dirksen) writing on his own behalf (1970: 270), and quoting critics (319, 332).

[71] I follow Popkin (1994: 63–64) in using this word as a shorthand for the particularist commitments mentioned above, a subset of what I call democratic sympathy. My use of the concept may differ from Popkin's in the details.

devoted to three values that might seem from the outside to lack a fully rational justification: the local mores of small-town Illinois, the fortunes of the Republican Party, and the distinctive glory of the United States Senate. These are the kind of mid-level justifications that we may expect from senators. By serving these goals, Dirksen served both himself and his country better than if he had been independent of geography, party, or institutional prejudice.

Dirksen valued "local interests" and once mused that "it would be strange indeed" if the defense of such interests had no place in the give-and-take of legislative negotiation.[72] But his attachment to his own locality was not merely philosophical but visceral. Dirksen was born, the son of German immigrants, in Pekin, Illinois, known as "Beantown" for the crop grown in patches on its north side.[73] Dirksen eulogized Pekin mores: "He had the idea that Pekin and nearby Peoria and the rural world that encompassed them had to themselves an essential goodness and salubriousness hardly to be found elsewhere."[74] As he himself once said in a speech, "Character has a chance. Everything by way of human attribute has a chance for better anchoring, better formulation, in a small town, better than [sic] the hurly-burly of a metropolitan center. . . . All the major decisions of my life have been made here [in Pekin]. This is my native city, where the family taproot goes deep, and it will ever be."[75]

Dirksen's biographer notes that this way of thinking was not to everybody's liking: "To the intellectual or agnostic in Chicago or the East, Dirksen's approach to life might smack of a bumptious Babbitt. He and his kind were foreign to cosmopolitan life, and proud of it."[76] The foreignness is not a requirement in a legislator, but the pride is: it was not necessary for Dirksen to look down on city mores, but it was good for politics that he looked up to those of his own state.

Dirksen's attachment to the rural life was reflected in his response to the "one man, one vote" decisions that diluted rural political power: he attempted to overturn them, with outraged fervor, first through constitutional amendment and then through a state-by-state campaign for a constitutional convention on the issue.[77] In an age of campaigns against activist judges, especially on issues of race and crime, he tried to reverse through amendment only one other constitutional decision: the ban on

---

[72] MacNeil (1970: 173).

[73] Schapsmeier and Schapsmeier (1985: 2).

[74] MacNeil (1970: 34).

[75] Dirksen, quoted by Schapsmeier and Schapsmeier (1985: 7); the two quotations originally came from different sources. One might note a peculiarly American irony: Dirksen, a child of immigrants, said of his home town that his family had "deep" roots there.

[76] MacNeil (1970: 40).

[77] MacNeil (1970: 289–90).

public school prayer, an issue that likewise ran deep among his constituents and his own instinctive set of values.

This unquestioned and somewhat narrow-minded grounding in small-town American values—his "pastoral sense of American traditionalism,"[78] as his biographer puts it—limited Dirksen's contemplative possibilities, but actually widened his persuasive abilities. No one could accuse him of selling out to urban depravity when he endorsed integrated housing, or to cosmopolitan alienness when he supported internationalist foreign policies. And in talking to rock-ribbed "constitutionalist" Republicans like Bourke B. Hickenlooper of Iowa, it simply made a huge difference that Dirksen had the background and values he did: "As a Midwestern conservative himself, [Dirksen knew] he would have to endorse the new product so strongly that some of his colleagues, who were fearful of criticism back home, could lean on him like a crutch."[79]

For a senator to lean on a prominent colleague "like a crutch" is not extremely high-minded—senators should defend their own positions—but it is sometimes necessary, and Dirksen's origins let him be a crutch in a way that, say, liberal Republican Jacob Javits of New York simply could not have done. The point here is not that Dirksen was an "interpretive" moral critic in Michael Walzer's sense: one who, because he speaks within a cultural tradition, is able to persuade people who live their moral lives in that tradition.[80] Dirksen's roots did not exactly make it possible for him to *persuade* others through an appeal to shared values; they provided the *substitute* for such persuasion that politicians, who must face constituents with limited time and knowledge, often need.[81]

Dirksen's Republicanism had roots just as deep. His father was a phenomenal partisan, who named his children after Presidents Harrison and

[78] MacNeil (1970: 264).

[79] Whalen and Whalen (1985: 159). Senator Hickenlooper, a Republican elder statesman with great influence among a crucial block of midwestern conservatives, was an almost dangerously serious believer in limited government. He is described as having "ranted" at one point that the powers of the attorney general under the Civil Rights Act would be "a gargantuan thing" (185, citing *New York Times*, 20 May 1964). His sincerity is evidenced by the obscurity of his constitutional objections: he demanded vociferously a vote on an amendment (defeated 40–56) to "delete the authority of the commissioner of education to finance technical and training assistance in the preparation, adoption, and implementation of school desegregation plans" (195)—an issue on which he presumably felt no organized pressure. Hickenlooper eventually voted for cloture (the cutting off of Senate debate) but against final passage of the civil rights bill.

[80] Walzer (1987).

[81] At least one senator testified that the crutch made the difference. "'I supported civil rights legislation personally,' said J. Caleb Boggs (R-Del.), 'but there was a lot of opposition to the bill in my state. Dirksen was a wonderful leader. He was able to understand our problems and operated in such a way that it made it easier for me to vote for cloture'" (Whalen and Whalen [1985: 202]).

McKinley (Dirksen's middle name), and then–House Speaker Thomas Reed.[82] As a youth in rural Illinois, Dirksen was surrounded by the myth of Lincoln, and when he began making speeches with a view to a political career, his favorite subject was a eulogy to Lincoln in front of American Legion chapters.[83] Normally wary of political labels (especially "conservative," which he thought connoted rigidity), Dirksen was always eager to call himself instead just a "Republican," or at greater length, an "old-fashioned, garden variety of Republican, who believes in the Constitution and the Declaration of Independence, in Abraham Lincoln, who accepts the challenges as they arise from time to time, and who is not unappreciative of the fact that this is a dynamic economy in which we live, and sometimes you have to change your position."[84]

To define "Republican" this way is to make it synonymous with Americanism and reasonableness as such, but not with any more contentious ideology. Dirksen in fact had *more* ideological consistency—particularly on fiscal issues—than this description implies, which makes his insistence on the mere partisan label all the more significant.

Dirksen referred constantly to the duties of the "Republican party" and the "minority party" (he had little patience for "movements," such as Barry Goldwater's fervent conservatism). Much as political scientists once did, Dirksen saw parties as the source of "covenants"—commitments that can be carried out and should be carried out—between legislators and the people. He admitted that he was "a little old-fashioned" on this score in an age when slick Republicans like Willkie regarded promises as mere "campaign oratory." In arguing in support of the atmospheric test-ban treaty in 1963, Dirksen quoted the 1960 party platform's stance in support of nuclear test bans and said,

> That is what my party said to the country. Oh yes, we have a party in this country. I do not subscribe lightly to party platforms. I have served on the platform committee of my party when such solemn words were indited [i.e., composed or set down]. They become lures to get the people into one's corner. There is something grave and solemn about it. I accepted the platform plank in that spirit. We said: "We advocate an early agreement by all nations to forego nuclear tests in the atmosphere." That is what we seek in the treaty today.[85]

Note again the mix of solemnity and realism in this passage. Dirksen appears to be saying that platform promises are lures to get the people's

[82] Schapsmeier and Schapsmeier (1985: 3).
[83] Schapsmeier and Schapsmeier (1985: 15).
[84] Schapsmeier and Schapsmeier (1985: 105).
[85] Quoted by Bauer (1969: 136–37; interpolation mine). It has been claimed that Dirksen actually changed his position on a test ban—from skepticism to support—after finding out that the 1960 Republican platform favored one (MacNeil [1970: 220]).

vote, but are in spite of that—or because of it?—"grave and solemn" statements which, once made as promises to the people, may not be lightly abandoned.

Dirksen changed his position on civil rights for the good of his party, and out of respect for his party's Lincolnian principles. (For the true partisan, there is little difference between interests and principle on such matters. To be a partisan is to assume that the triumph of one's party is a moral good.) In his 1964 civil rights speech, Dirksen approvingly quoted Hoover's description of the Whig Party as one which *died, and deserved to die*, because it "temporized, compromised upon the issue of freedom for the Negro."[86] He thought the same of the Republican Party: "the survival of our party and its ultimate victory" depended on its supporting action on civil rights. If the party did not pursue its fundamental purposes, it had no reason for being. Party allegiance provides moral purposes that transcend individual ambition but are more concrete and present to the imagination than abstract principle, and makes possible electoral and in-stitutional bases for pursuing those purposes. In this way parties ground action inspired by love of fame, and love of party is closely akin to love of fame as a legislative virtue. This is not to deny the ethical worth of action across party lines, but only to stress that such action, when it is necessary, should be called by the politicians' label, not the reformers' one: *bi*parti-san, not *non*partisan.[87]

As for love of the Senate and the office of senator, Dirksen came late to this love but only became a great senator when he found it. Dirksen's early career in the Senate was marked by pompous, exaggerated rhetoric, flip-flops on major foreign policy issues for short-term political motives,[88] support for McCarthy and McCarthyism even after many of his party colleagues had thought better of it, and a generally poor reputation that made him "almost as constant a target of the press as was Senator Mc-Carthy."[89] As a House member, Dirksen had been rated by his peers as

---

[86] Hoover's speech before the 1952 Republican convention, quoted in Everett Dirksen's 1964 speech in favor of the Civil Rights Act (Bauer [1969: 144]).

[87] Also in his great civil rights speech, Dirksen quoted a "great Georgian named Henry W. Grady" in support of the distinction between a "South of slavery and secession" and the new "South of union and freedom" (Bauer [1969: 143]. And when he cited the "living faith of our party"—"all men are created equal"—he did not describe this quotation as being from the Declaration of Independence, or from "those who fought in the American Revo-lution," but said "our party founds its faith in the Declaration of Independence in which a *great Democrat*, Jefferson by name, wrote the flaming words" (144; emphasis added).

[88] There is very good evidence that Dirksen switched his foreign policy position from internationalism to isolationism in order to please the powerful editor of the *Chicago Tri-bune*, Col. McCormick (MacNeil [1970: 86–87]).

[89] MacNeil (1970: 126). Even in his pro-McCarthy phase, Dirksen never went quite as far as McCarthy and avoided McCarthy's groundless accusations of communist sympathy. For

the second "ablest member of the House" for his hard work, knowledge of legislation, persuasive ability, and farsighted attention to matters that had not yet reached a crisis.[90] As a senator, he would eventually gain a similar reputation. So why in the Senate, from his election in 1950 until his reelection in 1956, did his actions, and his fame with them, slip so far?

One of Dirksen's biographers provides a double answer amply supported by the record of Dirksen's political maneuvers. First, Dirksen in the early fifties was looking to become president or vice president, and latched on to figures like Taft and McCarthy largely to this end. After the 1956 Republican convention, however, he realized that he had lost too many battles of maneuver in his party and had lost his real chances for national nomination. Second, Dirksen's convincing reelection in 1956, the attention he was getting from President Eisenhower, and the likelihood that he would become Senate leader made him confident that he could remain in the Senate without having to please extreme allies like Chicago Tribune publisher Col. Robert McCormick. (McCormick had by then also died, in 1955.) He knew that he could have power and influence without being president, and that "that power and influence were the fruit of his office as senator."[91]

> The Senate had been to Dirksen a means to reach ends beyond the Senate. Suddenly, to Dirksen, *the Senate began to appear an end in itself*. This is a mystic phenomenon that in time shapes the understanding of some senators, but not of all senators, by any means. Those who are struck by the mystique of the Senate come to believe that service in the Senate is an ennobling experience, and that service to the Senate is a calling worthy of selfless devotion. Those who sense the Senate in this wise traditionally have been men who have found in the Senate the summit of their own political careers, and Dirksen was now becoming one of them. . . . He worked now, in the late 1950's, on his legislative chores with the same prodigious energy that he had always given his work in Congress.[92]

---

instance, while McCarthy opposed the nomination of Charles "Chip" Bohlen as ambassador to Russia on the grounds that he was disloyal, Dirksen made no such accusations but based his opposition on policy disagreement: he "paraphrased the argument of Senator Bridges that the American people could have no confidence in a man so closely connected with the 'discredited' foreign policies of the Democratic administrations. 'Chip Bohlen was at Yalta.'" (MacNeil [1970: 114]). And Dirksen, ever the party man, opposed McCarthy's attacks on President Eisenhower—whom Dirksen had opposed as the party nominee (Schapsmeier and Schapsmeier [1985: 100]).

[90] MacNeil (1970: 77, and 63–82 passim).

[91] MacNeil (1970: 156).

[92] MacNeil (1970: 156; emphasis added).

Dirksen, whose personal ambition had previously made him (paradoxically) rather subservient to transient party moods (such as isolationism) and bits of popular support, became a good senator when this became not a stepping-stone but a vocation. Attachment to the institution was precondition for acting well as a member of it. Considering this fact as citizens and voters, we might do well to pay more attention to senators known for their "senatorial" virtues, as Dirksen was—and much less to those who have obvious ambitions for higher office.

ACTIONS: CIVIL RIGHTS AND OPEN HOUSING

Dirksen, it must be said, was no particular opponent of the influence of business and the wealthy in politics. This was a violation of the above standard, but should not deter us from the general conclusion: real people are not ideal types. In all other respects, Dirksen's acts revealed the uses of senatorial virtues in pursuing democratic political outcomes. Dirksen respected popular values; listened deeply to constituents and colleagues; persuaded rather than educated; was not too proud to bargain with his principles; cared about results; and was a master of legislative creativity. Dirksen's fights on behalf of the Civil Rights Act of 1964 and the Open Housing Act of 1968 demonstrate the kind of action that such dispositions are conducive to. A look at each will reveal the mix of democratic and fame-based motives that all good senators have—and that the best also understand their fellow senators to have.

Dirksen entered the debate on the Civil Rights Act of 1964 after the equality arguments for it were already well known in the Senate—and had *failed* to win over the two-thirds majority needed to invoke cloture. President Johnson, knowing this was likely, had told Hubert Humphrey that more personally charming and politically rewarding measures would be necessary: "The bill can't pass unless you get Ev Dirksen.... You make up your mind now that you've got to spend time with Ev Dirksen. You've got to let him have a piece of the action. He's got to look good all the time. Don't let those bomb throwers, now, talk you out of seeing Dirksen. You get in there to see Dirksen. You drink with Dirksen! You talk with Dirksen! You listen to Dirksen!"[93]

"Getting Dirksen" did not mean changing his mind on the main issue; he was a long-time proponent of anti–poll-tax and other civil rights measures.[94] But this was not all that was involved in his forming a personal

---

[93] Whalen and Whalen (1985: 148).

[94] The way Dirksen had previously phrased the moral arguments for civil rights to constituents is worth noting. While he would later quote the Declaration of Independence for the record, in a letter to a racist constituent he quoted the *Constitution* and made a democratic rather than a natural-rights argument: "The Constitution Preamble states that the

position, let alone a legislative strategy. Dirksen thought about his situation with Illinois segregationists and decided he could afford to take a tough stance "because he had renewed his credentials with this right-wing element by being an early supporter of Senator Barry M. Goldwater for president."[95] Having thus reassured himself politically, Dirksen told the administration that he supported the Civil Rights Act in principle but was determined, given the legislation's importance, to read it carefully and propose lengthy amendments to improve it.[96] A concern for substance rapidly fused with a concern for strategy. Writing notes on factors favoring cloture, Dirksen jotted down:

1. Faced with log-jam legislation.
2. 1964 an election year. Members will want some time to campaign.
3. July 13, 1964—Republican Convention—Hope it not necessary to dispose of unfinished business after convention.
4. Factor of weariness.
5. Group pressures—emotionalism.[97]

Of five factors the minority leader noted, not one had to do with the substantive merits of the bill: Dirksen had a fine sense of political pressures and humble human weaknesses.

Dirksen's strategy consistently played on both politics and human weakness, weaving into high-minded arguments political reassurances, personal appeals, party loyalty, quid-pro-quo legislative favors, and threats. Speaking to other Republicans, Dirksen "reminded them of past favors he had bestowed upon them, *and* he appealed to their sense of responsibility to try to quiet the gathering storm of racial upheaval in the nation."[98] (On the later Voting Rights Act, Dirksen reduced this appeal to pure personalism on occasion. "This involves more than you," he told one colleague. "It's the party. Don't drop *me* in the mud."[99] Having persuaded Senator Carl Curtis of Nebraska to vote for the bill in spite of being up for reelection, "Dirksen turned immediately to Curtis' Nebraska colleague, Roman Hruska. Hruska, Dirksen argued, could not em-

---

people of the United States do ordain and establish this Constitution. It does not say 'we the people with white skins or brown skins or black skins,' but all of the people" (Schapsmeier and Schapsmeier [1985: 119–20]).

[95] Schapsmeier and Schapsmeier (1985: 160). Goldwater, of course, would later ruin Dirksen's strategy of putting the Republicans on the right side, morally as well as politically, of the civil rights issue. Dirksen would end up pushing Goldwater, who opposed the Civil Rights Act, for president, while writing a pledge of "full implementation and faithful execution" of the act into the party platform (162).

[96] Whalen and Whalen (1985: 155).

[97] Whalen and Whalen (1985: 159).

[98] MacNeil (1970: 237; emphasis added).

[99] MacNeil (1970: 259; emphasis in original).

barrass Curtis by voting against cloture, and that argument worked.")[100] In seeking votes from a variety of regions, Dirksen stressed that thirty-two states had public accommodations or equal employment laws or both, and that the act would create no further burden on these states. He eventually won cloture votes from twenty-four of the twenty-seven Republicans from such states. Finally, the "substitute" amendments Dirksen finally offered (providing that states and localities would be given opportunity to enforce the act before the federal government would be granted jurisdiction) were designed as political cover for conservatives. Dirksen purposely exaggerated their substantive effect: "Because of the divergence in his party, Dirksen lacked the flexibility to effect any significant change in the House-approved bill. To keep peace in both philosophical camps, he had to bring out old H.R. 7152 [the House version of the act] *in disguise*—which, to maintain liberal support, would retain the substance of the original measure, but rewrite it in a way that would assuage the conservatives."[101]

In other words, the purpose of the Dirksen amendments was to mislead the public slightly for noble ends, and the pro–civil rights leadership of both houses welcomed this.

When Dirksen made his final speech in support of the Civil Rights Act, one might have expected it to be a set of platitudes stressing his and other Republicans' noble motives. In fact, Dirksen placed his mix of principled and political reasons in front of the public: he was not ashamed of politics. The speech quoted four reasons for his support of the bill. First, Dirksen spoke of an "idea whose time has come." But by these apparently idealistic words he meant not that the abstract persuasiveness of civil rights had become clear, but that military service and professional education had made blacks "status minded. . . . *They* feel that the time has come for the idea of equal opportunity."[102] This was a political argument as much as a principled one; it was at the very least an appeal to sentiments of esteem for a particular group rather than respect for persons in the abstract. Second, Dirksen spoke of the historical changes in state independence since the Supreme Court had struck down the last Public Accommodations Act in 1883: transportation, the income tax, and the automobile, as well as new state civil rights laws, had nationalized the country. He proceeded to quote Lincoln, of course (twice in a

---

[100] Ibid.

[101] Whalen and Whalen (1985: 186). As the Democratic head of the House Judiciary Committee put it, Dirksen had to enact "a lot of little niggling amendments that really didn't amount to much, so that the bill would come into law as a Dirksen bill and, more importantly, that he would be perceived as pouring the healing salve on the whole controversy. He did that very well" (189).

[102] Bauer (1969: 142; emphasis added).

short speech): this was a specifically Lincolnian argument, targeted right at "constitutionalist" Republicans concerned about states' rights, not just an abstract argument about moral progress (though it was that too).[103] Third, Dirksen called on Republicans to honor the "covenant with the people" that the party had sealed by putting civil rights in the party platform over the years.[104] This was an argument from party commitment, resembling the argument he had made on the test ban.

Finally, Dirksen made a purely moral argument *of a Republican kind*. Dirksen phrased the civil rights issue as one of *"equality of opportunity* in exercising the franchise, in securing an education, in making a livelihood, in enjoying the mantle of protection of the law."[105] Blacks were not to get reparations or substantive equality out of guilt, compassion, or recognition of their deprivation; they deserved instead equal opportunity, because they had developed economic and social status over time and had stood up for that opportunity. And they deserved the protection of the law in pursuing the American Dream like everyone else. This is a conservative theory of rights: rights, many conservatives believe, should be publicly recognized and guaranteed only after they have been earned.[106] These arguments made, Dirksen proceeded to call for cloture on the "substitute measure which is before us"—on his, Dirksen's, personal version of the bill.[107] He won that vote, not only by appealing to fellow senators' moral sense, but by understanding the varied and imperfect ways in which that sense operated, and making sure they had the political space to vote their moral conclusions.

Regarding proposals for Open Housing[108] legislation from 1966 to 1968, Dirksen was somewhat more ambivalent and his position more difficult, but his final decision and legislative style were similar. Dirksen had both constitutional and political reservations about the proposal. He had honestly thought that the Civil Rights Act was a matter of interstate commerce, but he initially believed that Fair Housing legislation had nothing to do with such commerce: he called the latter bill "absolutely unconstitutional."[109] Moreover, Dirksen "did not want to denounce his own constituents as racists" on an issue that presumably exercised the average

---

[103] Bauer (1969: 142–43).
[104] Bauer (1969: 143).
[105] Bauer (1969: 146; emphasis added).
[106] See Rossiter (1963: 26–27, 187).
[107] Bauer (1969: 146).
[108] That is, legislation banning racial discrimination in housing, later called Fair Housing.
[109] "If you can tell me what interstate commerce is involved in selling or renting a house fixed in the soil . . . I'll go out and eat the chimney off the house" (MacNeil [1970: 284]). "Absolutely unconstitutional": *New York Times*, 28 February 1968, p. 35.

Illinois voter far more than desegregation of public facilities in the South had, and he was wary of public alienation on the civil rights issue because of riots and Black Power.[110] Both these considerations—party-principled and political—were shared by many of Dirksen's colleagues, and his strategy, when he finally decided to work for the bill, reflected attention to them.

Chief among the amendments Dirksen introduced as his price for supporting the bill was the so-called "Mrs. Murphy" exemption. Named after the then-stereotype of Irish widows as owner-occupiers of houses, who let out rooms or floors of multi-family dwellings for income, the amendment let such owner-occupiers discriminate on the basis of race *if* they neither rented through a broker nor listed their discriminatory intentions in advertisements. This exemption did not greatly reduce the percentage of housing units available to minorities; by one estimate, the Dirksen amendment meant that 80 instead of 91 percent of the nation's housing units were covered.[111] The amendment was, however, a real concession on principle, for it said that people did not have to rent to blacks if this would require personal interaction in one's home.[112] At the same time, we can note (though Dirksen never defended it this way) that the advertiser and broker provisions did two things. First, without "calling constituents racist," they did send an implicit message that racial prejudice was shameful: those wishing to discriminate were not allowed to do so in the open air of brokerage listings or newspaper advertisements. Second, they minimized the *social* effects of individual prejudice by making sure that neither blacks nor racist whites could tell through brokers or newspaper ads that there were certain areas where blacks and other minorities were not welcome. Discrimination (even in rooms let in single-family dwellings) would be either individual, or if collective, would require a hard-to-implement private conspiracy.

Finally, although the exemption involved few *housing units*, it involved the maximum possible number of *voters*: a thousand single-family homeowners letting out rooms presumably represented at least a thousand voters, while a thousand high-rise units might be owned by only one. Thus, Dirksen's concession to racial prejudice pleased the most voters at the

---

[110] Schapsmeier and Schapsmeier (1985: 185); MacNeil (1970: 285).

[111] Metcalf (1988: 81–82).

[112] In negotiations with Attorney General Ramsey Clark just before crafting his own version of Open Housing legislation, Dirksen thought aloud, "It depends on how all-inclusive you make it, on what you excluded. For instance, if it does not apply to an individual. I have a house, and you want to buy it, and I don't want to sell it to you. That's one situation. When it's handled with brokers and agents—they operate under a license of the state. It's a different picture" (MacNeil [1970: 322–23]). MacNeil unfortunately does not give the source of this quotation.

least social cost; and allowed personal prejudice while letting the prejudiced know that their attitudes were not socially condoned. We have here
a textbook case of how to give some weight to even morally distasteful
voter preferences as they stand, without giving them more influence than
one has to or more respect than they deserve.[113] This is the kind of moral
compromise that good senators make. Dirksen will be remembered as a
senatorial statesman because he furthered Lincoln's principles of equal
opportunity while knowing how to deal with the uglier sentiments that in
his home state and the Senate chamber had votes behind them.

JOSEPH MCCARTHY: THE NEGATION OF SENATORIAL ETHICS

Joseph McCarthy is widely despised, "McCarthyite" used as an insult
barely below "Nazi" in intensity. "Perhaps no other figure in American
history," notes one biographer, "has been portrayed so consistently as the
essence of evil."[114] Without denying that McCarthy was a bad senator,
perhaps the worst of senators, in what follows I shall try to replace hys-
terical denunciation with systematic ethical analysis. McCarthy was not
the essence of evil but a flawed human being, not without real political
talents. Rather than condemning McCarthy for all the excesses of the
political age he lived in, the critic should judge McCarthy based on the
actual things he personally did or failed to do, and the concrete qualities
he displayed or failed to display. Most of all, one should judge McCarthy
not in terms of personal goodness or badness but in terms of his suit-
ability for the senatorial office he coveted and held. I shall even argue
that McCarthy, the disgraceful senator, would have been an excellent
organizer. If this conclusion confounds partisan biases and ideological
categories, so much the better.

Two points should be noted at the start. First, many widely believed
"facts" about McCarthy derive from two polemical biographies written
for political effect: Rovere's *Senator Joe McCarthy*, and Anderson and
May's *McCarthy: The Man, the Senator, the "Ism"*.[115] These books contain

---

[113] One could interpret Dirksen's actions not as concessions to voter anger but as matters
of principle: Dirksen could have been balancing racial equality against the principle of free
personal association. To sharpen the issue, imagine a society where free association and
small numbers of renters did not overlap: where most high-rise, multiunit housing com-
plexes were owner-occupied, and most single-family bungalows were rented out by ab-
sentee landlords, a different landlord for each unit. Then free association would require
exempting high rises but not bungalows, but attention to the largest number of voters
would require exempting bungalows but not high rises. I would submit that Dirksen both
would have and should have favored the latter. I am indebted to Dennis Thompson for
exchanges on this point.

[114] Reeves (1982: 674).

[115] Rovere (1959); Anderson and May (1952).

false details, unsourced accusations, and insupportable claims, some of which have been so widely and uncritically repeated, in books and articles, that they seem "well established." Careful scholars should consult the more recent and careful work of Thomas C. Reeves and David M. Oshinsky.[116]

Second, people often blame McCarthy for the anticommunist movement as a whole (first labeled "McCarthyism" by *Washington Post* cartoonist Herbert Block).[117] This makes little sense. "McCarthyism" as a political and social force—an exaggerated fear of subversion, guilt by association, harassment of communists out of private occupations—can hardly be blamed personally on McCarthy: the phenomenon largely preceded him and included a range of activities by private organizations that he did not control. The House Un-American Activities Committee was founded in 1938 and had gone through many chairmen before McCarthy became interested in the issue; names like Martin Dies and Richard Nixon made antisubversion famous long before McCarthy. As Robert Griffith points out, Dies "named more names in one single year than Joe McCarthy did in a lifetime"—over a thousand in total.[118] Thomas Reeves adds that rhetorical excess in associating opponents with communism was hardly invented by McCarthy: Republican politicians, business leaders, and the Catholic hierarchy had long done so by 1946. In 1950 political speeches, Republicans everywhere—and not just McCarthy in his famous speech at Wheeling, West Virginia—attacked Reds in government; in fact the Wheeling speech borrowed heavily from one by Richard Nixon, though it distorted absurdly Nixon's numbers regarding the number of communists and noncommunists in the world. In 1949–50, McCarthy was far from the leading Republican spokesman on the anticommunism issue.[119] Radical anticommunism is worthy of serious study and ideological debate.[120] The merits or vices of McCarthy as an individual, however, must be distinguished from those of the movement.

[116] Reeves (1982); Oshinsky (1983). Reeves (449) calls the Anderson and May book in particular highly inaccurate and cites several well-documented examples. The doctoral dissertation on which the current work is based unfortunately relied on these early, polemical biographies more than was wise.

[117] Reeves (1982: 267).

[118] Griffith (1970: 32); Reeves (1982: 101, 207). Reeves (209) considers Congressman John Ranking of Mississippi even worse than Dies.

[119] Reeves (1982: 101, 207, 222ff., 198–99). See also Oshinsky (1983: 102, and 85–102 passim).

[120] One common but dubious claim is that McCarthyism represents the dangers always present in "populist" or "mass" political movements. For able and sober criticisms of this line of argument, see Latham (1966) and Rogin (1967). Latham points out that the "mass politics" argument does not explain why an alleged general danger of demagogic or mass politics erupted into McCarthyism when it did, and not at some other time. Latham adopts a more skeptical thesis: McCarthy's rise reflected Republicans' frustration at having lost an

Those who blame McCarthy for the whole policy of anticommunism intentionally or unintentionally obscure a truth they might not like to admit: that anticommunism and a vigorous pursuit of the Cold War was the explicit policy of Democratic and Republican administrations, backed by overwhelming public support, from World War Two at least through the Vietnam era. (Stephen Holmes has not unreasonably called the Cold War "our public philosophy" during this period).[121] To the extent that there might have been advocates of communism in the State Department, it would have been their presence, and not good-faith attempts to find and fire them, that would have represented departures from the country's stated and thoroughly debated policy aims.

It is precisely by focusing on McCarthy, and abstracting from McCarthyism, that we can discern why McCarthy himself seems (rightly) worse than other politicians—even other antisubversive fanatics—of his age. Assume for the sake of argument that McCarthyism as an ideology was *precisely correct*: that the United States in the postwar era was in danger of being destroyed by communism; that communists abounded in all sectors of American life and particularly in the government, to the extent of endangering national security; and that formal legal measures had to be supplemented by public exposure and its attendant social sanctions if this threat was to be stamped out.[122] *Even then*, McCarthy was a very poor senator, because he lacked the pride in vocation to run serious, detailed investigations of communist activity; the democratic sympathy to place his own importance and that of the communist issue in perspective; and the associational sympathy to work well with other senators and his party to pursue effective legislation on national security and foreign policy.

Other legislators hounded witnesses, confused liberalism with procommunism, and encouraged blacklisting of those who would not testify against their friends. But McCarthy did these things without engaging in any independent investigation, without educating himself on the ideology, internal organization, or foreign policy of communist societies, without mentioning information that he knew proved the falseness or irrelevance of his charges, without a serious attempt to direct his inquiry towards the framing of legislation, and—famously—without caring who,

---

election (1948) that they expected to provide a usual rotation of power after sixteen years of Democratic rule. (Latham stresses, however, that the issue of subversion more generally was bipartisan in its leadership, its appeal, and its targets.) Rogin, looking more closely into the social basis of McCarthy's support, likewise stresses the Republican, conservative, and local-elite background of his supporters.

[121] Holmes (1997: 30).

[122] While I do not endorse these hypotheses, one must admit that recent scholarship proves very embarrassing to devoted anti-anticommunists. See in particular Klehr et al. (1995); Tanenhaus (1997); Weinstein (1997); and Radosh and Milton (1997).

or even how many, the alleged threats to national security might be. In other words, his inquiries aimed at exposure for its own sake, not legislative achievements; and he went far beyond what was necessary to assuage the considerable anticommunist sentiment among the public. Even staunch anticommunists, in fact even believers in conscientious efforts in the 1940s and 1950s to purge suspected communists from government posts, should condemn McCarthy's actions and the character flaws that led him to pursue them. Many, from J. Edgar Hoover to Richard Nixon to Whittaker Chambers, in fact did so.[123]

From the perspective of legality or personal morality, McCarthy is guilty of harming innocent individuals; that institutional and judicial mechanisms should have done more to prevent this is as true as it is obvious. From the standpoint of senatorial ethics, however, the more useful lesson is that McCarthy embodied none of the distinctly senatorial dispositions. This is why he engaged in reckless accusations rather than careful investigation, and this is what makes him a model of bad senatorial action. His ultimate betrayal of constituents' interests and constitutional purposes was rooted in his failure to love fame and to pursue the complex links between legislative prowess, democratic popularity, and senatorial respect.

McCarthy's Dispositions and the Senatorial Ethic

AMBITION VS. PRIDE; LOVE OF POWER VS. LOVE OF FAME

It is normally both difficult and dubious to say for sure whether a political figure is driven by ambition (love of power), by love of fame (a desire for esteem based on careful work and real achievements for the public good), or by some of each. McCarthy's career, however, represents a rare case in which the proper conclusion is quite clear. Both his record and the way he himself portrayed it show an unusually naked and unmixed ambition and an unusual disregard for real standards of achievement.

"Cramming" vs. Detail Work   McCarthy had a fine intellect, but it was the intellect of a crammer rather than a careful student, and he was proud of this. He finished four years of high school in a year of frantic work, earning mostly A's,[124] and went through college with similar quick-

---

[123] Reeves (1982: 249, 609); Tanenhaus (1997: 453–55); and see below. The books by Tanenhaus and Klehr et al. (see the previous footnote) do much to rehabilitate the anticommunist issue, but both works condemn McCarthy personally as having done nothing substantive to find communist spies.

[124] Reeves (1982: 9).

study methods, once doing a year's work in a few days.[125] McCarthy had no taste for "reading, study, or contemplation." He "put great store in hasty memorization, shortcuts, and the occasional bluff."[126]

This indifference to detail and careful work led experienced anticommunists to blanch at McCarthy's lack of serious knowledge. When McCarthy first made charges of loyalty whitewashes, what he said about existing loyalty procedures made clear his ignorance or misunderstanding of these procedures.[127] According to Reeves, J. Edgar Hoover, no friend of communism, was furious at McCarthy in 1950 "for his bluffing," his lack of factual knowledge to back his wild claims:

> Those experienced with the struggles of the Far Right were astonished and sometimes amused to learn of McCarthy's ignorance of Communism. At the meeting called by Styles Bridges, Joe revealed that he had never heard of former American Communist party leader Earl Browder. Ed Nellor and Don Suring discovered that the senator was completely unprepared on the subject of domestic subversion. Frank Waldrop of the *Washington Times-Herald* thought Joe a simple man, "an innocent." When the *Chicago Tribune*'s Willard Edwards first met McCarthy that summer he quickly realized that Joe knew virtually nothing about Communist theory, history, or strategy.[128]

This inability to think clearly about details or to plan carefully in advance stands, notes Reeves, in direct contrast to Richard Nixon's methodical, lawyerly style of building anticommunist cases. William F. Buckley, a well-known supporter of McCarthyism as a political movement, would later tell Reeves that McCarthy himself "drove [Buckley] crazy for his lack of intellectual precision."[129] Nor was this lack of precision limited to abstract or intellectual matters: McCarthy lacked the discipline to pursue legislative fact-finding. With the single exception of a housing bill he pursued in his first term,[130] McCarthy almost never attended committee meetings or took interest in legislation unrelated to communism.[131] A senator oriented to real achievement, with pride in her work, will naturally, as a matter of character, seek to investigate facts very carefully, in order to be sure that her differences of opinion with colleagues stem from superior knowledge and insight (or else legitimate differences in

[125] Oshinsky (1983: 12).
[126] Reeves (1982: 18).
[127] Reeves (1982: 241).
[128] Reeves (1982: 249).
[129] Reeves (1982: 401 and 738n63). Reeves (609) claims that Richard Nixon told him "years later" that J. Edgar Hoover came to believe that McCarthy was "impeding the investigation of Communists." But Reeves's documentation for this second-hand opinion is not fully clear.
[130] Reeves (1982: 137ff.).
[131] Oshinsky (1983: 286).

values and constituent interests), rather than just whim or naked opinion. McCarthy was not so oriented, and did not so act. McCarthy's "investigations" produced "names, documents, and statistics—in short, the *appearance* of diligent research."[132] Legislative achievement would have required more substance.

Exposure vs. Legislation Successful legislation, of course, requires more than factual investigation: it requires an honest attempt to effect the crafting of laws, rather than simply publicity or embarrassment of opponents. As the Supreme Court wrote in throwing out a contempt-of-Congress citation in an anticommunism investigation, "No inquiry is an end in itself; it must be related to, and in furtherance of, a legitimate task of the Congress."[133] Here McCarthy again falls short.

William F. Buckley and L. Brent Bozell, in their contemporaneous (1954) defense of McCarthyism, argued that there were real flaws in Truman administration loyalty procedures, and real danger of communist sympathizers' having influence on American foreign policy.[134] They submitted a legislative proposal that, however debatable on the merits, seemed honestly directed toward attacking weaknesses in executive-branch security without unnecessarily harming anyone's reputation. Buckley and Bozell proposed a distinction between "loyalty" and "security" risks so that people whose bad judgment endangered American policy could be fired for such misjudgment, without being tarred as traitors.[135] They proposed getting rid of security risks without fanfare and with language that did not distinguish their cases from those fired for lax work.[136] And they proposed giving those dismissed full financial compensation until they found private-sector jobs at their previous government salary level.[137] Buckley and Bozell gave two reasons for this apparent lenience toward those they saw as communist dupes. First, if a finding of security risk did not imply moral guilt or social and economic punishment, the presumption of innocence and other procedural safeguards could be more easily dispensed with. And second, it is hard to peer into people's

---

[132] Oshinsky (1983: 507).

[133] *Watkins v. United States*, 354 U.S. 178 at 187. For a quite convincing dissent arguing that the investigation in question was in the service of legislation barring communists in unions, see Justice Clark's opinion, *Watkins* at 217ff. But the dissent on the particular case does not impugn the principle.

[134] Buckley and Bozell (1995).

[135] Buckley and Bozell (1995: 251–52).

[136] "The State Department ought to dismiss the security risk and the 'policy misfit' the same way it dismisses an employee who is habitually late for work. And, for public consumption, the Department ought to have a stock phrase covering all separations" (Buckley and Bozell [1995: 256]).

[137] Buckley and Bozell (1995: 260–61).

souls and determine bad motives: "We are better off leaving matters of judgment and retribution to Providence. The function of a security program is to get misfits out of government—not to persecute them."[138]

These defenders of McCarthyism, however, would have had to admit that no part of their proposals was ever part of legislation proposed or pushed by McCarthy. Their defense of McCarthyism relied on assuming a hypothetical legislative program of which McCarthy's investigations *could* have been a responsible part. They never demonstrated that McCarthy himself had these responsible intentions. They conceded that they were defending the communists-in-government issue, not McCarthy's personal character. Their book contained, by a count they did not later contest, sixty-six criticisms of McCarthy's exaggerations.[139]

Since I am concerned here with McCarthy's personal actions and character, it is worth noting uncontested cases in which McCarthy's actions diverge completely from the legislative and moral responsibility advocated by Buckley and Bozell: (1) Buckley and Bozell question whether General Marshall's policies unwittingly helped communism; McCarthy called Marshall's *motives* procommunist.[140] (2) In accusing Judge Dorothy Kenyon of communist sympathies, McCarthy went beyond the evidence of her communist-front memberships and attacked her for "sponsorship of the doctrines and philosophy of this ruthless and godless organization"—something Buckley and Bozell admitted McCarthy "clearly had no business saying."[141] (3) Buckley and Bozell argue strenuously (and against the judgment of other scholars) that some of the people McCarthy alleged to be communists were in fact security risks in the State Department.[142] But McCarthy went beyond this to say he had the names of fifty-seven card-carrying communists, even though the list he was relying on contained no names, the Communist Party had long since recalled its membership cards, and the list contained accounts of unresolved security cases, not direct accusations of communist membership.[143] (4) Owen Lattimore, though not, as McCarthy claimed, a State Department employee, had had some influence on U.S. policy and was, according to Reeves, apparently "a fellow-traveler." But there is no evidence that he

[138] Buckley and Bozell (1995: 257).
[139] Buckley and Bozell (1995: xii-xiii).
[140] Buckley and Bozell (1995: 391).
[141] Buckley and Bozell (1995: 79).
[142] Buckley and Bozell (1995: 74–160). Contrast Reeves (1982: 235–85); and Oshinsky (1983: 115–29). The foreign policy issues involved here are complex, and most people who have ideological opinions for and against McCarthy—myself included—are frankly not well qualified to assess what would be sufficient evidence of communist sympathies to warrant dismissal from foreign policy posts in an age of rapid shifts in policy and strategy.
[143] Buckley and Bozell (1995: 52 and 52n); Reeves (1982: 227–28).

was what McCarthy called him: a Soviet spy and "the top of the whole ring of which Hiss was a part."[144] (5) Edward Rothshild, a bookbinder employed by the Government Printing Office, was according to Reeves's evidence a security risk found by the McCarthy committee. McCarthy, however, called him a spy who had access to hydrogen bomb secrets; there was no evidence of the former and the latter was false.[145] (6) Handed a judicious speech on possible communist influence on the National Labor Relations Board, McCarthy instead delivered a speech asserting "indisputable evidence" that the Board was "honeycombed with members of the Communist Party."[146] (7) Where Buckley and Bozell proposed compensating those fired from government posts until they found private work, McCarthy tried to hound not only documented communists but "Fifth Amendment communists" from private jobs at GE, Allis-Chalmers, Bethlehem Steel, and Westinghouse.[147]

Buckley and Bozell claim that McCarthy had a policy "vocation": to expose lax security practices in the State Department.[148] On the contrary: while they demonstrate such a vocation themselves, every case they cite makes clear that McCarthy's main interest was in exposure, not in any constructive program for changing policy or practices.

Love of fame motivates achievement; ambition motivates the appearance of achievement. Some ambition is necessary if love of fame, with its view to the long term, is not to get a politician defeated in the short term. (McCarthy's first primary opponent, Robert La Follette Jr., lost to McCarthy partly because he was too caught up in a complex and important congressional-reorganization bill to campaign or answer McCarthy's accusations.[149] The junior La Follette was a conscientious reformer and a "senator's senator."[150] His father, who was both a reformer and enough of a democratic campaigner to stay in office, was for this reason a better senator.) But a politician who is merely ambitious cannot be trusted, however clever she may be, to care about any political outcome that requires hard work or that the public is unlikely to notice immediately. Oshinsky, quite sympathetic to the anticommunist movement in general, nevertheless judges McCarthy's character harshly: "Reckless, uncompromising, bored with detail, he was ill-suited for lawmaking."[151]

---

[144] Reeves (1982: 255, 262, 282); Oshinsky (1983: 150–51).

[145] Reeves (1982: 511).

[146] Oshinsky (1983: 110).

[147] Reeves (1982: 525–26).

[148] Buckley and Bozell (1995: 57, 65, 75, 77).

[149] Anderson and May (1952: 96). There is no reason to distrust Anderson and May's account of La Follette's mistakes, since they are in general sympathy with his campaign.

[150] Reeves (1982: 86). Reeves (75) also notes that La Follette rarely visited Wisconsin while in office.

[151] Oshinsky (1983: 174).

DEMOCRATIC SYMPATHY

That McCarthy was populist in tone, and good for a time at winning public support, is not in question. He had the common touch and liked people. But true sympathy with public sentiments, and with the ideals of democracy, requires more than this. There is a kind of leadership, self-proclaimedly democratic but closely associated with fascism, that Hannah Pitkin has called "symbolic representation," under which the leader claims to have superior capabilities to define what the people want. Representation under this account of leadership "may be a matter of consent, but this consent is created by the leader's energy, intelligence, and masterful personality. For the fascist, no other conception is possible, because the people are amorphous and incapable of action or will."[152]

It is historically inaccurate to call McCarthy a fascist: he led no organized movement that would answer to that, nor did he have a developed fascist ideology. McCarthy's personal relationship to his constituents and larger group of followers, however, does resemble a fascist model: instead of taking direction from the variety and depth of popular sentiments, he took it upon himself to mold those sentiments in his image, and fancied himself the single virtuous leader whose burden it was to save the country.

The Prizefighter   McCarthy was prone to portray himself as the only politician capable of defending the nation against its enemies, attributing extraordinary virtues to himself and his causes. A former college boxer and Marine, he used images of combat and violence with abandon: "In virtually every address Joe spoke of his own courage and manliness. 'I will have to blame some of the roughness in fighting the enemy to my training in the Marine Corps,' he told audiences on several occasions. 'We weren't taught to wear lace panties and fight with lace hankies in the Marine Corps.'"[153]

McCarthy did not portray himself as having more knowledge or intelligence than the average American. He portrayed his *will* as qualitatively better: "McCarthyism is Americanism with its sleeves rolled up." "Supporters described him as a 'fighter,' a 'slugger,' a 'battler.'"[154] He proclaimed his unwillingness to fight with "kid gloves." He portrayed himself as a martyr who was being slandered for a one-man commitment to anticommunism.[155] Such claims are not as literally dangerous to democracy as McCarthy's opponents claim—it takes more than one politician to create the conditions for totalitarianism—but they are undemocratic,

[152] Pitkin (1967: 108).
[153] Reeves (1982: 325–26).
[154] Reeves (1982: 326).
[155] Ibid.

and almost certain to be false. In a country with 150 million citizens, it is certainly possible that some are smarter, harder working, or more far-sighted than the rest, but unlikely that only one person has the physical courage to understand and fight a clear foreign enemy. Even if it were barely possible that a leader at a given time could have unique qualities, for the leader *himself* to think so shows a dangerous tendency to despotic self-aggrandizement.

Single Issues vs. Plural Opinions   Oshinsky describes McCarthy in 1952 as the "classic one-issue candidate,"[156] and few would dispute this. Aside from a momentary interest in housing subsidies in his first term, McCarthy took little interest in issues other than communism. Perhaps most striking for a Wisconsin senator, he did not even understand the problems of dairy farmers: mistaking a satirical speech for a real one, he once proposed milk-price supports at 110 percent of the parity price.[157] I have suggested that democratic sympathy motivates listening to the diversity of views among one's constituents with a view to understanding their subtleties and complex roots: McCarthy preferred to use exaggeration and manipulation to make his constituents forget they had more than one concern. Rather than taking public concerns about communism and seeking constructively to address them (President Truman's establishment of an internal loyalty board to examine the executive branch could be placed in this category), McCarthy *fanned* fears to avoid losing on the issues that the people, left to themselves, might have cared about more. If a senator should act most of the time as a kind of advocate, McCarthy was a political ambulance-chaser.

ASSOCIATIONAL SYMPATHY

McCarthy cannot be accused of lacking the first aspect of associational sympathy mentioned above: an attachment to local mores and aspirations. Ever the Wisconsin farm boy made good, he had an inherent knack for speaking to his state's concerns. One could argue that McCarthy's eagerness to arrogate national and international importance displayed an inordinate impatience with the local, but I would not make too

---

[156] Oshinsky (1983: 231).

[157] Reeves (1982: 533). A parity price for an agricultural commodity represents, roughly speaking, the usual purchasing power of that commodity in relation to nonagricultural goods. In subsidy-based agricultural regimes, it is used as a baseline to set agricultural subsidies to farmers in times when prices are low; the farmer generally receives a subsidy that brings the total price to something less than full parity. In 1952 the parity price formula reflected the most recently available ten-year average of relative farm/nonfarm commodity values. A subsidy at 110 percent of parity would mean that dairy farmers would be paid one-tenth *more* than the prevailing (relative) market price, with no particular justification.

much of this argument. Yet McCarthy clearly lacked the other two aspects of associational sympathy: attachment to the Senate, and attachments to party.

McCarthy and the Senate: Calculated Contempt Every new senator needs a little time to adapt to the norms of the place; some remain self-defeatingly stubborn, indifferent to claims of experience, and individualistic throughout their first terms or longer.[158] But McCarthy went to extremes in this respect:

> He was motivated . . . by a need to confront established authority in a way that made *him* the center of attention. Where freshman senators usually seek the favor of influential colleagues with gestures of caution and respect, McCarthy took them on in raucous, often insulting public spectacles. Where freshman senators readily accept the ground rules—the creaking seniority system, the notions of courtesy, formal procedure, and team play—he went it alone, bowing to them when they served his purpose, trampling on them when they did not. Where *all* senators play up their familial attachments or remain discreet about their private lives, he accentuated his vices in ways that offended some colleagues and certainly baffled the rest. While this odd behavior may have aided his early successes, it also isolated him and established his reputation as a renegade. By any standard, his future prospects did not look good.[159]

McCarthy had contempt not just for Senate decorum but for Senate practice where it mattered: the staffing of committees, where policy gets made. He demanded complete power to hire and fire staff on his committee, an unprecedented usurpation of collective committee authority that led to an unprecedented Democratic boycott of the committee in 1953. The journalist William S. White called this "about as grave a step as can be imagined. To lose face in the club that is the Senate is, sometimes, actually to lose all."[160] In the Senate, McCarthy regularly called other senators who criticized him (as well as members of their staffs) liars, crooks, idiots, and, of course, communists.[161] When McCarthy was ultimately censured by the Senate, it was his flouting of Senate rules, not

---

[158] For an account of this, see Fenno (1991b). As Fenno's account makes clear, it is possible for those who ignore or alienate their fellow senators to win reelection—especially in recent times, when Senate norms and party loyalty have declined somewhat—but there is a cost in terms of legislative achievement. By refusing to build coalitions with fellow senators, Senator Arlen Specter guaranteed that the bill he cared about most, one to impose long mandatory federal sentences for "career criminals," would be approved only after many years and in a form that all but eliminated its original goals.

[159] Oshinsky (1983: 71).

[160] Oshinsky (1983: 321, citing William S. White article in *New York Times*, 12 July 1953).

[161] See Reeves (1982: 378–86, and passim).

his unethical statements about individuals, that are generally believed to have guaranteed the outcome.[162]

Perhaps the Senate could be said to have a procedural conception of ethics, and even of truth: senators trust that no clear untruth will survive forever in a context where opposing groups' partisans are seeking the most effective arguments and each party has a clear interest in undermining the other's assertions. Individual misdeeds can, except in flagrant cases where the public is aroused, be forgiven in the service of interparty comity. Whole societies cannot operate this way, but we should also not expect small assemblies whose members must work intimately with one another to punish severely each ethical lapse where milder remedies are possible.

But assaults on the intricate decision structure of committees, staffing, and senatorial privileges are more fundamental. McCarthy, both through his style and through his obsessive interjections, had "impeded the flow of Senate business, and this earned him [by the time of the censure vote] the wrath of many colleagues concerned with legislative achievements."[163] Like it or not, such achievements in the Senate require collective action. The dispositions required of senators must also be conducive to collective action and tested by collective approval.

McCarthy and the Republican Party: Maverick in an Elephant Shop When it came to the good of his party, McCarthy did not care. His actions on this point can be contrasted with Dirksen's in two respects. First, where Dirksen used reverence for the party platform to build a bridge between pledges made to voters in a campaign and actions pursued by senators once elected, McCarthy helped cement the destructive contemporary tendency to treat campaign promises as "mere" rhetoric. Buckley and Bozell attempt to defend some of McCarthy's extreme campaign statements on the grounds that he did not repeat them on the Senate floor. They accuse those who criticize McCarthy's assertions that "communists" or even "known communists" worked in the State Department of using an "irrelevant yardstick." Such charges, they argue, "were not repeated in the Senate and are unrelated to his later performances— for example, before the Tydings Committee. In the Senate speech which occasioned the creation of that Committee, McCarthy did not commit himself to reveal the names of 57 card-carrying Communists presently working in the State Department, but, rather, to present evidence against

[162] Oshinsky (1983: 481).
[163] Reeves (1982: 645).

individuals whose survival of the State Department's security program was a *prima facie* indictment of that program."[164]

This is not a fully accurate account of McCarthy's Senate speeches as a whole, which were somewhat less objective and less measured than Buckley and Bozell suggest. But in any case, Buckley and Bozell's argument proves the opposite of what they intend: if McCarthy's stated intentions in the Senate differed wildly from his rhetorical claims on the stump, this makes McCarthy's actions and character less, not more, ethical than they otherwise would have been.

Buckley and Bozell's argument makes sense only on an aristocratic view of governance, in which elections are a regrettable concession to the rabble and policy is made by the few who can handle the truth about the world. Under any democratic view, however, the people should be told during campaigns a version (necessarily shortened and simplified, to be sure) of what a legislator intends to accomplish. Love of fame differs from love of aristocratic glory in referring ultimately to public, democratic judgment as the standard of achievement. Not everyone has time to follow politics, but Dirksen's use of the platform as a pledge at least enabled activists and interested journalists to hold party leaders to a standard of popular control. To the extent that McCarthy's defenders show that he did not care what he told the public about his actions, they portray him as the very danger to democracy his opponents always claimed he was.

But McCarthy was a danger to his party in a larger sense: he failed to restrain his projects, or even the tone of his projects, for the good of the party. The career of Richard Nixon provides a useful (if perhaps surprising) contrast in this regard. In 1950, McCarthy ignored Nixon's advice to exercise more restraint in his charges.[165] In 1951, Nixon attacked McCarthy implicitly in warning that "indiscriminate name-calling and professional Red-baiting can hurt our cause more than it can help it."[166] Conservative Senate Republicans initially considered McCarthy an asset to the party who could help the GOP head out of the defeat of 1948, but soon after Eisenhower's election, and certainly after the Army-McCarthy hearings,[167] party leaders considered him a distinct liability and tried

---

[164] Buckley and Bozell (1995: 57).

[165] Reeves (1982: 247).

[166] Reeves (1982: 393, quoting *Madison Capital Times*, 24 November 1951).

[167] Buckley and Bozell's book predates the Army-McCarthy hearings. But Buckley, in his 1995 introduction to the book, does not alter his opinion in hindsight. Actually, a reading of the Reeves and Oshinsky biographies makes McCarthy's performance in the Army hearings look less shameful than it was later portrayed, and the Army less virtuous. McCarthy's most blameworthy offenses came much earlier.

without success to muzzle him.[168] It was once again Nixon, then vice president, who (as an administration spokesman who could not be accused of softness against communism) was forced to repudiate McCarthy more or less publicly: "When you go out and shoot rats, you have to shoot straight because when you shoot widely, it not only means that the rats may get away more easily . . . but you might hit someone else who is trying to shoot rats, too. So we have to be fair—for two very good reasons: one, because it is right; and two, because it is the most effective way of doing the job."[169]

Nixon would probably not have minded had McCarthy restricted his wild shots to Democratic "rat-hunters," but when McCarthy started attacking Eisenhower's hunting efforts, that was unforgivable. Nor is this partisan bias on Nixon's part completely indefensible. Interparty attacks may be answered in kind: experienced leaders of national parties are supposed to be able to defend themselves, or should be replaced by others if they cannot. But false, personal attacks *within* a party endanger the only institutions that can link broad majorities in the electorate with responsible policy-making in legislative institutions (of which the president, through the veto power, is a part). Every political party includes factions, policy disputes, even personal hatreds, but a constant leader who seeks legislative achievement must find ways of taming those divisions. Those who cannot should leave their parties, attempt to take them over, or enter politics outside legislative institutions; for inside those institutions, there is little chance that a freelancer will be able to claim real accomplishments.

Where McCarthy's Talents Lay

The above might make it appear as if McCarthy had no good qualities, or at least no politically salutary ones. This would be wrong. McCarthy's success and popularity were based on abilities that are invaluable in politics and not necessarily incompatible with praiseworthy political action. McCarthy was a brilliant conversationalist, if not a close reasoner. He had immense capacity for hard work, great physical energy, and little need for sleep. His self-reliance and toughness were legendary: as a farmer's son, he could easily have remained a high school dropout, but he completed those four years of high school in one hectic year (while working on the side) and worked sixty hours a week while attending college. As a judge McCarthy was not, as sometimes alleged, negligent

---

[168] Oshinsky (1983: 359) cites Arthur Larson as writing that Eisenhower's "'loathing and contempt' for McCarthy had 'to be seen to be believed.'" See also Greenstein (1994).
[169] Nixon speech of 1954 quoted by Oshinsky (1983: 394).

and arbitrary, but had a fine instinctive judgment of the justice of concrete cases (though little knowledge of law). He was garrulous and relentlessly friendly, and had an astounding memory for names and conversations. He was able to separate politics from personal relations, often shocking those he had called procommunist in Senate speeches by greeting them with great friendliness in person. He had a knack for publicity and for the rhythms of the press. And he was a "fabulous" poker player.[170]

These are the qualities of a superb politician—but not a superb legislative politician. McCarthy missed his calling as an organizer. His positive qualities as a person were positive qualities for organizers as well, and some of the qualities that made him a terrible senator—his disdain for authority; instinctive love of the vulgar expression; hard-drinking habits; impatience with book-learning, abstract theory, and detailed policy; and penchant for wild political rhetoric not backed up by sober facts—are often assets for organizers as well. Had he been born one or two decades earlier, or in Milwaukee rather than on a farm seven miles from Appleton, he might have acquired a reputation as legendary as that of John L. Lewis.

This is to stress, once again, the partial nature of each political office, and the plural nature of the ethics appropriate to different offices. One of the tragedies of political ethics has been a tendency to judge actions and characters as simply good or bad without attention to context. And one of the tragedies of a political discourse that relies on such ethics is that people with political drive and ambition grow up thinking that only formal office provides a proper outlet for such ambition—resulting in sad outcomes for themselves, their opponents, and the country.

CONCLUSION

Long and renewable terms for politicians, as we in the United States have for senators, are often thought to promote "professional" politics and professional politicians. So they do. The full implications of treating legislators like professionals, however, are not often noted. Professionals are supposed to have three devotions, in addition to their intellectual qualifications in the profession involved: first, to the wishes of those they serve—clients, patients, and so forth; second, to the standards and ends of the profession—health, the law, generally accepted accounting practices; and third, to their own prestige and well-earned esteem as people who practice their professions as well as their colleagues, or better. Pro-

---

[170] See, respectively, Oshinsky (1983: 302); Oshinsky (1983: 10), Reeves (1982: 5, and passim); Oshinsky (1983: 12); Reeves (1982: 35); Reeves (1982) and Oshinsky (1983, passim); Oshinsky (1983: 15); Reeves (1982: 401); Oshinsky (1983: 188); and Reeves (1982: 46).

fessional ethics, the study of good professional character, calls for professionals who have sentiments of attachment to people, aspirations to further professional ideals and standards, and enough noble self-interest to want to excel at pursuing both. A doctor who lacked the sentiment of attachment would be a sort of monster, animated by no love for patient wishes or welfare; one who lacked the aspiration to good medical standards would be a quack, who might have a certain charm but would be fraudulent as a doctor; one who lacked the desire for prestige or esteem would be professionally lazy: he would want to be a good doctor without keeping up with the journals.[171]

Current schools of political thought implicitly reject considering legislators as professionals. They downplay the sheer skill involved in making policy and crafting legislation well. For the reasons Aristotle mentioned, democratic citizens do not take it for granted that politicians' work is necessary, hard to learn, and not something everyone can master—which is why students of legislative "virtues" must remind us that these things are true. Beyond this, we are often unwilling to acknowledge that legislating requires *all* the professional dispositions: a desire to serve constituents ("clients"),[172] an attachment to professional principles (the public good and constitutional essentials), and the noble desire for advancement and adulation that comes from legislative duties well done (love of fame). Deliberativists tend to ignore the constituent service; populists tend to ignore the aspiration to serve higher principles; and both tend to ignore the fame, which Hamilton placed first.[173]

These differences of opinion are rooted in understandable sentiments. Democratic citizens do not want to admit that they sometimes lose sight of the public good and constitutional requirements and need to be reminded of them. Students of politics and policy do not want to admit that the principle of democracy is that numbers confer the right to rule,

[171] John Adams (1973: No. 5; see also No. 4) notes that scholars would not engage in the difficult and tedious preparations necessary for their work were it not for their sense of "emulation," which he defines as "a desire to excel another, by fair industry in the search of truth, and the practice of virtue."

[172] One difference between the ancients and the moderns is that Plato thought good politicians would be like doctors, looking after the souls of the people and making them better, while we tend to think they should be more like lawyers, protecting people's interests within limits set by the same people in a different capacity. When Madison used a doctor metaphor for politics, the lessons he drew were more liberal and choice-based than Plato's. See Rosen (1996: 580–81).

[173] Medical school interviews do not ask, "Why should there be doctors?" or "Why is medicine important?" but rather, "Why do *you* want to be a doctor?" In the 1996 presidential election, presidential candidate Robert Dole lost political popularity because he could not articulate why he wanted to be president, what he wanted to accomplish. Consideration of fame tells us why this flaw (rightly) mattered.

and that constituents have a legitimate claim to be heard even when politicians would rather not listen. And no one wants to admit that a desire for esteem based on political achievement is a good thing, possibly because students of politics either lack this desire themselves, or if they have it, would rather not be reminded that their positions give them little chance to satisfy it.

Theorists should examine more closely the accommodation among professional duties that theory tells us is necessary and that actually occurs in practice. Senators are quite aware of democratic demands. This is why they rarely act as "morally" as those with few stakes in the matter tell them to, but instead take account of voters' fears, prejudices, and angers. Theorists often regard senators' tendency to do this as a regrettable concession. It is, in fact, an ethical imperative: the first and most fundamental ethical imperative of democratic politics, where the people rule and demand government by consent.

From their side, constituents know what representation means. They know that not every voter, nor even the majority of voters, can get everything desired, for three good reasons: senators know more about some issues than the public and must use their judgment; different constituents have different interests and compromises must be struck; and there are matters of constitutional principle to which momentary public desires must sometimes be sacrificed. These reasons leave ample room for senators to use their intellectual discretion, to validate (quietly and within limits) their feelings of moral superiority, and to engage in the adversarial conflict and collegial deal-making that makes politics so interesting to do and to watch—in short, to win fame in the eyes of their colleagues and the public. Given a chance to evaluate these things, to hear about "stature," "effectiveness," and other legislative virtues, voters often re-elect a senator because of his character even when they disagree with him somewhat on the issues.[174] Here it is political scientists who lack perspective when they lament the end of "accountability" in politics: the people know that the whole polity benefits when legislative skill is valued for its own sake, and when legislators have room to act, without being punished for resisting their own supporters some of the time. People often prefer to elect the kind of person who will resist their wishes for the right reasons than the person who actually follows their wishes more closely. And those who long for the ideologically coherent parties of Europe should remember the disruptions to democracy such parties caused before melting into the issue-poor, catch-all parties seen in Europe today. Constancy, once again, is better for democracy than pure virtue, even an allegedly pure democratic virtue.

[174] See, for example, Fenno (1991a: 170, 190).

Doctors protect our wish to be healthy by giving unpleasant advice; conscientious lawyers protect our interests by telling us when not to sue; and legislators should protect our desires for money, freedom, and other political goods by telling us when, why, and to what extent there are not enough of these goods for us to get all that we demand. And there is little evidence that we citizens will necessarily punish them for doing so, as long as they tell us what is both true and pleasant to hear: that our opinions, not theirs, should set the agenda and serve as the basis for judging their performance.

CHAPTER FIVE

The Moral Activist and the Politics of Public Opinion

"By what means can the government get a hold on mores? I answer that it is by public opinion. If our habits in retirement are born of our own sentiments, in society they are born of others' opinions."

—Rousseau[1]

"While their enemy has brewed beer, they have brewed public opinion; while he distilled whisky, they distilled sentiment; while he rectified spirits, they rectified the spirit that is in man."

—Frances Willard, on women of
the temperance movement[2]

"The early Christians rejoiced when they were deemed worthy to suffer for what they believed. In those days the church was not merely a thermometer that recorded the ideas and principles of public opinion; it was a thermostat that transformed the mores of society. Wherever the early Christians entered a town the power structure got disturbed and immediately sought to convict them for being 'disturbers of the peace' and 'outside agitators.' But they went on with the conviction that they were 'a colony of heaven,' and had to obey God rather than man. They were small in number but big in commitment."

—Martin Luther King Jr.,
"Letter from Birmingham City Jail"[3]

IN CHAPTER 2, I distinguished between two informal offices that have to do with citizen or noninstitutional politics: organizer and moral activist.

---

[1] Rousseau (1989: 67). I shall use "mores" consistently to translate Rousseau's *moeurs*, and shall for the sake of consistency interpolate "mores" into Bloom's translation of this work where Bloom uses the awkward interpolation "morals [habits]."

[2] Willard (1889: 474–75).

[3] Cited in Washington (1991: 300).

Since the two terms are not sharply distinguished in common usage, it is worth explaining why the distinction is worthwhile and what it means.

The activist is a distinctly moral actor—oddly moral from the perspective of democratic constancy theory, which stresses the motivating power of interests and reputational rewards and tends to doubt the power of moral claims as such. But the theory in fact contains good reasons why even the mostly nonaltruistic citizens of a democratic regime long for activists. It also supports principles or rules that govern how activists may act to call a regime back to its principles, and what dispositions activists must have in order to reconcile their vocation with a larger political system that tends toward free-and-easy democratic skepticism toward moral absolutes.

The standard mode of democratic action might be described as the interest-based mode; its basic unit is the group or party, a set of citizens organized to vote, electioneer, demonstrate, strike, or boycott in favor of its interests. Whereas legislators and electoral politicians generally take the distribution of interest groups as given, organizers are those who refuse to do so: they seek to change existing levels of power and existing definitions of interests. An organizer can be intuitively defined, starting from the model of the labor organizer, as one who seeks to bring together large numbers of individually powerless people into coordinated groups that bring concrete pressure on powerful institutions, so as to improve the bargaining position of those organized and win tangible concessions. The next chapter will explore organizing in detail. For the moment, though, it is worth noting what this definition leaves out: a political figure is *not* an organizer if (1) the people she appeals to do not have the resources to bring pressure on the institutions targeted, or (2) she refuses, for reasons of tactics or principle, to concentrate on methods commonly understood as bargaining (i.e., negotiation grounded in threats to use or withdraw power resources).

Many successful reformers and radicals in the United States have shunned the politics of interest in this way, out of necessity or choice. In doing so, they have stepped outside the usual bounds of interest-based politics. They are *moral* activists; they seek to leverage fundamental principles and the moral bases of private life rather than throwing their weight on one side of the interest game. More thoroughly, an activist is *a citizen-politician, not holding formal office, who aims at achieving social change not through pressure tactics but primarily through moral and rhetorical appeals based on principles widely accepted by the political system and its citizens.* The activist appeals to the conscience, rather than the prudence, of those who have the power to bring about change. The qualifier "moral" stresses that such activists are seen by themselves and others as playing a special role, higher than mere persuasion to a personal or partisan point of view. The moral activist seeks not only to make the polity different, or more responsive to those currently powerless, but to make it *morally better*: to recall the citizenry to precious principles—justice, liberty, equality— that it has shamefully neglected. Many people we normally call activists will not be moral activists in the sense used here if their main activity consists in merely telling an interest group (e.g., consumers) about issues that affect its members.

To illustrate the moral activist, I have chosen the figures of Frances Willard and Martin Luther King Jr. Willard, the nineteenth-century pro- hibitionist and moral reformer, was head of the nation's largest organiza- tion of women (the Women's Christian Temperance Union, or WCTU) in an age when women had neither votes nor (if married) control over their own property. Given how few resources women had to bargain with, Willard quite naturally turned to moral appeals, hoping to "bre[w] public opinion" via the "Gatling gun of press, platform, and pulpit."[4] And Martin Luther King, though living in a time in which African-Americans could be with great difficulty organized (and were organized by others) on the basis of their limited voting rights and economic power, con- sciously left such methods to others. He concentrated on increasing pub- lic challenges to segregation and trying to rouse whites' consciences—a "spiritual strategy," as he called it, to complement the NAACP's legal strategy and other groups' political strategies.[5] Moral activists, lacking tangible resources with which to exert pressure, paradoxically are often perceived as having *more* power to effect change, since they lack the bur- den of connection to selfish interests.[6] In fact, democracies, and the

[4] Willard (1889: 436).

[5] Oates (1985: 120). Some of King's contemporaries, especially black student radicals, recognized the difference and criticized him for what they saw as insufficient commitment to organizer strategies. See, for example, Garrow (1988: 424, 441); Lewis (1978: 163, 250– 51); Oates (1985: 189, 299–300). The conflicts between King and the organizing tradition represented by the Student Nonviolent Coordinating Committee became famous when the latter, under Stokely Carmichael, began to reject nonviolence and universal rights in favor of "Black Power." But even before this, organizers had long felt uneasy with King because of his "arrogance," his "bourgeois" bias, and in particular his alleged reliance on personal charisma rather than patient and committed organizational work. Chapter 6 pursues this further.

[6] King's associate Stanley Levison—a former Communist Party member and no starry- eyed idealist—said King was "'one of the exceptional figures who attained the heights of popular confidence and trust without having obligations to any political party or other dominant interests. Seldom has anyone in American history come up by this path.' As a consequence, King had emerged as 'the great moral force in the country today,' an inde-

United States in particular, often revere their moral activists with a devotion they feel toward no other type of political figure. Why should this be?

The desire for activists is inherent in democratic politics (though the specific form it takes in the United States is relative to a particular history). Democracies are based on two principles: rule of the majority, and living as one likes. Majority decision—not an unmotivated procedure but a principle that follows logically from assumptions of equal political power—implies radical tendencies: to enlarge both the scope of activities to which rule of the majority is applied and the range of the population to which equal political power will be extended. Living as one likes, however, implies limits to what is permitted in pursuit of those tendencies. Democrats do not like to be dictated to, even in the name of more democracy.

The resulting tension has concerned all theorists of liberal democracy, a political system based on both majoritarianism and individualism. Thus Madison worried that majority factions would exert despotic power over minorities in the service of egalitarian measures like abolition of debts, and Tocqueville worried that American democrats would value equality more consistently and strongly than they valued liberty—a problem affecting all of public and social life, of which the "tyranny of the majority" was only one narrow manifestation.[7]

Though the tension between liberty and majoritarian equality is familiar, one consequence is less familiar: the desire to transcend this tension leads democrats to look for moral activists. Democratic citizens hope for activists who will advance democracy by voluntary means: not by making us live in ways we do not like but by making us come to like the (more democratic) ways in which we ought to live. The moral activist, not commanding the means of coercion, operates through *public opinion*. He or she embodies a *liberal* form of the democratic reform impulse. While an authoritarian democrat wants to enact majority opinions into laws, backed by punishments, a more moderate democrat prefers to rely on opinion, which injures no one and which the determined nonconformist is free to ignore. In a phrase made famous by political scientist Samuel P. Huntington, student leader Mel Levine told a commencement audience in 1969 that the actions of radical students embodied "our practice of your principles."[8] Note the rhetorical assumptions of the phrase: the activist does not claim a license to impose *new* principles on the listeners,

---

pendent leader utterly devoid of the taint of power and political ambition" (quoted by Oates [1985: 355]; interpolated summary Oates's).

[7] *Federalist*: No. 10; Tocqueville, *DIA*: II.2.1, pp. 503–6; *DIA*: I.2.7, pp. 246–61.

[8] Huntington (1981: 3).

nor even to question their old ones, but only to practice what the audience already believes. In this way, the activist's characteristic appeal is to guilt, and the activist's characteristic mode of speaking is not philosophical but rhetorical: he starts from the audience's premises, not his own.

Public opinion, then, both embodies a rational reform impulse and frustrates more radical attempts to legislate personal conduct. This paradox was a central concern of Rousseau, perhaps the first theorist to speak of "public opinion" as such and perhaps both the first and last to discuss the "instruments proper to direction of public opinion" as deliberate political tools notable for their liberality (though this is not Rousseau's word).[9] Public opinion can be called liberal both in its methods—"neither laws nor punishments nor any sort of coercive means"[10]—and in its ends, which as far as the magistrate is concerned concern not "man's perfection" but "only the good of the state insofar as it can be attained," not the judgment of individual moral merit (too great a power to give to magistrates) but the judgment of service to the State.[11] Following Aristotle and Thomas Aquinas, Rousseau argued that the laws cannot end all disorders and should not try to act without regard to the state of society and its vices: "For without remedying the evil, this degrades the laws too."[12]

Rousseau did not dogmatically assert liberal exceptions to democratic principles. He did not believe natural rights were retained in the civil state, and he believed that the sovereign had the right to do anything it saw necessary for the public good, and to judge for itself the necessity.[13] But he was determined to combine this radical theory of legitimacy with a wise doctrine of political possibilities and a prudent regard for the dangers of tyranny. (We might say he described the self-interest of democratic activists, properly understood.) Rousseau, of course, stressed the limits of purposeful appeals to public opinion, and the stubborn persistence of existing mores in the face even of justified moral appeals. Since the Tocquevillean theory of democratic activism is a response to Rousseau, it is worth going through the latter's argument in some detail. Briefly, Rousseau neglected the possibilities of moral activism because he was too enamored of unitary sovereignty: he assumed that moral reform had to come from a sovereign state or else a lawgiver, when in fact (as Tocqueville saw) it can only work if the activist is a product of voluntary civil society.

[9] Habermas (1992: 93) speaks of Rousseau as the first French thinker to write of *opinion publique*, though he attributes a similar meaning to the earlier English "public spirit."
[10] Rousseau (1989: 67).
[11] Rousseau (1989: 109); Rousseau (1964: 228).
[12] Rousseau (1989: 66).
[13] Rousseau (1978: II.4, p. 62).

ROUSSEAU: PUBLIC OPINION, MORES, AND LAW

In his writings on public opinion (scattered throughout several works) Rousseau occasionally speaks of opinion, along with mores and customs, as a kind of law, "which is not engraved on marble or bronze, but in the hearts of the citizens; which is the true constitution of the State."[14] In speaking of opinion as a kind of law, Rousseau is being metaphorical. Public opinion is not, as Rousseau thought legitimate laws had to be, created by the general will. Nor is its object the general will, since mores, which public opinion concerns, are synonymous not with general but with *"private* wills."[15] Rousseau calls public opinion a kind of law only to emphasize that it, like law, induces people to act a certain way and (in a sense) punishes them when they do not.

The mechanisms by which opinion does this, Rousseau stresses, are informal (or social), not formal (or juristic). The magistrate, says Rousseau in the *Second Discourse*, "is judge only of rigorous right; but the people are the true judges of mores."[16] This doctrine can have liberal effects. It is grounded, however, not in liberal principle but in prudence. Rousseau thinks that public opinion *cannot* be changed by deliberate political action of constituted authorities. (Lawgivers can do it, but they are semidivine, and there is never one around when we need one.) "Neither reason, nor virtue, nor laws will vanquish public opinion," says Rousseau, "so long as the art of changing it has not been found." But even this "art" is not easy to discover or employ: "Opinion, queen of the world, is not subject to the power of kings; they are themselves, her first slaves." Discussing a French administration's attempt to ban dueling through law, Rousseau concludes that the regime paid the price for not respecting the limits of its power when dealing with opinion: "For having wanted to mix force and laws in matters of prejudice and change the point of honor by violence, the royal authority has been compromised and laws which went beyond their power have been rendered contemptible."[17] Rousseau maintains that *chance* is the only thing that changes "public opinions," and even writes that "all that human wisdom can do is to *forestall changes*, to

---

[14] Rousseau (1978: II.12, p. 77).

[15] Rousseau (1978: III.1, p. 80; emphasis added). Habermas (1992: 97) seems mistaken on this point, as he identifies public opinion with the general will and claims that Rousseau regarded it as sovereign. This reading is not supported by Rousseau's work, especially since Rousseau himself (1978: IV.12, p. 123) explicitly contrasts the scope of public opinion with that of laws determined by the general will.

[16] Rousseau (1964: 228). The translator here uses "morals" to translate *moeurs*; I have changed it to "mores."

[17] Rousseau (1989: 69, 74, 73).

arrest from afar all that brings them on."[18] "Once customs are established and prejudices have taken root," he says in a similar vein in the *Social Contract*, "it is a dangerous and foolhardy undertaking to want to reform them."[19] Finally, in a passage that may seem question-begging, he asserts that "matters of mores and universal justice are not arranged, as are those of private justice and strict right, by edicts and laws; *or, if sometimes the laws influence mores, it is when the laws draw their force from them.*"[20]

These statements, though many-sided, are not contradictory. Through them runs a common doctrine: that mores, customs, and opinions are very *durable*, that astute magistrates can enlist them in the service of preserving the State as it is but cannot easily remake them for other purposes. The reasons for this are fundamental: public opinion, founded on traditions, prejudices, and common beliefs, can be conquered by "neither reason, nor virtue, nor laws." We might conclude that the legislator or citizen who relies on public opinion is relying on a truly intractable force: unreasonable, beyond virtue, extralegal.[21]

So to understand what Rousseau writes about political action based on public opinion, we must explore his accounts of the various political actors who successfully or unsuccessfully seek to appeal to public opinion: to change or build on social mores; to change custom through laws; or to reform laws through movements that build on custom. Rousseau gives strong reasons for activists to take up roles that preserve public opinion and mores rather than trying to revolutionize them. These roles include the tribune, who seeks a reform of current laws in the name of ancient principles, and the minister, who pursues the creative use of existing mores through appeals to the guilt, pride, and fellow-feeling of those who want to act a certain way but sometimes fall short.

The activist is best seen as a combination of these two roles: a demo-

---

[18] Rousseau (1989: 74; emphasis added).

[19] Rousseau (1978: II.8, p. 70).

[20] Rousseau (1989: 66; emphasis added, and I have substituted "mores" for Bloom's "morals [manners]").

[21] Habermas writes as if Rousseau, by identifying "public opinion" with the kind of private "opinion" that is akin to prejudice, had made a kind of historical blunder, had failed to discover public opinion in the "strict meaning of an opinion purified through critical discussion in the public sphere to constitute a true opinion" (1992: 95; see also 93, and on the "strict" meaning, 220, 241, 248). In fact, Rousseau is not ignoring the latter concept but denying its existence: public discussion is *not*, given people as they are, "critical" in the sense of reasoned, high-minded, or productive of a conclusion whose legitimacy is beyond reproach. The public—this is true of all publics—can have no standard for judging actions or arguments that is free of prejudice, and it is foolish to expect one. We cannot expose the actions of public figures or anyone else to public view for rational discussion without exposing them to irrational discussion—scandal, prejudiced moral denunciations, well- or ill-founded hero-worship, and so on—as well.

cratic tribune whose license to act as a tribune stems from her role as a minister. Moral radicals, who in spite of widespread resentment seek to use the powers of formal public office to coerce private behavior, are rightly criticized on Rousseauian grounds for ignoring the stubbornness of human habits, the limits of political coercion, and people's natural resistance to self-appointed authorities over their private lives. For Rousseau (as Judith Shklar has noted), authority is in tension not primarily with liberty (since Rousseau thinks the right authority makes us *freer* than before) but with principles of political equality that resist moral claims based on power and hierarchy. It is this tension, a democratic tension, that moral activists must negotiate.

The Tribune

When the word "tribune" occurs in popular usage, it generally refers to a kind of populist: more specifically, a voice of the masses, protesting against injustices that would otherwise be ignored by an uncaring elite. In this usage, a tribune expresses anger at the inequalities of an overly aristocratic political order, and tries to fight those inequalities. A tribune, though self-chosen and having no weapon other than public opinion, aims to affect a policy or range of policies directly, forcefully, and in a democratic direction.

This usage of "tribune" is actually a sort of compromise between two canonical treatments of the office. Machiavelli describes the tribunes of ancient Rome as fairly straightforwardly democratic officers with a power over policy equal (at least formally) to that of the Senate. The addition of the tribunate to the institutions of Rome, he claims, made what was previously an exclusively aristocratic regime more democratic and therefore better balanced.[22] Rousseau, on the other hand, characterizes the tribunate as neither part of government nor distinctively democratic. In general, he claims a tribunate can be instituted to defend the government *or* the people, or to balance each against the other, depending on the situation.[23] Rousseau describes the tribunes as not really a government office at all: the tribunate is a "special magistracy," "not a constituent part of the city," but instead a "preserver of the laws and the legislative power." A tribunate must restrict itself to this defensive and hortatory role of pointing out dangers to the laws and institutions rather than a policy or governmental role of making or enforcing laws. It "degenerates into tyr-

---

[22] Machiavelli (1950: Book 1, chapters 3 and 4).

[23] Rousseau (1978: IV.5, p. 120). Machiavelli (1950: 118) writes of the tribunate as a "powerful barrier between the Senate and the people" but tends in general to treat the tribunes as representing popular or democratic power.

anny when it usurps the executive power, of which it is only the moderator, and when it wants to dispense laws, which it should only protect."[24]

As a matter of history, Machiavelli's picture more accurately represents the ideology of Rome, with its "Senate and People" motto, and Rousseau's more accurately represents the realities of a Roman government in which the tribunes were artfully kept weak and divided, unable to exercise the direct governing power to which they were nominally entitled.[25] In any case, Rousseau's version of tribunal power is more useful to an unmixed republic with no aristocratic bodies and therefore no need to balance them democratically. (In the United States and other democracies, the people's direct interests and grievances are reflected in a democratically elected lower house, not in a tribunate.) The activist as democratic tribune naturally and rightly gravitates toward a role which stresses those elements of politics persistently ignored by the political process. She therefore speaks of the fundamental principles *underlying* the laws and the legal system, as opposed to the everyday forces and actions that determine the making and enforcement of law. The latter largely (and for the most part, rightly) involve the wielding of power and the brokering of interests.

Democracies that stress Benthamite, Hobbesian, or pragmatic doctrines of politics, whereby political right consists of sovereign action by the people in the present, may find little of relevance in the Roman office of tribune. For that office relied on the assumption that ancient laws and practices were best. Americans, however, tend to believe in a set of old and enduring political principles, those recognized in the Founding era. In American political argument—this is perhaps true of any "radical" polity that stresses its double origin in revolution and constitutional founding[26]—the Roman question "Is it the custom of our ancestors?" has weight. Such a politics has room for tribunes.

As Huntington has noted, American political conflict is popularly expressed (whatever its inner essence or substructure) not as a conflict among ideals but as an "ideas vs. institutions gap." This is a gap between universally held ideals of liberty and equality and the inability or unwillingness of current leaders and institutions to live up to those ideals.[27]

---

[24] Rousseau (1978: IV.5, p. 120).

[25] But see Machiavelli (1950: Book 1, chapters 47 and 48). Machiavelli often seems to portray history in different ways in different places to illustrate different theoretical points. This is not a problem as long as our object is theoretical insight rather than interpretive accuracy, and as long as we know what is going on.

[26] Arendt (1965).

[27] Huntington (1981: 10–12, and passim). Huntington does not endorse this tendency of American political argument: he regards it as a throwback to "Tudor" principles of natural rights and limited government that other democracies have rightly replaced with theories of

Sacvan Bercovitch has pointed out the links between this political style of political argument—which looks forward by looking backward—and the prophetic speech or jeremiad. In the typical form of the political jeremiad, a speaker reminds us that America was founded as a shining "City on a Hill" and can be so again, but only if we turn away from our current state of immorality and rededicate ourselves to our exceptional moral principles.[28]

This prophetic tradition in American political discourse consistently surprises and disturbs secular political commentators, not least because the homiletic method—deduction from authoritative biblical premises, most effectively conveyed through oral narratives—violates all the rules of Western philosophy and secular moral argument.[29] But to moral activists it is all but second nature and naturally appears side-by-side with, or even mixed in with, the secular political rhetorics of rights and constitutional tradition. Not distinctly sacred or otherworldly in character, such rhetoric is a basic element of the tribune's *political* appeal. Martin Luther King quoted Amos, Isaiah, and other biblical authorities at least as often as the Declaration of Independence, often in the same speech or same sentence.[30] As Branch notes, "To Americans grown weary of singsong slogans and campaign speeches, it was strange or even blasphemous to put the humdrum workings of democracy on a par with belief in God, but from the slave side of history they were comparable wonders."[31]

Both the moral authority and the political effectiveness of the tribunal activist are historically relative: in calling the laws and legislators to ancient principles, the activist must realize that only *certain* principles lend themselves to such uncompromising appeals. Which these are depends on the particular traditions of a given polity. As mentioned in chapter 2, this is a point in rhetoric and democratic ethics, not metaphysics. There may be universal moral principles, but a direct appeal to those principles that does not respect the convictions of those appealed to is neither politically effective nor respectful of the hearers' status as fellow citizens who have opinions of their own and are likely to regard *them* as univer-

---

state sovereignty (Huntington [1968: chapter 2]). But he recognizes the force of such appeals as a fact.

[28] Bercovitch (1978). Bercovitch does not like this form of American rhetoric any more than Huntington likes the secular form, but notes the persistence of the jeremiad tradition and doubts it is likely to go away. For a more sympathetic (and very influential) treatment, see Bellah (1992), itself a self-proclaimed jeremiad (xi).

[29] See Miller (1992: 112–17).

[30] Among other examples too numerous to list, see Martin Luther King, "I Have a Dream," in Washington (1991: 219, quoting Amos and Isaiah); the examples quoted by Branch (1988: 141, 215, 275, 843); and Miller (1992 passim).

[31] Branch (1998: 48).

sally valid. Jane Mansbridge wisely describes the essence of activism not as a discovery (or imposition) of new principles but as a kind of self-binding in the service of old ones: "The only way to get the public to pass what amounts to a self-denying ordinance is to stress the principle involved in an amendment rather than the specific substantive ways it would prevent the majority from doing what it wants to do."[32]

Not every principle of abstract right is credibly called a foundation of the constitutional order, and not every piece of biblical wisdom is widely accepted by the civil-religious but not theologically dogmatic temperament of American citizens. The constitutional and prophetic traditions are there to be called upon by the tribune to the extent that they resonate more broadly. Conservatives have foundered when they sought to define "constitutionalism" by fetishizing particular grants of power (such as the Second Amendment, which guarantees the right to bear arms) that are currently unpopular and have no special grounding in deeper principles. And radicals drawing on religion are mistaken when they hope to find in the American attachment to prophecy and "City on a Hill" aspirations an opening for utopian socialism and the brotherhood of humankind. King is to be congratulated, as we shall see, to the extent that he did not take rhetoric of the latter kind too seriously.

More concretely: an unmixed democratic republic, I have argued, will not support for long a program or a rhetoric too far removed from the goal of equal pursuit of interest. Stable democratic politics aims at ordered liberty and the managed pursuit of interest. Even in the United States, the most religious of the mature democracies, the Puritan "City on the Hill" ideal is now modest and bourgeois: even religious Americans aspire to membership in a city of sober churchgoers with their humble vocations, not a city of crusaders or saints.

The special force of the civil rights movement came from its simple pleas to let blacks pursue their interests in private life, and vote their interests in public life, just as whites did. (As I shall document, even King's appeals were more mundane, even mercantile, than is commonly remembered.) This is a force that could be matched by other movements for equal rights, but not by just any movement. When Frances Willard tried to prove that drinking alcohol was foreign to Christianity, she failed not only as a theologian but as an interpreter of what was essential in American moral and religious aspirations. The first task of a good tribune is to understand the constitutional and moral traditions embedded in the polity. An American tribune will therefore aim at reform rather than revolution; the inspiration of political choices by religion or organized moral action rather than the replacement of political principles by

[32] Mansbridge (1986: 35).

religious ones; action within democratic political institutions rather than in disregard of them. King recognized and practiced these distinctions; Willard did not. As King's example should show, one can be fairly radical in aspiration while remaining within a consensus on principles. If the tribune role is in a sense conservative, it replicates the familiar paradox of the American conservative who finds that all the principles traditional to his country are radical ones.

The Minister

Although it contains a well-known doctrine of "civil religion," Rousseau's account of what the clergy as concrete individuals should do in order best to serve the polity is fragmentary and hard to interpret. The civil religion, to start out with, is not an organized religion in the usual sense but a list of basic moral and theologically minimalist doctrines to which given religions must subscribe in order to deserve toleration.[33] Such "religion" tells us nothing about the nature and proper behavior of any clergy. Moreover, Rousseau's account of religious doctrines in the *Social Contract* addresses ancient civil religion, Roman Catholicism, and an ideal gospel Christianity, but leaves out the religion most familiar to him as a citizen of Geneva (and also most prominent in the United States): reformed Christianity, with its ministers who preached and (sometimes) practiced austerity and personal morality.[34]

That Rousseau might regard this last kind of religion as politically salutary is suggested by his criticism of d'Alembert, more specifically by what he does *not* criticize. Rousseau attacks d'Alembert for attributing to the Geneva clergy theological doctrines they do not profess (D'Alembert's article in the *Encyclopedie* has described them as Socinians who scarcely believe in the Trinity or Hell), but does not dispute d'Alembert's account of their mores ("exemplary"), their simple church structures, their toleration, and their hatred of superstition. Most important, Rousseau does not contest d'Alembert for saying that the ministers "do what is even better than being tolerant; they limit themselves strictly to their duties in being the first to give to the citizens the example of submission to the laws. The consistory, established to watch over mores, *administers only spiritual punishments*. The great quarrel between the priesthood and the state, which in ages of ignorance shook the crowns of so many emperors in enlightened ages, is not known in Geneva; the clergy does nothing without the approval of the magistrates."[35]

---

[33] Rousseau (1978: IV.8, pp. 130–32).

[34] Rousseau (1978: IV.8, pp. 124–30). The contrast is noted by Cranston (1997: 77).

[35] Jean le Rond d'Alembert, "Geneva," from the *Encyclopedie*, trans. Allan Bloom as appendix to Rousseau (1989), emphasis added.

Beyond refusing to criticize d'Alembert's description, Rousseau seems to endorse its thrust. He writes that "everything which is bad in morality is also bad in politics. But the preacher stops at personal evil, the magistrate sees only the public consequences; the former has as his object only man's perfection, to which man never attains; the latter only the good of the state insofar as it can be attained."[36] Rousseau's main point in this passage concerns the limits of the laws, but the limits of the preacher's role are also implied: ministers should concentrate only on personal evils and personal perfection, leaving distinctly civil concerns to civil magistrates. This does not mean that ministers must always be as apolitical as Genevan ministers; if this were the case, ministers could hardly be a kind of activist, as I am claiming. Rather, the political concerns of ministers must be of an indirect character, as the antidemocratic word "perfection" implies. The minister, not being a governmental or coercive entity, is free to regard politics and ethics as Aristotle did, as two components of a single effort directed at perfection of character. (Citizens who abhor such a view are free not to consult ministers.) Narrower police powers, looking after the safety of citizens while abstracting from their perfection, are the province of civil authorities. This is not to deny the reach or radicalism of what Genevan ministers did. As Michael Walzer has pointed out, the Genevan ministers had used Calvinist theology to invent nothing less than a new "office" that "involved the duty of moral censure," and "it was surely not difficult to see that the denunciation of kings by prophets and ministers was a political matter." Calvinist exiles in Geneva took this model of a "new office," based on Old Testament prophecy, back with them to Civil War–era England.[37] Their Puritan descendants brought it over to the New World in founding new cities, striving toward sainthood.

The idea that religious doctrines of the soul's perfection should be separated from public police power implies a Lockean view of the scope of the ministerial office. Religions are voluntary organizations separate from the government, and ministers derive their powers from the consent of their flock. The authority of a minister, and the possible scope of her moral arguments, should therefore be thought of as linked to her status in a particular religious/moral[38] congregation—not by virtue of

---

[36] Rousseau (1989: 109).

[37] Walzer (1965: 63, 98).

[38] I am using the word "minister" as shorthand for a general phenomenon of moral leadership. The theory fully allows for ministers who are not *religious* in the usual sense, who do not believe in a supernatural being or order. Any group of people that exists for moral purposes and appoints one or more persons to counsel members and look after their character is included here. Even some scholarly groups and their teachers would count, as would sufficiently intense philosophic communities such as those of Epictetus (see Nussbaum [1994: chapter 4]). Thomas Schelling, as noted in chapter 2, mentions "religious and fraternal" groups in this context. Social movements and political parties of a certain

metaphysical reasons having to do with which arguments are available within which narratives,[39] but by virtue of liberal, political reasons involving consent, trust, and enlightened self-interest. We let preachers preach at us sternly because we know we could leave if we found it too much. (For the same reason, if we belong to a church or moral society, it is probably one we find tolerable.)

As Tocqueville noted, this provides inherent limits on how stringent preachers can make their moral commands, lest they lose a flock that is still mostly worldly.[40] The people we trust to look after our true good are those whom we know, and to whom we have entrusted part of our moral life; from such people we allow much more moral scolding than we would ever tolerate from unknown and self-proclaimed moral saviors (including politicians). We seek, or some of us seek, moral communities and religious leaders to the extent that we suspect that our moral powers fall short of our moral aspirations—that we do not always act as well as we would like to upon reflection—and want someone to call us into line when this happens. What we seek from ministers is again a kind of increased constancy, voluntary in its basis though interventionist in its methods. Walzer has described the role of the Puritan church in similar terms—congregants "examined and admonished one another . . . in a close system of collective watchfulness"[41]—and Gerald Suttles has described a contemporary urban church as "a common establishment where a continuing group of people waive their individuality in favor of their common welfare."[42]

There are corresponding liberal, interest-based reasons for us to be suspicious of those who would preach outside their congregation and denomination. We have not consented to be ruled by clergy in this way; we do not necessarily trust these clergy, who perhaps espouse beliefs we

---

(highly ideological) type might play this role: one thinks of radical feminists, who freely engage in mutual moral criticism, and of various socialist, nationalist, and green political parties. In practice, it is rare for secular political or moral movements to play this role in the United States: virtually all such groups in America are in fact religious in nature, and their leaders are clergy or lay religious leaders of some description. Other types of moral leaders are recognized only among very particular groups, and this limits their effectiveness in the larger society. (If a football coach founds a moral crusade, it had better be one limited to men.) Scholars in the age of W.E.B. DuBois had an important moral standing in American society, no doubt stemming from their vestigial attachment to Victorian and nationalist principles, but that was long ago, and scholars are no longer politically relevant. Similarly artists, writers, and film directors have moral prestige in some countries, but not in the United States.

[39] For arguments to this effect, see MacIntyre (1988); and Gadamer (1994).

[40] DIA: II.1.5, p. 449.

[41] Walzer (1965: 221; see also 53).

[42] Suttles (1968: 42).

hate, to seek our good. And we have no need of self-appointed scolds: not because we seek total moral independence (a bit of a chimera) but because we are capable of appointing our own.[43] As democratic citizens who admit no standing superiors, we would rather live badly than be told how to live by those we have not chosen.

John Rawls's account of "public reason"[44] contains an important truth that need not depend on his neo-Kantian arguments: those seeking to persuade the political body as a whole must, morally and pragmatically, appeal to principles that are shared by that body, not to doctrines that seem outlandish to all but believers. Rawls, however, falls short in two ways.

First, Rawls fails to acknowledge Rousseau's and Tocqueville's reasons for seeing a certain kind of religion, including moral preaching, as not only consistent with the moderate liberalism of a constitutional democracy, but a likely *support* for liberalism, through its encouragement of characters able to follow through on plans and coordinate their plans with others. Martin Luther King saw and practiced both the liberal limits and the liberal uses of religion. He used mostly civic principles of justice (and theologically minimalist appeals to the civic American "God") when speaking on civic matters, and more stringent Protestant moral appeals only when preaching to his own congregation. This is why few of secular temperament objected to King's obvious religiosity. It is Frances Willard, who saw the world as her congregation and sought to bring about "Christ's reign on earth," who ended up seeming all but insufferable to those who did not share her unusual moral theology.

Second, Rawls underestimates how hard his standard of public reason is to uphold, largely because he underestimates the amount of cultural

---

[43] This voluntarist account of religious life owes much to Locke's *Letter Concerning Toleration* (1983), whose definition of religion limits, for the sake of liberty and civil peace, the permissible ways of conceiving of religious allegiance. Whatever one thinks of Locke's project on philosophical grounds, it has effectively been accomplished in the United States, where (as Will Herberg [1960: 86] has noted) Catholics and Jews have come to modify or abandon their traditional organic conceptions of Church or People and to recast themselves as Protestant-style "denominations."

This may be considered a dangerously irreverent way of considering our allegiance to clergy; many people regard such an allegiance not as "chosen" voluntarily but as expressing a preexisting conviction that a given group of clergy has insight into divine (or moral) truth. We are not autonomous but "conscientiously encumbered" (Sandel 1996: 65–71). Whatever value Sandel's description might have as an account of how people feel about their own religion or unchosen moral duties, however, it does not rule out a liberty-based account of why we resent the imposition of other people's religious and moral beliefs on us. At least politically speaking, such imposition is an infringement of our civil liberties and expresses contempt for our right of consent—whatever else it might violate and whatever else it might express. I am indebted to Talbot Brewer for discussion on this point.

[44] Rawls (1993: 212–54).

pluralism in the United States, and overestimates the extent to which liberal and reformist religion sees the world the same way that the secular liberalisms of Kant and Mill do.[45] Rawls hopes that the overlap among "reasonable" doctrines in the United States or a similar, constitutional democracy will make it possible for the members of a pluralist order to communicate without insincerity: the members of each religious or cultural subgroup need only stress those (considerable) parts of their beliefs that coincide with those of their fellows, and remain silent on the others.[46] But given that very reasonable people can disagree on points more fundamental than Rawls realizes—as King disagreed with fundamental secular and egalitarian assumptions of "mainstream" America—this is impossible. Moral dialogue across subcultures in fact requires carefully modulated rhetoric, and a degree of insincerity, practiced for the most moral of reasons. For similar reasons Rawls also underestimates the qualities of character needed to engage in successful moral debate. Such qualities are not possessed by every rational citizen but are, in fact, rare: they require the extraordinary restraint and democratic constancy practiced by those like King who make moral appeals day after day—without ever being able to say *exactly* what they think for fear of losing the audience. Moral activism is neither a universal requirement nor a universal possibility, but a *specialized skill* underpinned by an extraordinary type of character.

The office of moral activist combines the roles of tribune and minister. The need for this combination involves what might be called "moral capital." Given that democratic citizens are reluctant to take moral lessons, those seeking to impart such lessons must defend their prerogative to speak. Good moral activists who understand democratic legitimacy do this in two ways. First, they act morally themselves, and in particular, moral with respect to the behavior they preach. King's personal hard work, willingness to face danger, material self-denial, slow, careful speech, and conspicuous lack of personal race hatred earned him a hearing among the white Americans whom he was asking to pay more taxes, upset their everyday social patterns, restrain their prejudices, and grant rights to another race. He was grudgingly allowed to make moral demands largely because he asked others to make fewer sacrifices than he made himself. His personal behavior did not provide the reasons for political change—these came from moral arguments about justice, equality, democracy, and Christian charity—but it provided the license to put forth those reasons and be heeded. Tribunes must therefore practice public rectitude on matters where they make public appeals. Since King did

[45] On this see Leif Wenar's excellent article (1995).
[46] Rawls (1993: 169–71).

not urge Americans to greater chastity, his own sexual exploits were not directly relevant and rumors of them caused little change in his appeal. Willard's casual admission that she herself could be trusted with drink and had regularly drunk wine in Europe[47] was much more serious in this regard, and provided sufficient reason for people to stop listening to her on temperance. Moral activists, then, must restrain their desires in the areas they preach about; this is one sense in which they need constancy.

Second, and more important, democratic tribunes must generally be ministers because it is ministers who can draw on the currency of moral worth in a democracy: numbers. Ministers command the loyalty of groups of ordinary citizens who demonstrate collectively their commitment to a moral cause and their willingness to sacrifice for it. The example of those who belong to such groups gives others reason to think the sacrifice may be possible and justified.

Tocqueville's observations on the temperance movement illustrate how this works. Commenting on a petition he has read in which a hundred thousand people agree to abstain from alcohol, Tocqueville writes that on first seeing it he laughed, and wondered why they did not simply abstain privately. But soon he realized that this public combination transformed "isolated individuals" into "a power *conspicuous* from a distance whose actions *serve as an example*." The hundred thousand, "frightened by the progress of drunkenness around them, wanted to *support sobriety by their patronage*. They were acting in just the same way as some great territorial magnate who dresses very plainly to encourage a contempt of luxury among simple citizens."[48]

This "patronage" of a desired change in mores works on the public opinion of a given regime by associating the new mores with the social force that inspires respect. In an aristocracy, this force is represented by the local lord; in a democracy, moral respect comes from numbers. As Madison writes, "If it be true that all governments rest on opinion, it is no less true that the strength of opinion in each individual, and its practical influence on his conduct, depend much on the number which he supposes to have entertained the same opinion."[49]

Patronage of mores, like patronage of art, means using one's prestige to subsidize a valuable innovation that would not gain an audience on its own. (If the "power" made up of numbers did not speak, the cause would have few listeners.) By getting volunteers to line up behind a proposed change in mores, the tribune obtains democratic patronage for his rhe-

---

[47] Willard (1889: 334).
[48] *DIA*: II.2.5, p. 516; see also I.2.6, p. 242n.
[49] *Federalist*: No. 49; see also Hannah Arendt's (1972b: 140–41) appropriation of this idea.

torical art. The volunteers show by their own practice that the change in mores is possible. They show by their numbers that it is sufficiently easy to be consistent with democracy: that it involves ordinary constancy of purpose rather than a perfectionist standard of virtue.

The minister who induces people to do this leverages popular constancy behind a change in mores. Rousseau, in the example alluded to above, claims that the French state, in trying to ban dueling, erred in applying the force of law. The reform might have worked if it had been done differently: dueling should had been reformed not by the state but by a group of distinguished former soldiers (a "tribunate" or "Court of Honor") whose opinions about honor commanded immediate respect. Such men—to whom even the king must be subject—might have substituted for dueling their own solemn and conspicuous judgments of disgrace and honor—a new, workable set of mores.[50]

Tocqueville's associations provide the equivalent *democratic* solution to exactly the same problem. When a set of mores is too entrenched to be abolished by the state through laws, a respected social power should step in to substitute conspicuously its own alternative. Constancy is thus given a spur from outside without invading the right of conscience: the people in American associations, wrote Tocqueville in a letter, "mutually commit themselves to abstain from a vice and . . . find collective life to be a help to them in resisting what is most private and most peculiar to every man, his own inclinations."[51]

Why must it be a minister (i.e., a leader of a devoted moral community) who builds up this phalanx of volunteers? At most, the idea that moral movements requires ministers as their leaders might seem a contingent truth about the United States rather than a necessary truth about political action—even if "minister" is (again) used broadly to include moral and ideological leaders. But there is a simple reason for linking tribunal success to the ministerial role: moral organization based on numbers cannot have an infinite regress. To take Tocqueville's example again: once a hundred thousand had chosen to proclaim their abstinence from alcohol, this served everywhere as a conspicuous token that the cause must be taken seriously. But how did the first hundred come to take such a pledge, which at the beginning would have seemed quite nonconformist and austere? Such leaps of behavioral faith require the inspiration of a trusted moral leader—a minister, or secular analogue. In the late stages, a democratic moral movement wins listeners through numbers; in the early stages, it must win them through moral authority. (In fact, we know that this is more or less how temperance started: non-

---

[50] Rousseau (1989: 67–73).
[51] Tocqueville, quoted by Jardin (1988: 159).

conformist ministers in Britain, initially the leaders of a minority and persecuted sect, promoted it as the sign of Christian virtue in the midst of a fallen Anglican realm.)

One problem is that a minister does not easily admit that his moral authority is greater among his congregation than in the world at large: that he is the chosen head of a congregation, but merely one respected voice among others in the polity. An activist as minister-tribune must have the drive and spirit to inspire great devotion in voluntary followers, and then the constancy to clamp down on this drive and spirit and speak to a wider public in civic terms that *it* can accept. The tribune in public is not entitled to make all the moral demands that she regards as justified, even God-commanded. Few would-be moral activists have the strength required to live by this constraint: they end up preaching sectarian dogma to a public with neither the inclination nor the obligation to listen.

I have claimed, following Tocqueville, that a democratic polity is best off when the activist uses *moral* appeals for *civic* ends, to foster the character necessary for responsible citizen action and to induce the wider perspective and sense of civic duty needed to sustain such action.[52] In what follows I shall show that these theoretical claims apply in practice: that those we regard as great moral activists have sometimes understood the relation between ministerial and tribunal roles and have managed to fuse them into one political role that embodies the best of both. Martin Luther King, I will argue, used his fine sense of American principles to limit the practical scope of what might otherwise have been uncompromising, perfectionist, and highly annoying moral appeals. (He freely and properly made such appeals when addressing particular religious or racial audiences.) And he used his sense of hope and moral duty drawn from Christian traditions—liberal Protestant theology on the one hand, and the more distinctively black prophetic tradition on the other—to lend urgency to the tribunal appeal: to demand that American democratic and liberal principles be taken with full seriousness, rather than acknowledged but then ignored with a cynical chuckle. On the level of social practice, he appealed to American principles to demand that blacks be given rights and economic opportunity, and remained rooted in Protestant principles and mores so as to reassure whites and blacks alike that these rights would be exercised responsibly and the opportunities used wisely. And it would be hard to argue that this accommodation between civic and moral appeals limited King's vocation either as a moral minister or as a civic tribune.

[52] Chapter 2, above.

This is not to deny that the balance is fine, and hard to attain. It is very easy to end up, as Frances Willard did, with the worst of both worlds. Her sense of American principles became so distorted by moral fanaticism that she thought banning alcohol was necessary to preserve the polity, and her sense of Christianity became so distorted by political motives that she tried to claim that the Bible condemned alcohol and tried to dismiss as irrelevant those parts of everyday Christian moral life that conflicted with her political ideals. Disdaining both liberty of conscience and social restraint, she ended up as a hero to a huge sectarian following—and a distinct danger to pluralist democratic politics. Her example should remind us that not all activists are at all good for democracy. The moral activist, far from being above the compromises of politics, must work harder on compromise of a different type than any other political officer.

KING: PROPHETIC POLITICS AND POLITICAL MINISTRY

Activists at their best combine two roles which rely on the social and political effects of public opinion: the tribune, who calls the polity back to its founding laws or principles, and the minister, who reminds a voluntary religious-moral group of its aspirations in the realm of mores. Instead of trying to combine the highest or best of the tribune and minister roles, a good activist should do the opposite, using the limitations implied by ministerial principles to check the excesses of tribunal passion, and vice versa.

We can see the effect in the speech and practice of Martin Luther King, surely an exemplary activist. To a large extent, King was simply a deft tribune and an able minister as such: he had a fine understanding of the nature and meaning of the United States's founding principles, and a fine preacher's sense for how much could and could not be accomplished by stirring words and calls for self-sacrifice. But beyond this, King's fusing of the two roles was masterful, as he used moral standards derived from religion to check his utopian tendencies in politics, and used political principles to reinterpret in politically viable terms his more uncompromising calls for Christian charity. He combined religious and political passion to render compelling the conceptually modest but politically radical notion that liberty, economic opportunity, voting rights, and legal protection should be available to all.

King's minister and tribune roles will not be treated here as separate, both because good activists should in principle combine them and because King himself did not draw a clear distinction between his religious and political callings.[53] But by placing King's actions on a spectrum, start-

[53] As one scholar has pointed out, most of King's speeches were firmly rooted in the black

ing with his purely political principles and motivations and moving toward his religious calling, one can see how King's political wisdom and his religious calling strengthened and honed each other. In this way the religious and secular realms, rightly separated in the realm of government and law, are properly joined in the realm of independent social action grounded in conscience and a near-supernatural commitment to justice.

To start with politics: King recognized the place of constitutional, economic, and religious principles in the American political order. His consciousness of these considerations served not to blur or compromise his deep and radical aspirations on behalf of African-Americans, but to steer what remained a radical movement into constructive, credible, and practical channels.

Consider constitutionalism. King was a student and strategist of governing structures to an extent that his own sweeping rhetoric tended to obscure. While spurning electoral politics himself, he knew both which political forces were likely to benefit his cause (he called himself "neutral against Nixon" in 1960)[54] and how political forces work in the American system. His first major public speech was called, tellingly, "Give Us the Ballot—We Will Transform the South," and appealed to American self-reliance in saying that Negroes would rather vote in an antilynching law than beg for one.[55] And even when King's rhetoric seemed to get American governing structures wrong, his practical proposals got them right. When King spoke of a "Second Emancipation Proclamation," this usage might appear to mistake Lincoln's use of wartime prerogative to free the slaves for the kind of thing presidents are empowered to do in peacetime. But King's actual proposal for what the president should do respected scrupulously the limits of executive power. King called for President Kennedy to fight for legislation in his capacity as party leader; to call conferences on civil rights and lend prestige to the cause; to prohibit through an executive order discrimination by contractors and accommodations receiving federal aid; to restrict federal housing loans to those accepting an "open occupancy" policy; and to ask the Justice Department, backed by federal marshals, to "restrain lawless elements now operating with inexcusable license." All these demands were squarely within the scope of presidential authority.[56]

---

preaching tradition—and those that were not were not good speeches (Miller [1992: 148–49, and passim).

[54] M. L. King, quoted by Oates (1985: 153).

[55] King, "Give Us the Ballot—We Will Transform the South," in Washington (1991: 198). ("Negroes" was the respectful term for African-Americans at the time King spoke, and I shall use it when paraphrasing rhetorical statements made in the past.)

[56] King, "Equality Now: The President Has The Power," in Washington (1991: 152–59). It seems that King in fact adapted his position to political reality, letting the "Emancipa-

As for economic interest, the mainstream civil rights movement from the beginning acknowledged the importance of hard work and Protestant virtue. (Huntington, while adopting Louis Hartz's doctrine that the United States is based on a "Lockean" consensus, is surprisingly silent on this central Lockean concern.) King throughout his career could sound anticapitalist and antibourgeois. Hating the selfishness and inequality of capitalism unchecked, King often advocated a middle road between capitalism and communism, or a "modified" or "democratic" form of socialism. When in India, where anticapitalist rhetoric was acceptable, he said that "the bourgeoisie—white, black or brown—behaves about the same the world over."[57] At the same time King, himself an astoundingly hard worker, could put forth before black church audiences the most stringent version of the Protestant work ethic:

> In the new age we will be forced to compete with people of all races and nationalities. Therefore we cannot aim merely to be good Negro teachers, good Negro doctors, good Negro ministers, good Negro skilled laborers. We must set out to do a good job, irrespective of race, and do it so well that nobody could do it better.
>
> Whatever your life's work is, do it well. . . . If it falls your lot to be a street sweeper, sweep streets like Michelangelo painted pictures, like Shakespeare wrote poetry, like Beethoven composed music; sweep streets so well that all the host of Heaven and earth will have to pause and say, "Here lived a great street sweeper, who swept his job well."[58]

Elsewhere, King lamented Negroes' lack of "initiative," lambasted blacks for spending above their means, and expressed no patience with blacks who had "used their oppression as an excuse for mediocrity."[59]

This dichotomy in King's thought represents more than mere ambivalence, or even a willingness to hold his own race to higher standards than he thought others had a right to expect (though the latter played some role). Christopher Lasch gives the most compelling account in explaining King's distinctive "radicalism" as rooted in the social values of the black

---

tion" proposal evolve from an unrealistic demand that Kennedy simply "declar[e] all forms of racial segregation illegal" under the Fourteenth Amendment to the more orderly call for appropriate executive action (Garrow [1988: 161, 169–70]). There is nothing wrong with this. It merely shows that activists, like everyone else, can become more skilled at their vocations as they learn over time. Moreover, even King's original proposal had some constitutional referent and was not as extraconstitutional as the reference to the original Emancipation implied.

[57] King, "My Trip to the Land of Gandhi," in Washington (1991: 27). For other examples of anticapitalist rhetoric, see esp. Oates (1985: 25, 27, 127, 446); and Garrow (1988: 140, 364, 382, 585, 591–92).

[58] King, "Facing the Challenge of a New Age," in Washington (1991: 139).

[59] King, "The Rising Tide of Racial Consciousness," in Washington (1991: 150).

petite bourgeoisie: shopkeepers, other small businesspeople, teachers, and especially, black church ministers.[60] These independent black earners valued hard work and despised lower-class indiscipline. (Even Rosa Parks, we may note, was selected as a test case for desegregation after two other women who had been denied bus seats were rejected as morally lax and therefore embarrassing to the black community.)[61] The economic philosophy of the black ministers and petite bourgeoisie was in some ways anticapitalist, but in a populist rather than a Marxist sense. King's most detailed speech on economics evoked a populist rather than communist "American dream . . . of equality of opportunity, privilege and property widely distributed; a dream of a land where men will not take necessities from the many to give luxuries to the few."[62]

Finally, the black petite bourgeoisie's own discipline and religious faith gave it a strong sense of courage and just entitlement, and a determination to resist racial oppression. Lasch emphasizes the psychic benefits of this social outlook, with its sense of limits and its devotion to hope rather than optimism,[63] but one could also stress its *political* potency in America: the pillars of the black community, still being independent producers and proprietors, represented what Americans aspire to, even envy, as a way of life. If Americans hold Lockean values largely in a mode of nostalgia, the black bourgeoisie of the time lived them. King, preaching (simultaneously) constant self-denial and principled resistance to injustice, tapped this consensus in powerful and subtle ways. David L. Lewis has described the combination of "humility, forbearance, and black moral probity" and "gifted leadership and cautiously modulated militance" as a "unique and creative syncretism" invented by King, combining the best features of Booker T. Washington's forbearance and W.E.B. DuBois's agitation.[64] Lasch is probably right to say that King and the civil rights movement lost their way when they abandoned their grounding in this yeoman class and started to glorify the rebel, the dropout, and the unemployed youth, all "opposed to 'middle class values.'"[65] But as we shall see, this shift reflected King's larger disillusionment with mainstream American soci-

---

[60] Lasch (1991: 386–407).

[61] Lewis (1978: 48); Garrow (1988: 15–16); Branch (1988: 123). The case of a teenager named Claudette Colvin, in particular, was quietly settled when it came out that she used profanity freely and was pregnant but unmarried.

[62] King, "If the Negro Wins, Labor Wins" (1962), in Washington (1991: 206). The last clause could be seen as a direct paraphrase of John Winthrop's Mayflower sermon, "A Modell of Christian Charity," in which Winthrop warned that "wee must be willing to abridge our selves of our superfluities, for the supply of others necessities" (sermon reprinted in Bellah [1992: 14]).

[63] Lasch (1991: 386–93).

[64] Lewis (1978: 88).

[65] Lasch (1991: esp. 392–98).

ety, which eventually overcame even King's constancy and led him to embrace sincerity, expressivism, and unpopularity.

Finally, King's religious beliefs served to temper the radicalism of his political demands. King both embodied democratic constancy (in both the negative sense of self-restraint and the positive sense of perseverance) and sought to implant such constancy in his congregation. He inherited from one strand of the black preaching tradition "an exceedingly complex pastoral strategy designed to stimulate hope while deferring its reward"; he "visited the meetings in order to inspire commitment to the local movement *and* to insure that the commitment remained nonviolent, which meant that his speeches were always marked by the tension between exuberance and restraint."[66] As Lasch argues strongly, King's theology prevented him from the twin dangers of racial hatred and overoptimistic humanitarian utopianism. His "spiritual discipline against resentment," greatly influenced by Reinhold Niebuhr, helped turn the civil rights movement away from a natural search for revenge toward a highly disciplined determination to forgive the enemy as soon as he changed his ways.[67] Also from Niebuhr, King inherited a belief in human sinfulness that prevented him from having unrealistic hopes about the ability of social movements to end human envy, selfishness, or pride. Rather than supposing human beings were naturally good, as Rousseau did, King continually stressed their "duality," capacity for both good and evil.[68] In sum, King's theological sense of human imperfection kept him from inordinate utopianism, rationalism, or humanitarianism in politics.

If King's religious thought and action affected his politics, so did his political thought and action inform what otherwise might have been excessively controversial and uncompromising elements of his religion. In his "Letter From Birmingham City Jail," for instance, King makes the apparently troubling assertion that the individual conscience, informed by an Aquinas-style reading of natural law, can legitimately decide which laws are unjust and need not be obeyed: "A just law is a man-made code that squares with the moral law or the law of God. A unjust law is a code

---

[66] Lischer (1995: 29, 257; emphasis added).

[67] Lasch (1991: 369–93); see also King, "The Power of Nonviolence," and "An Experiment in Love," in Washington (1991: 12–13, 18). Participants in the Birmingham campaign were required to sign a pledge whose second "commandment" read: "REMEMBER always that the nonviolent movement in Birmingham seeks justice and reconciliation—not victory" (M. L. King, *Why We Can't Wait*, in Washington [1991: 537]). For a social movement not only to deny it seeks victory but to *require* this denial of all its participants is truly extraordinary.

[68] Lasch (1991: 376–78, 393). For King on duality, see King, "Love, Law, and Civil Disobedience," in Washington (1991: 47–48, quoting Ovid, Augustine, Plato's *Phaedrus*, and Carlyle).

that is out of harmony with the moral law. To put it in the terms of Saint Thomas Aquinas, an unjust law is a human law that is not rooted in eternal and natural law. Any law that uplifts human personality is just. Any law that degrades human personality is unjust. All segregation statutes are unjust because segregation distorts the soul and damages the personality."[69]

Though it is not (now) controversial that segregation "distorts the soul and damages the personality," to claim this as a basis for not obeying laws is to open the door to all kinds of lawlessness based on personal revelation or individual moral certainty.

King, who at the time of the Birmingham letter had been previously embarrassed by such charges,[70] quickly adds to the spiritual authorities (Aquinas, Tillich, and Buber) a "more concrete example" and "another explanation." These are in fact not examples and explanations at all but two completely separate, and political, doctrines of unjust law. The concrete example of unjust law is "a code that a majority inflicts on a minority that is not binding on itself." The explanation is that an unjust law is "a code inflicted upon a minority which that minority had no part in enacting or creating because they did not have the unhampered right to vote. Who can say that the legislature of Alabama which set up the segregation laws was democratically elected?"[71]

In a previous speech, King had put forward these political definitions of unjust laws as a response to a hypothetical skeptic who professed not to believe in moral laws and the law of God (being "not too religious") and *therefore* demanded something "more concrete, and more practical."[72]

[69] King, "Letter from Birmingham City Jail" (1963; henceforth "Letter"), in Washington (1991: 293). King's formulation here was not originally composed under great stress in jail but had been previously thought out. Similar statements appeared in speech in 1961. See "Love, Law, and Civil Disobedience" [henceforth "Civil Disobedience"], in Washington (1991: 49—"moral law of the universe," "law of God," "degrades the human personality"); and "The Time for Freedom Has Come" [henceforth "Time for Freedom"], in Washington (1991: 164–65—"moral law of the universe," "a law conscience tells [those engaging in disobedience] is unjust.").

[70] In a 1960 television debate, the prosegregation editor James J. Kilpatrick had homed in on the question of lawbreaking: "It is an interesting experience to be here tonight and see Mr. King assert a right to obey those laws he chooses to obey and disobey those that he chooses not to obey and insist the whole time that he has what he terms the highest respect for the law, because he is abiding by the moral law of the universe. I would prefer here on earth that we tried to abide by the law of the land, by the statutes, by the court decisions, by the other acts that establish law here on earth" (NBC-TV television show "The Nation's Future," 26 November 1960; transcript in letter from King to John H. Harriford, 31 March 1961, as quoted by Oates [1985: 162]).

[71] King, "Letter": 294. Both these formulations also appear in "Civil Disobedience": 49; and the first in "Time for Freedom": 164.

[72] King, "Civil Disobedience": 49. Interestingly enough, this early speech, like the "Let-

In the "Letter" as well, the political definitions do not so much specify or explain the religious definition as give completely new, secular reasons. King's "explanation" is calculated to buttress his case before those who lack either King's religious convictions on segregation or his readiness to use religious standards to justify political action.[73] Segregationists, King is arguing, demean blacks in ways that they themselves would not tolerate and do not have to tolerate (nobody builds a nice park or swimming pool and then prohibits *everyone* from using it). And the same segregationists adopt laws governing blacks without letting blacks vote on them. These are good political arguments—more precisely, *democratic* arguments. They have nothing to do with religion, and in fact strictly delimit the legitimate scope of civil disobedience based on religious conviction. (For instance, activists who trespass at nuclear testing grounds or abortion clinics fail King's political test for disobedience.) So why is religion needed in the argument at all?

Religion for King did not provide moral standards independent from secular or political ones, but provided reasons for *listening* carefully to arguments based on those standards, and *acting* conscientiously on the conclusion of the argument. In *Stride Toward Freedom*, King spoke of the need for churches, including white churches, to "work toward fashioning a truly great Christian nation," and for ministers to engage in "prophecy."[74] But in saying this he did not mean that ministers should work toward theocracy or even disrupt the political order in the name of spiritual mission. He demanded instead that ministers desegregate their own congregations, speak out on social issues, join interracial ministerial or-

---

ter," was addressed to an audience of liberal white clergy who professed opposition to racism but opposed some of King's methods (Washington [1991: editorial note to "Civil Disobedience," 43]). The divide here is not between religious people and avowed atheists but between people with different conceptions of what religion requires (always the interesting case in America). This does not mean that King was willing to let religious disagreements lie: by implying that only a near-atheist would doubt the moral-law standard for unjust laws, King is subtly tweaking his more cautious fellow-ministers, implying that they do not take their own religious ideas seriously. While *this* part of the appeal would not have worked before an audience of atheists or of believers in a wildly different religious tradition, by combining the tweak with a serious secular argument King was able to give a defense capable of persuading the widest possible audience, as the "Letter" did.

[73] Miller (1992: 159–68) notes that the "Letter" is the most "rigorously ordered, predominantly inductive" of King's works, and that its rhetoric is "classical," not like black church sermons. But he then draws the strange conclusion that the "Letter" was derived primarily from Black prophetic roots, when according to his own argument its style is clearly an attempt to *translate* this particular religious tradition into a more ordered style of argument that would appeal to a larger audience.

[74] Martin Luther King, *Stride Toward Freedom* (henceforth *STF*), in Washington (1991: 481).

ganizations (a serious and courageous undertaking in the South), speak against white fears of integration, and generally promote the church's role as "guardian of the moral and spiritual life of the community."[75]

King gave three reasons why only churches, not secular institutions, could do these things. First, accepting the unlikelihood of the law's reforming mores through coercion, King thought only the church could "get to the ideational roots of race hate, something that the law cannot accomplish." Following Kant, King stressed that the law could only affect external behavior,[76] but King expected churches to "give the popular mind direction" in more fundamental ways.[77] Second, the church had a traditional and well-motivated social role as a challenger of social convention. This role let it take direct action "to broaden horizons, challenge the status quo, and break the mores when necessary."[78] The early Christian Church, King was fond of pointing out, "was not merely a thermometer that recorded the ideas and principles of popular opinion; it was a thermostat that *transformed the mores of society*."[79] In terms of the present argument, we might say that transforming mores, not a job for the government, *was* a job for a church whose members looked to it precisely as a "guardian" of their moral life.

Finally, the kind of churches King was familiar with were intimately connected to the Old Testament prophetic tradition. This gave ministers a special authority (and stirring words from scripture) for denouncing injustice as contrary to a divine plan. More importantly, it gave them the kind of courage required to face "threats and intimidations, inconvenience and unpopularity, even at times . . . physical danger, to declare the doctrine of the Fatherhood of God and the brotherhood of man."[80] In short, King argued that some narrow and evil tendencies in human be-

---

[75] *STF*: 477–81.

[76] "It is not a question either of education or of legislation. Both legislation and education are required. Now, people will say, 'You can't legislate morals.' Well, that may be true. Even though morality may not be legislated, behavior can be regulated. And this is very important. We need religion and education to change attitudes and to change the hearts of men. We need legislation and federal action to control behavior. It may be true that the law can't make a man love me, but it can keep him from lynching me, and I think that's pretty important too" (King, "The American Dream" [1961], in Washington [1991: 213]. See also Branch [1988: 141, 213]).

[77] *STF*: 478.

[78] *STF*: 478; emphasis added.

[79] "Letter": 300. King was fond of the line and used it in several speeches.

[80] *STF*: 481. The "brotherhood of man/Fatherhood of God" formulation expressed a rather minimalist version of the American civil religion. It was widely acceptable in the 1950s and early 1960s, indeed such a cliché that New York Governor Nelson Rockefeller labeled it with the derisive acronym BOMFOG.

ings could only be addressed by turning people's minds away from what other people would think and toward what God thinks.[81] In this, he was doing no more than validating Tocqueville, who named religion as the only thing that could awaken Americans from their narrow concerns and call them toward greater purposes. King's political goal was not necessarily more than universal access to self-interest properly understood, but not even Tocqueville thought that a profound and action-inspiring regard for one's fellow human beings could be stirred by an *appeal* to self-interest properly understood. As Tocqueville agreed, such grand appeals could only (consistently) be made through religion—and not even religion could do it continually or to the exclusion of other goals.[82]

We turn finally to what King did as a "pure" minister, when he put aside his public and tribunal role and spoke religious and moral doctrine to a specifically Christian audience. Although it is understandable to focus on King's direct political role in advocating civil rights, one should not overlook the time he spent in the more traditional ministerial role of reminding congregants how to live. His spiritual advice was not limited to talks on love or the spiritual discipline of nonviolence, but extended to precepts about self-restraint, hard work, and delayed gratification (the bourgeois version of constancy—which mixes surprisingly well with the protest version, known as discipline or commitment). In a famous, or infamous, 1956 speech at Holt Street Baptist Church before the Institute on Non-Violence, King not only called for blacks to work hard at any job they had, but criticized the job they were doing at the time: "There is no excuse for our school teachers to say 'you is'—they're supposed to be teaching but they're crippling our children. . . . Too many Negro doctors have not opened a book since leaving medical school."[83] In front of the Urban League a few years later, while conceding that black inferiority was caused by racism, King said that the raising of black "standards" must start at home, said the black crime rate was by any criterion "much too high," and criticized blacks who lacked "that creative something called *initiative*," who "have used their oppression as an excuse for mediocrity."[84] King, whose commitment to racial justice was beyond doubt, could get away with moral criticisms that would have sounded simply prejudiced coming from whites. At the Holt Street speech he criticized

[81] *STF*: 478–79.

[82] Tocqueville (1969: II.1.4, pp. 444–45).

[83] Cited in Oates (1985: 123).

[84] King, "The Rising Tide of Racial Consciousness," in Washington (1991: 150). Elsewhere King noted that India, though desperately poor, had a very low crime rate, and attributed this to the "wonderful spiritual quality of the Indian people" (King, "My Trip to the Land of Gandhi," in Washington [1991: 27]).

overconsuming "Negroes with $2,000 incomes riding around in $5,000 cars."[85]

These remarks were not simply "moralism" in the sense of arbitrary strictures that others were supposed to obey out of respect for authority.[86] They were rooted in an understanding of the white-dominated society that blacks wanted to enter, one in which they would have to compete for economic gain and would need self-restraint in order to keep their new prosperity. The ministerial demands were rooted in mundane, middle-class social requirements. When King's editor embarrassingly describes the Holt Street speech as an attempt to mediate between King's middle-class and Christian commitments,[87] he misses the point: King's Christianity embodied, in the great tradition of the Protestant ethic, the middle-class aspirations of a not yet middle-class group,[88] and this accounted for much of his strength. Unifying a morally informed political activism with a socially rooted moral vocation, King called for blacks to be let into the mainstream of American life, while preparing them for the difficult life they would find there. King's combination of ministerial and tribunal skill made him more effective in moral politics than other rhetoricians, but also more realistic in religion than other preachers. Though black radicals sometimes accused him of idealizing whites, King's study of politics had taught him that whites would give blacks nothing unless they worked for it—and King gave *this* to his congregation as a hard moral lesson.

I have portrayed King as drawing on the constraints of American political life to restrain the least credible elements of his prophetic and religious message. This may also have been a deliberate strategy on King's part. According to Richard Lischer, a lauded scholar of King's rhetoric, King could be described as "adroitly playing both ends against the middle. By identifying the Movement with mainstream religious and cultural values, he was effectively cutting off two unwanted ends: the ultraconservative whites and the militant blacks. The trick was to maintain his posi-

[85] Oates (1985: 122). When President Clinton in his first term visited a black church to repeat some of King's comments on moral failings in the black community, he did not dare make such intimate remarks and restricted his comments mostly to the issue of crime. This was only right, though Clinton would have done even better, as nobody's chosen minister, not to preach there at all.

[86] King's occasional condemnations of sexual promiscuity (Garrow 1988: 376) were not rooted in an analysis of the social tasks facing blacks, and *were* close to being empty moralism in this sense. Significantly, this is the only area in which King's own behavior contradicted the ethic he advocated for others.

[87] Washington (1991: 135).

[88] Compare Walzer (1965: 303), on the appeal of Puritanism to protocapitalist classes in England.

tion on a constantly shifting field without alienating his supporters or compromising his bottom-line values."[89]

But this trick was very hard on King, who constantly had to restrain both his supporters and himself. Lischer stresses the extent to which King was *always* playing a role. As Lischer points out, Aristotle did not say (as commonly thought) that a speaker must have good character in order to be persuasive, but that a speaker must *appear* to each audience to have the character it expects—and this King did, no matter how difficult the constant mask became.[90] One friend of King's reported his saying, "I am conscious of two Martin Luther Kings. I'm a wonder to myself."[91]

This is a good thing from the perspective of a nonblack American whose attraction to the substance of black preaching is limited. Because of this performance, someone like Rawls can believe that King's message differed not at all from the secular, liberal-democratic principles and modes of reasoning that Rawls calls public reason.[92] But in fact King's real beliefs, rooted in black church theology, were not the same as secular liberal democratic principles, nor were the latter contained in the former as a sort of subset (as Rawlsian public reason suggests).

The conflict between King's theology based in the black church and the secular ideals of liberty, equality, justice, and reason represented by Rawls exists on many levels. (One could, for instance, contrast Rawls's philosophical individualism with the common black assumption that the important moral units in society will always be *groups*.) The problem for moral activism is clearest, however, in regard to two questions: the meaning of the American experience and the source of moral authority in politics.

On the first point: King as a Southern black person educated in Northern seminaries had access to two contradictory stories or myths about the meaning of America and its history. Most Americans, certainly including Rawls by implication, regard the fundamental story of the United States to be one of liberty and equality. Founded on liberal and

---

[89] Lischer (1995: 156). The account that follows is heavily indebted to Lischer's treatment.

[90] Lischer (1995: 163–64).

[91] Quoted from an earlier edition of Lewis's biography by R. King (1992: 96).

[92] "Religious doctrines clearly underlie King's views and are important in his appeals. Yet they are expressed in general terms: and they fully support constitutional values and accord with public reason" (Rawls [1993: 250n39]). Rawls quotes heavily from the "Letter from Birmingham City Jail" without noticing the tensions and contradictions between King's religious and constitutional criteria. And he exaggerates, as do many commentators attached to rational legalism, King's reliance on the *Brown v. Board of Education* decision as an authority.

democratic principles, the country has spent its history up to now work-ing out those principles, extending them to more and more people, and working out the tensions between them. Those evils that persist in America result from our failure to live up to our own noble ideals. Aris-tocracy and slavery never really had a chance in the United States: the South, elitist and inegalitarian, was never really "American."[93] This is the story celebrated in books of political science and political theory,[94] in popular myth, and even in the mainstream "civic" jeremiad, which stresses that America has fallen from the high ideal it is supposed to uphold. The tribune role I have outlined assumes the presence of such an ideal, and the desirability of making appeals to that ideal for the sake of social change.

King, to the great discomfort and anger of most whites, came to disbe-lieve this story after a noticeable break in his rhetoric that Lischer de-scribes as "after Selma and just before Vietnam."[95] King's late speeches and sermons could accurately be described as anti-American. King's oft-quoted claim that the U.S. government was "the greatest purveyor of violence in the world today"[96] was far from his most radical statement. In the course of calling on America to "reexamine its comforting myths," King wrote in a posthumously published essay that "the largest portion of white America is still poisoned by racism, which is as native to our soil as pine trees, sagebrush and buffalo grass. Equally native to us is the concept that gross exploitation of the Negro is acceptable, if not com-mendable."[97]

In the same essay King compared the United States to a decaying Rome and predicted a similar fate for it unless "the black man in America can provide a new soul force for all Americans, a new expression of the American dream" that did not depend on exploiting third-world peoples. This would require not only a revolution in American practice but, he said, a "correlative revolution in American *values*."[98] Elsewhere, in Lischer's (well-documented) summary, King "accused America of geno-

---

[93] Hartz (1955: 198).

[94] Adler (1987); Bloom (1987); Huntington (1981). Bloom, of course, has a highly ironic attitude towards the substance of American ideals and on balance could be said to despise them. But it is a measure of Americans' attachment to those ideals that few of his admirers have noticed this.

[95] Lischer (1995: 11). By "just before Vietnam," Lischer means before the height of mili-tary escalation and the antiwar movement.

[96] King, "A Time to Break Silence" (1967), in Washington (1991: 233).

[97] King, "A Testament of Hope," *Playboy* 16 (January 1969), 175ff.; reprinted in Washing-ton (1991: 316).

[98] Ibid.: 323; emphasis added.

cide and compared its conduct of war to the Nazis'. He warned an audience in Montgomery that any country that had treated its natives as America had would not blink at putting blacks in concentration camps."[99]

As Lischer summarizes, more or less approvingly, "The terrible secret that the prophet began to tell in his last desperate years was this: it doesn't matter if America has or has not lived up to its principles, because the principles themselves are a lie."[100] Or, as put more recently by John Hope Franklin, the African-American historian and head of President Clinton's commission on race, "Jefferson didn't mean it when he wrote that all men are created equal. The truth is that we're a bigoted people and always have been. We think every other country is trying to copy us now and if they are, God help the world."[101]

This is not really an argument about historical interpretation. The two stories about American history differ not regarding facts or even historical causes, but regarding the meaning of the facts. Whether slavery or the Vietnam War are fundamental to America or anomalous departures from noble ideals is not a question that can be settled empirically. Different groups in society will find one or the other interpretation (or neither) to be compelling, based on their respective experiences.

This means that the status of public reason is more controversial than Rawls would like. Rawls's naming of public values—like liberty, equality, and justice—is explicitly based on an account of history that stresses the badness of religious war and the need to avoid religious strife in politics.[102] To follow the later King's story is to draw very different lessons: it is not religious strife but *racism* that is the greatest threat to social peace, and any public philosophy that does not consciously mention racial reconciliation as a goal (and slavery as the profound historical evil that makes the goal necessary) is missing the most "obvious" fact about social consensus. Put another way: what appears to some as an arbitrary and tendentious appeal to particular grievances (racial discrimination) will appear to others as the most natural, universal issue in the world, one that affects us all fundamentally. To be an effective tribune requires respecting the public's view of its own values, where it must be admitted that those who command disproportionate numbers or power are allowed to call

[99] Lischer (1995: 11). The concentration camp comment is from a mass-meeting address from 16 February 1968, found by Lischer in the King archives in Atlanta (Lischer [1995: 159/301n]). With probably deliberate aim at Lincoln's national mythmaking in the Gettysburg Address, King in *Why We Can't Wait* (1963: 130–31) wrote that America was "born in genocide."

[100] Lischer (1995: 158).

[101] Quoted by Kersten (1997: 19a).

[102] Rawls (1993: xxiv–xxv).

themselves the public. King, devoted to truth, could not in good conscience continue doing so. Most whites, *equally devoted to truth*, could not understand King's increased tendency to make appeals that struck them as irrational. The "public reasons" of liberty and equality won out in the end, remained part of the mainstream American story, not because they were objectively more justified than King's accusations of fundamental American racism but because the people who preferred the former set of assumptions were more numerous and more powerful than those who preferred the latter.

The second crisis in King's activist role occurred when King came to dissent openly (as he perhaps had always dissented quietly) from the fundamental assumption, shared by both ordinary democratic citizens and liberal philosophers, that we are not subject to claims made by sources external to ourselves but only to those that we ourselves acknowledge. Rawls assumes as one of the axioms of political life that we regard truth not as stemming from "an external source, say from an order of values in God's intellect," but from requirements of human reason and feeling and the "requirement of our living together in society."[103] King did not agree with this: at least in his later years, he spoke as a literal prophet whose authority came directly from God and superseded human judgment.

Above I claimed that ministers in a democracy have moral authority as people chosen voluntarily by a group to look after its character and conduct. This is a frankly liberal reading of religious authority. In the black church tradition, while ministers certainly possess this kind of authority, certain black religious leaders are regarded as also having a supervoluntary, God-given, prophetic authority, akin to that of Moses or the later Old Testament prophets. As Lischer documents (and most Americans would be surprised to hear if they took the evidence seriously), King's associates quite matter-of-factly assumed that King was a prophet called directly by God to speak on His behalf.[104] More importantly, *King* took the prophetic role seriously. He believed he had not only the normal citizen's or minister's right and duty to speak up on political matters but a special calling to speak God's truth regardless of consequences and regardless of its reception by a corrupt nation. He compared his right and

---

[103] Rawls (1993: xxvi).

[104] As Lischer shows (1995: 173), this belief was held quite seriously by SCLC administrator C. T. Vivian, King's mentor Benjamin Mays, King's second-in-command Ralph Abernathy, Alabama SCLC preacher Fred Shuttlesworth—and King's own father. While many Americans might dismiss this as hyperbole and some (particularly Jews) might find it actively offensive, Lischer notes that "African Americans have traditionally decorated their leaders with messianic imagery and have given the name 'black Moses' to inspirational leaders" (174).

calling to do this to Saint Paul's calling to spread the gospel over the world.[105]

Once he became convinced of America's moral corruption, King began to "eliminat[e] the middle man"[106] of the congenial, Deist American civil religion and to speak directly of God's judgment on America. One began to hear statements like the following:

The judgment of God is on America now.

Our ultimate allegiance is not to this nation. Our ultimate allegiance is to the Almighty God, and this is where we get our authority.

Our government and the press generally won't tell us these things, but *God told me to tell you this morning.*[107]

The early King believed that he needed secular justifications to ground his authority to speak out on political matters. As late as the speech "A Time to Break Silence," his first prominent political speech against the Vietnam War, King found it necessary to give "seven major reasons" (by King's own reckoning) for speaking. Three of these reasons were nominally religious: King said he aimed "to save the soul of America," to live his "commitment to the ministry of Jesus Christ," and to express the "calling to be a son of the living God" that he "shared with all men."[108] But these were rather tame ways of phrasing a prophetic mission (King is not saying that *he* has a special calling or a personal message from God), and King rhetorically buried them by mentioning first three secular reasons for opposing Vietnam.[109]

"God told me this morning" is a different kind of appeal altogether. It contains none of the moderate skepticism regarding one's own moral judgment that Rawls demands of liberal citizens (under the heading of "burdens of judgment").[110] Nor should this surprise us. Leif Wenar has

---

[105] Lischer (1995: 185), citing the "Letter from Birmingham City Jail."

[106] Lischer (1995: 181).

[107] Cited from King speeches and sermons by Lischer (1995: 181).

[108] King, "A Time to Break Silence," in Washington (1991: 233–34).

[109] King (ibid.) argued that Vietnam was sapping funds from antipoverty programs; that a disproportionate number of black and poor people were being drafted and dying; that opposition to violence must include opposition to the American government's violence; and (later in the speech) that he had a special "commission" as a Nobel Peace Prize recipient.

[110] Rawls in *Political Liberalism* (1993: 55ff.) describes the burdens of judgment as a way of explaining the fact that "reasonable people can disagree." The basic idea is that there are many steps involved in making moral judgments: we must weigh evidence, assign weights to different moral considerations, deal with inevitably vague moral categories, try to account for the limits of our social experience, and deal as best we can with incommensurable or tragic moral choices. The fact that reasonable people can differ at any of these stages accounts for their differing on final moral judgments. Reasonable people must in turn

shown that the official creeds of most major religions, including most tolerant ones, deny the burdens of judgment, believing that the truth on moral and religious matters is in principle available to all "clear minds and open hearts."[111] Lischer writes even more bluntly, and perhaps with a bit of exaggeration, that "the African-American tradition of [biblical] interpretation ... did not pass through the Enlightenment." Enlightenment theology rather successfully aimed to turn religion from stories of salvation that "enveloped" the world to lessons in morality that "decorated" it. Blacks, however, *needed* the direct sustenance of knowing that God had a plan for their salvation. Since in a hostile society and polity "their only hope was to recognize their own suffering and captivity in the Bible stories," African-Americans never adopted the "distance" that theological liberalism assumes.[112] The black idea of God, as Benjamin Mays found it portrayed in black literature, assumes that God controls the world and actively intervenes in it, that God actively supports the cause of Right, and that God is quite clearly on the side of black people.[113] When King proclaimed God's judgment on an unjust nation, he was violating standards of religious skepticism to which the black church tradition was never fully committed and which many religious blacks would probably have been surprised to hear were expected of them.

In the difference between black prophetic leadership and the mainstream democratic skepticism toward self-appointed moral leaders lies a profound difference of opinion regarding the biggest danger of moral leadership. The black tradition fears, above all, insufficient moral commitment and societal indifference to clear injustices; the overall society fears above all the fanaticism that results from assuming that matters of justice and injustice *are* clear. Rawls's assumptions do not conflict with King's practice because one or the other made an unnecessary error. The conflict is real and fundamental: within the liberal-democratic polity, there are some groups (and African-Americans are not the only ones)[114]

---

admit that others can disagree, and must try to arrive at an accommodation with others in spite of the permanence of reasonable disagreement: "It is unrealistic—or worse, it arouses mutual suspicion and hostility—to suppose that all our differences are rooted solely in ignorance and perversity, or else in the rivalries for power, status, or economic gain" (58). This is exactly what the late King did suppose, at least regarding matters of economic and social justice.

[111] Wenar (1995: 43–48). Wenar presents evidence from current Baptist, Lutheran, and post–Vatican II Catholic doctrine.

[112] Lischer (1995: 200). Lischer uses italics for the words "enveloped" and "decorated."

[113] Mays (1938: 189–217).

[114] See the argument in Wolin (1996). Wolin claims that dispossessed people in general quite reasonably have little use for the standards of restrained, rational argument that Rawls regards as crucial. This is not to say that the only alternative is a kind of subrational bluster or flaunting of personal feeling, as some fervent critics of deliberation and rationality seem

who believe *for the best of reasons* that there are things much more important than the liberal quest for toleration and the democratic desire to live one's own life undisturbed by moral scolds. Reason can be "public" in Rawls's sense only by excluding to a great extent the validity of these groups' claims and perspectives. And one burden that makes activism so difficult, so rarely successful, such a strain on moral character is the need to swallow that exclusion, to pretend to accept it, in the service of equality and justice.

In short, the moral value of sincerity is overrated. Consistently practiced, sincerity would make moral activism impossible: it would require activists to eviscerate their effective rhetoric and to abandon the (conventional) sources of their moral standing. Judith Shklar has pointed out that hypocrisy is not an evil in a diverse society, but absolutely necessary if people of different backgrounds are to get along publicly while retaining very different private beliefs. "Liberal democracy," she writes, "cannot afford public sincerity. Honesties that humiliate and a stiff-necked refusal to compromise would ruin democratic civility in a political society in which people have many serious differences of belief and interest."[115]

Shklar tempers her attack on sincerity with the caveat that hypocrisy will hamper jeremiads in the cause of justice,[116] but even this might not be true. Hypocrisy as a social *value* might hamper jeremiads if it made the powerful more willing to flout their own ideals, but hypocrisy as an occasional *practice* might *help* jeremiads by encouraging moral activists to make effective arguments that might persuade others, *whether the activist believed those arguments or not.*[117] If full sincerity in politics involves rival social and racial groups telling each other openly that their premises are "a lie," we should practice less than full sincerity, and rediscover the very real version of respect that consists in not telling people that we regard their beliefs as worthless.

Frances Willard: Moral Reform and Political Zealotry

Frances E. Willard was an extraordinary individual: an intellectual who read Plato at a time when few women were educated, an orator at a time when few women spoke publicly, a formidable political force at a time

---

to claim (Sanders 1997; Fish 1999). There is such a thing as modulated militance; speech can be angry and still contain facts and arguments. The best response to a pervasive slant or bias in public argument is to change (through organizing, for example) the balance of power and confidence that causes the slant, not to embrace distorted or ridiculous claims by the disadvantaged in order to balance things out.

[115] Shklar (1984: 78).

[116] Shklar (1984: 86).

[117] This counsel may not be stable if universally known: perhaps it is activists who must be hypocrites while the rest of society remain believers in sincerity, even naïve believers. This would trouble a Kantian.

when women could not vote. As president of the Woman's Christian Temperance Union, she lived by a motto, "Do everything," that saw her take a hand in every major reform effort of her time: women's suffrage, child labor laws, socialism and the labor movement, sex education, rape law reform, eugenics. The political tactics pioneered by her and her colleagues were amazingly bold for her time: like the later civil rights campaigners, temperance women engaged in sit-ins, marched, prayed publicly—and faced everything from arrest to angry mobs to fire hoses for their troubles. And Willard did all this without evident personal rancor or resentment, winning at least a grudging personal admiration, if not political support, among people of all persuasions, from conservative to radical. At the time of her death in 1898, she was the most famous and admired woman in America. "When she died flags were at halfmast from the Atlantic to the Pacific: when her body was taken to Chicago every railwayman along the whole road came out to do her honour"; thirty thousand stood in the snow in Chicago to pay their respects at the funeral.[118]

Yet Willard is forgotten in our time, and with some reason. For she devoted most of her great talents and energies to a cause that was politically misguided, morally narrow, and predictably bad in its consequences: the drive to forbid all consumption of alcohol. In examining the character traits, social background, and errors in thinking that brought her to do this, we shall find a textbook case of the activist gone wrong—of the kind of activist, in fact, who makes some liberals and constitutional democrats distrust all mass movements and their leaders. While King used his tribunal wisdom to temper his religion and his religious insight to temper and toughen a political movement, Willard's lack of wisdom in playing both roles led her to utopian politics, naïve and unimaginative religion, and the recurrent American attempt to force small-town censoriousness on cosmopolitan populations that poisons our politics to this day. She provides a fine example of how a visionary and farsighted thinker on social issues can bring down history's contempt on herself and her cause if she does not understand how a politician in a constitutional democracy ought to translate ideas into action. Successful and loved in her time, Willard plays little part in the larger American story, because her life, rhetoric, and style of politics paid so little heed to the proper and enduring principles of democratic politics.

Willard was very well-read, "surprisingly well grounded in philosophy

---

[118] Reform efforts: Bordin (1986: 129–74); and Willard (1889: 375–442). Civil disobedience/demonstrations and their consequences: Willard (1889: 470); and Epstein (1981: 99). Public appreciation of Willard: Strachey (1912: 294–95), from which the text quotation is taken; Trowbridge (1938: 191); and Bordin (1986: 3–4).

and theology"; she read translations of Plato and other classics between teaching high school classes. She traveled extensively in Europe and the Middle East, where she learned foreign languages, studied ancient ruins, and noted comparative social conditions.[119] Thus it is striking that neither her seven-hundred-page autobiography nor other summaries of her studies and reading give any evidence that this most political of women ever studied a work of American government, politics, law, or political philosophy.[120] Her actions in this area mirrored her thought. She failed to appreciate, as will become clear, basic principles of American government like the role of conflict and difference of opinion in politics, the dependence of officeholders on popular vote, the legitimacy of self-interest and "pursuit of happiness," and the difference in principle between constitutional amendments and normal lawmaking.

Consider the last point first. Willard and her colleagues consistently seemed puzzled why some people could want temperance to be, as its name implied (and as it was when Tocqueville wrote about it), a movement of voluntary abstainers who sought to persuade others. In discussing how her movement changed its methods from moral suasion to legal prohibition to constitutional amendment, her tone was casual, as if the question were merely pragmatic:

> To the inane excuse of the seller [of liquor] that he might as well do it since somebody would, the *quick and practical* reply was, "To be sure; but suppose the people could be persuaded not to let anybody sell? why, then that would be God's answer to our crusade prayers." So they began with petitions to municipalities, to Legislatures and to Congress. . . . *Thus* the Woman's Christian Temperance Union stands as the strongest bulwark of prohibition, state and national, by constitutional amendment and by statute.[121]

In a speech called "Gospel Politics," Willard quoted at length New Hampshire Senator Blair's similarly pragmatic argument: local effort alone was a "waste of time," prohibition being a "national question." Blair endorsed the constitutional solution as a matter of course once he concluded that "the nation [could] act in no other way than by law."[122] The special status of fundamental law, which in retrospect seems a clear

---

[119] "Surprisingly well-grounded": Bordin (1986: 24). Plato and other classics: Willard (1889: 135). Travels: Willard (1889: 245–330); for their effect on Willard's education, Bordin (1986: 48–51). (Bordin calls Willard's travels her "finishing school and graduate degree program.")

[120] See Trowbridge (1938: 21), and esp. Strachey (1912: 71), where politics and law are not mentioned on an extensive list of subjects to study that Willard set herself in 1860. The list is otherwise exhaustive and includes everything from Conchology to Mineralogy to Rhetoric. Willard's reading in Plato does not seem to have included the *Republic, Laws, Statesman, Apology, Crito,* or *Gorgias.*

[121] Willard (1889: 472; emphasis added).

[122] Willard, "Gospel Politics" (1884), exerpted in Willard (1889: 404).

argument against the Prohibition amendment and its embarrassing repeal, did not occur to these activists. Convinced that their position was right absolutely, they saw no principled reason not to use the Constitution to forestall a future reversal of policy by a democratic majority.[123]

Next, consider the question of political conflict. King's outlook and personal experience let him reconcile a belief in the rightness of his causes with an acute awareness that not everyone would agree. In contrast, Willard's determination that politics should embody consensus and harmony left her shocked, frustrated, and angry when faced with those who opposed her "crusade" (her word). She believed the "contradiction and malignity of political debate," the "asperities of politics," were "altogether needless and unnatural."[124] This influenced Willard's preferences of political programs as well as styles. Her preferred organ of the labor movement was the Knights of Labor (which abjured strikes and spent most of its time founding cooperatives), rather than the pragmatic American Federation of Labor under Samuel Gompers; her favorite form of socialism was the technocratic classlessness of Edward Bellamy's *Looking Backward*.[125] Where King sometimes called for universal brotherhood or the reign of Christianity and then followed this with eminently practical proposals (often taken from other countries' existing policies), Willard talked of the "regnancy of Christ"[126] and the "prohibition of sin as against any alliance between sin and the government."[127] She proclaimed her goal as "the reign of Jesus Christ in Custom and in Law, . . . the *literal* adoption of His precepts as the only Code never to be outworn."[128] What the "ethics of Christ's gospel" required, she said in a mature speech, was "that the corporation of humanity should control all products," and put an end to "competition."[129] She wrote of the New Testament not as an inspiration for moral action but as "our best treatise on political economy."[130] "Only the golden rule of Christ," read an early WCTU principle

---

[123] Trowbridge (1938: 116–17) writes that by 1882–83 Willard "had been emphasizing the need of 'grounding' prohibition in a constitutional amendment, 'beyond the reach of demagogues.'"

[124] Willard (1889: 437).

[125] Knights of Labor: Bordin (1986: 137–144). Willard's attraction to Bellamy's ideas: Bordin (1986: 145–49). For an amusing and effective critique of nineteenth-century utopian solutions to class conflict, see Schlesinger (1945: 361–68).

[126] Willard, Speech before the Women's Congress (1885), quoted by Willard (1889: 478).

[127] Willard, Speech before the Prohibition Party convention (1888), quoted by Willard (1889: 450).

[128] Willard, WCTU President's Address (1897), in Leeman (1992: 183; emphasis added).

[129] Ibid.: 178.

[130] Willard (1889: 525). In general, Willard's view of religion, though politically "progressive," was theologically unsophisticated. In touring Egypt she talked without irony of "the visible hand of vengeance" which had caused God to smite the monuments built by tyrants (1889: 280).

laid down by Willard, "can bring the golden age of man."[131] Nor was this merely a concession to practices of her time. Ray Strachey calls Willard in fact the "pioneer of 'religion in politics' in America," and Willard herself triumphantly described the Prohibition Party platform of 1888 as the time "the word Christian occurs perhaps *for the first time* in American politics."[132]

Consistent with her belief that competition and conflict were not necessary in economics or politics, Willard could not account intellectually for opposition to her prohibition policies and always put it down to bad will, as consensus theorists of politics often end up demonizing those who stubbornly dissent. She professed shock at the idea that a politician would oppose prohibition out of fear of losing votes (even as she used this as a reluctant argument for women's suffrage).[133] She blamed another defeat on "A horde of ignorant voters, committed to the rum-power, [which] fasten the dram-shop like a leech on our communities."[134] She attributed defeats in 1882 to "an alliance with the rum-power," "Democratic treachery," and "the dictation of the Germans."[135]

The last remark points up how Willard's quest for harmony rather than ordered conflict led her to nativism. If all Americans were supposed to agree on Prohibition principles (and also socialist principles, in her later opinion) as representing the good of all, it stood to reason that opposition to Prohibition must ultimately be the result of foreign subversion and the immigration of bad characters. While she promised "an open hand for Catholic and Protestant, for the foreign as well as the native born,"[136] and worked on occasion with Catholic prohibitionists and even Jews,[137] Willard's idea of an open hand was to demand that immigrants adopt American mores (including abstinence from liquor) and to rail at them when they refused. She attributed the horrific state of municipal government to the United States's having become "the dumping ground of European cities," giving rise to "a hundred thousand anarchists among us." She spoke of an "ominous invasion on our wharves as these strange people come," and of eight hundred foreign-language newspapers, "a majority of which contain[ed] ideas concerning home and women, temperance and the Sabbath, that [were] European and revolu-

---

[131] Trowbridge (1938: 99).

[132] Strachey (1912: xviii–xix); Willard (1889: 442). Said platform begins by "acknowledging Almighty God as the source of all power in government" (ibid.).

[133] Willard, "Home Protection" (speech), in Leeman (1992: 132).

[134] Willard, First Annual Address to WCTU, quoted by Willard (1889: 370).

[135] Willard, annual Woman's Christian Temperance Union address of 1882, in Willard (1889: 386).

[136] Willard, speech to a committee of the Republican National Convention, 1884, in Willard (1889: 393).

[137] Strachey (1912: 255).

tionary, not American and Christian."[138] The very motto of the Temperance Union—"Home Protection"—played unsubtly on the nativist resonance of "home," and in a speech on the subject Willard made the point explicit: "Strengthen the sinews of old King Majority, by counting in the home vote to offset that of Hamburg and of Cork, and let American customs survive by utilizing (at the point where by the correlation of governmental forces 'opinion' passes into 'law') the opinion of those gentle 'natives' who are the necessary and tender guardians of the home, of tempted manhood and untaught little children."[139]

This represented a signal failure of tribunal wisdom. Abstaining from drink was not a universal or traditional sign of Americanism; indeed, liquor consumption was higher in the eighteenth century than in the nineteenth, and higher in 1830 than in 1870.[140] To demand that immigrants adopt this most arbitrary piece of evangelical morality was to see a fundamental principle of American society where none existed.[141] It was Willard's own weakness of character not to be able to abide opposition. And as Aristotle said of those who lacked constancy, this character flaw biased Willard's conclusions about the proper end the American polity should pursue: she sought not universal willingness to abide by American political principles, but absolute uniformity of mores.

As Willard's mention of "the correlation of government forces [where] opinion passes into law" implies, Willard's failure of wisdom as a tribune corresponded to a desire to play minister to the country and the world. Willard made no distinction between the social pressure of public opinion and the physical coercion that backs up law. When she spoke of achieving reform through changing public sentiment, she meant transforming the sentiment of lawmakers and law enforcers, who could then be trusted to coerce the populace.[142]

---

[138] Willard, "Tenth Annual Address" to WCTU, in Leeman (1992: 147–48). On the anti-immigrant sentiments of Willard and the WCTU generally, see Smith (1997: 385ff., 456). Smith summarizes Willard's ideology as "civic maternalism" (454).

[139] Willard, "Home Protection," in Leeman (1992: 124).

[140] Epstein (1981: 107).

[141] Willard's Americanism actually respected no national boundaries, but colored what might otherwise have been a humane and enlightened awareness of women's oppression in other cultures. Having encountered in her travels the cases of an Italian matron who had never heard of education (Willard 1889: 584), and an Egyptian "woman" sold as a child-bride at age ten (578), she still pursued the "polyglot petition," a multinational petition for prohibition of alcohol, as her only concrete international initiative (Bordin [1986: 191–93, 213]; see also Strachey [1912: 262]). She apparently did not stop to consider whether alcoholism was the root cause of women's oppression in a place such as Egypt.

[142] "The keystone of law can be firm and secure only when held in place by the arch—public sentiment. The more you can enlist in favor of your law the natural instincts of those who have the power to make that law and to select the officers who shall enforce it,

King, I have argued, managed the tensions of the tribune role by combining radicalism in outlook and aim with petite bourgeois habits and discipline. Willard's political moralism grew from the opposite combination: she hated the forms and requirements of society as such, but her ideas never questioned, or grew beyond, the small-town abstemiousness she grew up with. Instead of pushing justice for all in a restrained manner, she sought to universalize small-town mores in an unrestrained matter.

As argued in chapter 3, neither Willard's early life nor anyone else's is a reliable clue to his or her subsequent views or character. But what people *say* in mature years about their early lives is a different matter, and here Willard's opinions contrast instructively with King's. King grew out of the theological dogmatism and repressive mores instilled by his father. He thanked theological studies for removing the "shackles of fundamentalism" from his body,[143] and his education, which combined "Niebuhr and the Pool Tables,"[144] gave him an enduring empathy with imperfect and roguish characters that was of central political importance. Willard's frontier upbringing and later education in what she called the "prohibition village" and "Methodist heaven" of Evanston, Illinois,[145] was even more strict than King's. She was never outside the company of her parents until she was sixteen, and the future prohibitionist never saw wine offered in her own country until age twenty-five.[146] When she worked as a teacher, she never mentioned alcohol to her students until the Temperance Crusades of 1874 (the first and last time, Willard claimed, that she saw the inside of a saloon),[147] since she took their abstinence "always as a matter of course."[148] Her later reaction to such an upbringing mentions no "shackles"; on the contrary, she thanks her parents, at great length, for imposing such discipline: "With my naturally adventurous disposition I fear that but for a strenuously guarded girlhood I might have wandered into hopeless unbelief."[149]

Willard's political activism on the issue of prohibition was grounded not in an experience of an injustice that she hoped to remedy but in an

---

the more securely stands the law" (Willard, cited in Trowbridge [1938: 112]). Trowbridge glosses this to mean that Willard "had no illusions as to the impossibility of making headway without popular support," but the quotation seems rather to show that Willard sought *elite* support and thought that popular sentiments could only be changed through coercive laws.

[143] Quoted by Oates (1985: 17).
[144] The title of a chapter in Branch (1988: 69–104).
[145] Willard (1889: 332).
[146] Willard (1889: 637, 332).
[147] Trowbridge (1938: 75); Strachey (1912: 182).
[148] Willard (1889: 332).
[149] Willard (1889: 637–38).

assumption of unquestioned mores, which she hoped to politicize directly and to spread to communities where they were questioned. (This was not true of her activism on women's rights issues, which generally sprang from her personal experience of the limits women's conventional role placed on their aspirations.) Willard did not regard democratic majorities as having any moral weight: she considered "the public health" and "the public morals" as prepolitical goods that neither the legislature or the people could bargain away, and she once complained bitterly that the Prohibition Party was "despised for the single reason that it lacks majorities and commands no high positions as the rewards of skillful leadership or wily caucusing."[150] Other temperance women realized full well that small-town versions of public opinion were not to be expected in larger towns of even a few thousand, where people (and in particular women) did not all know each other.[151] But Willard simply saw this as a challenge. If face-to-face disapproval of others' behavior would not work, she would use other methods: "The Gatling gun of pulpit, press and platform."[152]

To do this Willard had to depart from the mores that she herself preached. Many authors have noted that she used conservative rhetoric in pursuit of an often-radical vision of social harmony and progress for women. For instance, in a famous address on the family, Willard endorsed the Victorian ideal of marriage for life, combining a man and woman into one entity through great and mutual love, with as little sex as possible—and then argued that this ideal required radical reforms: "co-education to mate them on the plane of mind; equal property rights to make her God's own free woman, not coerced into marriage for the sake of support," and legal equality that ended the ability of the husband to act in his wife's name.[153] Willard's manner, even on the platform, was "utterly feminine," even "coquettish,"[154] but her life, by the standards of the time, was not: never married, no children, a more-than-full-time career.

Such contradictions have led to debates about whether she, or her rhetoric, was progressive or conservative, radical or reactionary.[155] In fact,

---

[150] Willard, quoted, respectively, in Trowbridge (1938: 102, 117).

[151] Epstein (1981: 98).

[152] Willard (1889: 436).

[153] Willard, "A White Life for Two," in Leeman (1992: quotation from 169; speech in 159–72 passim). ("White" refers to purity and nobility: there was no racial meaning intended, though some might have inferred one.)

[154] Campbell (1990: 130), citing other work by Ruth Bordin.

[155] For contrasting views, see Leeman (1992: 69–76, emphasizing Willard's clear criticism of the status quo), and Campbell (1990: 121–32, emphasizing Willard's endorsement of traditional marriage and gender ideals).

Willard's own statements make the answer quite clear: she supported the traditional principles of her upbringing, but had no use for the traditional social roles that underpinned them. The Christian and feminine ideals of love, harmony, gentleness, and the like were genuinely Willard's ideals. But her aspirations for women's progress and her own rebellious nature led her to proclaim openly her contempt for existing social hierarchies,[156] for "purely artificial limitations" that keep women from professional careers,"[157] for "customs that immeasurably hamper and handicap the development of women."[158] And they led her to welcome "public rebuke and criticism," which she likened to the persecution of Joan of Arc and other martyrs.[159] Willard admitted to being ambitious and of aspiring toward heroism, and read about the renegade woman philosopher Hypatia "with admiration and a sort of reverential love."[160] When criticized for undermining existing social intercourse grounded in alcohol consumption, she went far beyond answering the charge, arguing for wholly new, "truer forms of society," grounded not in pleasure at all but in philanthropy, "highest thought and tenderest aspiration, in which the sense of selfhood is diminished and the sense of otherhood increased."[161] Willard herself called her conformity to traditional womanhood a kind of act to achieve greater political success: "I quietly accepted the inevitable; 'conformed' down to the smallest particular in wardrobe, conduct and general surroundings, confident that I could thus more completely work out my destiny in the midst of a crooked and perverse generation, having always for my motto, 'To *re*form one must first one's self *con*form.' "[162]

In Willard's own summary: "Under the mould of conservative action I have been most radical in thought. Christianity has held me as the firm bridle steadies the champing steed."[163] It was *Christianity* that "held her back," not a grounding in any concrete social structure or role, for Willard consciously ignored all the roles of her time (including the rebellious role of the more openly egalitarian suffragists).[164]

Willard employed traditional values in a radical attack on the gender mores and social roles of her time. The result was not without grandeur and pathos: Willard's "crusade" mentality gave her a genuine empathy

---

[156] Willard (1889: 130–31).

[157] Willard (1889: 692).

[158] Willard (1889: 693; emphasis added).

[159] Willard (1889: 388).

[160] Willard (1889: 688, 152).

[161] Willard (1889: 333).

[162] Willard (1889: 693; emphasis in original).

[163] Willard (1889: 692). The allusion to Plato's *Phaedrus* (253d ff.) was undoubtedly intentional, given Willard's love of Plato.

[164] This point is well made by Campbell (1990: 128–29).

for those despised and ignored by existing social structures, and a remarkable boldness in speaking out for them.[165] But the crusade mentality was ill-suited to the limits of democratic politics: it stoked Willard's utopianism and intolerance, making her determined to perfect the world but blind to the possible value of social practices she would have to overturn in order to do so. Willard saw public opinion as a weapon to be wielded, never as a warning to be heeded. She thought that she was called to revolutionize mores, never that she would do well to respect the limits represented in mores—her own or those of the poor cosmopolitans she hoped to "convert" by law. Trying to make Chicago into a temperance village, she pursued a course that would eventually make it a gangsters' battleground—since the open criminality of bootleggers, who catered to local habits and values, was preferred to a law that cast contempt on both.

Above was noted Michael Walzer's argument that Puritan political prophets—and thus, indirectly, their American counterparts—took as their model the same Genevan ministers praised by d'Alembert and Rousseau. There was, however, a crucial difference: where the Genevan ministers contented themselves with social and moral suasion, the Puritans were willing to use state coercion when they failed to control behavior through preaching and social pressure.[166] Two versions of moral activism can be seen as descending from these two models: a "Genevan" brand of prophecy recognizes the distinction between conscience and law; a "Puritan" brand (as Tocqueville saw) does not. King was, by and large, a Genevan. Willard was a Puritan, and the example of what her Puritanism led to stands as a warning to all those who see their calling as making fellow citizens into saints.

CONCLUSION

This chapter began with an attempt to get at the nature of moral activism, its proper methods, and its particular appeal. Against the idea that democratic activism necessarily required extrademocratic checks, I argued that democratic theory, as set forth by Rousseau, had its own resources for limiting moral activism and judging moral activists. Because moral activists command no resources but public opinion, they must (pragmatically as well as morally) have a view to when purposeful attempts at using public opinion are likely to succeed and when the public's existing mores and prejudices will thwart such attempts.

The activist's power is therefore strongest but most limited when she

---

[165] Willard noted the connection herself (1889: 130–31).
[166] Walzer (1965: 224–25, 301).

plays "minister." In religious affairs, a given congregation trusts a minister to be its moral guardian and to judge its actions and opinions; but only that congregation will see a need to listen to a minister's pronouncements at all. (In public opinion polls, political preachers like Jerry Falwell, who advocate repressive laws against immorality, tend to be disliked by all respondents who are not their active supporters—which is not true of other kinds of politician.) The role of political tribune is more general in scope but more restricted in content: as the price for having a broad national appeal, the tribune must try to render her message in terms that resonate with a few broad principles that most Americans agree with (equal opportunity, universal liberty, the orderly pursuit of interest). The activist role is an uneasy but possible combination of the two, combining authority within a voluntary movement with appeals to free people's existing beliefs in the public realm.

As I have tried to make clear, it is difficult for an activist to find the proper mix of minister and tribune. To bring it off, an activist must have both a distinctive intellectual outlook and distinctive ways of acting (dispositions or, if one likes, role-relative "virtues") rooted in a type of social background. For moral activists to be familiar with the limitations of activism, they must be intimately familiar with the principles of American government, especially the legitimate role of conflict and interest in it; be equally familiar with a particular moral or religious tradition as a resource to inspire and discipline action; be rooted in, and draw political strength from, an orderly social milieu, whose mores inspire confidence that the movement will respect limits; and be familiar with a wide variety of innocent variations in ways of life, so that no single set of mores will be confused with the only acceptable way to live. These conclusions are probably too abstract, in that they imply that any combination of political principle, moral depth, social rootedness, and cosmopolitan acquaintance will do. In fact, most combinations of these factors will probably not work together at all. For an activist to have the right outlook and background to make the right appeal on the right issue at the right time, an appeal that will build on the best of a democratic polity's mores while reforming the worst in its practices, seems to require a fortuitous and unpredictable mix; and we can probably only judge the appropriateness or inappropriateness of an attempt at activism after the fact of success or failure.

Moral activism is a risky business. When it succeeds, the result can be a far-reaching transformation of social practices, and a great gain in equality and justice. The successes, however, often blind us to the cases of failure: the average person who attempts a moral transformation of a democratic society ends up becoming either a conventional, interest-based politician or else bitter, disillusioned, and apathetic, prone to preach lack of trust for democratic methods and ideals.

In fact, moral activism is mostly failure, and we should take from this analysis a counsel of caution. If appeals to public opinion have, as I have argued, certain natural limits that should inform activists' actions, there is nevertheless a tendency for activists to be carried away beyond those limits. Moral activism tends to be illimitable as a matter of practice, not theory: having gained a few victories through the potent weapon of public opinion, activists tend to think they can reform every evil—whether public opinion in fact allows for such reform or not. Sometimes this happens even without initial success: many a would-be activist has built a successful but futile career on repeated, glorious failures. American history is littered with florid extremists like Father Coughlin and Emma Goldman, whose followers loved them fanatically but who have been judged by history as dangerous figures, their programs rightly rejected as contrary to democratic principles. It may be that there are only a few cases in the history of democratic politics of reform movements fully in accord with democratic and constitutional principles. Perhaps the exemplary models of democratic activism may be counted on both hands.

Moral activists can seem the purest, least corrupt figures on the political scene. This purity, however, can distract both themselves and others from critically examining their assumptions, aims, and methods. Activism is not contrary to democracy, but in its aversion to compromise and bargaining it is in a sense orthogonal to other democratic practices. It does not do what most people expect of democratic politics, and does not fully attend to the usual forms of democratic values—which embody a certain liberality and a willingness to let others do what they please, rather than openness to moral correction.

Democrats, I have claimed, long for activists as people who can transcend democracy's contradictions, creating reform without abolishing license. But the question is not whether we would welcome activism based on *our* values, aimed at reforming others, but whether we would welcome *other* people's activism, based on their view of moral rightness, aimed at reforming *us*. We should perhaps be careful what we long for, less willing to give the benefit of the doubt to self-appointed prophets of reform, and more willing to let democracy's tensions remain as they are. Democracies have, or should have, free speech, and all their members are allowed to try their hands at activism. But would-be activists should spend more time contemplating what is really required if they are to succeed, and to deserve success. The apparent sincerity and moral clarity of the moral activist might make it seem the easiest political office of all. In fact, it is the hardest, requiring more restraint, more willingness to compromise, and a narrower band of permissible social roles than most who expect a great deal from politics can stand.

CHAPTER SIX

The Organizer and the Politics
of Personal Association

"Aristocratic countries abound in rich and influential persons who can look after themselves and cannot be easily or secretly downtrodden. Their existence instills general habits of moderation and restraint in those in power.

"I am well aware that democratic countries do not naturally include persons of that sort, but something of like sort can be artificially created."

—Tocqueville.[1]

"Okay, you've convinced me. Now go on out and bring pressure on me!"

—Franklin D. Roosevelt to a reform delegation,
as quoted by Saul Alinsky.[2]

"I had always assumed that my role was to facilitate, which did not involve leadership. I didn't have a need for being considered a *leader*. And I think that got over to them in their original meeting. . . . And so they began to have that kind of confidence. So they felt they could trust me, to maybe further the matter of their independence."

—Ella Josephine Baker, on the first meeting of
the Student Nonviolent Coordinating Committee.[3]

"The way to bring our people home is by using patience, love, brotherhood, and unity—not force—love, patience, brotherhood and unity. We try and we try and we try. If they become a threat, we off them."

—Stokely Carmichael, on the black bourgeoisie.[4]

---

[1] Tocqueville, *Democracy in America* (1969: II.4.7, p. 697). Henceforth *DIA*.
[2] Alinsky (1971: xxiii).
[3] Quoted in Grant (1981; emphasis added).
[4] Carmichael, "Free Huey" (1968), in Carmichael (1971: 119).

THE PREVIOUS CHAPTER discussed the moral activist, who draws on rhetorical power and voluntary moral commitment in an attempt to shrink the gap between high moral principles and harsh political practice. With roots in voluntary societies, particularly churches, and a determination to bypass formal government in favor of direct popular appeals, moral activism is one kind of politics whose sphere of activity is civil society rather than the state. Indeed, those who mistrust the compromises and corruptions of government officials but remain ardent about politics often turn to the moral activist as the *only* model of good political action. They look forward (or backwards) to a better, purer age, in which all politicians will be as sincere as moral activists and all citizens will guiltily and voluntarily confess our moral shortcomings and resolve to make a better world.

There is, however, another kind of politics outside the electoral realm, and another kind of politician who holds no government office and draws power from masses of ordinary citizens. This is the organizer. Good organizers differ from good activists in their view of politics, in the actions that they take based on that view, and in the characteristic dispositions that make them good at those actions.

Activists are Christian or Kantian believers in moral dignity; they act on the principle that all people *should* act morally and *can* do so if properly reminded of their duties. Organizers are practical democrats who believe that power and legitimacy lie in numbers; they therefore base their strategy on how most people *do* act most of the time and for long periods, not on noble but rare behavior (e.g., self-sacrifice in the service of abstract principles). From this basic difference in outlook—fundamentally different perspectives on what makes government institutions and individual actions legitimate and effective—follow very different approaches to politics. Activists try to rouse people's conscience; organizers count, at least initially, on baser springs of action like anger, shame, resentment, pride, and greed. Activists believe that morality is the same everywhere (at least everywhere in the country they live in), and therefore prize media events that reach as many people as possible, especially those whose interests are *not* directly affected. Organizers think that where one stands depends on where one sits, and therefore concentrate on the allegiance of those who have a personal stake in their cause. Activists care about *why* people act—that is, from moral principles—while organizers are concerned with *how* people act: on their own initiative and in large numbers, so that the democratic regime becomes not necessarily more elevated but more democratic, issue debates not more refined but more contested.

This distinction between activists and organizers may be new to many political theorists, but it is common wisdom among those who act in social movements and those who study them. It is present in the work of Saul Alinsky, the founding saint of community organizing, who tried to convince frustrated student radicals to become "realistic" rather than "rhetorical," to adapt their methods to a world "not of angels but of angles."[5] It is present in civil rights activist Ella Baker's distinction between organizers willing to do "spadework" among ordinary people and those (like Stokely Carmichael, but also Martin Luther King) who would rather hear themselves talk.[6] It is present in Robert Moses' distinction between the "community mobilizing" tradition of the civil rights movement, represented by Martin Luther King, and the "community organizing" tradition, represented by Baker and the members of the Student Nonviolent Coordinating Committee (SNCC), who put in years of canvassing and voter education among blacks in the Jim Crow South.[7] It is present in historical works on the civil rights movement that go beyond our obsession with a relatively few speeches and demonstrations and with Martin Luther King.[8] It is present among partisans of the moral activist as well, for instance in the gleeful statement of King associate Hosea Williams (in response to criticisms by SNCC) that his fellow preachers in SCLC could "bring the press in with us," while the student organizers could not.[9] And it is present in the work of a student of leadership like Garry Wills, who compares King's rhetorical brilliance to Robert Moses' "antirhetorical" organizing style, and notes that some considered the latter more sincere, less "showy," than King's flamboyant preaching.[10]

Despite the scholarly and practical attention to organizing, however, recent political and moral theory has been much more drawn to the ethi-

[5] Alinsky (1971: 13).

[6] Cited in Payne (1995: 85, 264; see also 379–80). Payne's excellent work has greatly influenced the argument of this chapter.

[7] Moses et al. (1989: 424); see also Moses' comments in Grant (1998: 121). King himself admitted that "organizing solidly and simultaneously in thousands of places was not a feature of our [SCLC's] work"; SCLC-type organizations "were born as specialists in agitation and dramatic projects." Quoted by Miroff (1993: 33a). I thank Sharon Krause for pointing out the quotation.

[8] In addition to the works cited below, and other works specifically on SNCC and/or its founders and leaders, see Payne (1995) and Morris (1984).

[9] Quoted by Garrow (1988: 441). Organizers, including Ella Baker, often reverse the activist's preference for the press, and distrust media-seekers as unlikely to stay around once the showy moments are over (Grant [1998: 5, 139]).

[10] Wills (1994: 225–26). Wills ends up calling Moses' leadership style complementary to King's, rather than worse. But since he does not analyze the organizer role in its own right, but only as an "antitype" to the rhetorical leader, the effect is to slight the organizer as a kind of sidekick to the more inspiring rhetorical activist.

cal issues involved in conspicuous, public, religious and moral appeals. The reasons for this are unclear; they may include the prevalence of one-sided histories of the civil rights movement, which stress the marches and speeches but not the organizing;[11] the rationalism and legalism of much standard political theory, which tends to portray the claims characteristic of the recently organized and formally less qualified as too vulgar and partisan to be taken seriously; and the deliberate estrangement of academic life from all contact with economic interests, whether in business or in the labor movement. For whatever reason, those who believe in bargaining and the power of numbers are widely portrayed by political and moral theorists as unprincipled, vaguely heartless, and indifferent to the plight of the least well off—a conclusion that would have amused and shocked Mother Jones, John L. Lewis, and A. Philip Randolph.

This neglect of the organizer comes at a cost to theory as well as history. Activists and organizers are distinct not just as a matter of history and tradition but in what each can contribute to the democratic order. An organizer can do things that a moral activist cannot.

First, the organizer can attack the basic class problem of democracy—its tendency to divide into the rich and isolated few and the poor but passive many—through democratic methods. To uphold an interest theory of democracy, as democratic constancy theory in general does, does not imply approval for letting the rich run everything or neglecting those with little personal wealth and influence. But the only thing that prevents these implications is the ability of the less-well-off to organize, compensating for their lack of individual pull with the power of democratic numbers. If democratic constancy tells us that people are no saints and will at most pursue their enlightened interest, it is the organizer who *gives* the rich an interest in giving up some of their privileges so that they can keep the rest.

Second, the organizer attacks head-on the problem of democratic servility: the gap in power between the state and the unaided individual. Organizers believe that the powerless and passive should learn to act for themselves and demand their rights, while asserting their independence. Agnes Meyer referred to Alinsky's community organizing as "organized individualism."[12] As argued below, this is a productive paradox, not a contradiction.

Finally, the organizer attacks the isolation of the rich. Tocqueville noted that the rich tend to a prideful separation from the affairs of their fellow citizens—and that democracy creates a countervailing force in that the rich need the many to accomplish their aims. It is the organizer

[11] See the literature review in Payne (1995: 418, and passim).
[12] Quoted by Horwitt (1992: 179).

who creates this force, through associational practices that Tocqueville notes are artificial, not natural.

Thus the organizer's purpose is to unify effective power and individual assertion; to put pressure on the powerful not for charity but for jobs, votes, and the other attributes of dignified citizenship; to induce in the organized an impulse towards self-improvement and increased civic capacities; and to make the wealthy few part of a democratic order in fact as well as in rhetoric.

One can see in such activities, performed both by the organizer and in the organized, a clear example of the semi-virtues of democratic constancy—perhaps the purest example. Tocqueville's doctrine of "self-interest properly understood," as a quality opposed to narrow individualism and fostered by organizational life, is the essence of democratic constancy for ordinary people not serving in government (love of fame being the equivalent for formal officeholders). This essence is even more distilled in the practice of full-time organizers: this kind of political work may be regarded as the fullest development of democratic constancy.

It is still, however, a *particular* development of good political character and action, one that derives its shape from the institutional position of the organizer as a citizen provoker rather than a policy maker. Where senators need only to listen to what ordinary people already want and explain why they cannot get all of it, organizers must try to make people articulate latent demands and learn how to fight for what they want. And where senatorial love of fame consists in the pursuit of projects and policies, the organizer's love of fame consists in building ever-widening organizations: in fostering the growth of people who demand programs, not in legislating or executing the programs. Because of this, organizers must display more patience in personal interactions and more restraint in pursuit of their personal agenda than occupants of other political offices. If democratic constancy involves aspects of both "pagan self-assertion" and "Christian self-denial,"[13] organizing requires a particularly heavy capacity for both.

To examine the organizer's activity is to see that constancy is not a crabbed virtue of shopkeepers and dour pessimists, and does not mean mere "delayed gratification" in the form of postponed consumption. The common lore of social change movements once stressed that long-term success in organizing required discipline: a willingness to work endless hours, to accept momentary frustration and personal rejections, and to keep a check on self-indulgent longings for premature action. Tocqueville, likewise, discussed the virtues of association without making strong distinctions among social, political, and profit-making associations: all

[13] Mill (1975: 59).

have in some sense a similar end (a desire to accomplish important objects independently of the state), and all appear to inculcate similar useful habits.[14] To the annoyance, perhaps, of both the contemporary left and the contemporary right, Tocqueville denies the distinction between bourgeois and citizen—he gives more importance to politics and benevolent societies than libertarians would like, and more to private enrichment through self-denial than leftists would like.[15] In fact, constancy as a democratic disposition is flexible and widely applicable. Theories of democracy, with its free-and-easy principles, should not try to decide a priori whether the intelligent pursuit of interest should at a given time require pursuit of profit through economic partnership or a certain disciplined type of political activity.[16]

In the rest of the chapter I explore that constant activity: its theoretical rationale, found in Tocqueville, its characteristic forms in action, as found in the theory and practice of civil rights organizers, and the dispositions necessary to act according to those forms, as put forth by Alinsky. I then consider, as in the previous chapter, positive and negative examples of organizers in history: Ella Baker, the beloved practitioner and teacher of civil rights organizing, and Stokely Carmichael, a student of Baker's who rapidly became known as undisciplined, self-indulgent, and unable to create either pressure on the government or civic capacities in ordinary people.

Theory: Tocqueville on Democratic Association and Neo-Tocquevillean Organizing

Tocqueville's account of organizational action was rooted, as all his work, in basic premises about the nature of democracy and the characteristic dangers it is subject to. Most fundamentally, Tocqueville recognized that, in a democracy, the adherence of large *numbers* to an idea or position itself creates "collective power," even "moral prestige."[17] The government and its opponents both recognize this. The "moral strength of the government" is great in a democracy because universal suffrage guarantees that the opposition commands fewer numbers. Conversely, citizens

---

[14] *DIA*: II.2.5, pp. 513–17.

[15] See the exchange among Benjamin R. Barber, Milton Friedman, and various commentators in Evers (1990: 27–57). For an exceptional recognition of the relation between bourgeois and citizen virtues in Tocquevillean-style thought, see Fukuyama (1995).

[16] "Economic partnership," however, is the right phrase: Tocqueville's virtues of economic association seem to be associated with mutual cooperation, as found in partnerships or cooperatives, not with the deeply unequal wage labor relationships of an unchecked corporation, about which Tocqueville has some rather radical things to say.

[17] *DIA*: I.2.4, p. 190.

who find themselves in the minority associate "in the first place to show their numbers and to lessen the moral authority of the majority," in the second place to find out what arguments will persuade enough people on the other side that they can form a new majority.[18]

In fact, while accounts of "association" or "civil society" often define such terms according to the moral qualities and civic benefits these are supposed to promote, Tocqueville (whose definition will be followed here) defines associations in terms of numbers and cooperation before considering their moral qualities:

> An association simply consists in the public and formal support of specific doctrines by a certain number of individuals who have undertaken to cooperate in a stated way in order to make these doctrines prevail. . . . When some view is represented by an association, it must take clearer and more precise shape. It counts its supporters and involves them in its cause; these supporters get to know one another, and numbers increase zeal. An association unites the energies of divergent minds and vigorously directs them toward a clearly indicated goal.[19]

When Tocqueville talks of dangerous political associations (opposition parties) that have "almost equal moral authority" to the government, he means by this that they have equal *numbers*.[20] Thus, in a democracy, majority numbers confer the right to govern, increasing numbers holding an opinion confer increasing moral prestige; and the desire to win over greater numbers provides the motive for argument as well as the form it takes.

This does not mean, of course, that Tocqueville simply loved the American attachment to numbers, and in particular majorities. He noted two dangers of numbers-based democratic politics, both of which can be regarded as problems endemic to democratic politics that the organizer must recognize and combat.[21]

First was the well-known tendency to majority tyranny: "In the United States, once a party has become predominant, all public power passes into its hands; its close supporters occupy all offices and have control of all organized forces."[22] Because of this, *"unlimited* freedom of association"—a part of American "customs and of mores"—is a "dangerous expedient," but one worth risking: "The most distinguished men of the opposite party, unable to cross the barrier keeping them from power,

[18] Ibid.: 193–94.
[19] Ibid.: 190.
[20] Ibid.: 190–91.
[21] The need, or at least the desire, to reform public mores through conspicuous example, shame, and the collection of numbers involves the activity of the activist and has been discussed above.
[22] *DIA*: I.2.4, p. 192.

must be able to establish themselves outside it; the minority must use the whole of its moral authority to oppose the physical power oppressing it."[23]

Organizing of minorities, however dangerous and subject to abuses, was, and remains, the only possible check against organized majorities (i.e., democratic government). As Tocqueville noted, we have no aristocratic "secondary bodies" to "hold abuses of power in check," so we must "artificially and temporarily create something like [those bodies]" through voluntary action.[24]

Tocqueville's concerns on this score went beyond tyrannical government action on concrete matters, however: he also feared the effects of *societal* tyranny on thoughts and mores. In aristocracies average people tend to be guided in their views by "a more thoughtful man or class," but in democracies "public opinion becomes more and more mistress of the world. . . . In times of equality men, being so like each other, have no confidence in others, but this same likeness leads them to place almost unlimited confidence in the judgment of the public. For they think it not unreasonable that, all having the same means of knowledge, truth will be found on the side of the majority. . . . The same equality which makes him [the citizen of a democracy] independent of each separate citizen leaves him isolated and defenseless in the face of the majority." Thus individual opinions are suppressed by a "mighty pressure of the mind of all upon the intelligence of each."[25] The independent thought that liberals (rightly) hold up as a civic ideal is not natural to democracies but "artificial." We need, once again, voluntary, collective activity in order to provoke it: people's *natural* tendency in a democracy is to assume they have nothing special to contribute that others have not already thought of.

What kind of collective action this could be is a complicated question, since collective action must somehow be made to foster not just civic opinions but *individual* opinions. Organizers must keep this paradox from becoming a contradiction. Tocqueville suggests one way out when he notes and endorses the internal governance of the typical American association, which is civic and encourages a variety of views: "There is a place for individual independence there; as in society, all the members are advancing at the same time toward the same goal but they are not obliged to follow exactly the same path. There has been no sacrifice of will or of reason, but rather will and reason are applied to bring success to a common enterprise."[26]

Organizers must take care to do the same: to encourage discussion and

---

[23] Ibid.
[24] Ibid.
[25] Ibid.: II.1.2, p. 435.
[26] *DIA*: I.2.4, p. 195.

dissent within their organizations, even when taking all decisions upon themselves would be more tempting.

A second disease endemic to democracies is the temptation on the part of the rich or prominent to opt out, to dissociate themselves from a vulgar society that they feel is beneath them. But democracy also provides countervailing inducements for the rich *not* to do this: since the many control public affairs, "the rich in democracies always need the poor." In return for political and social support through their numbers, the poor do not want primarily material benefits—which, as Tocqueville noted, "by their very greatness spotlight the difference in conditions and arouse a secret annoyance in those who profit from them."[27] What the people want from the rich is "simple good manners," signs of respect: they demand of the rich "not the sacrifice of their money but of their pride." But this truth, if clear to the unbiased observer, is not immediately clear to the rich, who "will gladly do good to the people, but . . . still want carefully to keep their distance from them."[28] One of the jobs of the organizer is to explain to the rich that they need the people and cannot afford aristocratic disdain for them. One sure way to tell a good organizer is that he or she knows how to talk to the rich in the only terms that can lead them to sacrifice their pride: those of enlightened self-interest.

Tocqueville's doctrine on these matters can be called radically democratic in the true sense, not because Tocqueville loved democracy all that much but because he assumed that the problems of democracy required democratic solutions. Attempts to retain elements of aristocracy in government, or to replace them with oligarchy, Tocqueville's work rejects. He professes himself "firmly convinced that one cannot found an aristocracy anew in this world." To be sure, he calls associations "aristocratic bodies," but they are aristocratic in effect, not in form or motive power: they are "rich, influential, and powerful," but remain "associations of plain citizens."[29] To the extent that associations lend an aristocratic spirit to politics, they do so by encouraging that spirit in collections of ordinary individuals, not in rich and powerful individuals separate from the whole. (The latter must, on the contrary, learn how to give up some of their quasi-aristocratic pride, which in a democracy is no longer functional and only stands in the way of their achieving their goals.) And while Tocqueville recognizes that industry may lead to a quasi aristoc-

---

[27] *DIA*: II.2.4, p. 512. Compare Saul Alinsky's slogan (also a slogan of the labor movement): "Damn your charity—give us jobs" (Alinsky [1989: 59]). In general, the organizing tradition takes an ambivalent attitude toward the welfare state, preferring job opportunities to the dole.

[28] *DIA*: II.2.4, p. 512.

[29] *DIA*: II.4.7, p. 697.

racy, as division of labor separates the craft from the craftsman, he *attacks* the nascent industrial aristocracy that results from this process as uncaring, lacking in self-reflection, brutal, and destructive of all true association between industrialist and worker. Tocqueville rarely gives democracy egalitarian advice (he doubts that democracy needs it), but when it comes to the budding industrial aristocracy he warns the "friends of democracy" to "keep their eyes anxiously fixed in that direction," lest "permanent inequality of conditions" again take hold.[30]

Tocqueville restates in this way Madison's allegiance to an "unmixed republic" against those who seek to mix popular government with sources of authority independent of the people. Oligarchic and aristocratic responses to the dangers of democracy were available to Tocqueville (himself a born aristocrat who had read Burke as well as the Federalists), but at least when it came to his American travels and reflections, he rejected them in favor of letting democratic associations solve the very problems of passivity and tyranny to which democracy was subject. While these associations are not without risk, reliance on them is the least bad alternative. Because democratic associations will always recognize that they have in the end less authority than the constituted majority rule of the government, the risk of anarchy and violence inherent in unlimited associational freedom is ameliorated. "Thus in the immense complication of human laws it sometimes comes about that extreme freedom corrects the abuse of freedom, and extreme democracy forestalls the dangers of democracy."[31] This salutary pessimism is a long way from the optimism that the ills of democracy can be cured by "more democracy."[32] The solution to the problems of democracy for Tocqueville is a *certain kind* of democratic practice, and if we are not careful, associational life may in fact prove worse than the diseases it is supposed to remedy.

Corresponding to the two needs of a democracy were two modes of association that are not often distinguished in Tocqueville scholarship because in fact they go together in practice. Still, it is useful to separate out the two strands in order to discern the two separate activities that organizers must combine.

First is "organizing" the rich, or those socially advantaged in other ways, to sacrifice their pride as they need to in order to pursue common projects with the people. What Alinsky called a neighborhood organization or people's organization needs the money and social resources that such people (so-called pillars of the community) command, but the rich

---

[30] *DIA*: II.2.20, pp. 555–58; quotation from 558.
[31] *DIA*: I.2.4, p. 195.
[32] Dewey (1954: 144). To be sure, what Dewey meant by this slogan is less literal and more complex than what some of his more zealous followers have taken it to mean.

do not give such support naturally. Tocqueville famously believed that the way to get a prominent person interested in public affairs was to show him a concrete benefit to be gained by doing so: "If it is a question of taking a road past his property, he sees at once that this small public matter has a bearing on his greatest private interests."[33] One central task of an organizer is to persuade the rich that a new organization resembles the case of "a road past his property"—a matter of interest—rather than a matter of universal respect or caring for all people as such, which (as Tocqueville knew) is not a sentiment natural to human beings, particularly well-off ones.

Second is organization that might be called from the bottom and for the bottom. Against the passivity and willingness to accept majority opinion characteristic of mass democracy, the organizer aims to inspire the stubborn self-assertion and refusal to submit characteristic of *civic* democracy. The most conspicuous example of such assertion is voter registration, particularly in areas where registration is actively (often violently) discouraged by a ruling party. But a limited portion of the citizen body must learn to do more than vote—must become informed about issues and active in support of their own enlightened interests—if ordinary citizens as a whole are to salvage their own civic dignity and combat the complacent tyranny of the unchallenged administrative state.

Tocqueville's theory has limits, not because his central observations about democracy were wrong but because he could not put every possible problem of democracy at the center of his vision. Alinsky and other theorists of organization, even if they considered themselves followers of Tocqueville, have had to add to or modify Tocqueville's doctrines to respond to the problems of contemporary society and of the particular places where they were organizing. Five examples come to mind.

First, Tocqueville was so impressed with the pervasiveness of democratic conditions in America that he chose not to focus on the exceptions to these conditions, or on the social and economic forces that might endanger their continuation. First of these exceptions was *feudal inequality in the South*. Tocqueville found Southern aristocracy in the form of slave society immoral, antidemocratic, and anti-Christian, but he made these observations with a fatalistic attitude that sits uneasily with his usual appreciation of Americans' political resourcefulness. Tocqueville wrote that Southerners could never free their slaves unless they were prepared to intermarry with them. Otherwise, if the blacks were freed they would feel a demand for equal rights while "being unable to become

---

[33] *DIA*: II.2.4, p. 511.

the equals of the whites," resulting in a huge race war.[34] But during the Southern organizing struggle of the 1950s and 1960s, blacks freed themselves and solved their own problems of citizenship education in ways that Tocqueville could hardly have foreseen.

Second, the problems of *industrial capitalism* were something that Tocqueville considered more directly but did not tell us how to solve. As noted above, Tocqueville foresaw and decried the growing industrial aristocracy. But he did not flesh out (perhaps could not foresee) the prime solution to this problem—unions—and the many variations of union pressure tactics from which Alinsky and the organizing movement as a whole would draw inspiration.

Third, Tocqueville *assumed that the rich and prominent would want political power*: this is what let him predict that they would realize the need for alliances with ordinary people if they wanted to achieve their ends. At a time when the wealthy outside the South were largely Whigs with an attachment to internal improvements—not coincidentally is it a *road* that makes the complacent citizen seek his fellows' help—this assumption was fair. But things are no longer so simple. Several commentators have argued that the upper classes are now inclined to opt out of public services altogether in favor of private schools, roads, and security forces.[35] While such arrangements might require the rich to combine with each other, they leave them able to ignore people of lesser means (this is in fact the whole point of the separatist enterprise). To some extent, this strategy can be shown to be self-defeating, and we shall examine ways in which organizers have tried to persuade rich people that it is. But to some extent, the "revolt of the elites" (Christopher Lasch) *is* a rational response to those elites' situation and power calculations. Those who wish to restore communication between the classes must change the situation and the distribution of power. Again, this means direct pressure, which might be regarded as the creation by art of the natural common interests that used to exist. Those who regard this as (nonviolent) coercion are not wrong, but it is coercion with limits, and for civic purposes.

Fourth, because Tocqueville was concerned with political institutions, not the ethics of individuals, and moreover with institutions that were functioning well, he did not spend much time thinking about *rules for action*, or about what extraordinary and deliberate efforts might be necessary to restore the health of organizational life once the fortuitous habits and practices of early-nineteenth-century America had fallen into disuse. Tocqueville wrote of the "art of association," and thought that civiliza-

---

[34] *DIA*: I.2.10, p. 360.
[35] Reich (1991: 268–300); Lind (1995: 139–216); Lasch (1995: 25–49).

tion required that this art "develop and improve . . . at the same speed as equality of conditions spreads."[36] But he did not write much about the art itself: how to practice it, what actions it required, what temptations had to be overcome in order to do it well.

Some recent communitarian and conservative Tocquevilleans write as if they could restore the Tocquevillean state by restoring the necessary social institutions first (apparently by sheer force of collective will), and then waiting for the automatic processes that Tocqueville chronicled to take effect.[37] But this is to misunderstand not only Tocqueville but politics in general. Tocqueville thought that association was not natural (nor can its absence be blamed solely on the state): it draws people "out of their own circle," in spite of the fact that "differences in age, intelligence, or wealth, may naturally keep them apart."[38] Purposeful action must start from what is, and if we must create associations from scratch, it is often harder to resurrect old bodies whose social bases no longer exist than to create different associations that people may see as responding to their *current* enlightened interests. Associational life is based on habits: "Once [people] have met, they always know how to meet again."[39] But once the habit is gone, reinvigorating associational life requires purposeful organizing, not mere nostalgia.

Finally comes a problem that is not Tocqueville's fault: some observations that he meant to put forth as particular observations about democracy in his time have come to be exaggerated. People have mistaken contingent empirical observations for irrefutable dogmas.

First among these dogmas is the idea that organizational life depends above all on churches. Add to this some common stereotypes about African-Americans, and we have the common belief that black organizational life means a coalition among black churches as the only organized force in the community. Though Tocqueville did claim that only religion was capable of combating the tendency toward narrow *materialism* and focusing the mind on great objects,[40] there is no passage where Tocqueville claims that *political organization* rests particularly on churches. As mentioned above, he mentions social, economic, and political bodies as simi-

---

[36] *DIA*: II.2.5, p. 517.

[37] See Mitchell (1995); Bellah et al. (1985, 1992). Bellah et al. (1992: 179–219, on the "Public Church") are particularly frustrating on this score: after discussing how the kind of religion they want is in decline for several reasons that are not about to change, the authors say that churches "can, and must" increase their moral and political role. Apparently, they can *because* they must: a stance that entails a self-defeating refusal to discuss concrete possibilities for getting from one place to another.

[38] *DIA*: II.2.6, p. 521.

[39] Ibid.

[40] *DIA*: II.1.5, p. 448.

lar in nature and mutually reinforcing. In any case, it is empirically false that churches are always at the center of organizing struggles. Charles Payne notes that churches underpinned the civil rights movement only in urban areas; in the rural South, ministers were dependent on local plantation owners and often came to the struggle after everyone else.[41] Ella Baker regarded churches as valuable sources of organizational experience and discipline (especially for women, the ones who really ran them), but thought unions would do just as well as a source of "good leadership."[42] Even Saul Alinsky, who was so fond of working through Catholic churches that his enemies thought him a papist tool, tried to bring churches into coalition with unions whenever possible, and was willing to organize on other bases in communities that had low church membership (as with the FIGHT group in Rochester, New York).[43] A broad movement for civic action among the many will find and exploit individual initiative and civic virtue wherever it is found, and spurn institutions, including churches, if they in fact act in a dependent manner or lack the voluntary character that is required.

Practice: Civil Rights organizing the SNCC Way

In the early 1980s, Robert Moses (a celebrated former organizer for SNCC) and several co-authors distinguished between two traditions of civil rights organizing, traditions they distinguished not by their doctrines but by their characteristic practices. While the "community mobilization tradition," epitomized by Martin Luther King focused on "large-scale events" and "inspiring immense crowds in vast public spaces," the "community organizing tradition" was an "older, yet less well known" tradition that focused on careful work among ordinary people. This was "the tradition in the Civil Rights Movement of quiet places and the organizers who liked to work them."[44]

Moses writes of the organizing tradition as "organizing in the Spirit of Ella," meaning Ella Baker, whom he describes as the *fundi*, or traditional

---

[41] Payne (1995: 177, 191). See also Morris (1984: 5ff.).

[42] Ella Baker, cited in Grant (1981). See also Grant (1998: 19, and esp. 118, in which Baker while secretary of SCLC urges the organization to "stimulate religious bodies, civic and fraternal organizations" indiscriminately—neither neglecting churches nor giving them special emphasis).

[43] Horwitt (1992: 59ff.); Sethi (1970: 68).

[44] Moses et al. (1989: 424). I will attribute the article's initial observations on SNCC's methods of organizing to Moses rather than his co-authors, since he was himself a quite legendary organizer and a special protégé of Ella Baker's, and repeats the same basic sentiment in Grant (1981; 1998: 121). Moses would have needed help for the parts of the article dealing with educational theory.

African craft-teacher, of the organizers centered around SNCC.[45] Like a fundi, Baker built on those who went before her, wrote little about her craft, and left evidence of her role mostly in the actions of others. So before engaging in an assessment of Baker's own activities, we must infer from the actions and words of civil rights organizers—including those instructed by Baker—a model of what they thought they were doing when they were organizing successfully, ethically, and democratically. Some organizers wrote a great deal but did comparatively little organizing of their own (Alinsky in his later years comes to mind, and therefore may be more important as a theorist than as an exemplar of organizing). Baker did the opposite, and we must therefore use others' theory to illuminate her own example.

Moses defines the organizing tradition according to three basic principles: "the centrality of *families* to the work of organizing; the *empowerment of grassroots people* and their recruitment for leadership; and the principle of 'casting down your bucket where you are,' or *organizing in the context* in which one lives and works, and working the issues found in that context."[46] Family, grassroots empowerment, and organizing in context, when properly understood, remain the three basic concepts around which good organizers base their action. What do they entail?

Family: Trust and Action in Face-to-Face Societies

When Moses writes about the "family" of the civil rights movement, he does not mean literal families united by kinship and marriage (though in the immediate context of teaching schoolchildren math, this meaning of "family" is relevant). By a family relationship, Moses means a relationship among people who are personally acquainted and who trust one another on a deep level that goes beyond (and does not necessarily require) shared convictions. By a process Moses calls "informal absorption," Moses writes, SNCC organizers were taken in by local families, becoming honorary children of the community and thus negating the label of "outside agitator." In turn, the organizers "empowered their adoptive families by reinforcing and enlarging the connections between

---

[45] Moses et al. (1989: 424n1) define a *fundi* as "a Swahili term for a person who has an expertise valued by society, and who passes on his or her art to the young by example and instruction." (The Joanne Grant film *Fundi* [1981] gets its name from this label for Baker.) According to Moses, Baker's "art" was organizing.

[46] Moses et al. (1989: 425). The article where this appears gives these phrases an unusual context, since it is putting forth and advocating not a classic organizing movement but a new set of techniques for teaching math to black children. But the basic insights were based on earlier experiences with organizing that were more clearly political. "Cast down your bucket where you are" was, of course, a favorite saying of Booker T. Washington.

them and the larger Movement family, with its extensive networks across the land."[47]

This use of surrogate "family" for the purpose of building trust and enabling power can be explored through Peter Laslett's concept of a "face to face society."[48] A family is a face-to-face society, writes Laslett, because "all of its activities either are, or can be, carried on by means of conversation, conversation between members of the family." The family is the most familiar instance of such a society, but the Greek *polis* and the British House of Commons are others.[49] Such societies are characterized, first, by their members' "knowing" each other and, second, by a kind of suprarational decision-making. "Knowing" means that the members are "never called upon to co-operate in any other way than by being present at what is going on." When they are present and cooperating in this way they "respond with their whole personality, conscious and unconscious" and know that the other members are doing the same. When such societies get together to decide things, they do so by "meeting and talking," a process that *includes* "ratiocination" but is not limited to it. Exclamations, laughs, silences, and other nonpropositional expressions are part of the decision-making process as they are part of normal conversation. The process involves "intuitive psychology" and "total intercourse between personalities." (This contrasts with intercourse among people who do not know each other, which is a "matter of record" and involves ratiocination almost exclusively.)[50] Laslett seems to regard the trust and allegiance that builds up within such a society as natural—while the allegiance of people to distant government officials, or the state, is harder to explain (and seems to him quasi-religious). This seems to correspond both to Tocqueville's theory and to common sense: a family or a long-running group of intimate associates feels itself to be a unit bound together—for better or for worse—by mutual understanding in a way that a whole political movement, mass party, or country cannot be.

But the purpose of a face-to-face society is not trust for any purpose, but trust with a view to action. Laslett states that "any given sample of individuals capable of acting collectively" must discover within itself—or itself constitute—a "group of a critical size" that can act in this face-to-face way. Political scientists share this insight: they have often noted that committees capable of actually reaching decisions have to be very small.[51]

Community organizations are, or aspire to be, face-to-face societies.

[47] Ibid.

[48] Laslett (1956: 157–84).

[49] Laslett's account hardly seems to describe the life of a backbencher in the Commons; he might better have said the Cabinet.

[50] Laslett (1956: 157–60).

[51] See, for example, Dahl and Tufte (1973); and Olson (1971: 53ff.).

This is true, and appropriate, for two reasons corresponding to Laslett's. First, this is the only way to "act collectively," to form isolated and passive individuals into a body that takes initiative, makes decisions, and exerts pressure. This is a rather routine insight—that only small committees and not huge notional groups with a million members can take initiatives and make decisions—and will not be dwelt on. More important is the second point, that *nonrational* assessments of another's character are the best way to get people to trust one another when they have limited time and resources, limited formal education and ability to assess complicated propositions, and little political experience.

It is important to realize why there is a problem to be solved here. The label of outside agitator is often fatal to an organizer, because if it sticks it calls into question among local people the organizer's right to be listened to on political matters. From a theoretical standpoint, this attitude might be labeled as insufficiently cosmopolitan and open to new ideas. But organizers know that distrust of outsiders—however much it is fanned by powerful locals for bad purposes—is based on a largely *legitimate* suspicion of people who talk of great changes while their commitment to the welfare of locals has not yet been proven. Intelligent organizers accept that a good argument coming from one person is listened to more than the same argument coming from another.

Because of such concerns, many organizers have developed a principle of only going where they are specifically invited by large numbers of locals (or can wangle an invitation), for this provides "credentials."[52] But in black areas of the rural South this was not necessary, for locals developed another method for distinguishing unwelcome "outsiders" from prospective friends. Rural blacks in the South, notes Payne, were accustomed to evaluating someone's ideas based on an assessment of his or her character, not the other way around. Organizers counted on being judged by informal and ineffable ways of taking a person's measure. One organizer for the Congress on Racial Equality said that rural people

> deal more with the character of an individual rather than what he's saying. . . . When you met him, whatever way he was when you met, when you saw him ten years later . . . he would still be the same way, ten years down the road. . . . They knew who was strong and who was for real and who wasn't. . . . We would get caught up in words and logic. That didn't mean nothing to

[52] Alinsky (1971: 101). Even Martin Luther King, in his "Letter from Birmingham City Jail" (in Washington [1991: 290]), takes time to respond to accusations of being an outside agitator by noting that he has been "invited" to Birmingham and has "organizational ties" there—though he then, in the style of the activist rather than the organizer, goes on to contest the legitimacy of the accusation, comparing the scope of his moral calling to that of St. Paul.

them. They were dealing with motives and intent. Skip all the words and everything else. They brushed that aside and got right to what the individual was about.[53]

Organizers began their real political relationships with local people as soon as—and not before—"they were *judged to be worthwhile people*."[54]

This implies a requirement for the kind of self-control that we might compare to that of prospective family members (during courtship or an initial meeting with in-laws). Organizers, in Payne's account, "self-consciously strove to be on their best behavior around local people, best behavior as defined by local people." They tried to appear as "God-fearing, as respectful of women and the elderly, as men and women of their word, as principled."[55] Volunteers during the 1964 Freedom Summer had to keep up strict moral appearances—"no drinking, no dating of locals" (one was fired for insisting she should be allowed to hold hands in public).[56]

Similarly, the extension of the "family" into the larger civil rights movement can be quite seriously compared to the process of matchmaking, as Baker "set up" Robert Moses with Amzie Moore and other contacts in Mississippi. Matchmaking, a respected occupation in many societies, demands great judgment of character on short acquaintance. It also requires being more of a busybody than most ordinary people are comfortable with. Good organizers, like matchmakers, are thanked for their activities *and* regarded as a bit outrageous. The Jewish word for the disposition involved is *chutzpah*: "nerve" (in the good *and* bad senses). Baker explicitly named "nerve" as the virtue organizers needed to "invad[e]" beer gardens and night clubs in search of new organization members; she herself habitually accosted strangers in Harlem and said "Hello brother [or sister] . . . And where do you hail from?"[57]

Finally, the making of civil rights families often resembles something like counseling a married couple when that "family," like a marriage, is in danger of splitting up and no longer being face to face. Successful negotiation in organizations requires a mature understanding of face-to-face groups: like families, community or movement organizations involve intimate acquaintance, but not necessarily love at all times or in all directions. We hope to love our spouses, but are also required to get along with the in-laws. These things involve constancy in the form of patience, reticence, and the capacity for intelligent self-delusion. It is fatal to hope

---

[53] Matt Suarez, cited in Payne (1995: 238–39). Ellipses in original.
[54] Payne (1995: 239; emphasis added).
[55] Payne (1995: 243).
[56] Branch (1998: 493).
[57] Grant (1998: 49, 27).

for a pure and perfect "love" that is beyond the reality of real families, let alone artificial ones. What one can hope for instead is the enlargement of sympathies and growing awareness of common interests that Tocqueville hoped for in associations.

Empowerment and Grassroots Leadership

The purpose of a democratic organizer is to fulfill the promise of equal democratic rights, to fight tyranny, and to get ordinary people involved in social action in concert with one another. None of these things can happen if the organizer acts as a top-down "leader," telling the troops what to do while only he exercises independent judgment and initiative. Tocqueville noted that American organizations had a "civil government." But this is not a natural or inevitable state for organizations, especially new ones. On the contrary, for an educated, politically sophisticated organizer facing a group of uneducated political neophytes, the desire to take over is both natural and strong. A good organizer resists the temptation; in fact, the ability to resist it was seen by Baker as the central difference between "leaders" who keep others passive and organizers "interested not in being leaders as much as in developing leadership among other people."[58]

This does not mean that organizers are supposed to do nothing or merely stir up a "spontaneous" popular movement that is waiting to happen. Baker's and other radical democrats' talk of developing local *leadership* necessarily implies that somebody has to be leading in some respect. But there are three crucial differences between an organizer's leading the organization herself and her developing local leaders. Each of these differences points to the need to exercise difficult qualities of character.

First, the organizer of local leaders must be willing to acknowledge as a leader anyone who commands respect or has useful friends, whether or not the person is of high status. SNCC worked through bootleggers and recruited a former prostitute to run citizenship classes; Baker thought that failure to fight for the rights of social outcasts such as drunks stood in the way of effective organizing; southern radical Myles Horton found black beauticians excellent political contacts in the Jim Crow era because they were "relatively insulated from white community sanctions"; Alinsky sang the organizational praises of petty racketeers, and on at least one

---

[58] Baker (1970: 351). Alinsky (1971: 61), making a similar distinction between leaders and organizers, notes that this does not mean that an organizer lacks ego, only that his ego is directed at different things: "The ego of the organizer is stronger and more monumental than the ego of the leader. The leader is driven by the desire for power, while the organizer is driven by the desire to create. The organizer is in a true sense reaching for the highest level for which man can reach—to create, to be a 'great creator,' to play God."

occasion "had hookers doing fund-raisers" (giving new meaning to the currently popular phrase "social capital").[59]

Second, the organizer must acknowledge a distinction between local leaders and everyone else. She must realize that not everyone loves politics as much as she does, and accept the fact that mass participation in politics will be intermittent at best. Alinsky, one of the century's biggest boosters of participation, acknowledged from long experience that the most successful organizations had an active participation rate of around 5 to 7 percent of the community, and that participation at this rate, much higher than that of the CIO or political parties, conferred great power.[60] Robert Dahl has distinguished between *homo politicus*, a character type who likes being involved in politics, and *homo civicus*, the average citizen who has better things to do. "*Homo civicus*," he reminds us, "is not, by nature, a political animal."[61] The purpose of an organizer is not to make everyone into *homo politicus*, but to find *potential* political animals and make them into actual local leaders. Effective organizers are rarely seen complaining about the fact that most people are not active enough but "only" vote and contribute money. They consider these ordinary contributions the lifeblood of an organization, and feel happy to find what local leaders there are among a group of people used to exercising no power at all. And they are right. Many people who complain about mass apathy are students or full-time activists with no idea of the demands on ordinary people's time and money. Organizers work with the material they have.

Finally, an organizer must cultivate the link between action and education. Against "civic" educators who treat citizenship as a group of platitudes to be learned from a book, organizers know that people learn when they have an incentive to learn, and that local leaders must therefore be encouraged to assume serious tasks *before* they have the formal knowledge that might appear necessary for their responsibly doing so.[62] On the

---

[59] See, respectively, Payne (1995: 143, 166); Cantarow and O'Malley (1980: 70); Grant (1998: 54); Delgado (1986: 31); Alinsky (1989: 111), regarding racketeers; and Horwitt (1992: 402), regarding fund-raisers.

[60] Alinsky (1989: 181ff.).

[61] Dahl (1961: 225). Note that Aristotle did not mean "political animal" in this sense.

[62] Thus Stokely Carmichael, in organizing the Lowndes County Freedom Organization (the first party to use the Black Panther logo, though unaffiliated with the party of that name), encouraged barely competent people to run for offices like sheriff and tax assessor; then those people acquired an interest in learning what those offices did and developing a platform (Carmichael and Hamilton [1967: 111ff.]). Similarly, members of an Alinsky organization learned about the role of the federal government after they felt they had some power and might be able to pressure the government for grants if they found out what programs existed (Alinsky [1989: 165–69, 173]). This latter case is instructive as to means as well: Alinsky knew all about the government programs, but pretended to be less well in-

other hand, against some optimists who assume, or hope, that civic capacities will increase as soon as institutions are structured in a participatory fashion, organizers know that such development is not automatic—that institutions do not automatically call forth the capacities that would be needed in order for them to function well. Democratic institutions, including social movements and community organizations themselves, may simply act badly, irresponsibly, or stupidly if the people in them are not prodded to develop the capacities to run them well. Organizers believe in what is sometimes called "developmental democracy," but they regard this as a practice and a program rather than a state. Developing political capacities requires a level of involvement and clearheaded assessment that an aloof leader would be able to dispense with. Empowerment and development are *purposeful* activities, which will not happen unless someone acts to make them happen.

Organizing in a Context

Organizing "in the context in which one lives and works, and working the issues found in that context," means that both the organizer's goals and her methods must take direction from local wishes and expectations. Adjusting to context can be seen as having a general and a special sense, both requiring a democratic attitude toward human imperfection and a constant restraint of the organizer's own moralistic and ideological wishes.

In a general sense, the context in which one organizes is the context of human nature: an organizer has a knack for discerning human motivations like shame, anger, competitiveness, and the like, and a willingness to play on such motivations despite personal discomfort at the fact that people are not nobler. Alinsky recruited an important labor leader by inviting him to a baseball game but spending the whole game whispering with other people about the community organization: the boss's pride as a leader made him want to be a prominent person in the new organization, as he was in his union.[63] The racketeer mentioned above wanted above all to be respectable, and Alinsky got him more and more involved in an organization (and more willing to keep minors out of his gambling dens) by letting him pose for pictures with important political and social leaders.[64] Most instructively, in dealing with two business leaders who had joined an organization merely as good advertising, Alinsky put them on the children's committee, where they saw poverty first hand. Having

---

formed than he was so that local leaders would learn how to seek out and use government information on their own.

[63] Alinsky (1989: 109).

[64] Alinsky (1989: 112).

joined out of self-interest, they were quickly introduced to wider social interests and became dedicated to organizing around them.[65]

More particularly, organizing in a context means a willingness to find out and organize around the issues that the people *being organized* care about, rather than the issues that one cares most about oneself. This is a kind of self-denial. When Ella Baker was director of branches for the NAACP, she first found out what issues local people cared about—things as prosaic as street lights—and *then* explained how the political position the NAACP represented was related to these concerns.[66] The assumption is that the grievances people actually have are, if not fully informed or enlightened, at least a respectable starting point. This is a democratic assumption that starts with the premise that most people know at least something about their own interests.[67]

Putting this assumption into practice requires ideological flexibility and discipline at the same time. Flexibility, in that an organizer—generally an opinionated type—generally has preconceived plans or programs that he must keep silent about or ignore altogether if locals do not like them. (Later, after the organizer has gained trust and allies, he can suggest his own opinion from the position of one friend among equals, not from that of a know-it-all outsider with contempt for local mores.)[68] Discipline, with respect to local opinions and outlooks, to which an organizer must be constantly attentive. This latter kind of discipline—the opposite, by the way, of the centralized "discipline" of a totalitarian party—is in fact the way in which organizers keep from becoming rabble-rousing "subversives": most Americans like the democratic system and want to preserve it, and will not sign up with an organization that thinks otherwise. Those who preach Che, Fanon, or Mao generally turn out to be self-appointed "leaders" rather than organizers respected by large numbers of ordinary citizens. As Payne has written, "Some of the contentious and dogmatic behavior that came to characterize the [civil rights] movement in the middle sixties would never have been tolerated by local people."[69]

---

[65] Alinsky (1989: 97–98).

[66] Baker (1970: 347).

[67] "If you respect the dignity of the individual you are working with, then his desires, not yours; his values, not yours; his ways of working and fighting, not yours; his choice of leadership, not yours; his programs, not yours; are important and must be followed; except if his programs violate the high values of a free and open society"—Alinsky (1971: 122).

[68] Alinsky (1971: 94) gives the example of birth control. Liberal Protestants who combined their social gospel–inspired programs for the poor with birth control information were unable to gain even an initial hearing in Catholic neighborhoods. Alinsky supported contraception, but kept quiet about it in the service of pursuing more immediate goals and furthering the social, economic, and political development of the neighborhoods he worked in. Later, he was able and willing to broach the subject respectfully, and with quiet humor, even to priests.

[69] Payne (1995: 373).

Moreover, organizers must follow this mean between flexibility and discipline, not only with respect to ideas but with respect to people. As Baker noted, early SNCC volunteers were willing to deal with socially conservative locals, and often found them invaluable in organizing communities around far-reaching and courageous goals. Later black radicals often came in condemning certain attitudes and social sectors as "reactionary," thus dooming their chances to influence anyone.[70] Respect for people's opinions as they are is particularly important if one takes seriously the Tocquevillean mandate not only to organize the poor but to convince the comfortable that their interest lies in common action. Radicals hoping to persuade the rich to rejoin democratic life should sometimes start by warning them, but never by insulting them. Once again, there is a world of difference between a tough appeal to interest and an offensive charge of immorality.

These habits or techniques Moses seems to have found natural: he did not have to work at them. Because of his organizing skill, courage, and self-effacing dedication, he was thought of in the Mississippi movement as something of a saint, and in fact had to make conscious efforts not to be followed as the "Moses" his name evoked.[71] Many of the best organizers, Baker included, seem to have been equally saintly with respect to the qualities needed in organizing work. They therefore spent less time than they might have exploring what might lead organizers to act *in*appropriately: what dispositions and character traits would make them unable to make the right judgments, to sustain themselves in the steady, hard work of organizing while resisting its temptations. Fortunately, we have in Saul Alinsky a self-aware rogue and an acute student of human motivations who did little *but* explore the dispositions that good organizers needed. His "rules" for radicals (really not rules but dispositions of character he thought vital) describe the psychic preconditions for carrying out the activities of a good organizer.

CONSTANCY FOR RADICALS: SAUL ALINSKY ON ORGANIZERS' CHARACTER

When it comes to the strategic and ethical imperatives of organizing, Alexis de Tocqueville provides us with the underlying democratic theory, and Saul Alinsky tells us what organizers must do to fulfill that theory's

---

[70] Payne (1995: 199–200). Alinsky (1971: 184–96) makes a similar point about New Left radicals: their penchant for doing things like burning the flag, denouncing materialism, and spouting profanity guaranteed that they would win no followers among the majority of Americans from whom social change had to come—i.e., the patriotic, work-ethic-oriented, working-to-middle class, whom they thereby lost to Wallace and Agnew.

[71] Carson (1981: 149–50, 156); Burner (1994 passim).

imperatives. Alinsky considered himself a follower of Tocqueville and quoted Tocqueville's observations and warnings with such frequency that it became something of an inside joke.[72] Taking seriously Alinsky's intention to apply Tocqueville's theory of association in practice, I will read Alinsky's work as a serious study of the soul of organizers under democracy. There is nothing contradictory in regarding Alinsky, the self-proclaimed radical, as the heir to Tocqueville, the friend of chastened, liberal democracy. Alinsky, like Tocqueville, regarded it as in the interest of citizens and regime alike for ordinary people to act intelligently, forcefully, and with democratic methods in pursuit of their ends—and both feared the alternative: that people will eventually act either in blind service to a tyrant, or not at all.

Alinsky wrote *Rules for Radicals* as a way of warning New Left student radicals what they were doing wrong. But in the book he mostly criticizes them not for having mistaken *beliefs* about organizing but for having the wrong *character*. Qualities like impatience, arrogance, excessive asceticism, and a fanatical cast of mind impaired their success as democratic organizers. (We might add that it made them undeserving of such success.) Alinsky was not an organized writer. His formal list of the qualities organizers need is diffuse and repetitive, and leaves out some of the most important qualities because he took them for granted.[73] But by combining the list with some of his other observations, we can obtain a simple and persuasive account. It will turn out that organizers need a kind of democratic constancy in three broad senses similar to those mentioned above: (1) a "fame-interest" in doing *careful, steady work* in the absence of immediate rewards and the presence of immediate temptations; (2) an ability and willingness to *understand what people want* and to guide people toward larger definitions of their interest (while keeping in mind the Humean truth that one cannot expect people to do what they "ought" if they lack a motive or sentiment for doing so); (3) limited ambitions, the ability to *forswear the temptation to be too moral*, for excessive moralism is contrary to the modest, common-denominator values of a democratic regime.

[72] Alinsky (1989: 44–45, 218); Horwitt (1992: 284).

[73] According to Alinsky, a good organizer must have "Curiosity," "Irreverence," "Imagination," "A sense of humor," "A bit of a blurred vision of a better world," "An organized personality," "Ego," "A free and open mind, and political relativity"; be "A well-integrated political schizoid"; and be "constantly creating the new out of the old" (Alinsky [1971: 72–80; all these qualities but the last emphasized in original]). Some of these qualities will be described and analyzed in what follows; some of the others will not because they work better as descriptions of Alinsky's own peculiar character and that of his friends than as accurate accounts of qualities all organizers need. In particular, Alinsky's extreme irreverence is probably not a requirement; many fine organizers have been a bit more sober.

Alinsky thought that organizing was a rare skill that could not be taught: one more or less had it or didn't.[74] Considering the delicate psychic balancing acts that seem necessary for good organizing, one begins to see why good organizers are rare. Consider Moses' call for respecting family, empowering locals, and organizing in context. What dispositions of character are required to do these things?

The organizer's respect for *family*, I have argued, does not require respect for formal kinship structures so much as a willingness to live by codes of personal trust, informal reputation, and face-to-face relations. In the Rousseauian terms used when discussing the activist, the organizer must live by "opinion," regarded as a local, and personal force grounded in mores, rather than waiting for a government by (Habermasian) "public opinion," an entity allegedly rational, progressive, and impartial.[75] Such behavior requires forbearance, a willingness to wait until one is accepted, "unlimited patience in talking to and listening to the local residents."[76] (Alinsky expected an organizing drive to last two years at minimum.) But beyond this, it requires that one both be trustworthy and be able to prove oneself as trustworthy.

An organizer who wants to win a reputation for reliability among those he does not know needs commitment without fanaticism. Commitment is automatically assumed to be a virtue among organizers; it refers to palpable evidence that one will stick with a struggle when things get tough. (The need for this quality stems from the office: since the "office" of organizer is purely informal and part of voluntary society, the organizer faces every temptation to quit at times of hard work or risk.) Commitment is so essential to a movement that even those who are skeptical of an organizer's aims will often follow him if he displays more commitment than competing leaders.[77] At the same time, a prospective organizer

---

[74] Alinsky (1971: 71).

[75] Once again, Tocqueville means by "public opinion" something much more like Rousseau's "opinion" (only more universal and inescapable and therefore more dangerous) than like the ideal speech theorists' purer model of public discussion (e.g., Habermas [1991]).

[76] Alinsky (1971: 68).

[77] For instance, many radical blacks who were otherwise skeptical of Martin Luther King as being middle-class, overrhetorical, and out of touch with the grass roots, nevertheless venerated him for his unquestioned commitment to the civil rights cause (see Oates [1985: 405–6]; and Lewis [1978: 384]). This was a personal veneration for an individual's character, which is why these radicals' attachment to the SCLC model of political change generally ended with King's murder. On this issue, organizers are probably prone to look up to moral activists, since the latter with their ministerial roots may be able on average to draw on more sustenance in a long struggle (certainly King stayed in the civil rights struggle much longer than most SNCC members, Baker aside). For a general theory of the origins and importance of commitment in mass movements, see Chong (1991: chapter 4). Chong

must seem *reliable*—not a fanatic or hothead whose followers can expect to get killed for no reason, but someone who will pick the right battles, negotiate reasonable agreements, and use the least risky tactics consistent with success.

To have both these qualities is what Alinsky calls being a "well-integrated political schizoid." Such a schizoid is not a "true believer" (which Alinsky means in Eric Hoffer's sense: a fanatical ideologue with an irrational resistance to compromise).[78] But he is still able to act like a true believer in the service of building a movement: "Men will act when they are convinced that their cause is 100 per cent on the side of the angels and that the opposition are 100 per cent on the side of the devil."[79] An organizer must believe this to be true on one level—that is, must have commitment—but have another part, well-integrated with the first, that knows that the differences with the opposition are generally negotiable, bridgeable. Alinsky, in his usual mode, embraces this as a contradiction and a paradox. But in fact, the "political schizoid" merely embodies "active" and "passive" aspects of democratic constancy: unswerving in pursuit of a goal, the activist is also unwilling to get carried away in the worship of that goal. Constancy keeps the organizer from becoming an impotent "sympathizer" on one hand, or a destructive fanatic on the other.

Beyond this, establishing the metaphorical family of a movement requires that the organizer not only have the right desires but communicate them to others. Alinsky rightly considers the "art of communication"—or rhetoric, in the ancient, nonpejorative and nonhistrionic sense—not only the most important quality of an organizer but qualitatively above the others: "It does not matter what you know about anything if you cannot communicate to your people. In that event you are not even a failure. You're just not there."[80] "Rhetoric" in the sense of speechmaking is a learnable skill and a useful one, but Alinsky's "communication," like ancient rhetoric, also has a strong moral component. Establishing personal ties through communication requires understanding a particular person and pitching a message to the state of his or her soul.

---

(95) also notes that in the early stages of movements, when success seems speculative and participation is hard to justify rationally, building the movement requires a non-self-interested core: "purists, zealots, moralists, Kantians, what have you"—in my language, activists. This might also be important when time is of the essence. When Robert Moses wanted to build up the Mississippi movement massively in a few months before the 1964 Democratic convention, he abandoned his usual strong preference for organizing over mobilization and supported calling in Martin Luther King (Branch 1998: 412).

[78] Hoffer (1951).
[79] Alinsky (1971: 78).
[80] Alinsky (1971: 81).

The case of a large audience is obviously less finely tailored but is no different in principle: before different audiences, the *same* point must be made in different ways so that each audience will hear it.[81] In a contemporary context, this also requires understanding not just differences among individual souls but differences among cultures and social experiences. For, as Alinsky pointed out over and over, it is difficult to understand something outside one's own experience, often literally impossible.[82]

This requires, again, endless patience in getting to know which kinds of concepts and practices are common and which unheard-of in the particular cultural and social milieu in which one is organizing. But it also requires an extraordinary humility, democratic deference, with respect to one's own rightness. In democratic politics, having worked something out to one's own satisfaction is of no value in persuading others: one must be willing to prove it to *their* satisfaction. Considering that few intelligent, educated people do this among their peers, one can only admire the extraordinary democratic restraint of organizers who do this for years on end among people who have few formal credentials but only their democratic, individualist right to form their own opinions.

Empowerment, I have argued, requires organizers to accept people of any social status as leaders, to admit that not everyone can be made a leader, and to trust people with leadership before they may have all the necessary capacities for it. The first quality closely tracks what Alinsky calls "irreverence"—not a mere love of wisecracks but skepticism toward existing values and social structures.[83] This may be a rare quality among ordinary people but it is not among organizers, who after all are self-appointed radicals. (This might, however, serve as one more distinction between organizers and moralistic "reformers.") Given that irreverence is not rare in this context, more important are the qualities that enable the other two difficult modes of acting: how can a radical egalitarian accept the natural division between leaders and ordinary citizens, and how can an experienced politician stand to encourage civic responsibility in those who have never before been active?

Acknowledging that not everyone in a community will be an equally active citizen would seem a matter of common sense and good judgment, but, as Aristotle knew, judgment can be corrupted by extreme disposi-

---

[81] See Plato (1986: 277b–d); Aristotle (1991: Book 2, chapters 2–17).

[82] Alinsky (1971: 83–91). Alinsky uses many examples to prove this to skeptics. Once he demonstrated the point in person: he went onto a major city street and tried to *give away* ten dollars. He was unable to do so. Most passers-by assumed the maneuver was either a strange form of begging or a con game, since people do not just give away money for no reason. The reader is encouraged to reproduce the experiment.

[83] Alinsky (1971: 73).

tions of character, and the origin of good judgment must itself be traced to character. The beginning of an account of how this works lies in Alinsky's call for organizers with a "bit of a blurred vision of a better life." Notably, Alinsky does not mean by this an ideal or goal of a *better state of society*, but rather a bit of a vision that there *are other organizers out there* helping in the work: "What keeps him [the organizer] going is a blurred vision of a great mural where other artists—organizers—are painting their bits."[84] This blurred vision—"blurred" because a smart organizer knows he cannot prove it is true—deals with the need to believe in universal participation, not by making this belief a reality, but by making it unnecessary. An organizer who dreams of what herds of fellow political animals can accomplish feels less temptation to expect too much from *homo civicus*. (We can ask ordinary citizens, however, to take some notice of their interests, and to vote.)

What enables organizers to act this way is a quality Alinsky calls (bluntly) ego: "unreserved confidence in one's ability to do what he believes must be done." By this definition, even self-effacing, saintly people like Baker and Moses have ego; for it is not the same as *egotism*, the urge to dominate and assert one's own power, which "would make it impossible to respect the dignity of individuals, to understand people, or to strive to develop the other elements that make up the ideal organizer. Egotism is mainly a defensive reaction of [*sic*] feelings of personal inadequacy—ego is a positive conviction and belief in one's ability, with no need for egotistical behavior."[85]

Again, the restraints of democratic constancy are virtuous, enabling: once he stops believing that all citizens will be participatory civic angels, the organizer is free to pursue his proper mission, and his proper, well-motivated desires. And ego, like all other constant virtues, could be considered a well-ordered and properly limited desire, the "desire to create."[86]

Having ego, and lacking egotism, also drives the ability to pursue developmental democracy. Having the desire to create, the organizer wants to multiply the power of the organized rather than stunt it. Having more confidence in her own abilities than in those of others, the organizer knows that this multiplication will require deliberate coaxing and planning. Having little desire to dominate, the organizer will be able to ma-

---

[84] Alinsky (1971: 75).

[85] Alinsky (1971: 61, 79). Alinsky makes the strong claim that egotism makes the pursuit of organizational goals "impossible." Alinsky rarely makes so strong a claim, and it is noteworthy that though he is very tolerant toward organizers who want money, fame, or social status—and even seems to encourage these desires, after the model of his hero, CIO head John L. Lewis—he regards a *desire for personal power* over others as completely disabling for democratic organization.

[86] Alinsky (1971: 61).

nipulate democratic learning—as even progressive education is "manipulative" in the sense of planning the most favorable circumstances for learning—without manipulating *final* decisions, which will be free, independent, and vigorous. (As SNCC organizer Charles Sherrod said of his own goals in southwest Georgia, "Our criterion for success is not how many people we register but how many we can get to begin initiating decisions solely on the basis of their personal opinion.")[87]

This is not mere wishful thinking and it has substantive content: good organizers, like good teachers, really do value pupils who surpass them or even oppose their previous opinions. When the Alinsky-organized Back of the Yards Neighborhood Council in Chicago turned into a typical white homeowners group concerned with keeping out blacks, Alinsky refused to disown the organization as such. While he hated racism, he stood by the principle of an organized citizenry and the overall results of what the BYNC had accomplished.[88] Characteristically (and true to his roots in the collective-bargaining tradition), Alinsky thought that the remedy for exclusionary attitudes was not to rail at whites nor to attack their organized strength but to organize *black* neighborhoods into groups that would then be able to negotiate stable, integrated housing policies from a position of strength and orderly power.[89] Whites would live next to blacks when blacks gave them an incentive to do so and could cut a deal with the people in charge to get it done to everyone's satisfaction.[90] The democratic cure for white power was black power, and eventually integrated power—not no power or power only to those who could be trusted to do as the organizer thought best.

Organizing in a local context involves flexibility with respect to ideology, discipline with respect to local issues. To this end, Alinsky called for "political relativity," not only out of native skepticism and mistrust of ideologues but for positive, ethical reasons. He thought that the program of a community organization must come from the people being organized, and that to impose a program ahead of time—even a humanistic or "progressive" one—was to show contempt for the capacities of ordi-

---

[87] Cited in Payne (1995: 318).

[88] Alinsky (1989: xi–xii).

[89] Organizing the black neighborhood was Alinsky's next project. The group organized in Chicago's South Side, the Woodlawn Organization, was so successful that Charles Silberman (1964) used it as the only sign of hope in his otherwise bleak book. Unfortunately, Silberman's hopes were not borne out: the organization, which relied too heavily on angry young men, later transformed itself into a criminal gang. This cautionary tale should not make us mistrust organizing, but does demonstrate the need to think carefully about who is being organized, by whom, how, and to what purpose. I owe this point to Ernesto Cortes.

[90] Horwitt (1992: 366–68; 385).

nary citizens: "The actual projection of a completely particularized program by a few persons is a highly dictatorial action. It is not a democratic program but a monumental testament to lack of faith in the ability and intelligence of the masses of people to think their way through to the successful solution of their problems. It is not a people's program, and the people will have little to do with it."[91]

This does not mean that the organizer should not think deeply about political issues himself (Alinsky read not only Tocqueville but most major social thinkers of his time, and SNCC organizers were particularly fond of Camus), but that organizers should put their philosophy aside to a great extent when trying to engage the civic capacities of those with simpler experiences and immediate needs. The most ideologically laden phrase Alinsky used to describe his goals was "for the general welfare"— and he denied that greater specificity was desirable.[92] As for the rest, he expected organizers to respect the local issues and resentments that people actually felt and knew about, to display personal restraint in the service of democracy.

At the same time, the organizer must have basic attachments to democratic goals. Alinsky might not have attacked every segregationist group as quickly as others would have liked, but in his own organizational activity he rejected racial exclusion absolutely and was constantly maneuvering to make the organizations he worked with more inclusive and less bigoted.[93] In his personal life, Alinsky was able to work with a blinding array of ethnic and cultural groups, from American Indians to Mexican-American farm workers to black nationalists (Malcolm X once recommended him to a Black Power group as the man who knew more about organizing than anyone in the country)[94] to rich, white dispensers of foundation grants.

What sustained Alinsky in doing this was not a fanatical ideology, such as led the Communist Party to include blacks when few others would.[95]

---

[91] Alinsky (1989: 55); see also Alinsky (1971: 79).

[92] Alinsky (1971: 4).

[93] For examples, see Horwitt (1992: 68–79, 331ff.); and Alinsky (1989: 88–89). Some of Alinsky's inclusiveness was ignored because it did not deal with the cleavages that observers wanted to see. Thus the Back of the Yards Neighborhood Council in Chicago was all "white," in fact almost all Catholic, because the neighborhood was. But Alinsky's ability to get the various churches of different nationalities to work with each other—and with the left-leaning Packinghouse Workers Union—was little short of a democratic miracle.

[94] Horwitt (1992: 464). In Rochester this led to the phenomenon of the FIGHT organization, a black nationalist group prone to proclamations of mistrust toward whites, inviting a middle-aged white Jewish organizer into its city to help it fight Eastman Kodak. This was an organizer's democratic "family" in action: trust stemmed from personal recommendations and demonstrated effectiveness, not from racial or ascriptive similarity.

[95] Alinsky objected to communism as dangerous in practice, insufficiently respectful of

Rather, his explanation for what motivated his own work and what should motivate other organizers always mentioned *sentiments*: "When Egan [Jack Egan, a liberal priest with whom Alinsky worked closely] asked him how he happened to get into the kind of work he was doing, Alinsky summed it up by saying, 'Oh, Jack, *I hate to see people get pushed around*." He said a radical "personally shares the pain, the injustices, and the sufferings of all his fellow men."[96] This had to be more or less nonsense according to Alinsky's own theory of self-interest, but it is instructive nonsense: when Alinsky goes overboard he talks of shared pains—not dialectics, moral progress, or grand historic missions. Shared pains is in fact what Alinsky meant by his virtue of "imagination": not the ability to imagine worlds that have never been, but the ability to identify with other people and their concerns. Someone who does this "suffers with them and becomes angry at the injustice and begins to organize the rebellion," in a clear link between disposition, motive to act, and political goal.[97] (This identification is very close to the sentiment that Hume interchangeably called "sympathy" or "humanity.") Alinsky makes this more explicit in choosing the essential question for would-be organizers: "Do you like people?"[98] Alinsky points out that most people like people, with "exceptions" for blacks, Catholics, or some groups of people not their own—in fact "most people like just a few people, their kind of people, and either do not actively care for or actively dislike most of the 'other' people."[99]

Bonnie Honig has argued that Kantian humanism really consists of respecting the moral law that is supposed to exist in other people—rather than the people themselves, moral complexity and all.[100] Moral-law humanism, tolerant toward reasons but intolerant toward people, may keep Kantians from engaging in individual acts of tyranny, but it does nothing to solve the Tocquevillean problem of individualism, which afflicts those who would rather shut themselves off in their own family life than engage in real conversation, conflict, and debate with people they have little in common with. Alinsky made clear that the ability to talk to and respect pretty much any kind of person was an extremely rare disposition and that those who had it already had sufficient impetus to become

---

ordinary people, and liable to distract from the everyday work of organizing (Horwitt [1992: 395]). These reasons are distinct from more orthodox anticommunist sentiments not as much in content as in emphasis and attitude: Alinsky disliked not "communism" in the abstract but what he knew communists tended to do.

[96] Horwitt (1992: 270); Alinsky (1989: 15).

[97] Alinsky (1971: 74). See also Alinsky (1989: 6).

[98] Alinsky (1989: 6).

[99] Alinsky (1989: 6–7).

[100] Honig (1993: 18–34).

and remain committed organizers. That most of us lack this disposition should be clear to any follower of Tocqueville: *individualism*, lack of concern for any outside our own circle, is what democratic citizens feel by nature. Organizers, who are unnatural in this respect, must foster artificial organizations. These combat the natural unfriendliness that makes most of us little tyrants, or at least indifferent to tyranny.

We might call this the humanism of friendliness, and it holds the promise of being just as radical and challenging as more ideological humanisms, while being less cruel. (It buys these qualities at the cost of being demanding, depending on sentiments felt only by a few.) Alinsky displayed this humanism—and its benign lack of intellectual coherence—in his treatment of the rich. Alinsky was capable of great anger about the rich and the middle class (whom he called the "Haves" and the "Have-a-Little, Want Mores").[101] But as soon as he began to talk about real organizing, he made four concessions to the claims of the better-off, which in combination guaranteed that real "class warfare," with its suspicions and purges, could never be part of his program. These concessions were: first, and most important, that the middle class constitute the majority of Americans. Alinsky knew that it was impossible in the United States to be truly democratic and a despiser of the middle class.[102] Second, that the middle class and rich have money, without which organizing cannot get started: the first thing that Alinsky did when starting a neighborhood organization was to solicit money from local businesses.[103] Third, that poor Americans aspire to a middle-class lifestyle and will never be convinced by New Left assertions (however warranted) that material comfort is empty.[104] And finally, that the rich are, after all, citizens with interests like everyone else: calls for them to sacrifice some of their interests must be counterbalanced by demonstrations of how change, in the name of the common interest, would benefit them *in some way* along with everyone else. Neither the organizer's attachment to democracy nor his open disposition would allow him to ignore or disparage *anyone's* interests as illegitimate "grudgingness," or as below his notice.[105]

---

[101] Alinsky (1971: 18).

[102] Alinsky (1971: 184ff.).

[103] Horwitt (1992: 80).

[104] "At various universities members of the Students for Democratic Society [*sic*] have asked me, 'Mr. Alinsky, do you know that what you are doing is organizing the poor for the acceptance of these bourgeois, decadent, degenerate, bankrupt, materialistic, imperialistic, hawkish middle-class values of today's society?' There has been a long silence when I have responded with, 'Do you know what the poor of America or, I might add, the poor of the world want? They want a bigger and fatter piece of these decadent, degenerate, bankrupt, materialistic, bourgeois values and what goes with it!'" (Alinsky [1989: 229]).

[105] Contrast sharply Rawls (1972: 533–34, 540). For a much more sophisticated and sym-

On the last point, Alinsky claimed—and historical evidence confirms—that he could "sit down and talk with sophisticated leaders in business, religion, politics, and labor without any trouble."[106] This went beyond the businesslike mode of the labor negotiator who understands his enemies as people with whom one can deal through pressure: Alinsky firmly believed that for the rich to enter into dialogue and negotiation, and make concessions to the poor, would in the long run be in their interest—though an interest based on the presence of pressure. Man, said Alinsky, "is about to learn that the most practical life is the moral life and that the moral life is the only road to survival. He is beginning to learn that he will either share part of his material wealth or lose all of it; that he will respect and learn to live with other political ideologies if he wants civilization to go on. This is the kind of argument that man's actual experience equips him to understand and accept. This is the low road to morality. There is no other."[107]

This "low road" is the goal of the Tocquevillean organizer, who expects not altruism but universal canniness, leading to a society more acceptable to the organized majority, and therefore more just. The kind of justice we can shoot for is political, not Christian: the most we can hope for is a society in which a reluctantly civic-minded individual becomes *"in practice* his brother's keeper."[108]

ELLA BAKER: THE ORGANIZER AS TEACHER

Ella Baker was the most important civil rights organizer in American history. In the 1930s, she was a journalist and activist in black and Left circles in New York, and as national director of the Young Negroes' Cooperative League helped organize black consumer associations. In the 1940s, as director of branches for the NAACP, she was the most well-connected and vigorous civil rights organizer in the country, traveling twelve thousand miles a year (not by airplane), getting to know the members of local affiliates, and prodding complacent chapters to recruit more ordinary people by addressing their grievances.[109] (During this time Baker organized a leadership seminar that Rosa Parks attended; Parks, far from

---

pathetic treatment by an egalitarian of wealthy people's reluctance to change their lives fundamentally for the sake of equality, see Nagel (1991).

[106] Sanders (1965: 57).

[107] Alinsky (1971: 23).

[108] Ibid.; emphasis added.

[109] Accordingly to Payne (1995: 88), Baker was determined to involve the "uncouth MASSES [Baker's capitals]" in NAACP work. "As a case in point, the mass-supported beer gardens, night clubs, etc. in Baltimore were invaded on a small scale," in Baker's words (Grant [1998: 49]), and yielded up many NAACP membership subscriptions. The 12,000-mile figure comes from Payne (1995: 85).

the ordinary woman with tired feet portrayed in myth, was an experienced civil rights organizer and an administrator of the Montgomery NAACP.) Leaving the branch director post out of frustration at NAACP bureaucracy, Baker continued working with the New York office of the NAACP doing "strictly volunteer work which lasted until four o'clock in the morning, sometimes,"[110] and was particularly involved in early school-desegregation efforts. She organized In Friendship, a group of Northern supporters of the Southern civil rights movement whose members included Stanley Levison and Bayard Rustin, later close advisers to Martin Luther King.[111]

Baker herself was invited to serve as the first Executive Secretary of King's Southern Christian Leadership Conference—which was not a secretarial position (though the preachers sometimes treated it as one) but involved coordinating all administrative and financial affairs.[112] After becoming disenchanted with the egotistical and rhetorical excesses of SCLC—and frustrated at her inability to "turn [Martin Luther King] into an organizer" who talked to ordinary people in large numbers and developed their capacities[113]—Baker devoted herself instead to idealistic student demonstrators and called the founding conference of what would become the Student Nonviolent Coordinating Committee. Through Baker's contacts in Mississippi and other areas, SNCC organizers like Bob Moses forged initial relationships in the organizing movement that flowered and became known to northern whites in the form of the 1964 Freedom Summer. Baker was instrumental in organizing the Mississippi Freedom Democratic Party as an alternative to the segregationist Democratic party, and spoke at its founding convention in 1964. Many in the movement acknowledged her presence directly as the teacher or *fundi* who inspired and directed their own work.[114] No one, emphatically including Martin Luther King, had more influence on more aspects of the civil rights struggle than Baker. "Her circle of collaborators," wrote Julian Bond, "was enormous, a virtual who's who of civil rights history and progressive politics."[115] The fact that few have heard of her testifies to her

---

[110] Baker (1970: 348).

[111] By Baker's own account, perhaps not fully reliable, the idea of a Southern-based civil rights organization, which became SCLC, came from In Friendship and did not originate with King and his circle (Grant [1998: 100–101]).

[112] See the words of Rev. Wyatt Tee Walker—himself an administrative antagonist of Baker's—in Grant (1981).

[113] Grant (1998: 4; see also 103, 107, 108, 110).

[114] See the testimony by Vincent Harding, Robert Moses, and Charles McDew in Grant (1981); Moses' words in Moses et al. (1989); and James Forman's comments in Ransby (1994: 294).

[115] Julian Bond, "Foreword" to Grant (1998: xvi).

self-effacing determination to shun the limelight, but still more to our own laziness in preferring a story of television speeches and demonstrations to a more elusive story of minds changed, fears overcome, and citizens created one by one through personal organizing—the "spadework" Baker insisted on so strongly.

Baker's distinction as an organizer was founded on devotion to the democratic order, good, disciplined habits of day-to-day organizing activity, and dispositions that undergirded both her democratic outlook and her personal constancy.

As far as democratic theory goes, Baker was truly devoted to democracy, not as a utopian ideal in the name of which ordinary people could be sacrificed, but as the concrete reality of understanding the grievances of ordinary people and trying to help as many people as possible to organize against those grievances. Chief among those grievances was the denial of basic rights to security and life. She once said in a speech quite simply that she could not rest until "the killing of black men, black mothers' sons, becomes as important to the rest of the country as the killing of a white mother's son."[116] Unlike some later civil liberties activists, however, Baker regarded protection of individual security as a supplement to democracy, not a substitute for it. She noted how much easier organizing became when "the movement had developed to a point where cracking heads and brutalizing had to be paid for."[117] In 1960, asked about the civil rights movement's "chief objective," she answered in unabashedly *democratic* terms: "To secure for Negro Americans the basic rights and privileges that are supposed to be enjoyed by all Americans. We wish to be first-class citizens with its [*sic*] responsibilities and its opportunities. And our major drive—one of our major drives is for the *unhampered franchise*, to be able to register and vote at all elections, at all times and in all places."[118]

At the founding convention of the Mississippi Freedom Democratic Party—to an overwhelmingly black audience before whom bigoted or antiwhite appeals might have worked fairly well—Baker described the essence of the objection to the old Southern system by pointing out, in the words of one description, "that the Southern states *function as an oligarchy*."[119] While Baker did not talk very much about "majority rule" as such, she tacitly recognized the democratic status of majorities in her

[116] Baker speech shown in Grant (1981).

[117] Quoted in Grant (1981).

[118] Baker on 1960 television news program as shown in Grant (1981). Compare the electoral manifesto of SNCC as presented to the 1960 Democratic Platform Committee: "The ache of every man to touch his potential is the throb that beats out the truth of the American Declaration of Independence and the Constitution" (quoted by Zinn [1964: 37]).

[119] Quoted by Grant (1970: 61; emphasis added).

matter-of-fact talk about recruiting "masses" and "numbers": "If I have made a contribution," she said, "I think it may be that I had some influence on a large number of people."[120]

The way to end an oligarchy was to win for all citizens the right to vote and then give them an interest in voting: "There was no way of effecting a basic change without being able to produce some political clout. And the only way that Blacks could produce any political clout was to utilize the ballot."[121] While some organizers treated voting rights as irrelevant, as a tool of the white establishment, or solely as a rallying point for black self-assertion (as we shall see with Carmichael), Baker preached voting as the essence of democracy—and as a radical act if properly understood. The only way to fight the major parties' inaction and hypocrisy on civil rights, she wrote in 1959, was "to beat them at the old game of playing politics with civil rights. Their forward passes and field goals must be blocked by the strategic use of the Negro vote, North and South."[122] When, early in SNCC's career, a faction devoted to direct action, demonstrations, and nonviolent resistance wanted to abandon voter registration as insufficiently radical, Baker pointed out that resistance to letting blacks register was so universal and violent in Mississippi that people who engaged in voting rights would have the chance for all the courageous "resistance" to violence that they wanted. This incident says as much about Baker's practice as about her political theory. Normally reluctant to press her own opinions on those she was working with—particularly on the black students of SNCC, whom she thought were at once more imaginative than their elders and less confident in speaking up for their own opinions[123]—this was one issue on which she admittedly "did have something to say."[124] What she had to say was pragmatic: Baker did not speak for or against direct action *versus* voting as an

---

[120] Baker (1970: 346).

[121] In Grant (1981).

[122] Baker writing of 1959 quoted by Grant (1998: 160).

[123] "The older people ... they were tied up in legalism. And legalism in itself, I don't think you and I would have any argument about its ineffectiveness by itself. And if people aren't willing to take whatever step is necessary to move beyond a given spot, then you can't—you're stuck. And here were these youngsters, who not only were willing to take the kinds of stand—stands that I might have suggested, but they had gone even beyond that" (Baker on SNCC, interviewed in Grant [1981]). "Most of the youngsters had been trained to believe in or to follow adults if they could. I felt they ought to have a chance to learn to think things through and to make the decisions" (Cantarow and O'Malley [1980: 87]).

[124] Cantarow and O'Malley (1980: 87). Baker's modesty on this point was not merely after the fact; one of the participants in the meeting later simply noted, "Ella was there," and did not take an interviewer's hint that she in fact had a larger role (Interview with Charles Jones in Stoper [1989: 187]).

abstract strategy, but in the interests of organization, tried to explain why there was no conflict between the two goals in practice.[125]

And indeed, it would be strange in a democracy if those who voted were required to abstain from other initiatives—or (as SNCC activists were often eager to assume) vice versa. Baker believed that democracy implied not only voting but the ability to take collective, civic initiative for oneself. Democratic citizenship involved a balance between moral claims and personal political responsibility. "Nobody's going to do for you," Baker intoned, "that which you have the power to do and fail to do." In this context, an unnamed acquaintance referred to Baker as "nurturer of those who needed nurturing, scolder of those who needed scolding."[126] Baker preached not entitlement based on victimhood but the rewards that went with action. Baker's exceptionally wide sympathy did not extend to those who refused to work hard for their interests and those of people like them.

In line with democracy's modest pretensions, Baker did not believe that the moral nature of human beings could be greatly transformed or improved. While she valued the close cooperation and solidarity of the small-town community she grew up in, she knew that such altruism was not always to be expected when communities grew larger and people were no longer personally acquainted.[127] And though she often called for heroic action, she described the impetus of that action in terms of resentment and spirit, not altruism: "The natural resistance is there already. No human being, I don't care how undeveloped he is—no human being, I would be willing to say, relishes being sat upon and beaten as if he were an animal, without any resistance."[128]

Out of her determination to work with local people, Baker deliberately subordinated her ideological attachments to her devotion to democratic methods. Too much talk about democratic method can cover up a lazy reluctance to distinguish among ends and to stand up for a firm position, but democracy also has a real moral content. Baker provides a particularly clear case of this, for if left to herself she might have preferred to be a communist. She was at least an associate and conspicuous nonopponent of communists in New York Left circles in the thirties, and again in the late sixties and early seventies;[129] she was an "anti-anti-communist" in opposing purges of communists from southern civil rights groups

---

[125] In spite of this argument's plausibility, SNCC continued to have two wings corresponding to the two supposedly consonant goals. Later, after experience and reconsideration, the two branches merged again (Ella Baker interview in Stoper [1989: 269]).

[126] Quotations from Grant (1981).

[127] Cantarow and O'Malley (1980: 61).

[128] In Grant (1981).

[129] Grant (1998: 41, 191, 206ff.)

(though she carried one out when so ordered as an New York employee of the NAACP);[130] she admired the communists' cell structure "almost as an aside" ("I don't think we had any more effective demonstration of organizing people for whatever purpose");[131] she proposed to a SNCC meeting in 1966 that the group organize a "revolutionary ethics" course led by Third World revolutionary leaders.[132] But in practice, Baker never tried to turn SNCC or any other organization to a communist line and worked with great diligence for goals that had nothing to do with proletarian revolution. The FBI, not inclined to be forgiving of black radicals, decided in 1968 after twenty years of monitoring not to place her on its Security Index "'because in her speeches she has not advocated violence or revolution nor has she ever been a member of the [Communist Party]. Subject's activities reflect that she is interested in obtaining improvement of the Negro by peaceful means only.'"[133] We can infer that she pursued this peaceful approach because she practiced what the Communist Party only gave lip service to—real belief in the masses. The need to appeal to ordinary American blacks kept her from expounding a doctrine she knew they would reject.

Late in life, after SNCC disbanded, Baker (as her biographer euphemistially puts it) "stretched her horizons to encompass changing views in the society." She joined the Marxist revolutionary Mass Organizing Party; she advocated "liberation from the decadent values of 'the American way of life'"; and she spoke in front of a Puerto Rican solidarity rally against "capitalism and imperialism."[134] But by then, Baker no longer was trying to make a case to ordinary Americans (much less American citizens of Puerto Rico, only a tiny minority of whom have ever supported independence). Despite her call in the Puerto Rico speech for her listeners to go out and organize their neighbors, she was no longer an organizer herself. Her hard-working, self-denying disposition and devotion to democratic principles had served her in the role of organizer, but once she stepped out of that role, she was willing to relax both the disposition and the principles.

Baker matched the right political theory with the right habits. As a matchmaker of face-to-face societies, she had few peers, as shown by her multidecade organizing work and hundreds of contacts. Baker knew that organizing movements grew as a result of attachment to people as much

[130] Grant (1998: 99); also grant (1981: quoting comments by Anne Braden).
[131] "Almost as an aside": Grant (1998: 141); comments on communist cell structure taken from an oral interview also reported in Payne (1995: 94).
[132] Carson (1981: 202).
[133] FBI report cited by Grant (1998: 202: interpolation Grant's).
[134] Grant (1998: 206, 209, 211).

as belief in ideas.[135] However, the episode of "matchmaking" cited above (finessing the disagreement between those devoted to voting rights and those who favored direct action) perhaps demonstrates most clearly Baker's sense of intimate groups. Baker felt, as most SNCC members did, that the consensual style of the group—its attachment to the "general will," one observer called it—was precious.[136] But she also knew that it is precisely in small, consensual political units that political controversy has the tendency to be most bitter and divisive, as those who disagree appear to their enemies to be acting in bad faith and neglecting the common good.[137] The solon of the situation, she set forth a set of institutions that contained the conflict and subsumed it in a larger consensus, without either pretending there was no disagreement or trying to eliminate it. Baker got Robert Moses, a self-proclaimed "anarchist" who never believed in voting, to become a heroic, repeatedly wounded organizer for voter registration. This was the art of association.

In terms of organizing in a context, Baker was always willing to accept both human frailty in general and the temporarily limited aspirations of the particular people she found. She never wished away self-interest, pride, and similar motives, but instead adapted her appeal to take account of them. When trying to get a rich black woman to identify with the cause of poor blacks, she would talk about epidemics that could easily cross the tracks and kill her. Through such methods one could, she said, "point out where her interest lies in identifying with that other one across the tracks who doesn't have minks."[138] She was not above using yet baser appeals. She explained that a gifted fund-raiser approaching a possible contributor to the movement "might end up just saying, 'You ain't doin' nothing but spendin' your money down at that so-and-so place.' She may shame him."[139] Baker was even tolerant toward those who professed no time for political struggle because they had to support a family. She drew the line, however, at those who wanted to spend all their time

---

[135] Consider Harry T. Moore, a Florida principal whose house was bombed for agitating for black teachers' pay that whites had embezzled. In talking about him, Baker said, "There were a lot of people whom Harry T. Moore had benefited. We talked to them. He helped them get their pay when they had worked and didn't get paid. So you could go into that area of Florida and you could talk about the virtue of the NAACP, because they knew Harry T. Moore. They hadn't discussed a whole lot of theory. But there was a man who served their interests and who identified with them" (Cantarow and O'Malley [1980: 70; italics omitted]).

[136] The "general will" quotation is from Barney Frank (later a U.S. representative), who participated in the Mississippi Freedom Summer (Barney Frank interview in Stoper [1989: 283]).

[137] As noted by Dahl and Tufte (1973: 94).

[138] Cantarow and O'Malley [1980: 70–71].

[139] Cantarow and O'Malley (1980: 73). The "so-and-so place" is presumably a brothel, but a bar might have been shameful enough in some places.

piling up luxury goods.[140] Apparently, once it became a matter of pure discretion, she thought that a citizen's view of her interests ought to be a bit wider.

In acting in such ways, Baker displayed explicit *ideological* restraint: "On what basis do you seek to organize people? Do you start to try to organize them on the fact of what *you* think, or what they are first interested in? You start where the *people* are." Like Alinsky, Baker called the willingness to do this "identification": a sentiment, not an abstract reason.[141] Baker appreciated the value of identifying with local folk culture; though she had a fine education herself, she left its high-cultural lessons aside for political purposes.[142]

Finally, Baker very explicitly shied away from exerting "leadership" in favor of "developing leadership in other people." Her unwillingness to take over a meeting (though she was far from unwilling to speak) led, as mentioned above, to people's almost forgetting her presence. She was deeply interested in citizenship education. And she warned constantly against the charismatic leader who "has found a spot in the public limelight. It usually means that the media made him, and the media may also undo him."[143] At the same time, Baker did not oppose all leadership: making contact with particularly brave, committed, or perceptive local people was just fine with her, and she built a movement not by stifling such people but by putting them in contact with one another.

Baker was committed. A restrained but quietly prideful woman, she always said that the success of an organizer like her "depended on both your disposition and your capacity to sort of stimulate people—and how you carried yourself, in terms of not being above people."[144] She worked endlessly and for almost no money. She valued above all the slow spadework of organizing and the people ready to do it. As a rule she thought little of preachers, but she admired a preacher who, as she said, "will work" and would visit barbershops, gas stations, and housewives, "getting people to work" in turn.[145] Baker's suspicion of oratory and preference for prosaic substance involved tremendous self-denial, given that she herself was a superb orator—trained from childhood—and often called upon to speak.[146] Finally, Baker, though not eager for power or personal domination, had a healthy ego and knew it. Like Alinsky but independently of

[140] Cantarow and O'Malley (1980: 92).

[141] Cantarow and O'Malley (1980: 70).

[142] Payne (1995: 81).

[143] Payne (1995: 93). The intended target of the comment was probably Martin Luther King.

[144] Cantarow and O'Malley (1980: 71).

[145] Payne (1995: 85).

[146] Payne (1995: 80); Grant (1981) contains both Baker's testimonials to her own oratorical powers and some clear demonstrations of them.

him, she saw these two facts as linked: "I also think," she said, "you have to have a certain sense of your own value, and a sense of security on your part, to be able to forgo the glamour of what the leadership role offers."[147]

Baker was a great organizer and teacher but she was not perfect. There were lapses and flaws in her outlook and her character. First, she downplayed her own extraordinary qualities. This is often an estimable habit and of great use in organizing, but done excessively it could and did mislead some followers into unrealistically egalitarian notions. Highly educated herself (both formally and informally) and brought up to cultivate a perfect speaking delivery, she did not always realize how many advantages her own talents and education gave her over the generic "local leader." At the same time as she distrusted the standard set speech of black rhetoric as hackneyed and often content-free,[148] she ought to have noticed how frequently she was called upon to give such speeches: the people she trusted so much apparently regarded them as valuable, inspirational, and not necessarily a distraction from more humble day-to-day work. Second, Baker could be overly confrontational when diplomacy would have been more successful: so tolerant of the egos and personal concerns of ordinary people she was organizing, she was strangely intolerant of the extraordinary people (like Martin Luther King) who were trying to persuade *her*—and whose closer friendship could have been a great help even after she severed formal ties with them.[149]

More important, Baker's ideal of democracy was too pure. She tended to distrust large organizations as such, acknowledging their value only if they were formed by delegates from smaller ones.[150] As Bayard Rustin and others pointed out, the economic resources necessary for solving the problems of the black community lay mostly outside that community, and by standing purposely outside national pressure groups, black grassroots radicals (unlike their white counterparts like Alinsky and John L. Lewis) often undermined the very voting power and ability to challenge indifferent national authority that they had worked so hard to organize.[151] Baker's anxiousness to reach "large numbers" was apparently limited to her idea of the large numbers she knew personally. How to adapt the civic action of organizing bodies to a larger scale was a political question whose significance apparently escaped her.

---

[147] Baker (1970: 352).

[148] Grant (1998: 19).

[149] In Grant (1981), Wyatt Walker, Baker's successor as executive director of the King-led SCLC, comments that he, unlike Baker, knew how to deal with the "preacher ego."

[150] Payne (1995: 83, 369–70).

[151] Rustin (1964, 1971).

STOKELY CARMICHAEL: CHARISMATIC "ORGANIZING" AND THE FLIGHT FROM DEMOCRATIC DISCIPLINE

Stokely Carmichael (later Kwame Turé) popularized the phrase "Black Power" during a 1966 march in Mississippi. Many whites soon came to fear that he intended to kill them indiscriminately and to replace American democracy with a radical black dictatorship. Carmichael's speeches and writings sometimes gave support to these fears and sometimes tried to dispel them. (They varied by audience more than would be possible now, when information propagates more quickly.) But in phrasing the question as violence versus nonviolence or hatred versus love, whites have missed the important point about what Carmichael wanted to do, and who he was.

The criteria of nonviolence and love take Martin Luther King as the implicit standard. Carmichael would have been the first to admit that he did not want to be like King. What really bothered him were accusations of being out of touch with the masses. *This*, however, was exactly what he was. Carmichael's antidemocratic essence came through most clearly not in his ill-thought-out programmatic speeches but in his self-aggrandizing character and habits. Carmichael, in his most radical phase, never organized anyone: never did the slow work of talking to ordinary people and gaining their allegiance by finding out how their everyday concerns could be related to the program of a larger movement. His speeches, which caused such anger and terror in whites, caused him to be known among black organizers as "Stokely Starmichael"—as someone who would rather be famous than do effective organizing work. Carmichael's career reveals how some conservatives' fears of "radical" organizers, subverters of the republic, are precisely backwards. Revolutionary rhetoric thrives in the United States precisely when an "organizer" or "militant" survives as the darling of the media and celebrity-worshippers and has *no* real connection to the lives of most ordinary people. We have become so used to seeing Carmichael as a bad moral activist that we have failed to see that he was a bad organizer. The latter, not the former, should be blamed for his excesses.

Carmichael never conveyed a clear sense that he was operating in a specific political unit with a democratic structure. At times he spoke as if blacks would be satisfied with control over local communities where they formed a majority.[152] But when he became interested in issues that clearly required a larger perspective—particularly the Vietnam War—he still refused to take a national, American perspective but began to speak to blacks as a nation living within America, having more in common with

---

[152] Stokely Carmichael, "Toward Black Liberation" (1966), in Carmichael (1971: 41).

the Third World than with their fellow citizens. He denied the validity of the term "Black Americans."[153] Practicing what he preached, he accepted the Black Panther Party's grant of the title Prime Minister of the Afro-American nation, and accepted the honors of a head of state when traveling in Africa. (The honor was no doubt exciting for him but did little for his self-proclaimed African compatriots.) In short, he was little attached to the American democratic order; the vast majority of whites (and blacks), deeply committed to American democracy under some description, were rarely able to see what point was gained by his idiosyncratic national allegiances.

Carmichael was alienated not only from the United States' democratic order but from the politics of democratic numbers as such, the idea that those who seek to control the policies of a democracy should try to build a majority coalition. He rejected the "progressive coalition" strategy proposed by "pragmatic" (but still left-of-center and quite radical) blacks like Bayard Rustin, on the grounds that blacks would be "absorbed and betrayed" by any coalition then available.[154] Carmichael in his early phase professed to be interested in future alliances between blacks and poor whites. But as Martin Duberman pointed out, SNCC rhetoric under his leadership, which attacked whites of all political persuasions and emphasized blacks' superior "humanistic level," made it difficult to imagine how whites would ever be welcome, or why they should trust Carmichael as an ally.[155]

For present purposes, the moral issue of "black racism" is less important than what Carmichael intended to *do* with racial appeals. Nationalism can be a legitimate tool for rousing disaffected minorities to action in the service of democratic methods and tangible opportunities for themselves. (Before the right audience and for specific purposes, John L. Lewis regularly castigated corporate leaders as evil tools of the Devil. Once they agreed to sit down with him and formulate a mutually acceptable compromise, he shook hands. Alinsky took the same lesson, accusing Eastman Kodak in Rochester of "plantation" behavior for refusing to

---

[153] "We must break down the concept that black people living inside the United States are black Americans. That's nonsense! We have brothers in Africa and Cuba, we have brothers in Latin America, we have brothers all over the world. And once we begin to understand that the concept 'community' is simply one of 'our people,' it makes no difference where we are—we are with our people and therefore we are home" (Carmichael, "Free Huey," in Carmichael [1971: 115]).

[154] Carmichael, "Power and Racism" (1966), in Carmichael (1971: 25).

[155] Duberman (1968: 39). Duberman also notes that this rhetoric derived from a position paper that was not an "official" SNCC statement (given SNCC's chaotic decision-making structure, few things were). For current purposes, it is enough to note that Carmichael never disavowed it, and said even less ambiguous things within a few years.

deal with the black group FIGHT, then telling photographers after the final agreement that they should all use Kodak film.)[156] But by having no concrete plans for building an ultimate coalition or even a collective bargaining agreement with whites, Carmichael made a democratic victory in the United States mathematically impossible. It is hardly surprising that Carmichael is reported to have said "majority rule stinks," and declared in public that voting rights were a "honky's trick," that voting had no substantive benefits for blacks beyond the issue's past use as an organizing tool.[157]

Organizers need not have very specific goals, and public vagueness can add to one's bargaining power. But Carmichael's rejection of the basic goals of winning majorities and building numbers represented his death as an organizer. For it took away the reason for actual organizing: persuading as many ordinary people as possible to see their interests as connected to those of others. Carmichael was selected as head of SNCC because he had done a fine job organizing in Lowndes County, Alabama. (In that majority-black county, no blacks had been registered to vote before Carmichael started organizing, but black-backed candidates got more than 40 percent of the vote several months after SNCC voter registration began.)[158] But once he achieved leadership—and in particular, a national platform—Carmichael ran SNCC into the ground. Outside funding dried up as Carmichael began to refer to whites as "honkies" and engaged in anti-Semitic conspiracy theories.[159] More important, Carmichael never engaged in *any* grassroots organizing projects or canvass-

---

[156] Horwitt (1992: 502); see Sethi (1970) on the example of the FIGHT group in Rochester. This example reveals how Black Power ideology—including suggestions of antiwhite racism—need not on its own be crippling for a democratic organizer. Minister Florence, the head of FIGHT and an admirer of Malcolm X, repeatedly warned against trusting white people to do anything. But once his negotiating tactics (advised by Alinsky) had won concessions in the form of job-training and hiring agreements with Kodak, Xerox, and other corporations, Florence was more than willing to work with these white-dominated corporations on the basis of mutual advantage rather than love. As an end result, Rochester became more integrated, and its least-well-off black residents more prosperous.

[157] Barney Frank interview, in Stoper (1989: 283); Carmichael, "Free Huey!" in Carmichael (1971: 116–17).

[158] For a surprisingly measured account, see Carmichael and Hamilton (1967: chapter 5).

[159] Carmichael was particularly free with the "honky" epithet in his speech on behalf of Black Panther leader Huey Newton; see "Free Huey!" in Carmichael (1971: 112, 114, 116). As for anti-Semitism, Carmichael's repeated protests that his anti-Zionism was not anti-Semitic were always difficult to credit. Consider the statement: *The same Zionists that exploit the Arabs also exploit us in this country. That is a fact. And that is not anti-Semitic* (Carmichael, "The Black American and Palestinian Revolutions," in Carmichael [1971: 138; emphasis in original]). Unless Carmichael had special information that Zionists were *more likely than other American Jews* to be exploiters of blacks, "Zionist" can only be taken as a nonsubtle substitute for "Jew."

ing or voter registration after he started lecturing and becoming famous; by 1968, none of SNCC's field projects were active.[160]

SNCC organizers themselves—including serious "hard-liners" like James Forman, later author of *The Making of Black Revolutionaries*—complained that Carmichael's "actions indicated that he was more interested in building a cult of personality rather than a strong organization." For such reasons, SNCC in fact voted Carmichael out of office soon after he became a national figure, in the hope that his successor would avoid flamboyant public statements in favor of organizing.[161] At the time, Forman (like Baker an Old Leftist who believed in slowly organizing "the masses") blamed SNCC's troubles on its lack of constancy, on SNCC's foolhardy tendency "always to give in to the demands for the moment," giving its organizers little time for reading, reflection, and organizer training.[162] The result was that Carmichael, when asked for a concrete example of Black Power in action, could only name the success of the Rochester group FIGHT—a group that Alinsky, not Carmichael, had organized.[163]

Carmichael's lack of commitment to democracy rendered him unable to treat ordinary people as equals or develop their capacities—even as he claimed a keen desire to do so. The issue is not merit in some narrow sense. Some of Carmichael's writing attacked the idea of "qualifications" bitterly but effectively, claiming that the meritocratic system was a mockery to blacks trapped in pitiful schools, unable to afford college, and unable (if uneducated) to find even menial work in an automated economy. In response to this situation Carmichael at one point in his life advocated, in the organizer's prudent leap of faith, political participation *in advance of* formal education, and rightly argued that governments would not create opportunity without "pressure from below."[164] In white-run Lowndes County, where tax assessment was hopelessly corrupt and antiblack violence was common, the issues for blacks were indeed rather clear, and Carmichael was right to defend in such a context the "short speeches" of uneducated but determined local candidates; the quiet pride of a previously passive citizen who "had done his homework" and mastered the voting laws; and the "psychological need of [black citizens'] knowing that they could come together on their own, make decisions and

---

[160] Carson (1981: 285); compare Ella Baker's opinions reported in Grant (1998: 141, 210).
[161] Forman (1985: 521); Payne (1995: 378); Carson (1981: 234–35, 244). Those who hoped for a return to grassroots organizing and education rather than inflammatory media-grabbing speeches were a bit disappointed in Carmichael's successor, Rap Brown.
[162] Forman, quoted by Carson (1981: 235).
[163] Horwitt (1992: 508).
[164] Carmichael, "Who is Qualified?" (1966), in Carmichael (1971: 9–16; quotation on 16).

carry them out."[165] Such analysis displays the organizer's quiet faith that most groups of inert citizens contain at least a few people capable of much more.

But in later work, Carmichael showed either too much or too little tolerance for common wisdom. He started telling ordinary blacks they should define culture as James Brown rather than Bach or Beethoven.[166] Addressing a group of schoolchildren, he maneuvered them into arguing that the wider society should learn black English, rather than their having to master standard English; elsewhere he claimed that blacks' lack of proficiency in standard English stemmed from a conscious refusal to adapt to the culture of their colonial oppressors.[167] (Until he began using "street" terms on purpose, Carmichael himself, who had a West Indian background, spoke perfect standard English.) Carmichael apparently did not see any contradiction between giving this advice and berating black students for not reading enough Du Bois and Frederick Douglass[168]— though none of their books, and certainly not Carmichael's own *Black Power*, is written in the African-American dialect. Carmichael was thus partly responsible for a trend that is the opposite of civic development: he provided a justification for teaching students a language that guaranteed their inability to influence the political society of which they were citizens. But Carmichael did not even have enough of a practical program to valorize this inability with any consistency: in writing of Tuskegee blacks whom he hoped would become more radical, he wrote that the community there had the capacity to become examples to all blacks because of their "high educational level" (presumably in standard-English books) and "economic security."[169]

Finally, Carmichael's dispositions were not conducive to fulfilling the purposes of an organizer. Carmichael had egotism rather than ego, the desire to be on top of a movement rather than the patient fame-interest in building one. He preferred the reputation of a man who preached action to the pride of actually having given people the power to act. As Alinsky pointed out in a dig at radicals in general but implicitly Carmichael in particular, talk about black "manhood" is cheap, but the way for a black male to become a "man" and achieve "black identity" as an active and powerful person was to build organized power, with a view to

---

[165] Carmichael and Hamilton (1967: 114, 112, 106).

[166] Carmichael, "At Morgan State," in Carmichael (1971: 75).

[167] Jane Stembridge, "Notes About a Class" (1966), in Carmichael (1971: 3–8); Carmichael, "Free Huey," in Carmichael (1971: 114).

[168] Carmichael, "At Morgan State," in Carmichael (1971: 74).

[169] Carmichael and Hamilton (1967: 144).

confronting dominant institutions and forcing them to accord respect.[170] This is something Carmichael never taught anyone to do. Ella Baker understood manliness better than he did, or at least was better able to further it in action.

Carmichael's flaws stemmed from a failure of democratic constancy: a failure to accept the discipline of local organizing, and a failure to accept the limits of consciousness-raising. On the level of practice, Carmichael's distance from ordinary black citizens left him unable to understand "Black Power" in the sober sense they understood it—as a pragmatic program to address their needs. This was not unique to Carmichael. Joyce Ladner, a student of the Black Power movement in Mississippi, once distinguished between what Black Power meant to "cosmopolitans" like Carmichael—largely intellectuals—and what it meant to "locals" of a more grassroots origin. The cosmopolitans were devoted to black consciousness and treated Fanon's *Wretched of the Earth* as a Bible. "The locals," wrote Ladner, "are almost as committed to solving the pressing problems of inadequate income, education, housing, and second-class citizenship *practically* as the cosmopolitans are committed to solving them *philosophically*." Ladner noted the demographic differences between the two groups but did not interpret them: compared to the cosmopolitans, the locals were more likely to have been involved in electoral politics with the Freedom Democratic Party; were older; had more local organizing experience; and finally, were simply more numerous (two-thirds of her sample). In other words, the truly democratic portion of the Black Power movement was disciplined, experienced in politics, and had numbers on the ground. This faction, the constant faction, was not opposed to black nationalism but thought it was best expressed by blacks' getting things done. The difference between them and cosmopolitans like Carmichael was that the former were "committed to concrete economic and political programs, while the cosmopolitans—to varying degrees—endorse[d] such programs but actually ha[d] made little effort to realize them." Above all, locals knew what the right to vote meant. Said one, "Voter registration is black power. Power is invested in the ballot and that's why the white man worked like hell to keep you away from it."[171]

Lacking the discipline to adapt to ordinary people's desires, Carmichael became unable to accept realistic aspirations for human character. Lack of discipline in action led to lack of reality in aspiration. Because he

---

[170] Alinsky, (1989: 214). Again, Alinsky is talking about Minister Florence's experiences in Rochester. While Alinsky's formulations here are characteristically macho, there is no reason to think that this road to self-confidence and a sense of personhood should be in any way closed to women.

[171] Ladner (1967: 11–12). See also Payne (1995: 322ff.).

expected a utopian level of closeness among the black "family," Carmichael was unable to stay with face-to-face organizing as it was, rather than as he fantasized it. While he wanted all blacks to treat one another as family, he had a strange idea of how a family works and how widely family ties can be extended.

Carmichael took literally what he (dubiously) claimed was a habit among all blacks of calling each other "brother" and "sister"—in fact, "soul-brother" and "soul-sister." He insisted that this was not "ersatz" or "make-believe," but "real . . . a growing sense of community."[172] But the people he was talking about were, to come down to earth, not in fact related; they did not even know one another. To the extent that many blacks practice a certain solidarity and mutual aid on the basis of race alone, "brother" could have a benign and useful meaning here. (Committed labor union leaders call one another "brother" and "sister" for similar solidaristic reasons.) But Carmichael wanted more than this: he wanted "brotherhood" to be a real feeling of deep communion among blacks, and to imply agreement on a political ideology. Long-lasting face-to-face societies sustain themselves by negotiating agreements and preserving respect in spite of disagreements: no family, and certainly no parliamentary cabinet or committee, is so loving that everyone agrees all the time (and if one were it would be chilling). But Carmichael wanted a "united" black community to mean "*no fights* within the black community," and wanted to use "patience, love, brotherhood and unity" to bring the black bourgeoisie "home" to *his* position (which at that time meant Third World revolution and veneration of Mao and Che).

Hannah Arendt has pointed out the dangers of a politics based on compassion and love rather than respect: the politics of love threatens to eliminate the salutary distance between citizens with differing opinions and to result in terror when the desired unity is not forthcoming.[173] Carmichael's solution to a lack of unity and a failure of love followed this script: "There will be no fights in the black community among black people, there will just be people who will be offed! There will be no fights, there will be no disruptions. We are going to be united." As for the black bourgeoisie who would not be brought back by love, "If they become a threat, we off them."[174] Carmichael's lack of interest in expanding his circle of contacts and building an organization was related to his wrongheaded theory of love: he thought that love for black people, all

[172] Carmichael and Hamilton (1967: 38).

[173] Arendt (1965: 80–88).

[174] Carmichael, "Free Huey!" in Carmichael (1971: 115, 119). There can be no doubt in the context of the speech that "off" means "kill": later in the speech Carmichael equates being offed with taking a bullet (124), and refers to the assassination of Malcolm X as his being "offed" (129).

black people, required that one defend black people without stopping to think—as one would defend one's mother or brother from a beating by immediately killing the (white) person beating her.[175] Love for blacks implied hatred for whites: "If you don't have hate," he said, "you cannot differentiate love."[176]

As Richard King has argued, SNCC's commitment to ordinary people withered even as its talk of "the people" intensified. "The people" came to be thought of, Rousseau-style, as a unified totality—one either favored the program of the people or was a traitor. This guaranteed that diversity of opinion would not be welcome, and that the will of the people would be imposed from above rather than generated from below.[177] Alinsky, Baker, and other successful organizers were no dewy-eyed lovers of mankind, but they sustained a minimalist humanism that let them think that almost all ordinary people—with their usual self-interest, narrowness, and ignorance of others' lives—could in time, through face-to-face contact and with lots of patient effort, be induced to see at least a somewhat larger view and identify to some degree with other people. Carmichael's high aspirations for black consciousness led him to great depths of hatred for whites and blacks who could not or would not share in that consciousness. His insistence on fanatical love left him unable to "like people." Good democratic organizers seek to expand the realm of common interest; Carmichael wanted to contract it. In such a case, the organizer becomes not only an enemy of the political order but a danger to the civic capacities of every citizen he influences. Such a character should be treated as he treats others: he asserts no common interest with us, and we should stop trying to find any with him.

Conclusion: Particularist Organizing and the General Interest

Organizers aim at giving people power, and power can be dangerous. Developing civic capacities is not an abstract goal but one that culminates in actions that have consequences. Organizers think that people share many common interests and sometimes take this to mean that everyone's interests can be reconciled through bargaining. But bargaining, though distinct from violence, is also distinct from brotherly love. If people protect their interests through voting, they will appropriate resources that might have gone to someone else. Other methods of organizing—strikes, boycotts, and the like—are just as frankly coercive as voting is

[175] Carmichael, "A New World to Build," in Carmichael (1971: 148).
[176] Carmichael, "Free Huey!" in Carmichael (1971: 121).
[177] R. King (1992: 152).

(though still not violent), with the potential to harm some people's interests as they further others.

Organizers defend these methods from a position not of statesmanlike detachment but of identification: they are for the group they are organizing and see their main goal as furthering *its* interests (within certain limits). They are not generally concerned with the effect of such demands on the larger society: with the effect of political conflict on business confidence, the effects of wage demands on economic profits and growth, and the potentially immobilizing effects on the political system of having every voter *really* take an interest in her vote and the assumptions of democratic power that go with it. I have argued that an organizer's activity is largely self-limiting in one sense: antidemocratic aspirations will not be supported by large numbers, and the organizer seeking the power of numbers will have to abide by democratic rules. But while this effect prevents the formation of antidemocratic *demands*, it does not limit the damage that organizers can do to the political order by accident, by straining its capacity to respond to everyone's demands. We might be tempted to say that Tocquevillean organizers understand democracy less well than they believe: they understand the need for some citizen action if tyranny is to be avoided, but not the limits that must be placed on such action if democracy is to function.[178] We might initially conclude that our neglect of organizers is in fact salutary—that the last thing the polity needs is a group of righteous democrats stirring up civic movements to overburden our already hard-pressed institutions.

But organizers are not the only politicians present in a constitutional democracy. Indeed, they are not good at looking out for the general interest—nor should they have to. Other political officers, such as senators, have that job: the job of balancing interests and making deals that will reconcile their own constituents' interests with those of others. A legislator who cannot handle conflicting demands had better blame himself rather than blaming citizens for becoming as active as our civics books tell them to be. Senators often do stupid and demagogic things, but we rarely conclude from this that the office is bad for democracy. Our tendency to judge organizers by their worst effects rather than their overall function mostly reflects a bias against the organizer's style: more "vulgar," canny, and blunt than scholars are personally comfortable with. This in turn often reflects a quiet antidemocratic suspicion: we do not expect that ordinary people—even once educated, experienced in politics, and guided by hard-headed organizers' wisdom—can be trusted to speak for their own interests. The *Federalist* calls for "exclusion of the people, in their collective capacity," from "administration" of govern-

---

[178] Huntington et al. (1975: 59–118); Almond and Verba (1989: 186ff.).

ment.[179] But this is very far from the all-too-common belief that ordinary people should not even be trusted to organize locally, occasionally, in non-authoritative, non-lawmaking bodies, in defense of their interests.

The demands that organizers foster, after all, are not extreme. Tocquevillean democrats do not want to cripple government, only to challenge government and instill "moderation and restraint in those in power"; they do not think that all politics must involve direct citizen action, only that some kinds of politics should; they do not want to abolish political and social institutions, only to ensure that all have more equal power to influence them. The alternative is Tocqueville's fear: an administrative state in which many people's desires are satisfied (at least some of the time) but their civic capacities are destroyed. If organizers reduce the efficiency of government administration, we should accept this as the price of citizen engagement. And we cannot truly favor citizen engagement unless we recognize the need for those who promote it.

[179] Hamilton et al. (1992: No. 63).

Governing Pluralism, Office Diversity, and Democratic Ethics

> "Madison knew the secret of this disorderly system, indeed he invented it. The secret is the separation and balance of powers, men's ambition joined to the requirements of their office, so that they push those requirements to the limit, which in turn is set by the contrary requirements of another office, joined to the ambition of other men. This is not an arrangement whose justification is efficiency, logic, or clarity. Its justification is that it accommodates power to freedom and vice versa. It reconciles the irreconcilable."
>
> —Alexander Bickel[1]

THIS WORK HAS attempted to show the relations between political ethics, democratic and constitutional theory, and the theory of democratic offices. The treatment of each of these topics, and of their interrelation, has emphasized *plurality*: there is more than one political ethic; democratic theory must take account of more than one kind of politics; each political office embodies a particular political relationship, calling for its occupants to practice particular forms of action and to embody particular dispositions of character. The work ended by considering three very different kinds of politician and defending the fact that they were properly different: senators, activists, and organizers quite rightly serve different functions, act and look at politics differently, and have different dispositions. Transcending both parts and unifying them was an account of "democratic constancy": the idea that democracy flourishes by rejecting the goal of perfectibility and embracing a second-best ethic of decency, perseverance, patience, sympathy, and restraint.

The account so far has discussed each office in isolation; it has not said much about how each office relates to the others. In this section, therefore, I shall present reasons and examples supporting the conclusion that the good exercise of each office tends to have good effects on other offices and on democratic politics as a whole. (This does not always mean *comfortable* effects: political action is often measured by its ability to pro-

---

[1] Bickel (1975: 86).

voke constructive conflicts and tensions.) I shall then proceed to address some broad objections to the theory as a whole: that it is insufficiently principled, excessively political rather than ethical, too narrow in its definition of political office, too provincial in its focus on American values and institutions, and too quick to assume political apathy.

Some final remarks will clarify how the overarching theory and the particular judgments about political types relate to one another, and will draw out some wider implications of the view put forth here. I shall argue that the plurality of political ethics defended here corresponds to a theory of politics I call "governing pluralism." This theory in turn depends on a principle of democratic openness under which different modes of political life (though not *all* such modes) should be regarded as not only tolerable but valuable.

THE INTERRELATION OF OFFICES

Benjamin Constant described politics in terms of a division of labor between citizens and representatives: the latter engage in politics so that the former need not spend time doing so.[2] One could defend the offices described in this book in the same way. On such an account, the organizer would talk to ordinary people face-to-face so that senators could stay more distant; activists would stress moral principles so that organizers could forget about them; senators would discuss and trade off interests among one another so that activists could be blind to interest, and so on.

While this line of reasoning has something to it, it is not one I have followed or shall stress. Political issues are common to all offices: while it is possible (though unwise) for many ordinary citizens to be ignorant of affirmative action policy or the level of the highest marginal tax rate, activists, organizers, and senators must all be aware of such things. Nor do I regard a concern for ethics as the monopoly of one office: as I argued above, *all* political offices require ethical reasoning and call for the kind of people who are willing to engage in it. Finally, few politicians have the sort of ignorance of others' activity that the division-of-labor metaphor implies. As noted above, Martin Luther King did not think of his kind of politics as the only legitimate one but considered others' "political strategy" a supplement to his "spiritual strategy"; likewise, Alinsky and civil rights organizers were deeply attached to voting and focused much of their own activity in the informal, voluntary realm on canvasses that would give people more power in the realm of elections and, ultimately, legislation.

[2] Benjamin Constant, "The Liberty of the Ancients Compared with That of the Moderns," in Constant (1988: 325–26).

The division of moral responsibility discussed in chapter 1 makes a different sort of claim. Not the objects or issues of politics but specific modes of engaging in political action, and specific dispositions appropriate to those modes, are things in which particular types of politician can and should specialize. The organizer's character is rightly different from the senator's, because the two offices fulfill different purposes. Organizers, moral activists, and senators must all be in a sense good people, pursuing good actions. But they need not all define good the same way. No one can pursue all goods at once: it is fine for politicians, as for ordinary people, to emphasize those good actions that they (and those who place confidence in them) find most consistent with their own peculiar dispositions. Democratic constancy theory allows us to be comfortable with embracing variety and partiality in human characters because it does not aspire to make people fully moral. It makes concessions to human imperfections; it encourages people to cultivate the best parts of their character while avoiding situations that display the worst.

This brings up the natural question of why we should expect the different political offices to work well together: how they might further in common the good of a democratic polity, in spite of representing different goals and modes of action, and even to some extent fundamentally different ways of regarding what democratic political life is all about. There should be no presumption that the end of political action, particularly democratic political action, must be consensus or harmony. "In a democracy," as Richard John Neuhaus has argued, "the role of cooperation is not to be deemed morally superior to the roles of checking and competing."[3] Still, it is reasonable to ask whether a particular kind of competition will by and large produce decent outcomes. One can think of roles, such as that of roving assassin, that would certainly compete with other roles and check their authority, but that should not therefore win our approval.

These matters are not subject to cost-benefit analyses or other precise ways of calculating outcomes. There are not only too many variables but too much disagreement about what we want politics to look like. (Such disagreement represents one reason for accommodating diverse political offices in the first place.) But one can make reasonable arguments that the presence of each office enhances the work done by the other offices, and that the absence of an office harms the other offices' work and makes democratic politics as a whole worse-off. The judgments involved are (unavoidably) partly empirical, but so are all interesting judgments in political theory: we must do our best, and try to check our assertions against history, political science, and common sense.

[3] Neuhaus (1984: 84).

First, the presence of uncompromising moral activists can make people more comfortable with the necessary compromises of legislative politics and organizers' pressure tactics. John Rawls has argued that democracies must allow for civil disobedience so that those who have had their rights ignored may retain some confidence in a polity that civil disobedience gives them some hope of changing.[4] The point applies to activism more broadly, with or without disobedience. The activities of the moral activist make it more likely that excluded groups, which cannot count on exerting political power through the normal channels of interest aggregation, will be given access to political power and the nonpolitical things that go with it: will be able to vote, speak freely, join unions, be admitted to the Boy Scouts. Before the civil rights movement, most African-Americans considered not only elections but many of the opportunities of civil society a cruel joke: neither politics nor the most attractive civil and professional opportunities were realistically available to them. Blacks' later attachment to normal party politics and the social processes of individual and group bargaining was paid for by speeches and marches. Bayard Rustin, in later life the greatest advocate of a move "from Protest to Politics" by black Americans,[5] was before that the chief organizer of the March on Washington: he knew very well that successful "normal" politics presupposed successful protest. Arguments that feminists must now move from protest politics to "standard" political organizing have a similar character: no one denies that early agitation (for the right to vote, to own property within marriage, to divorce abusive husbands) was the precondition for later decisions to abandon agitation. In the absence of activism, however episodic, those excluded become understandably cynical about politics, regarding it as corrupt, unprincipled, and biased toward the few.[6] (This does not mean that they think politicians should follow their *own* principles: activists force them to respect the principles the *public* holds whether politicians like them or not.) Finally, in the absence of activism those whose rights *are* respected become complacent and ignorant. Activists who speak on behalf of other groups do us a service—intellectually as well as politically—when they make us realize the gap between the ideals of justice and equality we treasure and the realities of injustice and inequality, with which those of us with social advantages would normally feel quite comfortable.

In a similar vein, the presence of organizers can make people more confident that senators (and other legislators) will do what they should: will exert their vocational duty to delay or transform public demands

---

[4] Rawls (1971: 333–91). I explore this idea more fully in Sabl (2001).

[5] Rustin (1964).

[6] I thank Peter Euben for stressing to me the importance of this point.

only for public purposes, not because they are out of touch with those making the demands. In a polity like the United States, "underorganized" in the sense of lacking powerful groups representing the interests of the poor and uneducated, we tend to expect too much from activists and legislators. We want the former to make moral appeals so effective that they take the place of political pressure, and expect the latter to take constant account of powerless people who cannot reward them electorally, at the expense of those who can punish them severely. People then become disappointed and angry when the human disposition to altruism cannot bear the burden expected of it. It is far better to organize the unorganized, to provide direct pressure on elected politicians, who may then with a clear conscience do what they do best: bargain, compromise, draft bills, seek reelection. As Michael Walzer has written, in the context of chiding liberal activists who attacked President Clinton's stance on welfare, elected politicians "don't act conscientiously. They act politically. They make judgments about what will mobilize support and build coalitions. They do what pleases, or what they think will please, the most people. Advocates of real welfare reform need to find some way to make themselves the people who have to be pleased."[7] This is why Franklin Roosevelt, in the quotation cited as an epigraph to chapter 6, wanted to have organized groups put pressure on him in the direction he wanted to go. Knowing political reality, he needed political pressure in favor of the policies he himself favored, to counterbalance the pressure that would be put on him by enemies of those policies.

Finally, bad senators make people forget important democratic values: compromise, patience, a recognition that others have demands contrary to one's own. The result can be disaffection and a rush to extremes. Legislators who have too little democratic sympathy make people distrustful of legislative processes that they suspect of being mechanisms for selling out their interests, and eager to rein in their legislators through term limits, shorter legislative sessions, or lower salaries—generally intensifying the oligarchic effects against which they reacted in the first place. Legislators who do not listen deeply to people and try to understand them find themselves unable to sustain creative policies and coalitions. This only confirms constituents in the false belief that they have the right to have all their desires—including the most angry and ill-considered—enacted immediately. Senators who are unwilling or unable to broker legislative solutions and work for substantively good policy open the door to those who promise to "just fix" the political system through a quasi-dictatorial populism. Those who cast disrespect on their political parties and their own legislative institutions, calling them deca-

---

[7] Walzer (1996: 27).

dent and immoral, encourage extreme movements that seek to do away with parties and "revolutionize" institutions. And once again, activists and organizers are asked to bear too great a burden when these things happen: neither moral protest nor strikes and canvasses can create or sustain legislative institutions that make good policy by refining citizen demands.

Each of these offices is therefore useful, in fact necessary, if democracy is to sustain itself and not be transformed into something worse through ungovernability and anarchy, injustice and inattention to democratic principles, or feudal inequality and extreme civic disengagement. The political actors discussed above as negative examples each precipitated in his or her own way a serious crisis in the polity, a question as to whether democratic structures were still viable.

One should stress, however, just how different the three offices are. They differ in the dispositions they call for, the modes of rhetoric that sustain them, the habits of action they demand, and the ethical assumptions they rest on. It is commonplace to talk of political roles as hats that politicians can and should put on and take off. This work might be expected to conclude that senators must sometimes act like activists, that organizers must sometimes adopt the statesmanlike perspective of senators, and so forth. This is not in fact my position. Dispositions of character are not easily changed or put aside. Some people have conversion experiences, but nobody has one several times a week. In a hypothetical world of godlike, omnitalented politicians, it might be desirable for one person to be able to change his disposition often enough to fill all political offices in turn and as needed (though there would be great costs in political diversity, and questions of trust would still be acute). But given people as they are, incapable of doing everything well, such behavior—which in private life would be called schizoid, dangerously lacking in consistent character—would not prove compatible with capable and reliable performance in all of the many offices involved. Elective politicians who *try* to talk like activists are probably, unknown to themselves, not doing it very well. Perhaps we would be all the more frightened if they did do it well.

We might consider in this context the argument of Keith Miller (a student of rhetoric rather than politics) regarding Martin Luther King. Miller rightly claims that neither politicians like Hubert Humphrey nor organizers like Robert Moses were able to accomplish anything like what King did in the realm of moral rhetoric. When politicians spoke on civil rights, they fell into the factual, inductive style of political persuasion rather than the symbolic, sacralizing, deductive appeal to deep truths that King mastered. But the flip side of this, as Miller notes, is that when coming out in opposition to the Vietnam War, *King* tried to master the unfamiliar, fact-laden rhetoric of the policy maker *and could not*.[8] King had commitment and rhetorical skill, but his disposition was a bad match to the activity of foreign policy analysis. In a similar vein, Daniel Patrick Moynihan criticized the Johnson administration for letting Jack Conway, a former United Auto Workers organizer, run the War on Poverty: "Where the President hoped to help the poor, Conway wished to arouse them. That in a sense was his profession. He was a labor organizer on the militant wing of the labor movement." Conway, writes Moynihan, wanted to "create new institutions"; a federal bureaucrat should be the kind of person who wants to sustain and improve existing ones.[9] Moynihan has very kind words for organizers, including Conway. He singles out Saul Alinsky for praise. But he insists, following Alinsky, that organizers should shun policy jobs: "Social radicalism is not a civil service calling."[10]

The claim that every political rhetoric and every political relationship should be available to everyone assumes not only on an unusual view of human character but an unnecessarily narrow view of political argument. It reflects the quixotic desire that every political claim be commensurable with every other in a single forum of public debate and political decision. Once we realize that this is neither necessary nor desirable, we can stop hoping for political characters who have a protean ability to master with a moment's practice all possible functions and modes of action—and accept the need for a division of moral responsibility and moral characters.

Few take such lessons. Most political analysts grow attached to specific political goods and types of action, and rapidly become partisans of the offices that go with them. This often divides along ideological lines. Traditional conservatives study only the Senate and the presidency and want all politics to be "statesmanlike" and above the masses. They often claim that only these formal, institutional officers can be "deliberative."[11] This ignores the possibility that people who live for politics—just as reasonable, farsighted, and patient as senators, but to different purposes—might exist among popular movements, outside the formal policy-making offices. In a similar vein, what remains of the political Left (as well as the populist Right) worships organizers, wants to hear only about the "grass-

---

[8] Miller (1992: 10–11, 148–50, 193). King's popularity as a moral leader took its sharpest dive not, as commonly thought, after Black Power corroded his message and his base, but after he was perceived as meddling in foreign policy issues on which he had no particular expertise.

[9] Moynihan (1970: 96–98).

[10] Moynihan (1970: 187).

[11] "The people at large ... usually lack the time, information, and instrumentality for reasoning together about common concerns. Thus, deliberative majorities will not normally exist independent of the governing institutions themselves" (Bessette [1994: 36]).

roots," and quickly labels as a turncoat anyone who seeks electoral majorities. And the intelligentsia of Right and Left in academe, the press, and the clergy tend to assume politics is worthwhile only if it is unflinchingly moral, and want to remake all of politics in the image of moral activists (or morally "activist" judges).

We should reexamine all these partisan positions. Taking seriously the diversity of political life in a constitutional democracy requires taking seriously the fact that some people will seem more comfortable in one sphere of politics than in another, and perform one kind of office better than others. (Some will be good at no office: pluralism also values freedom from politics, or at least freedom from leadership.) Accepting this will help us appreciate the value of political actions, and political actors, that are not of our own favorite type.

If a former member of a moral movement for group justice, upon winning a Senate seat, begins to take into account a wide variety of opinions and interests and seeks legislative compromise, this should win praise, not blame, *even from those who support the movement*. The moral compromise that is rightly attacked as "selling out" when practiced by an activist is morally required of a legislator. As argued by Massimo D'Alema, the Italian communist-turned-reformist prime minister, there is a difference between the insider politics of governance and the outsider politics of "social commitment": this involves not a different moral universe but a "structural difference, different jobs." Governing, unlike social action, means commanding a majority of the votes, and therefore "a balanced platform that is *attentive to the* interests of outsiders but cannot be *centered on* their interests."[12] Instead of being angry at the new senator for not acting like an activist, the friend of the movement should be gratified—and a bit surprised—if he manages to recast his dispositions so thoroughly as to succeed and gain influence in his new office. (Such successful transformations are, again, rare.) Similarly, believers in the established legislative and executive powers should not be surprised or angry when observing leaders who seek to rouse the people independently of government. In a democracy, originally a contemptuous term meaning "rule by rabble," rabble-rousing has a place. Its presence represents a "crisis of democracy" only if this is the *sole* kind of politics taking place.

To ask what political leadership should be like is to ask the wrong question. We should ask instead what kind of politics should be practiced for a given purpose, in a particular sphere, by a certain sort of character, if the democratic polity is to fulfill its promise as well as possible. This does not imply that "anything goes." It does imply that many different political activities that actually exist might be valuable for reasons specific

---

[12] Bosetti (1998: 14; emphasis in original).

to an office, and should be judged by *those* reasons rather than those of a false universality.

OBJECTIONS

While no work can answer all possible objections, some are predictable and deserve a brief response.

First, the framework put forth here might look *unprincipled*. Instead of putting forth rules that must always be obeyed and then castigating politicians for not normally obeying them, I have started from the premise that current practices have some ethical value, and have tried to explain what that value is. I assume that political life often and rightly calls for rhetorical arguments that smooth over logical flaws; bargaining based on one's power position; appeals to cultural prejudice; small deceptions; and elements of manipulation. More broadly, this work has tried to explain why politicians who favor some groups, moral traditions, or partisan creeds above others might be performing vital roles for which we should praise them. Some will see these concessions to existing practices as an endorsement of ethical laxity and an abdication of the calling of moral theory.

One response is that the present project remains both critical of many existing practices and respectful of moral standards in the widest sense. To look for the reasons behind the roles we are used to is not to endorse everything that goes on. Some political goals that are generally considered important may in fact be indefensible, and some generally accepted means may be totally disproportionate to the (legitimate) ends they further. Moreover, some ethically dubious practices that might seem innocuous in single cases may be unjustifiable because they set bad precedents.

This will not be enough to satisfy everyone. The strongest objections are likely to come (broadly speaking) from the followers of Kant and Habermas: seekers of absolute moral rules, or else sociologically oriented proponents of "discourse ethics," who define a "political ethic" as the search for universally justifiable and egalitarian standards applied to political institutions, practices, and values.[13] Such critics will find even moderate concessions to particularism too strong: they are likely to claim that by likening politicians to "friends" of particular citizens and groups, I have given them too much license to abdicate their moral duties. A theory that looks to offices, moral roles, and relationships for moral justification may seem "hypothetical" or "instrumental," whereas morality on

---

[13] "A political ethic concerns the creation of institutions, the formation of practices, and the sustaining of civic values that cultivate the ability of enlarged thought and the universalist-egalitarian commitment that inspires them" (Benhabib [1988: 45–46]).

the Kantian account is to escape such categories and look toward what is right as such.

While such critics probably hold moral axioms very different from mine, making direct rebuttal difficult, some answers are possible. One common response that may work here too is to distinguish between the private and social realm on the one hand and politics on the other. "Never kill" is a laudable principle for individuals, and "never lie" is at least an acceptable one, but we should be glad that politicians make exceptions to these principles, for instance in times of war. A second response is to note that the present project endorses political roles for an atypical reason: not because they make a system "function" efficiently or with maximum utility but because they represent respect for democratic citizens' political prerogatives and the political structures through which they expect to exercise those prerogatives. In other words, means matter as well as ends, and values like universal dignity and freedom find a place here—though I argue for respecting these values in non-Kantian ways.

Finally, to the extent that the argument here does rely on hypothetical imperatives (citizens' expectations are respected partly because they already exist), this could be considered more congruent than strict Kantianism with democracy—with a kind of politics in which politicians recognize our ends and projects, not just their own. Michael Walzer has defended the hypothetical imperative as characteristic of commonsense reasoning, especially in regard to professional and political ethics. Doctors tell us to do something *if* we want to solve a certain health problem. If doctors tell us *merely* what we should do, without the hypothetical, they are abusing their office and assuming an inequality of wisdom between them and us that they have no right to assume.[14] We could make the same point about politics. Politicians have no *right* to adopt categorical imperatives; they must defend their actions not in terms of their own principles but in terms that respect the projects of ordinary citizens. Like Walzer, I find such ways of regarding political ethics congruent with common sense. Those who find them intolerable will differ with the assumptions of the current project. But they should also have to justify the fact that their view of morality seems to share few postulates with common sense, at least in the case of politics. Popularity is not the standard for judging ethical conclusions, but it is relevant in assessing the postulates from which one begins ethical arguments.

[14] Walzer (1983: 156). Nussbaum (1994), in her extended comparison of philosophy to medical treatment and philosophers to doctors, discusses many models of the doctor-patient relationship but strikingly fails to mention the right to refuse treatment—the patient's prerogative to have no relationship with physicians at all.

Second, the present project might be accused of *placing politics above ethics*. This is a book on political ethics, but it admittedly gives a certain priority to political considerations as opposed to ethical theory in the strict sense. The first chapter set forth the competing claims of universalism and particularism in ethics; the succeeding chapters, however, have abstracted from these theories, preferring to trace viable political compromises by which direct clashes between ethical imperatives could be avoided. The subject was changed from the question of *human* duties and purposes to that of *political* duties and purposes. Arguments about how politicians ought to live in order to be ethically good people were put aside as less relevant than arguments about how specific political officers ought to act in order to fulfill their purposes within a political regime. And the principles of that (democratic) regime were taken to be largely given, rather than subject to critical moral examination or construction: democratic political principles like equality, majority decision, living as one likes, and democratic stability were taken as the starting point for ethical reasoning about character (or at least political character), not the other way around.

The serious and even radical nature of this move should be stressed. For the move from moral to political reasoning amounts to a refusal to consider moral arguments on the merits. Moral arguments are regarded, for present purposes, as political claims that must be accommodated in the polity for the sake of peaceful accommodation and the principles of democratic politics—not as philosophical claims that must be examined with a view to their truth. Nor is there the comfort of asserting that philosophical claims on these issues are false, indemonstrable, or meaningless, or that speculation about them is a waste of time.[15] They may very well be true, demonstrable, and meaningful, and examining the truth of ethical claims may be part of a worthy human life—but abstracting from their truth is necessary for the sake of *political* life. In a democratic regime, we cannot demand of others the kinds of moral argument that seem noble, attractive, and even necessary when we try as best we can to consider our own, private ethical actions.

As I have suggested above, this "cannot" has both an empirical and moral content: it represents not a mere concession to political baseness but a certain defense of that baseness in the name of democracy. Empiri-

---

[15] Here I differ strongly with the position of Richard Rorty (1991: 175–96; 1993: 31–50). Compared to Rorty, I am less willing to proclaim that certain people have mastered the whole philosophical tradition and have demonstrated that all its ultimate questions are meaningless or badly posed.

cally, most people are not used to engaging in abstract, philosophical moral reasoning and do not expect to be required to. One can even define "culture" as a repertoire of behaviors and possible decisions, thinking outside of which is hardly even conceivable most of the time.[16] Closer to home, one could apply Socrates' finding that most Athenians did not enjoy having their convictions about virtue and their accustomed ways of life questioned by an obtrusive philosopher. Liberal democracies have ended the practice of killing people like Socrates, but they have never succeeded (as Mill noted) in making them popular.[17]

I have argued that such attitudes embody the principle of consent applied to social as well as political life. As noted throughout this work, democratic citizens generally require those seeking to challenge their beliefs to win their consent for engaging in this challenge. The would-be reformer must use the right rhetoric, occupy a social role that we respect, and appeal to principles that we share. Absent such consent, democratic citizens deny that strangers are entitled to ask them to justify anything. And this denial is what protects them from the projects of self-appointed moral superiors, otherwise known as aristocrats.

Or we could consider, and generalize, Tocqueville's observation that Americans regard all honest occupations as honorable.[18] Though an aristocrat like Tocqueville found this standpoint extraordinary, it was natural to the citizens of a democracy based on equality of conditions. In a democratic political order, Aristotelian assertions about the good life or Hegelian assertions that soldiers and civil servants lead more complete ethical lives than ordinary workers are all but incomprehensible—and highly offensive if comprehended.[19] The desire to reason about the goodness of one's life and to defend one's moral beliefs and practices against all comers is largely limited to philosophers and those with similar dispositions, and distinguishes such dispositions from those of ordinary people. Most democratic citizens do not share this love. They will put up with the chore of defending their beliefs and practices occasionally and to some extent in the context of relations with intimates and confidantes, but certainly do not welcome being asked to do so by random strangers.

The demand that ordinary people justify all their public opinions, aims, and aspirations through moral reasoning is therefore elitist in a special sense: it does not necessarily require a rare skill or benefit a small group, but it appeals to a rare taste. In demanding that democratic citizens justify themselves with the kind of arguments philosophers are used

[16] Swidler (1986).
[17] Mill (1975: chapter 2, p. 32).
[18] Tocqueville (1969: II.2.18, pp. 550–51).
[19] This point is made (quietly) by Shklar (1988: 106).

to, we are not asking ordinary people to do more than they are capable of but asking them to do more than they want to do, feel they have to do, or expect others to do. Those who criticize as elitist the demand for too much moral reasoning in politics are not attacking the *skills of the masses* as insufficient but attacking the *demands of the elites* as excessive and artificial (and, I would add, contrary to the free-and-easy spirit of democracy).[20] I might have a desire to justify myself to others in reasonable terms, or to reflect about the good life for human beings, or to find my true vocation or source of meaning in the life of a soldier, civil servant, or professor. But to turn these first-person desires into third-person demands directed at others is to offend the democratic taste for being left alone and for having one's way of life more or less accepted along with everyone else's.

Third, the theory could be accused of being *too narrow*, of excluding too many important political roles. I have concentrated on three political offices: senator, moral activist, and organizer. In doing so, I have of course left out other roles, offices, or political functions that are vital to politics. Most conspicuously, I have left out the president, and Supreme Court justices. This reflects a division of scholarly labor. The proper actions and dispositions of the president and Supreme Court justices have been discussed extensively. In fact, as I argued in chapter 1, the approach of this work takes direction from well-known and respected works on the presidency and the Supreme Court. Senators, activists, and organizers are comparatively under-studied.[21] For similar reasons, I do not discuss the roles of others who affect politics: bureaucrats, lobbyists, campaign managers and consultants, volunteer canvassers, political journalists, interns—or even more broadly, bond traders, oil company executives, publishers, and so on. One could also argue that "the political" includes the personal and the social: one could inquire into the proper (democratic? undemocratic? pre-democratic? extrademocratic?) purposes of family and corporate institutions, and draw appropriate conclusions about the actions and dispositions appropriate to them. (Feminist theorists, among others, take on the former case; business ethicists, the latter.) But one has to stop somewhere. If others like my approach, I encourage them to adopt it in studying other offices.

Fourth, this work could be accused of *provincialism*. My examples have been taken from the United States, which might be said to distort the analysis. Because of weak party-discipline, a United States senator is much more of a free agent than are occupants of upper houses in other

---

[20] To this extent, the rebuttal made by Gutmann and Thompson (1996: 132–33) is, I think, a response to arguments that are not those their opponents intended to make.

[21] My own Whiggish political prejudices may also play a role.

countries. The organizer flourishes in the United States, with its tradition of independent associations, much more than in countries with strong statist traditions and distrust for nonstate associations. And the moral activist could be seen by citizens of other countries as a uniquely American invention, closely related to Americans' odd piety and moralism, and to the insufferable assumption that the United States has a distinctive moral mission.

While conceding the objection in part, and acknowledging that some of my conclusions will not apply directly to other countries, I would still make two responses. First, other countries may in coming years become more like the United States than they are now (assuming they were ever as different as portrayed: both Americans and non-Americans have cultural interests in exaggerating U.S. political exceptionalism). To engage in admitted speculation: many major parties in advanced democracies currently seem to be facing great turmoil over cultural and national issues, and party discipline may over time yield to fragmentation and greater opportunities for free agency.[22] Nor are "Westminster" institutions— highly centralized, with parliamentary supremacy, and based on a strict two-party system ensuring legislative coherence and accountability— either as "normal" as some political scientists assume or as permanent as sometimes supposed. Almost all democracies have senates or upper houses that have at least a delaying power and affect calculations of policy, and the power of such institutions is by and large increasing rather than waning.[23] Some, like France, combine an ethic of parliamentary sovereignty with an incongruously strong, independently elected president. Most democracies have multiparty systems that provoke questions of party loyalty, fidelity to constituents, and the ethics of negotiation. All these factors will bring the issues discussed in chapter 4 (on the senator) increasingly to the fore.

The organizer role may become less exceptional as well, as confidence in the state slowly erodes and the dominance of economic interest groups and distributional issues in the political arena is increasingly contested. As many countries see declining confidence in both states and labor unions, and those interested in issues such as feminism and environmentalism seek outlets outside party systems that are too rigid to accommodate their claims, theories of association are suddenly popular, Tocqueville is newly read, and organizers may become increasingly relevant as people must consider where to turn for political power.

---

[22] As of this writing, the prime ministers of both Australia and Germany have in the past three years had to engage in American-style arm-twisting and compromise in order to pass vital tax bills through upper houses in which their governing coalitions were a minority.

[23] See the evidence in Patterson and Mughan (1999).

Finally, the increasing popularity of universal human rights (and Europe-wide rights in the EU) as a legitimating principle is starting to bring to many countries' politics an unaccustomed—and to parliamentarians, unwelcome—amount of American-style moral activism. Judicial review is increasingly common and powerful;[24] even Britain has passed legislation empowering courts to proclaim laws in violation of EU human rights principles. In these and other ways, the present politics of the United States may seem less and less "exceptional" over time.

Nor should one regret this. (This is the second response.) Charles Fried has argued (see chapter 1) that the adversary system of justice is not just pragmatically justified but morally worthy; that a system in which lawyers are not allowed to represent aggressively the legal interests of their clients is morally inferior to one in which they are. Only personal and zealous legal representation sufficiently respects the client's status as a "responsible, valuable, and valuing agent."[25] The contrapositive implication has been fleshed out by David Luban: those who attack the adversary legal system and prefer a Continental model (sometimes called "inquisitorial") may not understand fully the values according to which such systems operate. Taking the German system as an example, Luban shows that it rests on close cooperation between judges and prosecutors, on fixed schedules of payments in civil trials that do not attempt to track closely the circumstances of particular cases, and above all on a pervasive elitism in which lawyers are remote from ordinary experience, the court system makes little attempt to explain itself to those whose interests it affects, and working-class and uneducated persons are treated, sometimes to their face, with undisguised condescension. The system requires a profound trust in the impartiality and competence of lawyers, judges, and academic legal commentators (whose work is consulted in lieu of precedent).[26]

In a legal system, such things might in fact be tolerable (and Fried might be wrong). Luban concludes that, in spite of its flaws, the German system might still be on balance superior to the American—though so remote from American expectations of the legal system and of social structures more generally that adopting it in the U.S. would cause much more inconvenience than it would cure. But in politics the loss of moral agency has even higher costs than in a legal system. Once again, the question is whether we want the political system to represent our will and judgment as agents, as well as our interests as passive recipients of

---

[24] Tate and Vallinder (1995); "The Gavel and the Robe," *Economist*, 7 August 1999, 47–48.

[25] C. Fried (1976: 1069).

[26] Luban (1988: 92–103).

government services. The American answer is yes, and this, I submit, is the democratic answer. As Judith Shklar has argued, we should seek a system that asks the least-well-off what they want and think, instead of just giving them what others decide they need. The alternative—practiced in most places and times—is political paternalism of a kind we would never accept in any other realm.[27] The American system of democracy cannot claim to maximize efficiency. But it gives a huge diversity of people an opportunity to advance their claims and ideas forcefully (whether or not they have the assumed skills and narrow assumptions of a "political class"), and forces political leaders to pay some attention to the vast majority of ordinary citizens who are not active members of a party. These are great democratic goods and may be generally recommended.

Finally, the present work may seem to be *time- and culture-bound.* Some might call democratic constancy theory a crabbed philosophy for an exhausted age. It could be accused of doing justice to the political apathy of a single generation or the narrow perspective of a lackluster set of political leaders, but of being false to politics generally. Those who remember the politics of the 1960s might claim that political argument is inherently interesting, and has only been stifled by forces of consumerism, conformity, and manufactured media consensus. Or one could level another version of the previous objection: Americans may hate politics, but people, particularly educated people, in other countries love it.

This objection mistakes both the nature of the current theory and the nature of political engagement. The theory assumes not that people do not like politics, but that they do not like having their political beliefs and social practices *challenged*, except episodically and under certain conditions. I would submit that this was the case in the 1960s as well: rebellious students did not spend much time listening to those who thought Aron was wiser than Adorno, or Haydn better than Hendrix. This is not to blame them, only to put them in the same category as everyone else: people seek social validation and communities of the like-minded, rather than constant challenges from people whose beliefs are radically different from their own. Nor can it be said that the 1960s were an age of constant political engagement: even in that decade, or any other, a small proportion of the population was actively involved in politics, or actively changing its minds on political issues, at any given time. Political activity remained occasional for most and consuming only for a few.

This is also the response to those outside the United States who describe their own citizens as more politically engaged than Americans. The citizens of other countries might enjoy talking about politics and

---

[27] Shklar (1988: 115ff.).

social issues, but such talk tends to involve either limited dialogue within a broadly shared framework ("Which kind of Marxist analysis is appropriate here?" "How should we neoliberals think about pollution?") or heated ideological argument intended to overpower others' beliefs rather than learn from them.[28] In no country, at no time, does the average person regularly and routinely modify his or her deeply held beliefs in response to uninvited philosophical objections. As Tocqueville pointed out, to engage in such examination, a rather caricatured version of the enlightenment ideal, would make it impossible to live life. We could not carry out the simplest action if doing so required justifying our first principles from the ground up.[29]

DEMOCRATIC VALUES AND GOVERNING PLURALISM

The above account of political offices has attempted to stay rooted, though indirectly, in common opinions. It has tried to make sense of the inarticulate and intermittent public awareness that many different kinds of politicians each serve a real purpose in a democracy—either in promoting equality and the rule of the majority, or in reformulating and rendering into good policy the hasty demands that the majority sometimes puts forth. To ask that all political offices serve a *single* purpose, or that each be shown to promote efficiency, social stability, role contentment, or other shibboleths of sociological functionalism, is to miss the point of pluralist, democratic politics. A pluralist regime is not an organism; or if it is, it is one that can only survive as long as it has indigestion. Democracy has *many* purposes—though all of them must, if they are to sustain their claims, be made consistent with democracy's basic egalitarian principles. Equality and stability, change and continuity, are both needed in democracy, but they are not the same, nor is either supreme. Nor does the political theory of Tocqueville, Madison, and Aristotle promote or even allow a politics devoted to efficiency or role contentment. Tyrannical administrative regimes may be highly efficient at different moments in history, and people may come to feel content in them. But a democratic constitutionalist is willing to sacrifice a little efficiency for the sake of active liberty, opposition to tyranny, and the toleration of diverse human opinions and interests.

I call the resulting ethics "governing pluralism" or "democratic pluralism": it involves extending the nonjudgmentalism characteristic of democracy as a whole to the study of what our political figures should do. (This is not the same as *moral* pluralism, the idea that there are multiple,

---

[28] For a perceptive and very funny analysis of the latter, see Gambetta (1998).
[29] Tocqueville (1969: II.1.2).

incommensurable values, with no single one being overriding—though the two ideas are certainly consistent).[30]

As long as each officer serves her purpose, it is not even absolutely necessary—though it is common and no doubt desirable—for the occupants of each office to realize the need for other offices and the values served by those who fill them. It is presumably a good thing if *someone* understands the value of this diversity, however: after all, every democratic citizen must choose, and evaluate, more than one officer. Here, and for the most part only here, is where political theorists are useful: in criticizing and praising political actions and actors so that citizens can choose the best possible political leaders. But we must remember that those leaders have qualities of character that we lack. Even Madison, an unparalleled constitutional theorist, was a weak and ineffective president.

Responding to these facts about what democratic citizens will allow in their politics, democratic constancy and the office ethics that follow from it are motivated by one social outlook and two moral values: reality, sympathy, and toleration. The claim to be pursuing these fine values is not mere boastfulness if one freely admits what is thereby rejected: justification based on absolute moral principles, the conviction that everyone has high moral capacities (or that we do ourselves), and the hope for moral progress. Governing pluralism is a difficult perspective to adopt—and so often abandoned in a crisis—precisely because it requires giving up so much. Consider what are required by reality, sympathy, and toleration in turn.

By *reality* I mean what Camus meant: a willingness to ground our political programs and intellectual criticisms in a way of life that people have actually led and a set of social values that they have expressed in concrete actions (and have found frustrated by concrete injustices) in a particular, identifiable time and place. This does not in the least imply conservatism (though a democratic polity must entertain that too). For Camus, reality meant identification with the aspirations of trade unionists—with their ethic of productive work and free labor—and of the Paris Communards. His preferred political mode was not conservatism but syndicalism.[31]

---

[30] For an excellent summary and defense of moral pluralism see John Kekes (1993), and the citations therein. I regard moral pluralism as both correct and a good foundation for the theory presented here—but it is not the only possible foundation. Moral theories such as rule-consequentialism, as well as political ideologies ranging from democratic radicalism to progressive conservatism, could all be broadly consistent with the current work. I do not, by the way, agree with Kekes that the political ideology most consistent with moral pluralism is conservatism.

[31] Camus (1991: 297ff.).

A Camus-like attachment to reality is, however, opposed to the philosophical doctrine called constructivism. The work of some theorists takes pride in its freedom from existing social institutions and practices, in its willingness to label as unjust any conventional practice or set of rights that cannot withstand the test of reasonable public justification.[32] The standpoint of reality does the opposite: it proclaims its freedom from the claims of moral philosophers to the extent that these claims are divorced from solidarity with actual people's lives and aspirations. The status quo contains great conflicts—in particular, always the conflict between rich and poor—and reality as a political outlook in no way licenses the existing social order.[33] Reality does, however, for the sake of respect for those who find comfort, stability and meaning in their (unreflective) daily lives, refuse to disrupt those lives unless the comfort, stability, and meaning of other actual people requires it. When reasoned argument alone confronts a group of people's prephilosophic opinions about the way it lives—positive or negative—reason essentially deserves to lose. Camus is right to regard the alternative to a grounding in lived life and concrete demands as "Caesarism," government by commissars. When Nussbaum, for instance, lauds the "lawgiver" who acts without caring that everyone in the regime disagrees with his (ascetic) values,[34] we should consider carefully the undemocratic implications of such a conclusion.

Democratic constancy does not oppose social change, even at times radical change, as long as it is founded on the actual opinions and demands of identifiable individuals whose program cannot be accommodated within existing public policies and economic structures. Still, despite its nonrelativism and unusual openness to radicalism, democratic constancy has a clear and deliberate ambition to be tolerant toward ordinary mores and public opinions, as reflecting ways that people have found to live adequately the lives they find worth living.[35] Democratic constancy is in this way more liberal and humane than rationalist forms of liberalism, for it believes that if one intends to ignore—or still more, to modify—people's personal opinions and diverse ways of life, one should do so only because they render unlivable other ways of life, or the health of the polity that sustains all ways of life.

Sympathy means taking some pleasure from others' happiness, and some uneasiness from their unhappiness, whenever either is directly pre-

---

[32] See, for example, Cohen (1989: 22–23).

[33] See the fine arguments on this point made by Walzer (1984), whose position is clearly seems to be greatly influenced by Camus though he does not use the term "reality."

[34] See chapter 3, above.

[35] See similarly Constant, "Of Uniformity," in Constant (1988: 75).

sented to us.[36] Beyond this, it includes the ability to identify with the aspirations of groups of people as they are, as in the senator's identification with constituent wishes and the mores of her state, the activist's identification with the life of a congregation unified by moral and spiritual beliefs, and the organizer's identification with the latent desire of a particular group of people to fight oppressive social and political forces and put forth their own idiosyncratic opinions.

Sympathy, a tendency to share the feelings of other people, is often contrasted with equal respect. Respect means in this context the belief that everyone has "a capacity for working out a coherent view of the world" (a "perspective" in Charles Larmore's terminology) and the associated moral duty to treat everyone equally by virtue of this.[37] One can argue for sympathy or for respect on the basis of which is more effective and universal: the partisans of sympathy have usually claimed that real feeling for a few is more likely to motivate real and difficult action than a diffuse respect for all, and the partisans of respect argue that respect gives us reasons to listen to the claims of those who lack the "similarity or power" to arouse our fellow-feeling or self-interest.[38] But once again, an appeal to the suppositions of democracy settles the issue on different grounds.

Sympathy is something that everyone feels to some extent and that can be enlarged by the unintrusive (and largely automatic) means of daily social intercourse, as well as the more intrusive but consensual means of careful political argument.[39] To demand that others exercise equal respect, on the other hand, is to demand of them both a strenuous moral practice and a complicated philosophical belief. That people have certain metaphysical capacities is a complicated doctrine; that we often feel for other people and understand how they feel as they do is simply a fact. There is nothing philosophically wrong with preferring metaphysics to experience, but democratic citizens in the course of everyday politics cannot be expected to do so and will not be able to support a mode of politics premised on their doing so.

[36] Hume (1983: Section 5, Part 2). Sen (1977: 326) notes that "behavior based on sympathy is in an important sense egoistic, for one is oneself pleased at others' pleasure and pained at others' pain." Larmore's (1987: 62) use of sympathy to mean the ability to imagine ourselves in the position of others, and thereby to treat them "acceptingly" even when we disagree, is a small but important subset of this.

[37] Larmore (1987) 62–65.

[38] Hume, (1983: Section 5, Part 2, note 22); Larmore (1987: 65). It should be noted that the Kantian tradition is not just indifferent to sympathy but hostile to it, for it endangers impartial justice. See Kant (1957: Ak. 379), and esp. Kant (1960: 102–4): Kant treats instances in which children help the suffering rather than fulfilling their strict duties as textbook cases of bad moral impulses that must be extirpated.

[39] Hume (1983: Section 5, Part 2, note 19).

Most people value the everyday mores and practices of people with whom they are in sympathy. They value what Kenneth Dover called "Popular Morality"—the "principles, criteria and values" that underlie their accustomed ways of resolving conflicts among people's wishes— rather than moral philosophy.[40] We can certainly demand that unpopular and baffling forms of morality, including the morality of philosophers who reject popular mores in the name of coherent moral worldviews, be tolerated. But one can hardly expect ordinary followers of convention to understand very thoroughly these philosophic bohemians, nor can we demand that they derive from others' ability to be more coherent than necessary and less conventional than normal an obligation to engage in such people's preferred style of moral argument. Some reformulations of Kantianism, which stress the moral value of publicity and communication rather than the metaphysics of moral dignity, are more accessible to our everyday understanding. Yet even these appeal to tastes that are, in fact, specialized. Taking other people's interests into account is mere human kindness, but few people believe they must canvass hundreds of political and social viewpoints before making a personal moral decision or entering a voting booth. Todd Gitlin has written of participatory democracy, "Freedom as an endless meeting was only alluring to those who had the time and taste to go to meetings endlessly."[41] Of moral validity as an endless meeting the same might be said.

This might seem a merely practical or unprincipled objection, one that regards certain kinds of moral evaluation as bad because they can never be popular. While one can defend the idea that moral premises that find no support in public feeling should not be trusted,[42] the case for sympathy does not require such an argument. There is a more general objection from the standpoint of democratic ethics. The objection applies, in fact, to all forms of obligation that advocate duty without sympathy, "commitment" to the moral worth of an action without regard for the happiness of those whom the action benefits.[43]

The objection is that someone who acts from sympathy faces a built-in democratic check. If a political officer motivated by sympathy finds that a

---

[40] Dover (1994: 1). I recommend Dover's further discussion of the difference between popular morality and moral philosophy (1–5).

[41] Gitlin (1993: 175). For an extended treatment of the theme, see Walzer (1970).

[42] See Hume (1978: 546–47, 552–53).

[43] I take the term "commitment" from Sen (1997), who defines it as a non-sentiment-based propensity to fulfill duties that may or may not be universalist in scope (a commitment may involve duties to neighbors or fellow union members, for example). A moral commitment, as Sen defines it, has force regardless of whether fulfilling it actually makes us feel good. In fact, we know we have one to the extent that our actions lack such feelings, are "counter-preferential" (326ff.).

huge number of constituents regard her actions as useless or disagreeable, this response will disturb her and make her think twice about proceeding. But one who acts from commitments that do not depend on others' feelings cannot, it would seem, acknowledge such checks. On the contrary, such a person takes perverse pride in the fact that he neither likes what he is doing nor is motivated by the feelings of those he hopes to benefit.[44] We might therefore welcome the fact that a stable democracy rarely sees politicians acting out of abstract moral duty, beyond the bounds of sympathy. Moral duty as such, as suggested in chapter 5, normally plays a background, "framework" role, influencing what kinds of practices people think are justified but not typically inspiring people to heroic self-sacrifice.

Finally, the advantages of *toleration* are well known: it conduces to social peace, everyone's liberty, and the self-knowledge that is gained when people learn to avoid, as much as possible, coercing others on the basis of conclusions drawn from imperfect human reasoning. It is less commonly pointed out, however, that toleration requires forswearing a competing value, moral progress: "Citizens go their separate ways, keeping their moral reasons to themselves, avoiding moral engagement. This may sometimes keep the peace (though often only temporarily, as the violent confrontations over abortion show). But mere toleration also *locks into place the moral divisions in society* and makes collective moral progress far more difficult."[45]

Toleration indeed stands in the way of moral progress. From this we should conclude, however, that democrats generally will, and should, reject the demand for moral progress. Hannah Arendt has pointed out the philosophical inconsistency of liberals who retain loyalty to progress but reject the "glorification of history in Marxian and Hegelian terms, which alone could justify and guarantee [progress]."[46] But just as telling, and more relevant, is the *democratic* objection to moral progress: to believe in progress is to deny that the average person's moral beliefs are more or less all right as they are. As argued above, activists can, by engaging in

[44] Sen (1977: 329) rightly notes that action based on commitment must be truly austere if it is to avoid charges of sympathy: one who acts on commitment, in a literary example he quotes, does so "in cold blood," lacking both "motive" and "interest." Attachment to this severe or "monkish" view of moral duty, then, is not limited to orthodox Kantians.

[45] Gutmann and Thompson (1996: 62).

[46] Arendt (1972b: 127). In a similar way, recent assertions of moral progress have a self-undermining character. To the extent that a desire for progress (with respect for values such as autonomy, equality, or deliberation) leads some theorists to reject toleration—perhaps the highest value and proudest achievement of modern political and moral thought—their own work demonstrates that such progress tends to come at a price, and is therefore not unambiguously progress.

careful and indirect arguments, engage in such denial in ways that respect democratic values—but not easily, and not all the time.[47]

Some aspects of liberalism are compatible with democracy and even strengthen it, but the old rationalist dream of sure, constant moral progress probably just contradicts democracy, for it promises a standard of morality completely separate from that of majority decision and requires modes of moral engagement that are too intrusive to be accepted by democratic citizens fond of being left alone and willing to let others mind their own business. Democratic constancy, and its close cousin enlightened self-interest, are a *lingua franca* of democracy, not because they provide a common currency to which all conflicting claims can be reduced (the old utilitarian claim), but because they provide a common *rhetoric* with which almost anyone can be addressed without taking offense or shutting out the appeal.

At the price of perfect philosophic rationality, the advocate of democratic constancy gets a politics that encourages people to engage in styles of moral argument that are intelligent, if not unimpeachably rational; that treats everyone's plans and opinions democratically, giving each some consideration regardless of its content or philosophical quality; and that deals with the aims and aspirations that people actually do have, rather than the ones that a style of argument alien to them demonstrates they should have. Philosophers are free to have higher aspirations than this, as long as they pursue these aspirations in ways consistent with democratic practices. Discussions of the good, the noble, the self-actualizing, and the morally obligatory are both good in themselves and pleasant to experience, and are among the many activities that liberal or constitutional democracies allow their citizens to engage in. But philosophers ought to recognize just how *strange* extended, reasoned, serious argument on such subjects seems to ordinary people. We can perhaps posit some future society in which the desire to engage in such arguments would not be extremely rare (though I confess I cannot imagine what such a society would look like). But until we see one, we should take Socratic advice and accept that only the rare citizen has a philosophic *daimon*.

PLURALISM AND THEORY: How POLITICS RESCUES PHILOSOPHY

I began chapter 1 by discussing universalist and particularist philosophies of office, and ended it by promising that politics could resolve the dichotomy between the two. Now we can see what this means. Politics cannot, and should not try to, eradicate adherents of either particularism

---

[47] In addition to the above discussion, see the subtle argument of Sreenivasan (1998).

or universalism. In particular, we will always have with us partisan advocates of particular groups' views and dedicated believers in universalist values like safety, utility, and equal rights; we must for the sake of sympathy, reality, and toleration find ways in which both extraordinary political vocations and ordinary citizens' demands may be met.

To engage in such a search is to assume that the political order we are accustomed to is more or less worth preserving. This requires rejecting for the moment some of philosophy's critical edge. We consider preservation of the democratic polity as a good in itself, as the source of principles for action that should be followed—thus replacing, as Aristotle would say, justice and virtue simply with justice and virtue relative to an existing and imperfect regime. This could be called a sort of political idolatry. But it is a benign idolatry, far from the Hobbesian state-worship that requires submission to a tyrant as the price of avoiding religious war. To base one's principles on the goodness of a constitutional, democratic, pluralist political order is to base them on an order in which many ways of life can be lived, though with more compromises and less social distinction than some of its occupants would like.

In particular, pluralism and democratic constitutionalism make possible many different kinds of *political* life: those stemming from a desire for political preeminence based on public service, those stemming from a moral impulse for reform, and those stemming from identification with ordinary citizens and their desire for self-assertion. Constitutional regimes are not just anxious to avoid war over universalism and particularism, but anxious to give the friends of universalism and particularism in their various forms some actual satisfaction, real opportunity to put their practical convictions into practice. Constitutionalism's "accommodation" of the diverse philosophical schools does not fully respect either school's *conclusions*—for a modern democracy cannot hope for agreement on such divisive matters—but it does respect the fervency and sincerity with which human beings *hold* such conclusions and try to live in accord with them.

The result is not so open and pluralistic that it makes judgment impossible. The judgments of democratic constancy theory are modest and particular but clear: certain types of political action and the characters that lead people to them are to be rejected as harmful to democracy. The demagogic senator who has no love of fame and no serious plans for achievement; the impatient and self-serving organizer who slakes her own thirst for glory while failing to promote citizens' interests or capacities; the moral activist who confuses a calling to lead a congregation for a calling to turn the government into a moral theocracy—all are bad for democratic politics by almost any criterion.

These judgments are rooted, however, in empirical analyses of who is harmed, as the values of reality, sympathy, and toleration would suggest. Frances Willard greatly harmed the interests of American social drinkers and slandered the mores of particular immigrant groups, while having no idea of how a democracy could possibly function under the Christian realm she advocated. Joseph McCarthy lacked both common cause with the citizens of his state and true devotion to legislation; he ignored his constituents' real interests in the service of pursuing his own ambition, and ignored the serious question of communism in favor of slandering individuals as communists. And Stokely Carmichael set himself apart from American democracy as a whole, abandoning not only the development of democratic citizens but the whole democratic political order (based on popular pressure and voting majorities), in favor of a pan–Third World fantasy that did nothing for those he considered his people. These figures should be condemned not because their arguments were not philosophical enough, but because they betrayed many actual people, harmed others, and made it harder rather than easier for the democratic process to guard the interests of ordinary citizens and extend its equal privileges more widely. We should remember, however, that the penalty for violating the principles of the regime is, in a democracy, light. Those who do not respect the ethics of their office should be punished by loss of office, or lack of public attention, but they always keep their freedom, as well as their ability to gain more influence by returning to democratic principles.

When it comes to practical advice for political leaders, it becomes clear that democratic politics—the politics of openness to various aspirations—requires openness as well to different kinds of character, to different dispositions that lead people to disagree on what goals and actions are fit to aim at. In terms of life as a whole, these differences are so various that they probably defy a thorough theoretical analysis. (Aristotle and Hume did not just disagree about how to evaluate the passions: they saw *different* passions.) But if we narrow the question to political office, we can usefully employ the scheme of a tension between universalist attachment to utility, security, and equal rights, and particularist attachment to vigorous advocacy on behalf of a group or cause to which the politician feels deep kinship. Or we could consider a similar tension in an institutional context, as when Madison sought to tame the tyranny of the legislature by creating different branches and making them "by different modes of election and *different principles of action*, as little connected with each other as the nature of their common functions and their common dependence on the society will admit."[48] The different principles involved are apparently the principle of democratic rule, which requires the

[48] *Federalist*: No. 51.

House to express popular feelings as they are, and that of democratic stability, which requires for our own good that we do not get what we want right away but are required to pass our program through a group of constant senators. One principle says to give the people what we want; the other says to give us what we need, and what we will eventually miss if we do not get it. Both bold political dispositions and sober ones find obvious places in such a scheme. Add to the story the complexities of partisan, regional, ethnic, religious, and other differences, and one sees just how fully a pluralist democracy lets political diversity flourish.

Diversity of character is in this way supported by a political order that sustains diverse public spheres. "Pluralist" theories of ethical life often emphasize the multiple allegiances and goals of ordinary *citizens* in a democracy. They do not acknowledge, however, that these multiple allegiances and goals imply many different forums for those with *extraordinary* passion for public affairs. Governing or democratic pluralism includes the debates and compromises of legislation, the moral appeals of church meetings and mass marches, and the slow persuasion of organizing work in fields, factories, and homes out of the public eye. Some believers in a single "public sphere" are surreptitiously intolerant in their assumptions: there should be one public sphere because only one kind of action (rationally justifiable in a potentially universal discourse) and one kind of rhetoric (moral argument about propositions) is legitimate. Actual people with their actual allegiances resist, and should be allowed to resist, not only unitary requirements for how they should think as individuals, but unitary requirements for how they should arrange their public lives with others.

With a diversity in public spheres comes a diversity in forms of political rhetoric and justification. Senators work in the large sphere of a nation with great regional variation in mores, representing opinions and interests that can hardly be made uniform through moral persuasion. In this sphere they must use the flexible rhetorics required to tally and trade disparate opinions, bargain for votes, appeal to party ideologies that paper over important differences for important reasons, and cultivate a mysterious but very real institutional respect. Good senators either gravitate to these rhetorics naturally (by disposition) or are at least willing to learn. Activists work in a sphere of religious and moral commitments that are strong in a liberal democracy precisely because they reflect consent. Such a sphere implies a principled rhetoric that calls for sacrifice, justice, and equality, and provides a public place for the moralistic temperaments that exist in any polity. Organizers work in civil society, a sphere of economic interest and informal local politics. This sphere involves such a diverse "system of needs"—civic as well as material, noble as well as selfish—that it calls for politicians who can understand whole human beings through personal interaction and induce people to find their common interests amid their clashing ones. That is, it calls for politicians who find themselves much more drawn to diverse personality and social types than are most people, and even most political officers.

A plurality of governing principles and governing offices reflects, then, the plural spheres of social and political life. Here we see both the attractive, free and easy benefits of democratic politics and the serious philosophical restraint required to appreciate those benefits. The move from single standards of political judgment to multiple ones involves a move from doing justice to our own, overly rigid theories to doing justice to politics as a whole. It requires valuing sympathy, toleration, and reality above ideals that are not of this world.

References

Adair, Douglass, 1974. "Fame and the Founding Fathers." In *Fame and the Founding Fathers: Essays by Douglass Adair*, ed. Trevor Colbourn. New York: Norton.

Adams, John, 1973. *Discourses on Davila*. New York: Da Capo Press.

Adler, Mortimer, 1987. *We Hold These Truths*. New York: Macmillan.

Alinsky, Saul, 1946. *Reveille for Radicals*. New York: Random House. Reprint 1989.

——, 1971. *Rules for Radicals*. New York: Vintage Books.

Almond, Gabriel A., and Sidney Verba, 1963. *The Civic Culture*. Newbury Park, Calif.: Sage Publications. Reprint 1989.

Anderson, Jack, and Ronald W. May, 1952. *McCarthy: The Man, the Senator, the "Ism."* Boston: Beacon Press.

Applbaum, Arthur Isak, 1999. *Ethics for Adversaries: The Morality of Roles in Public and Professional Life*. Princeton: Princeton University Press.

Arendt, Hannah, 1961a. *Between Past and Future*. New York: Penguin Books.

——, 1961b. "What is Authority?" In Arendt (1961a).

——, 1965. *On Revolution*. New York: Penguin Books. Reprint 1987.

——, 1972a. *Crises of the Republic*. San Diego: Harcourt Brace Jovanovich.

——, 1972b. "On Violence." In Arendt (1972a).

——, 1972c. "Civil Disobedience." In Arendt (1972a).

Aristotle, 1984. *Politics*. Trans. Carnes Lord. Chicago: University of Chicago Press.

——, 1985. *Nicomachean Ethics*. Trans. Terence Irwin. Indianapolis: Hackett.

——, 1991. *On Rhetoric*. Trans. George A. Kennedy. Oxford: Oxford University Press.

Baker, Ella, 1970. "Developing Community Leadership." In *Black Women in White America: A Documentary History*, ed. Gerda Lerner. New York: Random House.

Barber, James David, 1992. *The Presidential Character: Predicting Performance in the White House*. Englewood Cliffs, N.J.: Prentice Hall.

Barry, Brian, 1990. *Political Argument*. Berkeley: University of California Press.

Bauer, Fred, ed., 1969. *Ev: The Man and His Words*. Old Tappan, N.J.: Hewitt House.

Bellah, Robert N., 1992. *The Broken Covenant: American Civil Religion in Time of Trial*. 2d. ed. Chicago: University of Chicago Press.

Bellah, Robert N., Richard Madsen, William M. Sullivan, Ann Swidler, and Steven M. Tipton, 1985. *Habits of the Heart*. Berkeley: University of California Press.

——, 1992. *The Good Society*. New York: Vintage Books.

Benhabib, Seyla, 1988. "Judgment in Arendt." *Political Theory* 16, No. 1 (February): 29–51.

——, 1992. *Situating the Self*. New York: Routledge.

Benjamin, Martin, 1990. *Splitting the Difference: Compromise and Integrity in Ethics and Politics*. Lawrence, Kan.: University Press of Kansas.

Bentham, Jeremy, 1926. "Anti-Senatica: An Attack on the U.S. Senate." *Smith College Studies in History* 11, No. 4 (July).

————, Jeremy, 1962. *Works of Jeremy Bentham*. Ed. John Bowring. Volume 9. New York: Russell and Russell, Inc.

Bercovitch, Sacvan, 1978. *The American Jeremiad*. Madison, Wisc.: University of Wisconsin Press.

Berke, Richard L., 1991. "The Education of Paul Wellstone." *New York Times Magazine*, 10 November.

Berlin, Isaiah, 1969. "Two Concepts of Liberty." In *Four Essays on Liberty*. Oxford: Oxford University Press. Reprint 1991.

Berrigan, Philip, with Fred A. Wilcox, 1996. *Fighting the Lamb's War : Skirmishes with the American Empire*. Monroe, Me.: Common Courage Press.

Bessette, Joseph M., 1980. "Deliberative Democracy: The Majority Principle in Republican Government." In *How Democratic is the Constitution?* ed. Robert A. Goldwin and William A. Schambra. Washington, D.C.: American Enterprise Institute.

————, 1994. *The Mild Voice of Reason*. Chicago: University of Chicago Press.

Bickel, Alexander, 1975. *The Morality of Consent*. New Haven: Yale University Press.

————, 1986. *The Least Dangerous Branch: The Supreme Court at the Bar of Politics*. 2d ed. New Haven: Yale University Press.

Bloom, Allan, 1987. *The Closing of the American Mind*. New York: Simon and Schuster.

Bordin, Ruth, 1986. *Frances Willard: A Biography*. Chapel Hill: University of North Carolina Press.

Bosetti, Giancarlo, 1998. "Reinventing the Left: Interview with Massimo D'Alema." *Dissent* 45, No. 2 (Spring): 11–17.

Bradley, F. H., 1988. *Ethical Studies*. 2d ed. New York: Oxford University Press.

Branch, Taylor, 1988. *Parting the Waters: America in the King Years*. New York: Simon and Schuster.

————, 1998. *Pillar of Fire: America in the King Years 1963–65*. New York: Simon and Schuster.

Brookhiser, Richard, 1996. *Founding Father: Rediscovering George Washington*. New York: Free Press.

Buckley, William F., and L. Brent Bozell, 1995. *McCarthy and His Enemies: The Record and Its Meaning*. New edition with a new introduction. Washington, D.C.: Regnery Publishing, Inc.

Burner, Eric, 1994. *And Gently He Shall Lead Them: Robert Parris Moses and Civil Rights in Mississippi*. New York: NYU Press.

Burns, James MacGregor, 1978. *Leadership*. New York: Harper & Row.

Campbell, Karlyn Kohrs, 1990. *Man Cannot Speak for Her: A Critical Study of Early Feminist Rhetoric*. New York: Greenwood Press.

Camus, Albert, 1991. *The Rebel*. Trans. Anthony Bower. New York: Vintage International.

Cantarow, Ellen, and Susan Gushee O'Malley, 1980. "Ella Baker: Organizing for Civil Rights." In *Moving the Mountain: Women Working for Social Change*. Old Westbury, N.Y.: Feminist Press.

Carmichael, Stokely, 1971. *Stokely Speaks: Black Power Back to Pan-Africanism.* New York: Random House.

Carmichael, Stokely, and Charles V. Hamilton, 1967. *Black Power: The Politics of Liberation in America.* New York: Vintage.

Carson, Clayborne, 1981. *In Struggle: SNCC and the Black Awakening of the 1960s.* Cambridge: Harvard University Press.

Carter, Stephen L., 1998. *The Dissent of the Governed.* Cambridge: Harvard University Press.

Chen, Martha Alter, 1983. *A Quiet Revolution: Women in Transition in Rural Bangladesh.* Cambridge, Mass.: Schenkman Publishing Company.

Chong, Dennis, 1991. *Collective Action and the Civil Rights Movement.* Chicago: University of Chicago Press.

Cicero, Marcus Tullius, 1991. *On Duties.* Trans. and ed. M. T. Griffin and E. M. Atkins. Cambridge: Cambridge University Press.

Coady, C. A. J., 1993. "Dirty Hands." In *A Companion to Contemporary Political Philosophy*, ed. Robert E. Goodin and Philip Pettit. Oxford: Blackwell Publishers.

Cohen, Joshua, 1989. "Deliberation and Democratic Legitimacy." In *The Good Polity: Normative Analysis of the State*, ed. Alan Hamlin and Philip Pettit. Oxford: Basil Blackwell.

———, 1996. "Procedure and Substance in Deliberative Democracy." In *Democracy and Difference*, ed. Seyla Benhabib. Princeton: Princeton University Press.

Constant, Benjamin, 1988. *Political Writings.* Trans. and ed. Biancamaria Fontana. Cambridge: Cambridge University Press.

Converse, Philip E., 1964. "The Nature of Belief Systems in Mass Publics." In *Ideology and Discontent*, ed. David Apter. Glencoe, Ill.: Free Press.

Converse, Philip E., and Gregory B. Markus, 1979. "Plus ça change . . . : The New CPS Election Study Panel." *American Political Science Review* 73, No. 1 (March): 32–49.

Cranston, Maurice, 1997. *The Solitary Self: Jean-Jacques Rousseau in Exile and Adversity.* Chicago: University of Chicago Press.

Dahl, Norman O., 1984. *Practical Reason, Aristotle, and Weakness of the Will.* Minneapolis: University of Minnesota Press.

Dahl, Robert A., 1956. *A Preface to Democratic Theory.* Chicago: University of Chicago Press.

———, 1961. *Who Governs?* New Haven: Yale University Press.

———, 1971. *Polyarchy: Participation and Opposition.* New Haven: Yale University Press.

———, 1979. "Procedural Democracy." In *Philosophy, Politics and Society*, ed. Peter Laslett and James Fishkin. New Haven: Yale University Press.

———, 1989. *Democracy and its Critics.* New Haven: Yale University Press.

Dahl, Robert A., and Edward R. Tufte, 1973. *Size and Democracy.* Stanford: Stanford University Press.

Delgado, Gary, 1986. *Organizing the Movement: The Roots and Growth of ACORN.* Philadelphia: Temple University Press.

Dewey, John, 1954. *The Public and its Problems.* Athens, Ohio: Ohio University Press.

Dickens, Charles, 1991. *Bleak House*. New York: Knopf.

Dietz, Mary G., 1994. "'The Slow Boring of Hard Boards': Methodical Thinking and the Work of Politics." *American Political Science Review* 88, No. 4 (December): 873–86.

Donagan, Alan, 1983. "Justifying Legal Practice in the Adversary System." In Luban (1983).

Dover, K. J., 1994. *Greek Popular Morality in the Time of Plato and Aristotle*. Corrected ed. Indianapolis: Hackett.

Downs, Anthony, 1957. *An Economic Theory of Democracy*. New York: HarperCollins.

———, 1991. "Social Values and Democracy." In Monroe (1991).

Duberman, Martin, 1968. "Black Power in America." *Partisan Review* 35: 34–48.

Du Vair, Guillaume, 1598. *The moral philosophie of the Stoicks*, written in French, and englished for the benefit of them which are ignorant of that tongue. By T. I. [Thomas James] Fellow of New Colledge in Oxford. At London Printed by Felix Kingston, for Thomas Man.

Dworkin, Ronald, 1978. *Taking Rights Seriously*. Cambridge: Harvard University Press.

———, 1985. *A Matter of Principle*. Cambridge: Harvard University Press.

———, 1999. "The Moral Reading and the Majoritarian Premise." In Koh and Slye (1999).

Edsall, Thomas Byrne, with Mary D. Edsall, 1992. *Chain Reaction: The Impact of Race, Rights, and Taxes on American Politics*. New York: Norton.

Elster, Jon, 1984. *Ulysses and the Sirens*. Revised ed. Cambridge: Cambridge University Press.

———, ed., 1998. *Deliberative Democracy*. Cambridge: Cambridge University Press.

Ely, John Hart, 1980. *Democracy and Distrust*. Cambridge: Harvard University Press.

Epstein, Barbara Leslie, 1981. *The Politics of Domesticity: Women, Evangelism, and Temperance in Nineteenth-Century America*. Middletown, Conn.: Wesleyan University Press.

Euben, J. Peter, 1997. *Corrupting Youth: Political Education, Democratic Culture, and Political Theory*. Princeton: Princeton University Press.

Evers, Williamson M., ed., 1990. *National Service: Pro and Con*. Stanford: Hoover Institution Press.

Faludi, Susan, 1991. *Backlash*. New York: Crown Publishers.

Fenno, Richard F., 1973. *Congressmen in Committees*. Boston: Little, Brown.

———, 1978. *Home Style: House Members in Their Districts*. Boston: Little, Brown.

———, 1991a. *The Emergence of a Senate Leader: Pete Domenici and the Reagan Budget*. Washington, D.C.: Congressional Quarterly Press.

———, 1991b. *Learning to Legislate: The Senate Education of Arlen Specter*. Washington, D.C.: Congressional Quarterly Press.

Fiorina, Morris P., 1989. *Congress: Keystone of the Washington Establishment*. New Haven: Yale University Press.

Fischer, David Hackett, 1989. *Albion's Seed: Four British Folkways in America*. New York: Oxford University Press.

Fish, Stanley, 1999. "Mutual Respect as a Device of Exclusion." In Macedo (1999).

Fishkin, James S., 1991. *Democracy and Deliberation*. New Haven: Yale University Press.

Flaumenhaft, Harvey, 1992. *The Effective Republic: Administration and Constitution in the Thought of Alexander Hamilton*. Durham, N.C. and London: Duke University Press.

Forman, James, 1985. *The Making of Black Revolutionaries*. Washington, D.C.: Open Hand Publishing.

Frankfurt, Harry G., 1988. "On Bullshit." In *The Importance of What We Care About*. Cambridge: Cambridge University Press.

Freud, Sigmund, 1958. "Two Principles of Mental Functioning." In *Standard Edition of the Complete Psychological Works of Sigmund Freud*, trans. James Strachey and Anna Freud. Vol. 12. London: Hogarth Press.

———, 1961. *Civilization and its Discontents*. Trans. James Strachey. New York: Norton.

Fried, Charles, 1976. "The Lawyer as Friend: The Moral Foundations of the Lawyer-Client Relation." *Yale Law Journal* 85: 1060–1989.

Fried, Richard M., 1976. *Men Against McCarthy*. New York: Columbia University Press.

Fukuyama, Francis, 1995. *Trust: The Social Virtues and the Creation of Prosperity*. New York: Simon and Schuster.

Gadamer, Hans-Georg, 1994. *Truth and Method*. 2d revised ed. Trans. Joel Weinsheimer and Donald G. Marshall. New York: Continuum.

Gambetta, Diego, 1998. "'Claro!': An Essay on Discursive Machismo." In Elster (1998).

Garrow, David J., 1988. *Bearing the Cross: Martin Luther King, Jr., and the Southern Christian Leadership Conference*. New York: Vintage Books.

Gerring, John, 1994. "A Chapter in the History of American Party Ideology: The Nineteenth-Century Democratic Party (1828–1892)." *Polity* 36: 729–68.

Gewirth, Alan, 1988. "Ethical Universalism and Particularism." *Journal of Philosophy* 85, No. 6 (June): 283–302.

Gilligan, Carol, 1982. *In a Different Voice*. Cambridge: Harvard University Press.

Gitlin, Todd, 1993. "The Rise of 'Identity Politics.'" *Dissent* 40, No. 2 (Spring): 172–77.

Glendon, Mary Ann, 1987. *Abortion and Divorce in Western Law*. Cambridge: Harvard University Press.

Gomberg, Paul, 1990. "Patriotism is Like Racism." *Ethics* 101: 144–50.

Goodin, Robert E., 1985. *Protecting the Vulnerable*. Chicago: University of Chicago Press.

———, 1992. *Motivating Political Morality*. Oxford: Blackwell Publishers.

———, 1995. *Utilitarianism as a Public Philosophy*. Cambridge: Cambridge University Press.

Grant, Joanne, 1970. "Mississippi Politics: A Day in the Life of Ella Baker." In *The Black Woman*, ed. Toni Cade. New York: Signet.

———, 1981. *Fundi: The Story of Ella Baker*. Film. Franklin Lakes, N.J.: New Day Films.

Grant, Joanne, 1998. *Ella Baker: Freedom Bound.* New York: Wiley.

Green, Donald P., and Ian Shapiro, 1994. *Pathologies of Rational Choice Theory.* New Haven: Yale University Press.

Greenberg, David, 1999. "The Mark of McCain." *Slate,* 14 December.

Greenberg, Stanley B., 1995. *Middle Class Dreams: The Politics and Power of the New American Majority.* New York: Times Books.

Greenstein, Fred I., 1994. *The Hidden-Hand Presidency: Eisenhower as Leader.* Baltimore: Johns Hopkins University Press.

Griffith, Robert, 1970. *The Politics of Fear: Joseph R. McCarthy and the Senate.* Lexington, Ky.: University Press of Kentucky.

Gutmann, Amy, 1983. "How Liberal is Democracy?" In *Liberalism Reconsidered,* ed. Douglas MacLean and Claudia Mills. Totowa, N.J.: Rowman & Allanheld.

———, 1999. "Deliberative Democracy and Majority Rule: Reply to Waldron." In Koh and Slye (1999).

Gutmann, Amy, and Dennis Thompson, 1996. *Democracy and Disagreement.* Cambridge: Harvard University Press.

Habermas, Jürgen, 1992. *The Structural Transformation of the Public Sphere.* Trans. Thomas Burger. Cambridge: MIT Press.

Hamilton, Alexander, James Madison, and John Jay, 1992. *The Federalist Papers.* Cutchogue, N.Y.: Buccaneer Books.

Hardimon, Michael O., 1994. "Role Obligations." *Journal of Philosophy* 91: 333–63.

Hare, R. M., 1981. *Moral Thinking.* Oxford: Oxford University Press.

———, 1989. *Essays on Political Morality.* Oxford: Clarendon Press.

Harris, Fred, 1993. *Deadlock or Decision: The U.S. Senate and the Rise of National Politics.* New York: Oxford University Press.

Hartz, Louis, 1955. *The Liberal Tradition in America.* New York: Harcourt Brace Jovanovich.

Hegel, G. W. F., 1974. *Vorlesungen über Rechtsphilosophie.* Vol. 3, ed. K.-H. Ilting. Stuttgart: Fromman Verlag.

———, 1991. *Elements of the Philosophy of Right.* Trans. H. B. Nisbet, ed. Allen W. Wood. Cambridge: Cambridge University Press.

Held, Virginia, 1983. "The Division of Moral Labor and the Role of the Lawyer." In Luban (1983).

Herberg, Will, 1960. *Protestant-Catholic-Jew.* Revised ed. New York: Doubleday & Company.

Hirschman, Albert O., 1977. *The Passions and the Interests.* Princeton: Princeton University Press.

Hoffer, Eric, 1951. *The True Believer.* New York: Harper & Row.

Holmes, Stephen, 1988. "Precommitment and the Paradox of Democracy." In *Constitutionalism and Democracy,* ed. Jon Elster and Rune Slagstad. Cambridge: Cambridge University Press.

———, 1997. "What Russia Teaches Us Now: How Weak States Threaten Freedom." *American Prospect* 33 (July-August 1997): 30–39.

Honig, Bonnie, 1993. *Political Theory and the Displacement of Politics.* Ithaca, N.Y.: Cornell University Press.

Horwitt, Sanford D., 1992. *Let Them Call Me Rebel: Saul Alinsky—His Life and Legacy.* New York: Vintage Books.

Hume, David, 1978. *A Treatise of Human Nature*. 2d ed. Ed. L. A. Selby-Bigge and P. H. Nidditch. Oxford: Oxford University Press.

———, 1983. *Enquiry concerning the Principles of Morals*. Ed. J. B. Schneewind. Indianapolis: Hackett.

———, 1987. *Essays Moral, Political, and Literary*. Rev. ed. Ed. Eugene F. Miller. Indianapolis: Liberty Fund.

Huntington, Samuel P., 1968. *Political Order in Changing Societies*. New Haven: Yale University Press.

———, 1975. "The United States." In *The Crisis of Democracy*, by Michael Crozier, Samuel P. Huntington, and Joji Watanuki. New York: NYU Press.

———, 1981. *American Politics: The Promise of Disharmony*. Cambridge: Harvard University Press.

Jackman, Robert W., 1993. "Rationality and Political Participation." *American Journal of Political Science* 37 (February): 279–90.

Jackson, Andrew, 1837. *Messages of Andrew Jackson with a Short Sketch of His Life*. Boston: Otis Broaders & Co.

Jardin, André, 1988. *Tocqueville: A Biography*. Trans. Lydia Davis with Robert Hemenway. New York: Farrar Straus Giroux.

Kant, Immanuel, 1957. *Perpetual Peace*. Trans. Lewis White Beck. New York: Library of Liberal Arts.

———, 1960. *Education*. Trans. Annette Churton. Ann Arbor: University of Michigan Press (Ann Arbor Paperbacks).

———, 1965. *Metaphysical Elements of Justice*. Trans. John Ladd. Indianapolis: Library of Liberal Arts.

———, 1983. "Metaphysical Elements of Virtue." In *Kant's Ethical Philosophy*, trans. James W. Ellington. Indianapolis: Hackett.

Kekes, John, 1993. *The Morality of Pluralism*. Princeton: Princeton University Press.

Kenny, Anthony, 1979. *Aristotle's Theory of the Will*. New Haven: Yale University Press.

Kerson, Roger, 1998. "Get on the Bus." *In These Times*, 19 April, 20–22.

Kersten, Katherine, 1997. "Founders Among the Early Foes of Slavery." *Star Tribune* (Minneapolis, Minn.), 26 November.

King, Anthony, 1997. *Running Scared*. New York: Free Press.

King, Martin Luther Jr., 1963. *Why We Can't Wait*. New York: Harper & Row.

King, Richard, 1992. *Civil Rights and the Idea of Freedom*. New York and Oxford: Oxford University Press.

Kitschelt, Herbert, 1994. *The Transformation of European Social Democracy*. Cambridge: Cambridge University Press.

Klehr, Harvey, John Earl Haynes, and Fridrikh Igorevich Firsov, 1995. *The Secret World of American Communism*. New Haven: Yale University Press.

Koh, Harold Hongju, and Ronald C. Slye, eds., 1999. *Deliberative Democracy and Human Rights*. New Haven: Yale University Press.

Kraut, Richard, 1989. *Aristotle on the Human Good*. Princeton: Princeton University Press.

Ladner, Joyce, 1967. "What 'Black Power' Means to Negroes in Mississippi." *Trans-action* 5: 7–15.

Larmore, Charles E., 1987. *Patterns of Moral Complexity*. Cambridge: Cambridge University Press.

Lasch, Christopher, 1978. *The Culture of Narcissism*. New York: Norton.

———, 1991. *The True and Only Heaven: Progress and Its Critics*. New York: Norton.

———, 1995. *The Revolt of the Elites and the Betrayal of Democracy*. New York: Norton.

Laski, Harold J., 1997. *The Rise of European Liberalism*. New Brunswick, N.J.: Transaction Publishers.

Laslett, Peter, 1956. "The Face to Face Society." In *Philosophy, Politics and Society*, ed. P. Laslett. Oxford: Basil Blackwell.

Lasswell, Harold, 1936. *Politics: Who Gets What, When, How*. New York: McGraw-Hill.

———, 1948. *Power and Personality*. New York: Norton.

Latham, Earl, 1966. *The Communist Controversy in Washington*. Cambridge: Harvard University Press.

Leeman, Richard W., 1992. *"Do Everything" Reform: The Oratory of Frances E. Willard*. New York: Greenwood Press.

Lewis, C. S., 1952. *Mere Christianity*. London: Geoffrey Bles.

Lewis, David Levering, 1978. *King: A Biography*. Urbana, Ill.: University of Illinois Press.

Lind, Michael, 1995. *The Next American Nation*. New York: Free Press.

Lischer, Richard, 1995. *The Preacher King: Martin Luther King Jr. and the Word that Moved America*. Oxford: Oxford University Press.

Locke, John, 1960. *Two Treatises of Government*. Ed. Peter Laslett. Cambridge: Cambridge University Press.

———, 1975. *An Essay concerning Human Understanding*. Ed. Peter H. Nidditch. Oxford: Clarendon Press.

———, 1983. *A Letter Concerning Toleration*. Indianapolis: Hackett.

Luban, David, 1988. *Lawyers and Justice: An Ethical Study*. Princeton: Princeton University Press.

———, ed., 1983. *The Good Lawyer: Lawyers' Roles and Lawyers' Ethics*. Totowa, N.J.: Rowman & Allanheld.

Macedo, Stephen, ed., 1999. *Deliberative Politics: Essays on Democracy and Disagreement*. New York and Oxford: Oxford University Press.

Machiavelli, Niccolò, 1950. "Discourses on the First Ten Books of Titus Livius." In *The Prince and the Discourses*, trans. Christian E. Detmold. New York: Modern Library.

———, 1985. *The Prince*. Trans. Harvey C. Mansfield, Jr. Chicago: University of Chicago Press.

MacIntyre, Alasdair, 1984. *Is Patriotism a Virtue?* The Lindley Lecture, Department of Philosophy, University of Kansas, Lawrence, Kansas. Pamphlet.

———, 1988. *Whose Justice? Which Rationality?* Notre Dame, Ind.: University of Notre Dame Press.

MacNeil, Neil, 1970. *Dirksen: Portrait of a Public Man*. New York and Cleveland: World Publishing Company.

MacPherson, C. B., 1962. *The Political Theory of Possessive Individualism: Hobbes to Locke*. Oxford: Oxford University Press.

Madison, James, 1987. *Notes of Debates in the Federal Convention of 1787*. New York: Norton.

Mansbridge, Jane, 1980. *Beyond Adversary Democracy*. New York: Basic Books.

———, 1986. *Why We Lost the ERA*. Chicago: University of Chicago Press.

Mansfield, Harvey C., Jr., 1978. *The Spirit of Liberalism*. Cambridge: Harvard University Press.

Marshall, T. H., 1965. "Citizenship and Social Class." In *Class, Citizenship, and Social Development*. Garden City, N.Y.: Anchor Books.

Mason, Philip [Philip Woodruff, pseud.], 1964. *The Men Who Ruled India*. New York: Schocken Books.

Mayer, William G., 1998. "A Typology of Campaign Strategies." Paper delivered at the 1998 annual meeting of the New England Political Science Association, Worcester, Mass., May 1–2.

Mayhew, David, 1974. *Congress: The Electoral Connection*. New Haven: Yale University Press.

Mays, Benjamin E., 1938. *The Negro's God as Reflected in His Literature*. Boston: Chapman & Grimes. Reprint, Westport, Conn.: Greenwood Press, 1969.

Metcalf, George R., 1988. *Fair Housing Comes of Age*. New York: Greenwood Press.

Meyers, Marvin, ed. 1981. *The Mind of the Founder: Sources of the Political Thought of James Madison*. Hanover, N.H.: University Press of New England.

Mill, John Stuart, 1975. *On Liberty*. Ed. David Spitz. New York: Norton.

———, 1986. *The Subjection of Women*. Ed. Susan Moller Okin. Indianapolis: Hackett.

Miller, Keith, 1992. *Voice of Deliverance: The Language of Martin Luther King, Jr., and Its Sources*. New York: Free Press.

Miroff, Bruce, 1993. *Icons of Democracy: American Leaders as Heroes, Aristocrats, Dissenters, and Democrats*. New York: Basic Books.

Mitchell, Joshua, 1995. *The Fragility of Freedom*. Chicago: University of Chicago Press.

Monroe, Kristen Renwick, 1991. *The Economic Approach to Politics: A Critical Reassessment of the Theory of Rational Action*. New York: HarperCollins.

Morris, Aldon, 1984. *Origins of the Civil Rights Movement*. New York: Free Press.

Moses, Robert P., Mieko Kamii, Susan McAllister Swap, and Jeffrey Howard, 1989. "The Algebra Project: Organizing in the Spirit of Ella." *Harvard Educational Review* 59: 423–43.

Moynihan, Daniel Patrick, 1970. *Maximum Feasible Misunderstanding*. New York: Free Press.

Nagel, Thomas, 1979a. *Mortal Questions*. Cambridge: Cambridge University Press.

———, 1979b. "Ruthlessness in Public Life." In Nagel (1979a).

———, 1986. *The View from Nowhere*. New York: Oxford University Press.

———, 1991. *Equality and Partiality*. New York and Oxford: Oxford University Press.

Neuhaus, Richard John, 1984. *The Naked Public Square*. Grand Rapids, Mich.: W. B. Erdmans.

Neustadt, Richard E., 1990. *Presidential Power and the Modern Presidents*. New York: Free Press.

Nussbaum, Martha C., 1986. *The Fragility of Goodness*. Cambridge: Cambridge University Press.

——, 1988. "Nature, Function and Capability: Aristotle on Political Distribution." *Oxford Studies in Ancient Philosophy*. Supplemental Volume.

——, 1990a. "Aristotelian Social Democracy." In *Liberalism and the Good*, ed. R. Bruce Douglass, Gerald M. Mara, and Henry S. Richardson. New York: Routledge.

——, 1990b. *Love's Knowledge*. New York and Oxford: Oxford University Press.

——, 1992. "Human Functioning and Social Justice: In Defense of Aristotelian Essentialism." *Political Theory* 20: 202–46.

——, 1993. "Equity and Mercy." *Philosophy and Public Affairs* 22 (Spring): 83–125.

——, 1994. *The Therapy of Desire*. Princeton: Princeton University Press.

——, 1995. "Aristotle on Human Nature and the Foundations of Ethics." In *World, Mind, and Ethics*, ed. J.E.J. Altham and Ross Harrison. Cambridge: Cambridge University Press.

Nussbaum, Martha C., and Amartya Sen, 1989. "Internal Criticism and Indian Rationalist Traditions." In *Relativism: Interpretation and Confrontation*, ed. Michael Krausz. Notre Dame, Ind.: University of Notre Dame Press.

Oates, Stephen B., 1985. *Let the Trumpet Sound: The Life of Martin Luther King, Jr., and the Southern Christian Leadership Conference*. New York: Mentor Books.

Olson, Mancur, 1971. *The Logic of Collective Action*. Cambridge: Harvard University Press.

"On *In a Different Voice*: An Interdisciplinary Forum," 1986. *Signs* 11: 301–33.

Ordeshook, Peter, 1993. "The Development of Contemporary Political Theory." In *Political Economy: Institutions, Competition, and Representation*, ed. William A. Barnett, Melvin J. Hinich, and Norman J. Schofield. Cambridge: Cambridge University Press.

Oshinsky, David M., 1983. *A Conspiracy So Immense: The World of Joe McCarthy*. New York: Free Press.

Parfit, Derek, 1984. *Reasons and Persons*. Oxford: Clarendon Press.

Patterson, Samuel C., and Anthony Mughan, eds., 1999. *Senates: Bicameralism in the Contemporary World*. Columbus, Ohio: Ohio State University Press.

Payne, Charles M., 1995. *I've Got the Light of Freedom: The Organizing Tradition and the Mississippi Freedom Struggle*. Berkeley: University of California Press.

Petracca, Mark P. "The Rational Actor Approach to Politics: Science, Self-Interest, and Normative Democratic Theory." In Monroe (1991).

Pitkin, Hanna Fenichel, 1967. *The Concept of Representation*. Berkeley: University of California Press.

Plato, 1986. *Phaedrus*. Trans. C. J. Rowe. Warminster, England: Teddington House.

——, 1991. *The Republic*. Trans. Allan Bloom. 2d ed. New York: Basic Books.

Popkin, Samuel L., 1994. *The Reasoning Voter*. 2d ed. Chicago: University of Chicago Press,

Post, Robert C., 1987. "On the Popular Image of the Lawyer: Reflections in a Dark Glass." *California Law Review* 75: 379–89.

Putnam, Robert D., 1988. "Diplomacy and Domestic Politics: The Logic of Two-Level Games." *International Organization* 42: 427–60.

Radosh, Ronald, and Joyce Milton, 1997. *The Rosenberg File.* 2d ed. New Haven: Yale University Press.

Ransby, Barbara, 1994. "Ella Josephine Baker," In *The American Radical*, ed. Mari Jo Buhle, Paul Buhle and Harvey J. Kaye. New York: Routledge.

Rawls, John, 1971. *A Theory of Justice.* Cambridge: Harvard University Press.

———, 1993. *Political Liberalism.* New York: Columbia University Press.

———, 1999a. *Collected Papers.* Ed. Samuel Freeman. Cambridge: Harvard University Press.

———, 1999b. "Justice as Fairness." In Rawls (1999a).

———, 1999c. "Two Concepts of Rules." In Rawls (1999a).

Reeves, Thomas C., 1982. *The Life and Times of Joe McCarthy.* New York: Stein and Day.

Reich, Robert B, 1991. *The Work of Nations.* New York: Vintage Books.

Renshon, Stanley A., 1996. *The Psychological Assessment of Presidential Candidates.* New York: NYU Press.

Resnick, David, 1979. "Justice, Compromise, and Constitutional Rules in Aristotle's *Politics.*" In *Compromise in Ethics, Law, and Politics*, ed. J. Roland Pennock and John W. Chapman. New York: NYU Press.

Riker, William H, 1982. *Liberalism Against Populism.* Prospect Heights, Ill.: Waveland Press.

———, 1990. "Political Science and Rational Choice." In *Perspectives on Positive Political Economy*, ed. James E. Alt and Kenneth A. Shepsle. Cambridge: Cambridge University Press.

Rogin, Michael Paul, 1967. *The Intellectuals and McCarthy: The Radical Specter.* Cambridge: MIT Press.

Rorty, Richard, 1991. "The Priority of Democracy to Philosophy." In *Objectivity, Relativism, and Truth.* Cambridge: Cambridge University Press.

———, 1993. "Trotsky and the Wild Orchids." In *Wild Orchids and Trotsky*, ed. Mark Edmundson. New York: Penguin Books.

Rosen, Gary, 1996. "Madison and the Problem of Founding." *Review of Politics* 58, No. 3 (Summer): 580–81.

Rosenblum, Nancy, 1987. *Another Liberalism.* Cambridge: Harvard University Press.

———, 1998. *Membership and Morals: The Personal Uses of Pluralism in America.* Princeton: Princeton University Press.

Rosenthal, Jean-Laurent, 1998. "The Political Economy of Absolutism Reconsidered." In *Analytic Narratives*, by Robert H. Bates, et al. Princeton: Princeton University Press.

Ross, W. D., 1953. *Aristotle.* 5th ed. London: Methuen.

Rossiter, Clinton, 1963. *The American Presidency.* 2d ed. New York: Time Inc.

Rothstein, Bo, 1998. *Just Institutions Matter: The Moral and Political Logic of the Universal Welfare State.* Cambridge: Cambridge University Press.

Rousseau, Jean-Jacques, 1964. *The First and Second Discourses.* Trans. Roger D. and Judith R. Masters. New York: St. Martin's Press.

———, 1978. *On the Social Contract, with Geneva Manuscript and Political Econ-*

omy. Trans. Judith R. Masters, ed. Roger D. Masters. New York: St. Martin's Press.

Rousseau, Jean-Jacques, 1979. *Reveries of the Solitary Walker*. Trans. Peter France. London: Penguin Books.

———, 1989. *Politics and the Arts: The Letter to M. D'Alembert on the Theatre*. Trans. Allan Bloom. Ithaca, N.Y.: Cornell University Press.

Rovere, Richard H., 1959. *Senator Joe McCarthy*. New York: Harcourt, Brace and Company.

Rustin, Bayard, 1964. "From Protest to Politics." *Commentary* (February), 25–31.

———, 1971. *Down the Line: The Collected Writings of Bayard Rustin*. Chicago: Quadrangle Books.

Sabl, Andrew, 2001. "Looking Forward to Justice: Rawlsian Civil Disobedience and its Non-Rawlsian Lessons." *Journal of Political Philosophy* 9, No. 3: 307–30.

Sandel, Michael J., 1982. *Liberalism and the Limits of Justice*. Cambridge and New York: Cambridge University Press.

———, 1996. *Democracy's Discontent*. Cambridge and London: Harvard University Press.

Sanders, Lynn, 1997. "Against Deliberation." *Political Theory* 25 (June): 347–76.

Sanders, Marion, 1965. "A Professional Radical Moves in on Rochester." *Harper's*, July, 37–59.

Scalia, Laura J., 1991. "Self-Interest and Democratic Theory." In Monroe (1991).

Scanlon, T. M., 1982. "Contractualism and Utilitarianism." In *Utilitarianism and Beyond*, ed. Amartya Sen and Bernard Williams. Cambridge: Cambridge University Press.

Schapsmeier, Edward L., and Frederick H. Schapsmeier, 1985. *Dirksen of Illinois: Senatorial Statesman*. Urbana, Ill.: University of Illinois Press.

Schattschneider, E. E., 1960. *The Semisovereign People*. New York: Holt, Rinehart and Winston.

Scheffler, Samuel, 1994. *Families, Nations and Strangers*. The Lindley Lecture, Department of Philosophy, University of Kansas, Lawrence, Kansas. Pamphlet.

———, 1997. "Liberalism, Nationalism, and Egalitarianism." In *The Morality of Nationalism*, ed. Robert McKim and Jeff McMahan. New York: Oxford University Press.

———, 1999a. "The Conflict Between Justice and Responsibility." In *Nomos XLI: Global Justice*, ed. Ian Shapiro and Lea Brilmayer. New York and London: NYU Press.

———, 1999b. "Relationships and Responsibilities." *Philosophy and Public Affairs* 26, No. 3 (Summer): 189–209.

Schelling, Thomas, 1984. *Choice and Consequence*. Cambridge: Harvard University Press.

Schlesinger, Arthur M., Jr., 1945. *The Age of Jackson*. Boston: Back Bay Books.

———, 1949. *The Vital Center*. New York: Houghton Mifflin Co. Reprint, Da Capo Press, 1988.

Schlozman, Kay Lehman, 1984. "What Accent the Heavenly Chorus? Political Equality and the American Pressure System." *Journal of Politics* 46: 1006–32.

Schumpeter, Joseph A., 1950. *Capitalism, Socialism, and Democracy*. 3d ed. New York: Harper and Brothers.

Sen, Amartya K., 1977. "Rational Fools: A Critique of the Behavioral Foundations of Economic Theory." *Philosophy and Public Affairs* 6 (Summer): 317–44.

Seneca, 1963. "De Constantia Sapientis" ("On the Firmness of the Wise Man"). In *Moral Essays*, trans. John W. Basore. Cambridge: Harvard University Press.

Sethi, Prakash, 1970. *Business Corporations and the Black Man: An Analysis of the Kodak-FIGHT Controversy*. Scranton, Penn.: Chandler Publishing Co.

Shklar, Judith N., 1972. "Rousseau's Images of Authority." In *Hobbes and Rousseau: A Collection of Critical Essays*, ed. Maurice Cranston and Richard S. Peters. Garden City, N.Y.: Anchor Books.

———, 1984. *Ordinary Vices*. Cambridge: Harvard University Press.

———, 1986. *Legalism: Law, Morals, and Political Trials*. Cambridge: Harvard University Press.

———, 1988. *The Faces of Injustice*. New Haven: Yale University Press.

Shugarman, David P., 1990. "The Use and Abuse of Politics." In *Moral Expertise: Studies in Practical and Professional Ethics*, ed. Don MacNiven. London: Routledge.

Sidgwick, Henry, 1981. *The Methods of Ethics*. Indianapolis: Hackett.

Silberman, Charles, 1964. *Crisis in Black and White*. New York: Random House.

Singer, Peter, 1979. *Practical Ethics*. Cambridge: Cambridge University Press.

Smith, Adam, 1982. *The Theory of Moral Sentiments*. Ed. D. D. Raphael and A. L. Macfie. Indianapolis: Liberty Classics.

Smith, Rogers, 1997. *Civic Ideals: Conflicting Visions of Citizenship in U.S. History*. New Haven: Yale University Press.

Sreenivasan, Gopal, 1998. "Interpretation and Reason." *Philosophy and Public Affairs* 27, No. 2 (Spring): 142–71.

Stembridge, Jane. "Notes About a Class." In Carmichael (1971).

Stoper, Emily, 1989. *The Student Nonviolent Coordinating Committee*. Brooklyn, N.Y.: Carlson Publishers.

Strachey, Ray, 1912. *Frances Willard: Her Life and Work*. London: T. Fisher Unwin.

Sunstein, Cass, 1984. "Naked Preferences and the Constitution." *Columbia Law Review* 84: 1689–1732.

———, 1985. "Interest Groups in American Public Law." *Stanford Law Review* 38: 29–87.

———, 1993. *The Partial Constitution*. Cambridge: Harvard University Press.

Suttles, Gerald D., 1968. *The Social Order of the Slum: Ethnicity and Territory in the Inner City*. Chicago: University of Chicago Press.

Swidler, Ann, 1986. "Culture in Action." *American Sociological Review* 51: 273–86.

Tanenhaus, Sam, 1997. *Whittaker Chambers: A Biography*. New York: Random House.

Tate, C. Neal, and Torbjörn Vallinder, eds., 1995. *The Global Expansion of Judicial Power*. New York: NYU Press.

Tavris, Carol, 1992. *The Mismeasure of Woman*. New York: Simon and Schuster.

Taylor, Charles, 1989. *Sources of the Self*. Cambridge: Harvard University Press.

Thompson, Dennis F., 1987. *Political Ethics and Public Office*. Cambridge: Harvard University Press.

———, 1995. *Ethics in Congress*. Washington, D.C.: Brookings Institution.

Tocqueville, Alexis de, 1969. *Democracy in America.* Trans. George Lawrence, ed. J. P. Mayer. New York: Doubleday. Reprinted 1988.

Tribe, Laurence H., 1992. *Abortion: The Clash of Absolutes.* New ed. New York: Norton.

Trowbridge, Lydia Jones, 1938. *Frances Willard of Evanston.* Chicago and New York: Willett, Clark & Company.

Truman, David B., 1951. *The Governmental Process.* New York: Knopf.

Tulis, Jeffrey, 1987. *The Rhetorical Presidency.* Princeton: Princeton University Press.

Waldron, Jeremy, 1999. "Deliberation, Disagreement, and Voting." In Koh and Slye (1999).

Walling, Karl-Friedrich, 1999. *Republican Empire: Alexander Hamilton on War and Free Government.* Lawrence, Kan.: University Press of Kansas.

Walzer, Michael, 1965. *The Revolution of the Saints.* Cambridge: Harvard University Press.

———, 1970. "The Obligation to Disobey." In *Obligations: Essays on Disobedience, War, and Citizenship.* New York: Simon and Schuster (Clarion Books).

———, 1973a. "In Defense of Equality," *Dissent* 20 (Fall): 399–408.

———, 1973b. "Political Action: The Problem of Dirty Hands." *Philosophy and Public Affairs* 2: 165–66.

———, 1981. "Philosophy and Democracy." *Political Theory* 9: 379–99.

———, 1983. *Spheres of Justice.* New York: Basic Books.

———, 1984. "Commitment and Social Criticism: Camus's Algerian War." *Dissent* 31, No. 4: 424–32.

———, 1987. *Interpretation and Social Criticism.* Cambridge: Harvard University Press.

———, 1996. "Opportunism Knocks." *New Republic*, September 16 and 23, p. 27.

Washington, James M., ed., 1991. *A Testament of Hope: The Essential Writings and Speeches of Martin Luther King, Jr.* San Francisco: HarperSanFrancisco.

Weber, Max, 1946. "Politics as a Vocation." In *From Max Weber*, ed. H. H. Gerth and C. Wright Mills. New York: Oxford University Press.

Weinstein, Allen, 1997. *Perjury: The Hiss-Chambers Case.* Updated ed. New York: Random House.

Wenar, Leif, 1995. "*Political Liberalism*: An Internal Critique." *Ethics* 106, No. 1 (October): 32–62.

Whalen, Charles, and Barbara Whalen, 1985. *The Longest Debate: A Legislative History of the 1964 Civil Rights Act.* Cabin John, Md.: Seven Locks Press.

Willard, Frances E., 1889. *Glimpses of Fifty Years: The Autobiography of an American Woman.* Chicago: Woman's Temperance Publishing Association.

Williams, Bernard, 1981. *Moral Luck.* Cambridge: Cambridge University Press.

———, 1985. *Ethics and the Limits of Philosophy.* Cambridge: Harvard University Press.

Wills, Garry, 1981. *Explaining America: The Federalist.* Garden City, N.Y.: Doubleday.

———, 1994. *Certain Trumpets: The Call of Leaders.* New York: Simon and Schuster.

Wolin, Sheldon, 1996. "The Liberal/Democratic Divide: On Rawls' *Political Liberalism.*" *Political Theory* 24: 97–119.

———, 1989. *The Presence of the Past.* Baltimore: Johns Hopkins University Press.

Zinn, Howard, 1964. *SNCC: The New Abolitionists.* Boston: Beacon Press.

Index